PROSPERITY AT CALVARY

Calvin L. Swindell

ACKNOWLEDGMENTS

Many of my friends and family were supportive when I announced I would write this book. I want to thank my trusted friend David Rice who on several occasions suggested things I should include in this book. I am indebted to Walsh College, Professor Michael Curry for his ranting and raving on the subject of business ethics to the point of amusement where I began to understand what he meant. Thanks to economics Professor Joseph Weglarz for his brief confirmation that prosperity affects all forms of religious worship. The seed for writing this book and others was planted by Dr. Pao Yu Chou, Professor emeritus at Marygrove College she had faith in me long ago.

Mr. Gerald Jeffries and Mrs. Evelyn Hankins were two of my biggest supporters. I want to extend a special thanks to Mrs. A Ford for her assistance with editing the first draft of this book. I am grateful for Reverend Opal Simmons encouraging words and Bible study. Bruce Hunt and Harold Edwards have supported me like brothers. Without reading the manuscript Dewey Foshee thought the book would be good based on conversations we had. I am especially grateful to Robert W. Stewart, Chairman emeritus Primark Corporation for his insight and permission to include events in his life in this book.

I could not have completed this book without the support of my wife Paulette and my sons Arbari and Hasani who served as computer consultants when problems arose and designed the book cover.

TABLE OF CONTENTS

ACKNOWLEDGMENTS iii

INTRODUCTION vii

CHAPTER ONE 21
   Pyramid of Prosperity

CHAPTER TWO 37
   Calvary

CHAPTER THREE 53
   The Mountain Top

CHAPTER FOUR 87
   Sowing and Reaping

CHAPTER FIVE 113
   Faith in Action

CHAPTER SIX 137
   Links

CHAPTER SEVEN 167
   The Desire to Fight for Prosperity

CHAPTER EIGHT 211
   Where Is the Love?

CHAPTER NINE 243
   Giving Away Prosperity

CHAPTER TEN 267
   Invisible Substance

CHAPTER ELEVEN 285
    Forgive Us Our Debts

CHAPTER TWELVE 311
    Money: a Liar and a Cheat

CHAPTER THIRTEEN 341
    True Atonement

CHAPTER FOURTEEN 371
    Treasure in Heaven

EPILOGUE 401
    A Celebration of Many Mansions

REFERENCES 433
ABOUT THE AUTHOR 437

INTRODUCTION

On the road to prosperity, former slaves complained and resisted God. They left Egypt with gold and other precious items, and more importantly, their freedom, but in many ways they were poor. True prosperity escaped them as they clung to the rationale that the old ways of slavery were somehow better. Their spirits became weary and they lost their GPS (God Pointing System) directions to the Promised Land, wandering in the desert for 40 years. Their constant complaining and murmuring planted seeds of discontent for their present situation, and motivated them to wish for the contentment they had had as slaves. But the only way "God's children" could enter the Promised Land of prosperity was if they purged their negative thoughts.

Out of several thousand people who left Egypt as slaves, only two were able to overcome the seeds of negativity - a form of slavery – and enter the Promised Land. Even Moses got caught between his stagnant beliefs (a rock) and thoughts (a hard place), leading him to misinterpret what God wanted to teach him; hence, Moses could not enter the Promised Land. The several thousand people who perished in the desert over a 40-year period represented thousands of personalities deeply rooted in the old "slavery way" of thinking. Those personalities, along with their accompanying thoughts, had to die in order for the people born of a new birth to receive God's new covenant – a new consciousness of the prosperity God had in store for them.

FALSE PROSPERITY

As a child I witnessed a form of "false prosperity" as it was defined by local radio ministers. One radio preacher spoke of sending his listeners "a blessing" if they sent him a love offering. He spoke of the righteousness of God, and explained that God had spoken to him of a blessing for all those who participated in his 20-dollar love offering. He told his audience about all the testimonies he had received from the previous week's participants; good fortune smiled upon those who had sent in their money. He went on to say how "God put the Spirit on him this week" even more powerfully than the week before. He continued, "You owe it to yourself to receive this special blessing."

The special blessing of holy water was free; he claimed it was "direct from the Holy Land." He only asked for a 20-dollar love offering to help cover the cost of his radio ministry and other outreach ministries. The preacher threw out one last line to overcome any objection, saying, "How can a 20-dollar love offering compare to a guaranteed blessing from God through our Lord Jesus, the Christ?"

When listeners met the preacher in person, he spoke fast, like a salesman peddling numbers straight and boxed. He would then meet with his associate, the street numbers' banker. The men came to a meeting of the minds with a little something on their hearts. They colluded on the subject of prosperity, mainly theirs. The cover of God was a natural avenue to exploit prosperity through three digit numbers. One encouraged a sure-bet blessing. The other banked on misinformation given out by his pastoral associate.

God does not play the street numbers! He enters the inexplicable that men call "randomness" with a sense a humor. God allowed calamity to turn into prosperity. The preacher's sermon inspired those considered "the marks" or "the suckers" to act on the false information. However, God turned this situation around by letting "the marks" hit the numbers in masses, thus putting a hurt on the numbers banker's bank.

Then there are the modern-day televangelists who preach boldly that we are the righteous children of God, "entitled to prosperity." It is a feel-good religion; it makes us feel good about the Word of God, but it relies too heavily on the power of positive thinking. The television prosperity preachers believe success is hidden in our subconscious minds, but the viewer is confused, having no idea where the subconscious lives.

These T.V. evangelists preach that the answer to achieving prosperity lives deep within the crevices of the conscious and subconscious mind. But they fail to mention the limited power of positive thinking. Their sermons are more like lectures, along the lines of packaged speeches, which urge their viewers to learn to "believe in themselves."

My reaction to these prosperity preachers was that of a true non-believer; I'd change the channel or turn off the T.V.

HUMAN CAPITAL

I spent a great amount of time in my adult life studying economics, seeking an answer to a burning question of my youth that will become evident in Chapter Six. After years of cross-referencing theory, gathering data, plotting graphs and reviewing statistical reports, a pattern emerged which indicated that the whole of economics is a function of human capital. Human capital consists not only of the talents we develop, but also our beliefs, and more importantly, our behavior.

How we worship God plays a key role in shaping the productive and consumptive forces of economics.

I noticed religion has it own set of economic references. Both subjects are derivatives of philosophy. Over the years I have wondered, after discovering that the Bible is full of economic references, why had I gone through the pain of searching for the main ingredients of prosperity through the intricate nuisance of economic theory when I could have just read the Bible and arrived at the same conclusions?

The reason was I deeply distrusted religion to deliver any definitive work on prosperity. Had I relied on religion alone, the final product (conclusion) would have turned out differently.

The richness of religious characterization, with its common interpretations, would have lost the ordinary reader and bored those who see the world from a practical point of view. The reading of this book would have excluded from the storyline that "Prosperity is a *combination* of *practical knowledge* in this world, and *God's promises*." From a strictly religious point of view, I would have had to abandon the many interdisciplinary subjects that make up human capital, arriving at a conclusion that would skip over many of the details contained in the process of finding what prosperity really is. We certainly would have lost, in translation, the impact of beliefs, behavior and stewardship on the prosperity process. That is why I did not write this book from a purely religious perspective, but also included the secular world of everyday living.

WHAT IS PROSPERITY?

In our interpretation, the Church represents all religions that worship one God. We see God as having the ability to enter any means of worship because God transcends the man-made rituals of religion. The search for prosperity is the search for our daily bread, and the search for life's meaning. Prosperity is defined as "being successful, well-to-do, receiving good fortune, experiencing growth in vigorous ways, to thrive and to flourish."

Prosperity can mean different things to different people. To some who are currently experiencing long-term unemployment, prosperity means a stable job. For a family struggling with its basic needs of food, clothing and shelter, prosperity can mean an increase in wages. For the person looking for salvation, or understanding into the ways of God, prosperity is that indescribable feeling when God touched them with His spirit. To the fearful, and those experiencing injustice, prosperity comes in the form of comfort and justice.

Prosperity is a constant, steady flow of daily bread to those looking for security. Prosperity means "great wealth" to individuals seeking the satisfaction of abundant living through high finance and upscale lifestyles. To those suffering from ill health and physical pain, prosperity is when healing takes place. And for those who wish to help make the world a better place, prosperity is in the small victories that come from enhancing human achievement and loving thy neighbor.

PATTERNS OF BELIEFS

The most fascinating part of the journey, in the search for prosperity through worshipping God, began with the realization that beliefs directly influence our behavior, and our behavior influences the development of our stewardship - our talents. Beliefs have the ability to affect emotions, which then influence the metaphysical outcome through physical manifestations. The patterns of belief are rooted in the accumulative thoughts of those before us, in addition to those thoughts that come to us through intuition...that is, uneducated or sometimes educated guesses. Our beliefs are also influenced by our contact with divine intelligence or "intelligent design" (as it is now being called). It is our contact with the divine that opens up multi-faceted avenues of feelings, emotional urges, imagination, and a profound inner-knowing that departs from logic or rational inquiry.

Our beliefs shape our thoughts!

Thoughts have the ability to help create the quality of life we live. As a child I heard the saying, "if thoughts could kill." As I grew older I realized thoughts *do* kill. All actions are preceded by beliefs and thoughts. There is no action in this world that happens without a prevailing belief filtered through thoughts preceding the action.

I had a client say to me that he had been driving for 50 years until he had his first accident. He went on the say, "It was one of those things that just happened." I pointed out to him that the seeds of his accident had accumulated over those 50 years of driving. In fifty years of driving he had passed several million parked vehicles - all potential accidents waiting to happen. He had also encountered several million moving vehicles, along with several million stationary objects and pedestrians, all of which were potential accidents. The seed of his accident was planted 50 years ago when he conceived the idea or thought that he could drive. His accident was not a random event because by simply driving, he placed himself into the pool of potential accidents.

Anything that can happen to any other human being can happen to you as well. The question is, "How will you interpret it?" or "How will you react to it?"

REACTIONS

If you react negatively to events that happen to you, then you can expect to receive a negative response from the nature of things. If you react positively with a sense of "there must be some blessing behind what has happened," then the universe will respond with an eventual positive outcome...provided you interpreted the lessons behind the events correctly.

Thoughts become things through ideas endowed with the power to rearrange matter, heal bodily functions, and aid in the enjoyment of a more fulfilling life. The hidden clone of thoughts is their ability to think on their own. In the Artisan Studio movie "Terminator," the machines (robotic computers) began thinking on their own through artificial intelligence, thus developing the ability to create other machines. The frightening part was that the machines saw humans as weak, insignificant and expendable. The machines thought it was their rightful place to replace human beings as stewards, thus subduing the earth, becoming fruitful and multiplying.

STEWARDSHIP AND BEHAVIOR

On this journey to learn what prosperity is I encountered some colorful mentors who taught me the art of stewardship. My mentors also taught me things I should not do.

The most important thing, the essence of stewardship, is *how we administer our talents*!

Our stewardship is in conjunction with our behavior (which has a direct influence on our blessings). We are charged with the duty of making the most of our talents and our ability to learn. I believe the doors on Earth and the doors in Heaven that Jesus referred to are the ability to open and close our thoughts (the doors). I also believe that God's original call to duty set forth in Genesis – for us "to be fruitful and multiply" and especially "to subdue the earth" – is a call for us to figure things out and act on the duties of stewardship.

Stewardship and behavior go hand in hand. One is predicated on the other; both are founded in our beliefs that are filtered through the Spirit of God.

WHY DOES GOD WANT OUR PROSPERITY?

I embarked on this journey out of curiosity, to find God after feeling His presence and yearning to learn more. I searched with fascination, discovering that many of the claims Jesus made are now being proven by science. Was He really the Son of God, or was He just a prophet? Where did He learn the profound philosophy He left to the world? Why has the "Jesus' way" of thinking sparked brilliant minds around the world to analyze and re-analyze His parables with renewed meaning? After years of study, contemplation and insights from ideas contained in the universe, I realized that Jesus could not have known the things He spoke of without having intimate contact with universal intelligence.

My curiosity took another turn when I noticed the *same theme*, from a Christian perspective of God being the source of prosperity, was also present *in other religions*. So I asked, "Why does God seem to want us to have prosperity?" The question gained momentum when I noticed that God's promise of prosperity is referenced in the Bible at a five to one ratio over seeking Him through prayer. The answers I arrived at in the process of looking at God's promise of prosperity led to more questions, and each answer led to the conclusion of this book.

MY EARLY ENCOUNTERS WITH ECONOMICS

I was fortunate to attend college and study economics under some unusual circumstances. In my search for God, and eventually, for the meaning of prosperity, I crossed paths with a high school teacher who guided me to the subject of economics. He told me, "If you want to understand how wealth is produced and distributed, you should look into the subject of economics." What seemed like a misfortune, that I was not able to attend college immediately after high school, became a blessing in disguise. On the road to prosperity, you will often cross paths with one or more persons who enter your life for the purpose of helping to change the course of your life. Had I gone straight to college from high school, I would not have met those people who altered my life.

I went to a small liberal arts college in Detroit where there were no more than three students at any given time majoring in economics. Because the college setting was so small, my adviser served as the Department Head and primary Professor of Economics. This setting allowed me to learn in a one-on-one teaching environment. I would joke to other students that my matriculation was straight out of the television series "Kung Fu." She was the master teacher and I was "grasshopper" who knew little at first; slowly, my mind caught fire.

Her name was Dr. Pao-yu Chou. She encouraged me to write research papers; she seemed genuinely interested in my offbeat analogies fitting economic theory to the observable challenges of life. When she asked, "How can you tell when the economy is progressing?" I would respond with answers like "Observe the bus stop. If there are many people at the bus stop in the mornings and evenings, the economy is doing well. If the opposite is true, then the economy is not doing so well." I wrote some of the zaniest research papers (I look back on them with amusement), papers such as "The Economic Self-Interest of the Legal System to Assist in the Perpetuation of Crime," or "The Economic Implications of The Saturday Night Special Hand Gun," or my favorite, "The Economic Theory of the Being Sexy." Dr. Chou seemed to especially like my papers on poverty and the plight of the poor. I connected things that did not seem to connect, and noticed that Dr. Chou would wait anxiously for my next paper. I think she knew I was writing my papers "on the fly" because so many other things were going on in my life at that time. (I was also involved with a charity to help kids read).

Surprisingly, the seed of discovery connecting prosperity to God came from a nun! Dr. Chou insisted that I take this nun's class (she happened to be a noteworthy economist and Financial Minister for the IHM sister order). She was responsible for managing and investing the vast financial affairs of the sisters' order, and had a reputation for being hard-nosed, keenly intelligent, and a no-nonsense instructor. I saw it as an opportunity to match wits with an economist who had put the economic advisers of the Reagan Administration to shame in a televised debate that made supply-side economics look like a sham.

In class I picked this nun's brain for what she had to offer, and there were moments when I felt she was picking my brain. The revelation came during one class when I inquired into the extent of the IHM sister order financial holdings; I discovered just how vast those holdings were. "How could a group of nuns, who took a vow of poverty, be so wealthy?" I wondered. The sister order of the IHM's owned a substantial block of stock in Detroit Edison (now called DTE Energy) which later acquired Michigan Consolidated Gas Company (the connection will become clear in Chapter Seven). The vast holding of the IHM's planted the seed of curiosity in me to draw a conclusion that there must be *a connection between God and prosperity*.

Economics is a subject in dire need of new ways of thinking. All the formulas, graphs, charts and theory cannot capture the true spiritual natural of the human dynamics that influence the way humans make their living and worship a varied God. The beliefs we develop, and the way we worship God, play a profound role in our way of thinking and the decisions we make.

Just before graduation I went to Dr. Chou for career advice.

She told me to go to graduate school, pursue an advanced economics degree, and write a book. Of course I discarded her advice. My thoughts were, "Why would I ever want to write a book?" As time passed, I did take her advice and continued my education. The thoughts about writing this book incubated over time, but the icing came about after what I observed on two occasions that left an impression on my mind, and interfaced with my constant search for meaning through God.

Two Significant Occasions

On one occasion, while in the commercial teller line at the bank, I was making multiple deposits into my business accounts. I noticed a young lady counting a substantial number of coins she wanted to exchange for dollars. Just about every person in the bank who was waiting in the long line became irritated, complaining impatiently about the young lady counting her coins. Even the bank teller displayed disgust with the young lady's situation. It was obvious that the coins being exchanged for dollars were all she had. The irony was that my deposits, and those of others in the commercial banking line, took as much or more time than the young lady's transaction, yet the teller greeted us with a smile because we had more money to deposit.

The other incident was similar; it occurred in a supermarket when a man counted pennies and cashed bottle deposits to buy baby formula. The people in the cashier's line became overly critical, and the cashier was flat out mean. I asked God, "Why are people so irritated by the poor? Why do we feel inconvenienced by their plight?" Like all questions put forth to God, He always provides an answer to those who have an ear to hear it. His answer was that both the rich and the poor do not know that God never intended for any of us to be poor.

Later I did something out of character...I watched a televangelist preacher. I disagreed with many of his concepts, but agreed with his position that God decreed that we should have prosperity.

WHY WRITE?

I talked about my idea to write a book with an associate, and he said, "Writing such a book is just a waste of time. People don't read anymore. Any book about God and money will be met with criticism, so it's not worth the effort."

I responded to my friend that "it is worth the effort, even if only one person understands that God does not want us to be impoverished. Prosperity is not a concept I have conceived, but it is what I have come to believe as God's intent. Coming from the background I come from, I would be the first person to admit that this whole promise of prosperity set forth by God was a lie if it were not true."

I went from skepticism to lukewarm belief; back to skepticism, then to rational belief; back to skepticism and then more skepticism in search of more proof and more proof. Finally, I came to wholeheartedly believing. It was a journey where I surely wore both God and other humans out with my multitude of questions.

This book examines the spiritual side of prosperity as it relates to our beliefs, our thoughts and behavior, and the development of stewardship. If I was pinned down and asked to describe what category this book should come under, I would say it is a form of *spiritual economics*. On the other hand, it is a book about church life and the things that are wrong with the church. The lessons encompass how to obtain prosperity, how to lose it, how to maintain it, and how the invisible hand of God enters the process.

Above all else, this book is a perspective on how and why prosperity is God's decree. I also attempt to clarify why there will always be the poor.

I make no claim to know exactly how God thinks, or claim any exclusive knowledge of His will. I wrote several accounts of life in the church from 15 years of experience as a member of the governing body of a multi-million dollar organization. It was in the church where I experienced the highs of God and the lows of the internal problems within the church. It took years for me to come to terms with the grief of remaining silent on certain improprieties within the church. Finally I did the right thing, and with God's help the grief was removed.

The events contained in the book are sizzling collections of anecdotes. I use both illustrations and biblical parables to drive home certain points. Fictitious illustrations are surrounded by non-fiction narratives. In many cases, I did not give the true names of real people.

The decision to incorporate the message in the form of fiction was based on the fact that truth really is stranger than fiction. When speaking of God it is hard for many people to fathom what is true.

I wrote this book with the understanding attributing words to biblical characters beyond what is written will open doors to criticism. But I thought about the plight of our Lord Jesus; any criticism I may receive would be mild compared to what He went through for our sins so that we may live life abundantly. I also understand that the biblical teachings as a whole seem preposterous to some, and therefore to them all that is written on the subject is fiction anyhow.

Near the end of the completion of my manuscript, I encountered a young lady who made me aware of the extent of stagnant religious beliefs held by some worshippers. I saw this young lady when I went to the place of business where she works. She is mostly melancholy, and rarely has much to say of a positive nature. One day I suggested that she go to God with her complaints since she said, "There is no one to complain to here on Earth."

She replied to me in the most serious demeanor that, "It would not do any good to petition God because what is written is written."

I then asked her, "Do you believe that God can create variations and change things, and that God can come with a new covenant?"

She responded, "No." She had been taught, "What is written is written." I left the shop that day with doubt in my mind.

For a brief moment I thought I should not attempt to publish this book. But I only seek to share my personal experiences, and the questions I presented to God, and the intuitive answers I received. It is my belief that the reader will have to decide what to believe, and what is fiction, as well as what kind of relationship they wish to have with God.

A BRIEF CHAPTER SUMMARY

- Chapter 1 describes the attributes that work together to form a prosperity consciousness.
- Chapter 2 projects what certain biblical characters (not overly discussed in the past) may have talked about at Calvary.
- Chapter 3 examines the mystery of the poor, wise person who knows God and human hearts, but who never achieved prosperity in accordance with God's decree.
- Chapter 4 examines if we really reap what we sow, and how seeds grow into their kind. Chapter 5 takes a close look at the role faith plays in prosperity.
- Chapter 6 looks into the life and times of my mentors, and sees stewardship in action as it relates to the prosperity process.
- Chapter 7 encounters an "up close and personal" perception of an historical event that highlights the practical and political side of prosperity in action. It looks at the life, flaws and successes of a controversial Chief Executive Officer and his relationship with God.

  We proceed from the first seven chapters to enter the emotional side of prosperity.
- Chapter 8 attempts to explain how love plays a role in the prosperity process.
- Chapter 9 gives a better understanding of why giving is an instrumental part of the prosperity process.
- Chapter 10 attempts to uncover how the invisible hand of God enters the prosperity process.

- Chapter 11 changes direction and enters the practical side of prosperity, looking at the attributes behind debt.
- Chapter 12 looks closely at the undercurrent of money.
- Chapter 13 examines why true atonement is necessary in the prosperity process.
- Chapter 14 takes a glimpse into why it is important to lay up treasure in Heaven.

The epilogue wraps things up.

I am sure the reader will end this book with many questions, all of which I am certain God is ready, willing and able to answer.

PROSPERITY REQUIRES WORK

I believe the world would be a happier place if people would learn to understand and accept prosperity as God's promise. Prosperity is the process of developing our God- given talents and knowing that with peaceful joy our daily needs are always met. Prosperity is not a form of wishful thinking like some self-help books would have you believe. This book does not advocate chanting certain words or mental mapping as ways of achieving success, although words and visions do have merit. The principles in this book believe that *work is a requirement for achieving prosperity.* Human capital is the fuel behind all human endeavors, and if you turn to God, you have chosen the best source available to help you develop your human capital and achieve prosperity.

This is not one of those self-help books that will instruct you on how to achieve prosperity yesterday or the day after tomorrow. What it does advocate is that you are worthy of achieving prosperity. It seeks to knock down old beliefs that have stood in the way of the prosperity of many. We also seek to help you to understand that prosperity is very important to your quality of life. It is so important that the Bible contains over 2000 references to prosperity!

CHAPTER ONE

Pyramid of Prosperity

The greatest gift - above all other gifts - is the gift of life! God used His imagination to create us in his image. In so doing He planted in us seeds of success. The seeds He planted require a combination of factors to grow. In the physical world a seed alone has no power. It must be connected to other complimentary factors. It will not grow without nurturing soil or water alone. Nor will it grow with the sunlight alone. It will grow with the combination of nurturing soil, water and sunlight and protection from harsh elements.

Prosperity bears fruit with the same complimentary elements as a seed. It requires a combination of nurturing factors that play a role in helping us grow into a prosperity consciousness. At the fullness of certain combination factors the spirit of God's transmute His promise into a reality. Prosperity is a process.

GOD AS FATHER

The first seeds God planted in us were the seeds of the soul and reasoning. It is these seeds we must nurture more than all others to experience God's promise. In time the nurturing of reasoning coupled with experience evolved to the point of giving God a personality. The image of God as a Father grew out of a comparison to the attributes of what constitutes a good father. The fact that man made an assumption about God's gender coincides with God taking on the role of the Father. In explaining that God is personal, John C. Bennett writes:

*God is unique. One cannot describe God by com-
paring Him with anything else of the same kind.
The most that we can do is find suggestions and
symbols in the world of our experience...which
seem fruitful in our thoughts about God...To say
God is personal is to say that God is more like a person than like a thing, more like a person than like
a mathematical proposition, more like a person
than a tree...When we use the word "personal" as a
description of God we mean to include only a few of
the characteristics of persons: awareness, intelligence, purposefulness, the capacity to appreciate,
the capacity to respond to persons.*

Over time, the human imagination has produced many versions of God. We incorporate our versions of God into our way
of worshipping, and factor our image of Him into our decision-
making process. It is the image we have of God that influences
our resistance, acceptance and rejection of various forms of worship.

GOD VERSUS JESUS

In creating different versions of God we have created the
God of tradition who conflicts with Jesus – who broke traditional rules. The God of the godly battles Jesus for being too
down-to-Earth. The God of the occult and sect battles Jesus for
proclaiming the captives are free from their oppression. The
God of the self-righteous battles Jesus for exposing hypocrisy.
The God of the word is still fighting Jesus for His dynamic views
and creative meanings. The God of songs is still fighting Jesus
for being bigger than the choir. The God of the atheist fights
Jesus through denial. The God of the guided whom this book
embraces battles Jesus because His will, at times, conflicts with
ours.

What we see most often are human versions of God that do
not make sense. We are witnessing versions of God that come

from the pulpit of churches, discouraging many from believing our sins are forgiven and that God is prepared to give prosperity to all who give Him first place in their lives.

The most interesting version of God is the God of war. I had the occasion of talking to a man who echoed the God of war shortly after 911 in 2001. He spoke of God being on our side in the coming war. I suggested to this gentleman that God is progressive and if God goes to war with us this time He may update His weaponry to modern times. Instead of God putting on His heavy metal armor in the Old Testament and taking up His sword, this time God would put on His bulletproof vest and rack his AK-47. It must have been something I said because I have crossed paths with this same gentleman on several occasions since and each time he will not speak to me.

First of all, it is absurd to think God would need any man-made weapon to deal with us. Secondly, the image of the God of war is the cupid that fuels on-going wars and this image is contrary to the God of peace.

HOW WE VIEW THE WORLD

Our concept of God is factored into the way we go about pursuing our daily bread. One of the most intriguing philosophies in the pursuit of acquiring our daily bread is "survival of the fittest." I wrestled with the concept of survival of the fittest while witnessing many situations where people who embraced this philosophy "do unto others before they do it to you." On many occasions, people around me practicing this concept engaged in backstabbing and double crossing, selling out friends and relatives for personal and financial gain. This philosophy encourages an atmosphere of constant cutthroat competition, deception, thievery and, sadly, violence.

There was a time when I thought the concept of survival of the fittest resonated with negativity; that it relied on physical dominance or mental manipulation as a right of passage in order to be declared fit.

Later in life I realized this approach to producing our daily bread has more to do with how we view the world and our relationship to it than anything else.

This led me to recognize that the formulation of beliefs is the foundation of human ideas. Beliefs are defined as convictions or the acceptance that certain things are true. Beliefs come in the form of doctrines, creeds, tenets or opinions and imply complete unquestioning acceptance. The acceptance of a belief is embraced even in the absence of proof, sometimes lacking supporting evidence or reason. Ideas resulting from these beliefs not only influence how we pursue our daily bread, but also help formulate our sense of belonging and our image of God.

The belief in the existence of God may be founded on intuition, trust and faith. Beliefs start with a premise that may or may not be true. Coincidental occurrences provide reinforcing evidence to move the premise from the formulation stage to establishing roots that become beliefs. In the process of moving from the formulation stage to establishing roots all supporting occurrences become apparent in the mind's eye of the believer. The belief is firmly established from that point on through repetition of thoughts, feelings and words.

BEHAVIORAL CLUES

Once beliefs become firmly established, other residual effects take place, developing behavior clues which correspond to those beliefs. Behavior is defined as the way a person acts: the conduct or manners that can be observed. Behavior implies conformity with a required standard.

Under the heading of behavior there are subheadings such as demean, deport, comport and acquit. Demean suggests behavior or appearance that is indicative of specific negative character traits. Deport behavior implies alien behavior whose presence is undesirable or illegal. Comport is agreeable behavior, whereas one conducts themselves with dignity and without bigotry. When behavior is in the acquit mode our conduct is declared not guilty after evidence that has been presented.

The avenues and methods we utilize in pursuing our daily bread are directly linked to our beliefs in conjunction with the behavioral clues that are instrumental at creating the blueprint for stewardship. The way we go about establishing our stewardship is influenced by the last ingredient, which is the economic era we were born into, which dictates the avenues and methods we use to pursue our daily bread.

DEFINING STEWARDSHIP

Stewardship means to be put in charge of a duty or duties. On a physical level, it is supervising or managing property or finances. It also means supervising our environment, which consists of nature and other living things.

On a spiritual level stewardship means we are keepers of our brothers and sisters with a mandate to look after them and bring comfort to their lives. Jesus came to show us the connection between this world and the spiritual world. He came to prove Himself and us worthy of supervising the spiritual side of human behavior. He came to teach us and comfort us, heal us and show us that if we are responsible with small things such as mercy, compassion, empathy, ethics, morality, decency and love, we would become worthy to be put in charge of eternal life, where abundant living is the true meaning of prosperity.

When Jesus said He was put in charge of the human souls given to Him by the Father, He was speaking of stewardship. His stewardship was the supervision of the souls of God's children. His duties were to comfort us and reconnect us to the righteousness of God. Jesus came to teach that survival of the fittest is interconnected with the small things such as mercy, compassion, empathy, ethics and morality, love and decency, and by being those things we would become worthy to be put in charge of God's abundance, wealth and the power to transform things with our imaginations. His message was clear for those who had an ear to hear: the riches of life are contained in things within.

RECOGNIZING OUR TALENTS

God provides us with a way to make a living by giving each of us a talent or talents. Stewardship is the process where we learn to develop our talent or talents. The gift of talents is intended for us to make life better and to earn a living while adding beauty and joy to life through esteemed accomplishments.

The methods we use to go about fulfilling the mandate of God to be fruitful and multiply while replenishing the earth has more to do with how we see the world and how we see ourselves fitting into the world than the profession we choose. If we see the world from a purely physical perspective of limited resources and predatory economics, then our stewardship will fall in line with the limited view. When viewing the world from this standpoint of limits, we may miss seeing things from a higher spiritual view. Our behavioral adjustment to these limits may motivate us to engage in cutthroat tactics to make a living. Or we may see limits and lean on the spiritual nature of things without exerting any effort to change our views or condition.

Once we establish our views of life and where we fit in, the next step is the recognition of our God-given talents. The most important aspect of stewardship is early recognition of these talent(s). One of the main reasons that people live unfulfilled lives of poverty and unhappiness is their inability to recognize and act on their God-given talents.

I have witnessed people who are uncertain of their talents in their 20s, 30s, 40s, 50s, and even in their 60s. They have not accurately assessed what they are good at, are unable to decide what to do with their lives or to bother to invest in themselves to develop what they are good at in terms of making a living. In most cases they landed in jobs because the places where they applied were hiring. As time passed, they remained in jobs they hated. Many ended up living life on the negative side of things and grabbed hold of bad habits as a result of being stuck in an unfulfilled life.

Some blamed God for their shortcomings, some chalked it up as the nature of things and some attempted to change things by admitting the results of their lives were their fault.

The truth is God will not provide you with the things He has given you the talents to obtain on your own. If you ask God in the right manner, He will show you how to overcome the barriers that block you from becoming your gift-talented self.

THE PERCEPTION OF TIME

The perception of time has convinced us to believe it is to be worshipped as a god. How we view time has a direct influence at shaping our views concerning God. The only time that exists is right now where you and God share this life. Your prosperity and struggles will come and go but the time you spend with God is eternal and all you will ever really have. Some people are blessed with long life as a reward and other are granted long life because they are slow learners at the things that are of God.

Time has two sides: one is reality and the other is fear. Time becomes a fearful experience when it dominated our thoughts to the point of anxiousness where God cannot enter our life. Time becomes an illusion when it dominates our thoughts to the point of anxiousness and fear. Jesus warned us in Mark 6:34 not to be anxious about tomorrow because His Father has tomorrow covered. No matter what we do to direct the outcome of things, time will take care of itself.

The illusion of time has more to do with the perception of the finality of things than the continuation of things. Colossians 1:15-19 gives us an interesting perception of time: Christ is the exact likeness of the unseen God. He existed before God made anything at all, and in fact Christ himself is the Creator who made everything in Heaven and Earth. The things we see and the things we cannot, the spirit world with its kings and kingdoms, its rulers and authorities; all were made by Christ for His own use and glory.

If Jesus existed before there was time, then how could He be physically born again, then die a physical death, then be resurrected again and return to Heaven? The point is Jesus consistently bypassed the finality of time. When you look at it this way Jesus' suggestion not to worry or become anxious about time makes sense.

THE WORK OF THE SPIRIT

It is imperative that we understand the intricate workings of spiritual things, because God is Spirit. In God's Spirit we possess a frame of mind, disposition or mood that is separate from matter. In the Spirit of God, we experience life by thinking, feeling and being motivated by parts of the human dynamics that are distinguished from the body. We become part of a consciousness beyond tangible intelligence animated by the principles of life; godly principles that are essential for developing the characteristics for living a supernatural life. The Spirit contains the principles in human life regarded as inherent in the breath of God, or as infused by God.

When we understand what spirituality is, we become influenced by divine inspiration where we are encouraged, cheered on, and experience vigor and courage. We then live a life of the soul where we are carried away often and secretly to a special place where we are touched by God.

PROPER USE OF TALENTS

When we engage in the dogmatic view of an impersonal God where God does not have a hand in our prosperity, there is a tendency to hide our talents and engage in lower behavior that destroys our sense of stewardship and duty and seeks to get what we see as ours without any regard for others. In Matthew 25:14-30, Jesus used the parable of the authority figure (who by consensus is God) who gave talents to various personalities to invest and then report their success upon his return. A talent is equivalent to over a thousand dollars. Each personality was given an amount according to their character and dutiful responsibility.

All of the personalities except one invested the funds entrusted to them in a positive way, thus doubling their original investment. The one personality that refused to invest the funds hid his talent. When the authority figure returned and asked each personality to give an account of their success, the personalities that put forth an effort reported 100% returns on their original investments, while the one who had hid his talent reported no gain. When the authority figure asked why the one had not at least put the funds in the bank and earned some interest, his defense was to criticize the authority figure by saying "Master, I knew you to be a harsh and hard man, reaping where you did not sow, and gathering where you had not [separated] the grain. So I was afraid and went and hid your talent in the ground. Here you have what is yours."

The authority figure in the parable took the one talent away from the wayward personality and gave the funds to the one with multiple talents and the greater return. Jesus concluded the parable by saying "To those that have; more will be given and to those who have little even that will be taken away."

This statement puzzled me for a long time. It is one of the most controversial statements Jesus made; one that has caused an ongoing debate among biblical scholars. The controversy is this: how could Jesus, who came to give the poor hope and justice, impart a teaching that seemed like an about face to His previous teachings?

However, the meaning of this statement became clear to me after observing the behavior of an acquaintance.

To say this acquaintance had low self-esteem is an inaccurate statement. Modern research is returning some interesting conclusions in the area of self-esteem and self confidence. When ideas of old are looked at with renewed insight we see things differently. More up-to-date research in the area of psychology has concluded that people with very high self-esteem and self confidence are more likely to commit silly acts of destruction and self-destruction than those of low self-esteem.

We will call this acquaintance "Billy." He is a little self-absorbed, but so are most of us. Sometimes those gifted with genius IQ's tend to over-analyze things, in so doing they can miss the point and operate under false premises. When operating under false premises all subsequent reinforcing information may or may not be true, but the conclusion is usually based on false information. Billy's talent was that most things of learning came to him too easily.

Suffering is not a prerequisite to prosperity; in fact, Jesus said we are to have light burdens. The positive side of suffering and struggle can leave us with the residual effect of proper discipline. The negative side of suffering and struggle can cause many to give up and quit. But for those who have never suffered or struggled, a vacuum sometimes develops in the mind, along with an attitude of advantage or superiority. Humility cannot enter the personality unless there is suffering or struggle. Billy never struggled to learn and understand tangible formulas and concepts.

The years went by and Billy did nothing but intellectualize, acquire more information, philosophize and learn more. Prospective employers offered Billy positions which he refused one after another until the offers stopped as employers assumed he was not interested. Surprisingly Billy survived his short life without ever holding down a job. He developed high-minded ideas; he would have seen himself as a sellout had he taken a job; any job would have eventually evolved into boredom.

On top of Billy's high-minded views of himself, he developed socialist views because he refused to work; he convinced other people to take care of him. Billy saw capitalism as the root of all evil. If you gave him one talent to invest and thus multiply the principle, his reaction would have been the same or worse than the personality in the parable. Billy would have interpreted the gift as the gesture of a hard-hearted capitalist pig wanting him to use his mental talent to make more money to further the capitalist's oppressive craft: capitalism.

Notice how both personalities, one biblical and one real, criticized the authority figure, God, with a smug, superior demeanor. In both cases they judged the one giving the talent as a sinner and unworthy of their effort.

Jesus stated a just law; "to those who have more, more will be given and to those who have little, even that will be taken away." The law rewards effort. Perfecting our talents motivates the mind to dream of higher heights all while discouraging slothfulness (laziness), one of the seven deadly sins. But a just God will provide for the lazy as well as the dutiful.

Solomon said in Proverbs 26:10, NKJ:

The great God who formed everything gives the fool his
hire and the transgressor his wages.

Billy seemed mentally superior to the rest of us, yet he died of a drug overdose. In the scheme of things he was just another fool who hid his talent.

The talents God gives us are to be cultivated through ideas that will come to us now and in the future. By virtue of the gift of free will we are connected to ideas that come from universal intelligence by faith. When we hide our talents we cut ourselves off from the flow of God's plan and dam the abundant waterfall of ideas. Instead, we are to use the ideas God gives us to develop our talents and make our dreams a reality. Otherwise, we will gradually lose our God-given talents from lack of use or refusal to use. When we consistently hide our talents it diminishes our ability to connect us with the spirit of God's ideas.

THE EVIL OF MONEY

My first encounter with the concept of money left me in a state of confusion. An older Muslim gentleman asked me to show him a dollar. He pointed to the eagle and said it was an evil beast representing the blue-eyed devil. On the other side of the dollar he spoke of the pyramid and the ever-seeing eye that he said represented God. To top if off, in the middle of the dollar were the words "In God we Trust" which he explained represented hypocrisy. He went on to say that "the beast is an evil predator out to get your money and steal your soul; whatever you do in life, keep you some money." He kept my dollar and handed me a *Muhammad Speaks* newspaper.

His words of wisdom were very confusing because I was just a child of 11 years. My beliefs were shattered because I was sure that the devil's eyes were bloodshot red.

As the years passed and my knowledge of life evolved, some old ideas were dismissed and replaced with new ideas, some clues about life were modified, and I gained a better understanding of the spiritual nature of God. The Muslim's words of wisdom contained some truth but many untruths. An eagle is not a beast but a majestic bird. Yes, this bird does prey upon other living things. But like all living things the eagle was created to fulfill a role of replenishing the earth by giving and taking. I grew to understand that evil grows out of the hard hearts of selfish human beliefs. And God knows we don't need any more mean or evil people. What this Muslim did with his example of a dollar was pointed me in the direction of the pyramid which I will use as an illustration of how prosperity is connected to God.

A pyramid is a fitting symbol for clarifying the mechanical connection between God and prosperity. The pyramid served as a royal tomb in ancient Egypt. It has a square base with four triangular sides that meet at a point. In financial terms the pyramid represents a gradual increase in expense or revenue at the margin. It also represents financial schemes whereas each person in the pyramid recruits another person whereas the first participants in gain the bigger rewards and those who are last in lose. The concept of each one recruiting others is also an important attribute of Christianity.

At the top of the pyramid is God. All the sides ascend upward toward blessings or downward as we move away from God. At the base of the pyramid are our beliefs that contain faith which is inherent in us. As our beliefs grow, we learn more about God which prompts a corresponding movement up the sides of the pyramid in the form of modified behavior and a greater sense of stewardship duty. (See Illustration 1)

Illustration 1

THE PROSPERITY PYRAMID

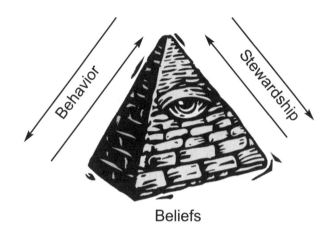

Beliefs

The process of achieving prosperity operates through a trilogy that corresponds to the sides of the triangle. All human beings start out with core beliefs formulated through inherent faith. Beliefs contain faith that is the foundation of our existence. As our faith increases we are influenced in two ways. In one way our behavior becomes modified, in another way we become more acutely aware of our stewardship responsibilities. If our beliefs ascend upward, our behavior is modified and if our stewardship correspondingly ascends upward then we are assured prosperity. Our beliefs descend downward our behavior also spirals downward when we view God's resources as limited.

When we see God's resources as limited we can still ascend up the side of the pyramid representing stewardship but we tend to approach the prosperity process with a survival of the fittest or cutthroat mentally. In this case we may become good stewards of material things but our spiritual power is grounded. So we may not love as we should or give as much or practice mercy; we may become prone to practicing avarice.

If we ascend upward along the lines of the pyramid by increasing the beliefs that are more in line with Jesus, it is possible for our behavior to ascend upward but not necessarily our stewardship. It is possible that our beliefs increase and our behavior is to be modified yet we still believe that God's resources are limited.

We can also achieve a point on the pyramid where our beliefs become stagnant and our behavior is modified but it does not translate into an increase in stewardship.

Our beliefs and behavior and stewardship can become stagnant ceasing to grow beyond a certain point through miss-education or stubbornness or lack of self-knowledge.

It is also possible for our beliefs to become more in line with Jesus and our behavior modified by His teachings so that we are assured to gain other benefits mainly of a spiritual nature, yet only achieve relative prosperity.

The process also works in reverse. If our stewardship declines and we neglect our duties of administration of ideas, talent formation and prudent allocation of resources, our prosperity declines. If our behavior become un-Christ like and we are not trustworthy with spiritual things such as love, giving, honesty and a tender heart, our prosperity will eventually decline; we may even experience infirmities in the body and soul. Every point along the ascending pyramid sides where we stop striving to reach the top is the point where we have reached our prosperity contentment. Some may call this point our point of competence or incompetence. It is the point where we can handle only so much God and only so much prosperity.

On the other hand, certain behaviors or demeanors can exclude us from inclusion in groups that influence prosperity. I have noted this occurrence in many entertainment groups. The members are fine as long as the group is playing the local entertainment circuit, but as soon as national or international recognition is about to strike, one or more members' behavior changes or some unusual circumstance appears that is the seed for that member or members to drop out or get kicked out of the group, just at the point where the group is about to strike it big. Check out the history behind many success stories and you will see this pattern over and over again. What happened was one or more people developed a negativity that caused them to drop out or get kicked out of the success story at their point of contentment, below what God had in mind as a blessing.

The optimum situation is achieved when we obtain ascending balance between our beliefs, behavior and stewardship. When this balance is achieved, our prosperity increases. The extent that we strive to increase our prosperity level is in accordance with how discontent we are with our role of co-creating with God. If we are content we stop the prosperity process at some point. If we are discontent, we seek greater upward mobility on the pyramid. However, at whatever point of contentment of discontentment we aim for our efforts can only achieve so much movement, because the Spirit of God is essential for pulling us upward, especially if we seek to make it to the top. Any ascension is achieved by the grace of God.

It is possible, however, to break into the prosperity process without petitioning God's grace. This means there is no effort put forth to believe in God, to perfect God-given talents inherent in stewardship or to modify behavior in accordance with the teachings of Christ. However, remember the ever-seeing eye atop the pyramid is watching. There are extreme consequences that accompany breaking into the Kingdom of God like a thief.

CHAPTER TWO

Calvary

THE GREAT EXCHANGE

A great exchange occurred at Calvary. On the spiritual level the Father released His blessings on His Son as He hung on the cross, sacrificing for our sins. The Son, being of the same substance as the Father, looked upon His mother, Mary, releasing His spirit of love as He gave her to His disciple, John. In the spirit of a loving mother, Mary released all the love she held dear for her dying son. And with His last breath, Jesus released His spirit into the heart of His Father. This act of releasing simultaneous multiple loves formed a circle, placing human souls in the center of circle where the guiding light of the Holy Spirit lives.

To release ourselves to the Father is to let go of our human frailties. It means to set ourselves free from pain and suffering. To release ourselves into the hands of the Father is to surrender our wills to Him. To release ourselves in the hands of the Father is to set ourselves free from the captivity of false images. To release ourselves into the hands of the Father means we have been granted permission to go in and take out what we need from God's treasury.

When Jesus' mother released her love for Him in conjunction with the Father, the Son and the Holy Spirit, it meant the portals of the heavens had been reopened and God's greatest creation, human beings, could now travel back and forth between Heaven and Earth. The sacrifice of God's Son was payment for the debt of our sins, thus allowing the Holy Spirit or

Comforter to enter human endeavors and release abundant ideas that would teach us the nature and ways of God. More importantly, the strength of the ideas would allow us to ascend and descend between Heaven and Earth with the power to open and close doors on Earth as they are in Heaven.

As our beliefs grow, so will our closeness to God. On that day at Calvary the seed was set for us to reconnect directly with God in Jesus' name. The multiplier effect was set in motion. The people of God could now experience natural regeneration and procreation under God's grace. The intensity of a new force was set motion on that day at Calvary, and the souls of human beings would multiply in many ways. The sacrifice of Jesus was the cause of the increase; the effect is the multitude that would result from the spirits of abundant believers.

A FATAL BLOW

What does this all mean to those who lack knowledge of spiritual things? The sacrifice was a fatal blow to the spirit of death that held us captive, that stood as barrier to entry into the spiritual dimension of God's Kingdom. It was the answer to millions of prayers calling for God do something to give us new hope. On this day at Calvary the new covenant between God and human creation, who would now be called children of God, was unsealed. It was the beginning of a transition into the new promised world where there would be no more tears.

The only thing that can slow down the promise of God's world to come is us, through our contentment. If we are content with the ways of the world our ideas will stagnate into the mode of conserving the ways of old. If we succumb to the ways of the world we are then in opposition to God's plan and true prosperity escapes us because we are not in the flow. If we are discontent with the ways the world our ideas take on momentum and connect us with God's plan. In our discontent there is progress through hope.

THE TWO THIEVES

The two thieves on either side of Jesus, the crowd and the Roman soldier at Calvary are appropriate characters to illustrate the thinking patterns of those who are content and discontent.

To illustrate my point I have added words and personalities beyond what we are given in the biblical depiction.

Thief on the left: "So You are the Son of God? You can't even save yourself or us."

The Crowd: "Yeah, come on down if you are the Son of God! He said He would destroy the temple and rebuild it in three days. That's preposterous! Only a fool would say such a thing. This guy had us fooled when He fed us. He tricked us. I am still hungry. Hey Jesus, King of the Jews, come on down."

Thief on the right: "Don't you fear God, in the wake of facing death? We deserve to die for our evil deeds, but this man has done nothing wrong. Jesus, remember me when You come into your Kingdom."

Jesus: "Behold this day you will be with Me in Paradise."

Thief on the left: "Why did you say that to Him? Where is paradise? We are nailed to a man-made tree and near death. This is more like Hell than Paradise."

Thief on the right: "Don't you have any shame? He is the Messiah."

Thief on the left: "Then let Him prove it by freeing Himself and us. Better yet, free us and throw in a treasure chest of loot. Now that's Paradise to me."

Thief on the right: "I now realize after all the years we've been together you've lost your soul and you are stupid."

Thief on the left: "Stupid! Stupid! We wouldn't be here if you had followed the code: no witnesses. You let a witness live, that testimony was our death sentence."

Thief on the right: "I was so tired of the violence: robbing, hiding out. I was tired of justifying it; it was wrong. We've spent our lives justifying taking from others. We felt entitled not to work nor go without. We were envious. We called those who worked an honest day's work 'Suckers.' And my inner self tells me this man Jesus is innocent."

Thief on the left: "Have you heard the saying 'he who is without sin'? He is just a man. He is probably just another prophet looking for a following. And I am not a thief; I am a political prisoner."

Jesus to John: "He is your son. She is your mother."

Thief on the right: "Jesus entrusted the care of His mother to His friend. And our mothers are ashamed that we were born. This is a criminal death."

Jesus: "I thirst!"

Thief on the left: "The soldiers gave Jesus wine and He refused it. Now that's gratitude. If the soldiers would just give me a drink, I would surely be grateful. Hey, over here, give a dying man a last request!"

The Roman soldier then gave the two thieves wine laced with incense that acted as a drug.

Thief on the right: "The pain from these spikes is tearing into my flesh. I think we should pray."

Thief on the left: "I am not going to pray. If we must die I am going out with dignity."

Thief on the right: "There is nothing undignified about two men praying as they face their Maker. It occurred to me some years ago that you were evil. Don't you see the devil has possession of your soul? Listen, Jesus is speaking."

Jesus: "It is finished!"

Thief on the right: "My pain is severe! The earth's movement is tearing my flesh at the spikes. Jesus! Jesus! Oh, Jesus is dead."

Thief on the left: "Why is the sky so dark? Am I dead?"

Thief on the right: "He was special. My heart reveals to me: He was the Son of God."

Thief on the left: "Why are you crying? What has this man ever done for you?"

Thief on the right: "He gave me hope in our brief encounter. For a moment I thought when He released His spirit, He released me from the blood on my hands. He released me through His words, His presence. What man have you ever seen do that? His breath is tied to the elements and the windstorms seem to brew heavenly thunder. I am not sure what we have just witnessed. He may not be a king but I am certain He is innocent."

Thief on the left: "So are we. We came into this world without a chance: raised by abusers and introduced to crime by those we looked up to. And now we hang here like carcasses nailed to a tree, mocked in shame just like Jesus."

Thief on the right: "Why is the sky still so dark? It is hard to tell what time of day it is. The signs in the sky are all out of whack. Did you see that? The soldiers pierced Jesus' side with their spear even after His death."

Thief on the left: "Those dirty dogs."

Thief on the right: "I am in deep pain and breathing is difficult."

Thief on the left: "Hang in there, Brother. We've been in tight situations before and prevailed."

Thief on the right: "It's funny how we see our lives in their entirety at the moment we face death."

Thief on the left: "It's better to truthfully examine your life daily. Each day is an opportunity to vary your path. On this day whatever minutes and hours I have left, time has slowed – it is in no hurry. It is another page, another saga in my life story. I beg the gods for death to come quickly; they dine at lunch and ignore my plea. While I suffer, seeing my wretched life in clear retrospect, it is better that I die as soon as possible; surely a compassionate God would grant me that."

Thief on the right: "Look, Joseph the rich man and Nicodemus come to take Jesus' body away. It seems strange that a leader of the Sadducees comes to bury Jesus while His disciples are nowhere to be found."

Thief on the left: "The Roman released Jesus' body to this Joseph because he has money and that is clout. Nothing else matters in this world."

Thief on the right: "Money is not everything."

Thief on the left: "What money cannot buy me, I can't use. This whole thing is about money. Why do you think Rome is interested in this Hell-forsaken place? It is because of money through taxation. And why do you think those Sadducees wanted Jesus dead? It's because they want to maintain their elite status over the church and the church donations and the heredity of the priesthood. And why do you think the Pharisees wanted Jesus dead? It is because He was a threat to their honored place as religious leaders. Their honored place translated equals a comfortable living. A comfortable living is achieved with money."

Thief on the right: "Money cannot buy you peace of mind or good health. Nor can money buy you love. And tell me when money stopped anyone from the grip of death or brought anyone a place of honor in God's Kingdom."

Thief on the left: "I know a few men and women who will love you if you have money. Love is overrated anyway. I heard it said that this Jesus fellow was loved, and look what happened to Him. His disciples abandoned Him. Only the women stayed. Now that's a brave crew. As far as peace of mind goes, give me the money so I won't have to scratch out a living for my daily bread in a land of weariness and despair."

Thief on the right: "That still does not gain you entry into the Kingdom of God."

Thief on the left: "Why should I worry about the afterlife? I still say: give me the money. And with my money I will give to poor, donate comfort to the sick and bribe those Roman soldier dogs so they will treat me with respect. And since I don't have to worry about food, clothing and shelter I can afford to pray. Beyond this, if Heaven is denied me, then I would ask the gods one last request."

Thief on the right: "And what would that request be?"

Thief on the left: "There is a drink made from the finest grapes of the west lands that is so exquisite and yes, expensive. Even the container is made of the finest material. Surely the compassionate gods would grant a poor soul this drink to drink to satisfaction so that Hell would not be so bad. The container of this drink is heavy enough to double as a weapon, just in case I should encounter demon robbers in Hell. I assure you if the gods were to grant me this last request I would feel no pain and depart this world with drunken honor going to Hell a mellow fellow."

Thief on the right: "I did not know you were that shallow in your knowledge of God. You have enlightened me: to remain in the status quo is to decline. I did not know you went through life in such a mental state: without hope, without a dynamic view of life."

Thief on the left: "Hope is just wishful thinking and yes, I wish I were not here. You cannot say I did not have faith because all of us have faith in one way or another. Every decision is an act of faith. I always had faith that I would get away with each caper. And in our business, uncertainty is a change of plans. So don't tell me about faith. We all have faith. Being a robber, my faith was that I would always get away. All criminals and sinners have the same faith: the faith of getting away with it."

Thief on the right: "Here come the soldiers. Oh no!"

Thief on the left: "You bastard, you broke his legs! I'll come down from this cross and kick your butt. No, don't hurt him."

Thief on the right: "Help me!"

Thief on the left: "Get away from me! I will spit on you."

[A scream, then silence]

Thief on the right: "Jesus, Jesus, save us! May Your paradise come now!"

First Roman soldier (to a second soldier): "We need to speed up their deaths so we can go home. Did you break their legs? What do you think about this Jesus fellow?"

Second Roman soldier: "I don't know what to think. Some strange things happened today. I heard the curtain in the temple where the Jewish priests pray for intercession split down the middle at the exact moment of Jesus' death."

Third Roman soldier: "I have been studying this Jewish religion. Symbolically, the curtain is very important."

First Roman soldier: "Do you have an explanation for the earthquakes and the sky turning dark and the storm?"

Second Roman soldier: "Those things are probably just a coincidence."

Third Roman soldier: "Look here, under my uniform. The two scars I received in battle are gone. I draped Jesus' robe over my shoulders and the scars are gone."

Roman soldiers all together: "Surely this was God's Son!"

Thief on the left: "How are you holding up, my brother?"

Thief on the right: "I am in great pain!"

Thief on the left: "This slow death is not easy."

Thief on the right: "Let us spend our final moments avoiding conversations of death. Let our words be positive and our thoughts the same."

Thief on the left: "Positive thinking is a trap. The eternal optimist is susceptible to missing the real point or truth. And positive mental mapping can project images in the mind that can leave you blind. The chanters of positive affirmations are really programming themselves with rituals in many ways. But I will not deny you the last request of soothing words and tranquil thoughts. What good words do you want to talk about while we wait to die?"

Thief on the right: "You have to put everything in black and white. I guess you cannot see the positive side of things."

Thief on the left: "I am not all bad; in my unconscious state I know everything. But when I am conscious, I am limited and confused. Even the worst of us are capable of love. I love the same as other human beings. I just don't believe any man has the ability to save this world."

Thief on the right: "Do you ever think about why we were put on this earth? Maybe our purpose is to make things better than we found the world. Maybe we have powers beyond our earthly limits. Just maybe we have an understanding far greater than things down here on Earth. Just maybe this Jesus fellow knew something we do not know; that there is another dimension to this world, one where there are no more tears."

Thief on the left: "My mind is not that vivid. Earthly wealth and power impair my minds' eye. They keep me grounded. The worst lies are the ones you tell yourself, because you believe them more readily. The gods know how much I have lied to myself. I honestly believed I could make a living being a thief. I thought the big score was just around the corner. In truth I lived poorly, more poorly than the poorest because at least the poor honest man has some moral and ethical capital."

Thief on the right: "Let's talk about something else. Do you have any other plans for later in the day?"

[Both laugh]

Thief on the left: "Stop! It hurts so much to laugh; little movements hurt so much. It seems strange that we laugh in our final hour."

Thief on the right: "What else do we do?"

Thief on the left: "We could cry for ourselves."

Thief on the right: "Let's talk about life. If I could come back to life again and have a second chance, I would be a gardener."

Thief on the left: "Why a gardener?"

Thief on the right: "Because a gardener is directly involved in the process of creation. A gardener selects his seeds and plants them in faith to grow in Earth's darkness. He nurtures the soil, aims water at the seeds, watches over the seedlings and nurtures their growth. This seems to me what God does."

Thief on the left: "I knew you were soft."

Thief on the right: "What would you want to be if you came back to life?"

Thief on the left: "I wouldn't want to come back to this world."

Thief on the right: "Okay! Then what are you views on life?"

Thief on the left: "I think about being born. Just think about what it takes to be born. You're in the womb comfortable and at peace when your world suddenly starts to erupt. You are being pushed outward toward the light. Once your head reaches the opening, you feel the coldness of this world. Your temperature in the womb was nice and warm and now, no matter what the temperature is outside, it is still colder than inside. Someone from the outside is pulling your head while you are being pushed by your mother's contracting muscles. As you move through the process you are smothered in slime and blood. You are being pushed, pulled and squeezed, and upon entering this world you are slapped on the behind. Welcome to the world, here is your first beating.

"On the dark side something deeper is going on, but you don't remember. You see, there were two other voices beside the human voices present. These voices take place on the subconscious level where the child has no fixed set of boundaries between this world and the next. One voice is subtle and smooth saying, 'Don't breathe; live life in the abyss.' The other voice is saying, 'Breath and live life abundantly.' This goes on for what seems like eternity, because the child has no sense of time and everything is moving slowly. The child must listen to one voice or the other; there is no in-between. If the child acknowledges the first voice and does not breathe or delays breathing, death or birth defects is certain. If the child breathes and chooses life, safety is still suspect because the evil voice of anti-life remains in the darkness for a lifetime. The pro-life voices appear every now and then, often ill-timed and distant yet vaguely reassuring; limited voices saying 'go this way' and 'don't go this way.' In many ways we are all God's sacrifice."

Thief on the right: "I did not know your thoughts were so deep. I don't know what to say."

Thief on the left: "Let us conserve our strength and say no more. I am in great pain and find it difficult to breathe. I must admit this world is in need of a Savior."

Thief on the right: "Hang in their, Brother."

Thief on the left: "Yeah we are hanging."

[Both laugh]

[Silence]

Thief on the right: "Oh my Lord! I understand, I really understand. 'It is finished' is not the end but a new beginning. It is the end of this harsh reality that you and I have struggled with all of our lives. We depart from this world with the Crown Prince at our side. Don't you see His mission was to end death so that we may have an everlasting life of abundance? We are in Paradise when we connect with the heart and mind of God where souls touch and grace has a place in every fiber of our being. Can you see it? It is the blood of reconciliation. It is the blood. Are you there? Speak to me. Oh no! You died before ever knowing Jesus: the saddest of all deaths."

Thief on the right: "Farewell, my friend, my brother and my partner in crime. May your soul find peace in Jesus."

Thief on the right: "I have found salvation in the blood. This man Jesus who died next to me has shown me deliverance from sin; that is the ultimate paradise. Those after me will find His presence. Hopefully future generations will accept this supreme sacrifice of my Lord Jesus, a sacrifice granting Him the rights to woo us, entice us and plead with us, and to pursue the abundant rebirth of our souls. The Kingdom of Heaven is a state of consciousness. All the stored up goodness in Heaven was released on this day."

[Silence]

First Roman soldier: "Is he dead yet?"

Second Roman soldier: "No, I wish this last one would hurry up and die."

Third Roman soldier: "An idea just came to me. We need to come up with a faster execution system."

First Roman soldier: "I thought about that too. We are soldiers; let's face it, we say our wars are in the name of the gods, conquest and glory for our country. The truth is after all the killing, plundering and pilfering; returning home alive with money in our possession is our best hope for glory."

Second Roman soldier: "If not for the belief that we fight for the gods and country then our souls are doomed from the start. So the spoils of war become our contentment and ultimately our prosperity."

Third Roman soldier: "We should get ours before there is nothing left. These executions weigh heavy on the economy of Rome. These are interesting times. Rome may become bankrupt."

First Roman soldier: "I'll bet the empire will consider outsourcing these executions if we could show them a more cost-effective way."

Third Roman soldier: "I have a feeling the occult followers of Jesus will one day become big business."

Second Roman soldier: "If we mention this while we are still soldiers our ranking superiors will steal our idea and cut us out."

Third Roman soldier: "Then we will wait until our military duties are over."

First Roman soldier: "In the meantime we should work on our business plan."

Second Roman soldier: "I envision the imprisonment and execution of the occult followers of Jesus will become a growth industry."

Third Roman soldier: "I see it now. We saw how fanatical those followers of Jesus were. We may be on to something big. I predict Jesus' followers will multiply and spread His creed."

First Roman soldier: "Yeah, there will be no shortage of Jesus' followers to imprison or execute."

Second Roman soldier: "The multiplier effect."

Third Roman soldier: "Prosperity."

First Roman soldier: "This may be the beginning of new conquest, adventure, imperialism and laws written for the express purpose of accumulating wealth: a blessing from the gods."

Third Roman soldier: "What about taxes?"

First Roman soldier: "There is opportunity in greasing the palms of tax collectors. We will flirt with government and prostitute his doctrine, then gather our money gifts from favorable taxes rulings."

Second Roman soldier: "It is the time into which one is born that dictates economic opportunities. And we stand at the forefront of an industry of imprisonment and death where poor souls now have added value."

Third Roman soldier: "We can vertically integrate into burial plots and assure our cash flow from prison to execution to the grave. This is shrewd business."

First Roman soldier: "Gentlemen what we are witnessing here today is a miracle."

Thief on the cross: "Jesus, I release my soul to you. It is finished!"

First Roman Soldier: "What would we call ourselves?"

Second Roman soldiers: "Angels!"

[All the Roman soldiers laugh!]

Third Roman soldier: "How about we call ourselves Murder Enterprise?"

First Roman soldier: "That does not sound right. It may scare potential customers away and give us a negative image."

Second Roman soldier: "How about Roman Reality!"

49

Third Roman soldier: "Rome's days are numbered. Every great society will fall in due time. We need to position ourselves beyond the fall of Rome."

First Roman soldier: "How about we call ourselves Capitol Punishment!"

Third Roman soldier: "That may be debatable."

First Roman soldier: "If this Jesus thing takes off like we envision, maybe we should disguise ourselves as a church."

Second Roman soldier: "You may have something there."

Third Roman soldier: "I am not sure we can make money being tied to a church."

First Roman soldier: "Are you kidding? Just look at all those church factions that wanted Jesus dead; they live comfortably."

Second Roman Soldier: "Just keep in mind we are on to something big."

First Roman soldier: "If exterminating Jesus' followers takes off, achieving explosive growth, how will we keep up with the demand?"

Second Roman soldier: "We can line them up against the wall and shoot them with our arrows."

Third Roman soldier: "How about we make a sport out of it and feed them to hungry lions? We can charge admission and pick up additional revenue from concession stands."

Second Roman soldier: "Are we missing something? We agreed that this Jesus fellow is the Son of God and God may not approve of this business. We may not be doing the right thing in the eyes of God."

First Roman soldier: "Did you see Jesus forgive His accusers and executioners?"

Third Roman soldier: "Yeah. If God is forgiving, we can do anything and then repent."

Second Roman soldier: "I guess it's okay to be evil then repent."

First Roman soldier: "Gentlemen, those are all good ideas. It is ideas that make this world go around. I suggest we keep churning our ideas around in our heads and write them down. Ideas are fleeting; it is best to write them down while they are still fresh in the mind."

Second Roman soldier: "What about this thief still hanging here?"

First Roman soldier: "What about him?"

Third Roman soldier: "He is just a thief; how much is he worth to anyone? In the scheme of things, the world won't know his name."

CHAPTER THREE

The Mountain Top

THE POOR WISE PERSON

One of the great mysteries of life is the poor wise person. This becomes a greater mystery when we study the rise of Solomon after he asked God for understanding and wisdom. In Ecclesiastes 6:7, NKJ Solomon writes: *"All people* [wise men and fools alike] *spend their lives scratching for food, but they never seem to have enough."* Both have the same problem, yet the poor man who is wise lives a far better life.

As great as wisdom is, does wisdom block the mechanisms in the mind that formulate concrete ideas, thus killing prosperity? In this world where wealth and lifestyle are the measurement of success and the poor are in the same boat as the rich, the poor wise person at times resembles the fool on the hill who sees everyone with a smug belief that they hold the promise and answers to life.

On the subject of abundant living, does wisdom get in the way of prosperity? If the poor wise person made a conscious choice or vow to live an impoverished life because it is better, then the question becomes: is poverty what God decreed for us? Another question is: does God want us to suffer in our search for our daily bread, or does He want us to enjoy the fruits of His labor? The world of Creation belongs to God and the conscious choice to exclude his goodness through creativity is limiting Him.

Jesus clearly stated that He is the vine and we are the branches, and that whoever lives in Him shall produce a large crop of fruit...His true disciples produce bountiful harvests. This brings glory to the Father (John 15:5 and 8). The question that remains is: does the poor wise person live a far better life?

Perhaps the poor wise person in the following illustration can provide some answers. I believe that after digesting what he has to say and then petitioning God for an answer, we will better understand that God wants us to be prosperous.

THE HOLY MAN

My soul feels dry. This inner feeling of being disconnected from God preys heavily upon my peace. It seems that God has abandoned me. I searched for His counsel, to engage Him while He engages me. What is the nature of this perceived inequity between being rich and poor? Will I accept His answer or will He tell me this is just His way without reason or explanation? Did I ask too much of God in search of the reason so many are weary and so many suffer in search of daily bread?

Could this be my moment of depression, or am I selfish for believing God owed me an answer? Could this be one of life's unanswerable dilemmas where God has the answer and He is not talking to me?

THE SEARCH BEGINS

The holy man sat at his writing table wrestling with the question of behavior as it relates to God's biblical promises to grant us prosperity. He asked: is it better to be poor and wise than rich with problems? He was also in search of how God could make good on a promise of prosperity to all that come to Him if the world's resources were limited. He prayed to God: "Father of Greatness who fashioned the Heavens, able to turn shame to honor, tragedy to triumphs, death to life, sickness to health and poverty to wealth, I surrender."

The holy man narrowed his search for the foundation of behavior to biology, specifically DNA. He gathered all he could find on the subject of DNA and immersed himself into the subject of human genetics. The multi-cellular organism is a double helix of deoxyribonucleic acid (DNA) that contains all of our genes. DNA is made up of four chemical bases, pairs that form the twisted, ladder-shapes called DNA molecules. All genes are made up of stretches of these four base chemicals arranged in different ways in varying lengths. Human genes are made up of a series of chemical building blocks represented by A (adenine, T (thymine), G (guanine) and C (cytosine). The number and order of the chemical bases determine the form of life, its appearance and the diseases the species may be susceptible to. Humans possess altered genes; endowed with a larger brain, they are able to perceive variations in things, analyze and formalize ideas, verbalize languages and consciously recreate life forms. This is the mystery.

The holy man remembered his chemistry and realized the four base chemicals in human genes all have an organic origin. He asked himself; "Did God really imagine us in His mind and form us from Earth's organic matter?"

He noticed a footnote in the material he was reading that referred to the human genome project. He asked himself: what is this human genome project? The holy man was led in another direction, searching for the meaning of the human genome project. He was astonished at what he found. He learned that the human genome project is the process of sequencing overlapping cloned segments of DNA from known locations on chromosomes. The genome project's goal is to seek to identify and order the chemical components of DNA and the 23 pairs of chromosomes that are found in human cells. Genes influence ethnic make up, diseases and behavior patterns. Behavior!

THE GENETIC CODE

The holy-man stopped reading to digest what he had read. He asked himself is behavior coded in genetics. His mind drifted back to his missionary days in poor countries. Being stationed in one place for extended periods allowed him to befriend families and get to know the family history from one generation to the next.

He recalled two situations that had puzzled him for many years. A son abandoned by his father before birth committed the exact same sin of his father at the exact same age, despite never having had any contact with the father. He also remembered the daughter who had committed the exact same sins of her mother at the exact same age in the exact same way. He reasoned to himself that finally his questions of long ago had been answered. Genes are one thing and environmental learning is another, but could spiritual seeds transcend all of them? He asked himself: could it be our biological genes have memories that are carried backward and forward by a form of invisible spiritual genes?

The holy man pieced together all the information he could find about the human genome project and concluded that DNA is our contact with the Creator. He continued to read, discovering that science could not explain the gaps between DNA chemical building blocks. The holy-man reasoned God is the force that stands in the gaps as the umbilical cord of divinity. He was sure there is a connection between the mind, body and soul of man and God that has an affect on our behavior. For the first time the holy man firmly understood what Jesus meant when he had said; "I am in the Father, the Father is in me, and I am in you."

The holy man was lost for words. He said, "Wow, it is true."

THE MISSING PIECES

He reasoned that there are many things within us that will always remain a mystery. We have looked outwardly for so long, how can we look within without surrendering ourselves? His thoughts went beyond what he had learned until his body collapsed from exhaustion. He prayed before the point of sleep, "God I release all I have obtained in hope of gaining divine understanding. Grant me the wisdom to see beyond what I know." He then fell into a brief deep sleep.

His dreams took over, connecting the missing pieces. In a half-asleep, half-awake state, he thought: "Thoughts and beliefs are handed down from one generation to another. The knowledge of God is programmed into every living thing handed down before there was a beginning. The distance between God and us is the distance we place between His soul and ours through our minds and words. The gap between us and God is but a marker of the degree we should know Him. Between the gaps of our experience and our higher thoughts God's love lives within us. Between the gaps of our desires and our yearnings we are connected to the soul of the Father, the Son and the Holy Spirit. Like wireless receivers, souls are implanted with Divinity. There is no escaping; we are heirs to God's abundance by way of inner knowledge passed on through the compass of time and ideas. All that we are, can be or need to be is contained within."

COSMIC FORCES

The holy man awoke and heard the still small voice speak. It was a voice he recognized. "I am God, there is no other. I will speak to you by way of cosmic forces."

The holy man sat silently in a state of meditation.

Peaceful silence!

He thought: what if there are cosmic forces in the universe that affect our behavior?

The holy man ruled out astrology because he felt it was the pseudoscience of fortune telling. He said to himself: maybe astronomy has some answers. The universe is God's creation the same as human beings, surely God is in the universe as He is in man.

The holy man logged on to the Internet for material on the subject of astronomy. He found and read bits and pieces from various websites. Time, space and matter all came into existence simultaneously; this was the start of time. We do not know what happened before because there was no before. The same ten hydrogen nuclei for every nucleus of helium that should have been present during a big bang are present today in the same ratio. There are particles called quarks and anti-quarks that are the exact opposites. When they collide they annihilate each other. Had these quarks been equal they would have cancelled out one another and there would be no universe as we know it. There are slightly more positive quarks than anti-quarks [negative], with the surplus forming matter.

THE POSITIVE WILL ALWAYS PREVAIL

The holy man stopped reading and thought about this in terms of the Scriptures. There are 247 negative confessions in the Bible and over 8000 positive promises. He wrote notes in his journal: "Life is biased on the side of good. The positive energy contained in the universe will always prevail over the negative!"

He continued to read. About 300,000 years after the Big Bang protons combined with electrons to form complete atoms. Radiation was unlocked, allowing atoms to travel freely across the universe. Galaxies rotate, creating a vast quantity of material that we cannot see. This missing mass makes up 90 percent of the universe's total mass. It may be locked up in black holes. It is different from ordinary matter and plentiful. Because the matter is invisible it is unrecognizable to us.

The holy man stopped reading in order to digest what he had learned. He wrote more notes: "There is no scarcity of resources in the universe. We are watching God in action through the phenomenon of black holes and invisible matter. This phenomenon is no accident or random act of chance. There is an intelligent force directing the universe!"

The holy man was not sure how science played a role in the many promises God makes on the subject of prosperity. He had to admit that he was astonished to know that the universe is being directed by an all-knowing intelligent source. His thoughts begin to race. God is not limited by the same parameters as humans. God created mathematics and devised the universe for us to discover. We know so little yet claim to have the answers. He asked: how do black holes operate?

A NEW HEAVEN AND A NEW ORDER

The holy man researched black holes and found they are an efficient process for extracting energy from matter in the universe. This regeneration of matter and energy is more efficient than nuclear fusion. His thoughts posed the question: "Are black holes or black energy the point of no return in the universe? Could this be the makings of a parallel universe?" He wrote more notes: "It appears that God has created new planets and a new universe. It seems that God is creating a new Heaven and a new order. Could this mean that the time is near for God's world of no more tears?"

The holy man discovered that black holes orbit the center of the galaxy at a distance of several light years. Black holes process the merging and releasing of gravitational waves. Time is influenced by gravity. Time is slowed and possibly absent in the jet cone gravitational pull at the center of black holes. Black holes pull on surrounding stars. The stars pull back on the black holes and pair up with the black holes while ejecting companion stars. The holy man wrote: "Everything in the universe is recycling itself. There is no waste in the universe."

Quasars are remote luminous objects at the core of the galaxy. Quasars are created when two galaxies violently interact and collide. Quasars are powered by black holes. Black holes or dark energy appear to play a hand in expanding the universe and taking galaxies with it. The sun and the earth are insignificant to the infinity of the universe.

The holy man dropped the reference book he had in his hand, then dropped to his knees and prayed, "What a marvelous God You are, creating an ever-expanding super abundance of all things."

"This is amazing," he prayed to God. "You divided the light from the darkness and made the sea have its boundaries and stop at its appointed place. Scarcity is a by-product of the limitations within the human mind." He recalled Psalm 8:1 and said "it is true, O Lord our God, the majesty and glory of Your name fills all the earth and overflows the heavens."

There is abundance piled on top of abundance and life piled on top of life. I am looking at the unimaginable power and intelligence of God. Out of the darkness came the light. The elements of light are particles and waves. I understand now "I am the light." He wrote more notes: "The prophecy of the sun and the moon not being needed any longer as a source of earthly light is coming true. The universe is infinite and a new light of Jesus is spreading toward the final hour."

THE STRANGER

Out of the corner of his eye the holy man noticed a person who appeared in the room. He was puzzled; how could anyone enter his attic writing room? The doors were locked, the windows secure. How could the stranger make his way up the mountain to the isolated monastery? "Who are you?" the holy man asked?

"I am."

"I am who?" the holy man asked. The stranger's manncrism was kind and smooth. He spoke with a calm, reassuring tone.

"I came to bring you clarity," said the stranger.

"What kind of clarity?" the holy man asked.

"I come bearing the gift of clarity that transcends your knowledge, far greater than the rationalization of a feeble mind, on a plane of the divine." The holy man confessed this stranger was very convincing. For a moment he thought the stranger could read his mind.

"Who are you?"

"You have been fasting, pondering the meaning of this world and writing for days; you must be tired and hungry!"

The holy man thought about how Jesus would approach characters in the Bible with unmet needs on their minds and heal them. So the holy man asked, "Jesus, is that You?"

"It is I; I came to praise you for your fortitude. The uniqueness of your gift has not gone unnoticed. I praise your ability to gather bits of information and connect them to a greater understanding; and you pursue this for the sake of giving good news to the poor. Only a true soldier with noble intentions and courage would embark upon this task to correct the injustice in this world. I am truly proud to be in the presence of such a talent."

The holy man was so excited he thought he was dreaming. Was Jesus actually acknowledging him and speaking to him in human form? "He is magnificent in appearance," the holy man thought. He said, "I am honored that You came down from the throne of God to speak to one as lowly as me." The holy man dropped to his knees and said, "Oh my Lord, Your grace surpasses all understanding and rests upon me as unworthy."

The stranger spoke by quoting Scripture: "I came to fulfill the Word.
You will make your prayer to Him, He will hear you...
You will also declare a thing, and it will be established
for you...

(Job 22:27-28, NKJ)

I can grant you your wish. I ask one small thing – that you show your humility and worship only Me."

"Yes my Lord, I shall worship You with all my talent, my heart, my mind and my soul, declaring my life to You."

"Then worship Me by abandoning your work. This is not the time to bring hope to the poor and right the wrongs of injustice."

CONFUSION CLOUDS THE ISSUE

"I have spent countless hours saturating my whole person to be like Jesus. I have given my mind, my body and my soul, and have vowed poverty for the sake of being close to the Lord. I have released my soul to all that I know is godly, hoping to gain entry into the Kingdom of God. It is disheartening that You ask me to abandon what I thought was Your will. Now I don't know what to feel. Should I feel drained upon discovering that all my beliefs were for naught, or shall I feel redeemed that You corrected me in the nick of time? With all my heart I believe life in this world is not fair. But I refuse to believe there is no fairness and justice in God."

"The ways of the spirit world are higher than your understanding. There is a bigger picture than your mind could conceive. Test your faith by abandoning this work."

The holy man said, "If it is Your will, I will stop searching for the reason we will always have the poor. Correct me if I am wrong."

"It is my plan, Holy Man, to keep secret, hide or charge a fee to those who seek the internal workings of prosperity. What kind of world would this be without the poor? Who would work, who would serve the grand plan of their masters? Who would give Me glory? Who would be left to sing praise to a God that does not answer? What would happen to character stories of triumph over evil and who would be the lost souls without hope? Who would go through life never minding or finding their own business? Who would see a few thousand dollars as all the money in the world? Where else can we acquire undervalued souls so cheaply? Who else would accept small wages for backbreaking labor? And who would spend their entire lives never deciding what they want to be? Who would spend all their money feeling good? Where else would we manufacture love and the love of consuming by autosuggestion? And who would retire from a job but never retire from their thirsty pursuit of sex? It is our money. How can we forget the poor souls that just don't give a damn? It was for these reasons that it was said, 'We will always have the poor.' They are the money of the rich."

"Jesus would never suppress the hopes of anyone. So who are you?"

"I am an angel. I was just testing you."

The holy man responded, "Yes God does test us from time to time to make us aware of how far we've come by faith, to pull our faith forward. Your test seems absolute and with a sense of urgency, somewhat pushy, whereas God pulls us into His presence."

"The difference between those that have and those that do not is a matter of faith. Don't get left out in the cold because your faith is lacking."

"Your light, your aura is growing dim. I see you in another light. It is an evil dimness."

"What if I say to you, 'Repent or go to Hell.' Would you think I was being too pushy?"

THE TRUTH COMES OUT

The holy man said, "I can't imagine you representing God or being an angel from Heaven. Your aura is getting darker. Everything about us is a clue into our nature. So who are you?"

"Your disobedience will convict you and prevent you from achieving your goal. The poor have had enough spokespersons stretching from the beginning to now. Besides, poverty is their conviction and injustice their life sentence. Have you heard the saying 'Grant me the serenity to accept the things I cannot change, the courage to change the things I can and the wisdom to know the difference?' It is wise to understand the poor are permanent fixtures in the scheme of things. You should beg me to grant you your heart's desire. I know what you want."

The holy man started to feel uneasy with this stranger who had appeared from nowhere. He started to feel heaviness in the pit of his stomach, set off by alarming intuition indicating something was out of order. He responded to the stranger: "The prayer starts off with the words '*God* grant me' and it is odd that throughout your conversation you cannot bring yourself to say God's or Jesus' name. And to speak of the poor as being convicted sounds evil to me. In spite of your good looks, calming manner and knowledge of the Scriptures, your light appears even dimmer. I now see an aura of darkness about you. Who are you?"

"Do you recall what Jesus said to Thomas the disciple? He said, 'Don't be faithless any longer. Believe!' I am a messenger of God."

The holy man replied, "Thomas was like many of us; we need proof, especially in times like these when both the familiar and the strange seek to lead us astray, proof is best exercised. If you are God's messenger, then what is your message?"

"I am here to offer you prosperity."

"Prosperity comes in many forms and at some price. What kind of prosperity do you offer?"

"My wealth is of gold, power, and the satisfaction of being a part of the new revolution in pursuit of happiness. With my wealth you can help the poor."

"If you were sent from God you would know I have no need for prosperity or fame. I see myself at the forefront of a Jesus revolution. Now I know who you are. You are the devil."

An Aberration

"I came bearing gifts, offers of great wealth; where is your gratitude? You respond by calling me names, when did I offend you? I can see you are a man in need of forgiveness. You call me such a name, a negative name with negative implications, a name not associated with wholesomeness. What is in a name? It is a name that oozes with evil when spoken. Did I do or say anything evil to you?"

"No, you did not do anything that I could say with certainty is evil, but your mannerism is overtly enticing, even consuming. There is a sense of urgency in your tone that seems contrary to the ways of God. You push too hard while God pulls us into His presence with contemplating thoughts that led us to cognitive diversity."

"I am a man of forgiveness when falsely accused. I forgive you. I must ask you this question, since you search for answers through science: explain to me from a scientific point of view how an evil spirit can exist in a universe that is positively dominated."

The holy man thought about the question placed before him, and conceded "I have no answer." He wrote a note to himself: "The negative particles in the universe by nature are short lived. They are aberrations that are eventually defeated by the positive particles in the universe."

"You fall short in your knowledge of these things and appear confused. Some pursuits in life require you to roll the dice and lay down your life to find an answer."

"We lay down our lives every day by discarding old ideas because they no longer have merit. We must die to unforgiving thoughts and sins that take so many people out daily. We must discard our habits of saying the wrong things that deeply hurt and scare others for life. Through it all we pray and fall short and pray again. We must lean on Jesus in spite of the fact that no matter how hard we try we still are not at the brink of sainthood and under certain circumstances miles away from truly being humane. Now you tell me why should I die for an aberration when most of us are unwilling to die for God?"

"Holy Man, you are breaking my heart by jumping to conclusions. You know an ignorant man jumps to conclusions without evidence or facts. First you call me the devil and now you use that word 'aberration.' I forgive you because I know you need some help. I know you have issues. Why else would you be here in the mountains alone in pursuit of a lost cause? I know a good psychologist; you seem to have some problems with the double-mindedness of wisdom. There is still time to get you some help."

"You *are* an aberration. Why should I talk to an aberration, especially one that is a liar?"

"I am not a stranger; my name is Belial."

"That is the name of Satan."

"Who? I don't think I've met the gentleman."

"You are the devil."

"I have other names."

"Why so many names?"

"It's a power play. My greatest moments are convincing people I do not exist. I have created so many names most folks have no idea who is who. Some people call me the Dragon; others say I am the Serpent. 'Satan' has a certain ring to it. Some people give me the name 'Belial.' Some call me 'Beelzebub'; I am still not sure what that name means. 'Lucifer' is popular with some folks. I prefer 'Belial.' Besides, what is in a name?

"Nevertheless, it works; it throws people off, making the world think I can be in several places at the same time, sort of like the other fellow does, using the multiplier effect. It is fun. Remember, I am the devil and I know how to have fun."

"But you are a spirit without form or substance, an aberration, for lack of a better word."

THAT JESUS COURAGE

"I can tell you have been getting high off of your religion. I am not an aberration, I am quite real. I have the power to grant wealth. Did you notice Jesus did not dispute my right to confer the kingdoms on Earth to anyone I choose? Jesus knew they were mine to give.

"I have the power to enter the minds of human beings, is that an aberration? When I enter a person's mind their reasoning abilities are acutely enhanced. Their thoughts have more clarity and their logic is more pronounced than ever before. What about my ability to incite sin against that which is holy? I could summon a legion of psychopaths to kill you without mercy. Don't forget I can cause mental and physical illness. By the way you don't look very well. Are you sick?"

"Stop it; your auto-suggestive evil won't work on me. Indeed you could do those things to me; the thing that stops you is the blood and resurrection of Jesus Christ our Lord. His sacrifice absolved the world of sin and decreed His righteousness to us. His sacrifice was so great that He took back from you possession of our souls and became the governing body on Earth as He is in the Heaven. And I admit that the forces of evil are more than I can bear, so I rely on His words and protection as a shield of grace where God will cradle me from you and my fears."

"Look at you. You've got some of that Jesus courage. So you think you are a man? You whine and say I am not a punk! With some luck you just might make it to Heaven with your manu-factured courage in tow. Your error is in your interpretation of wisdom. When inspired men like you were writing the words of God, I was there. Granted, many words slipped through but I was able to keep a portion of His words from being published. There will always be weak holy men and editors for me to manipulate. Some I will simply ask, 'Do you want to be like God?' and watch their egos take flight.

"Slavery was rampant in the early stages of this world. The slave owners and traders requested my services to help down-play God's Word and of course I assisted them. That is what I do: assist evildoers and bring them under my umbrella of sin. Then I pass judgment on them, convict them and condemn them. I hid lost Scriptures and withheld secret Bible texts that few will ever read. I hid many ancient scrolls and missing Scrip-tures still yet to be discovered. Jesus came along and started speaking to the hearts of the people but they did not under-stand.

"What is wrong with the world is its belief in entitlement. Have you noticed how people strive and act when they feel they are entitled to something? In some ways they are more evil than I. The self-righteous, like you, feel entitled to their smug, mis-guided beliefs in wisdom. The poor feel they are entitled to a greater spirituality and are prone to believe they will live a bet-ter life through socialism. The rich and powerful feel they are entitled to their greed, wealth and privilege. The clueless feel entitled to their way of life, if they could just figure it out. And those that seek to live alternative lives feel entitled to live as they choose. In a universe that grants every strong wishful emotion of entitlement, you humans still got it wrong. It is true that there are more things going on in the spirit world than you can ever imagine."

PROCEEDING WITH CAUTION

The holy man was curious and wanted to know more about the things in the spirit world. He knew he had to proceed with caution, however, and not tip his hand that the devil had information he needed.

"The beauty of the sacrifice of Jesus is that with the help of the Holy Spirit we have His ability to dismiss the devil at will. I don't see us ever being friends because you are a liar. I could say 'get behind me, you devil' and you would be compelled to vanish."

"Most man-made things are a lie. Do you remember when Pilate said to Jesus 'What is truth?' Did you notice Jesus did not respond? Because there was no way He could have responded to that question with an earthly response. It would have confused the situation to state what is true in the spirit world as it relates to holy things. It is the way the question is posed that leads to no answer. How do you dismiss what is in your soul?"

What Do You Want with Me?

The holy man thought about what the devil had said, then replied, "My question to you is: what do you want with me?"

"I want you to abandon your work for a greater good. Give evil a try and be like a god. This is my standard enticement presented to everyone. There are no rules to being evil, just acts and responses. It is still significant today as it was long ago, because people still want to be gods."

"I thought you would be more creative than to offer me the Adam and Eve proposition. I am not stupid."

"Let's change the subject, Holy Man."

"Okay, Devil, how about we don't talk at all, unless you can be truthful. I may also add that foul language is off limits. If you can agree to those terms we can continue to talk."

"My name is Belial. Call me Belial. I can show you the vastness of my wealth with a picture. A picture is better than many words. Let me show you something. Close your eyes and take a journey of the mind with me. I want to show you my treasure."

"I don't trust you enough to close my eyes. It is wise to keep at least one eye on the devil at all times."

"It's Belial! My name is Belial. It is disrespectful for you to call me something else. I suggest you get it right; I could cause you great harm. Watch your tone and realize whom you are dealing with. I could slap you into Hell. Besides, you want to learn from me. Remember I can read your mind. If you don't trust me fine, trust your God."

The holy man thought for a moment, "If I fear God enough and pray enough and ask Him for enough protection I have a chance. If I seek God with enough love, clinging to Him and crying out to Him, I can make it with His help." The holy man thought: "How convincing the devil is! He has mastered the art of putting people at ease. Surely God will protect me. Maybe this is all a test from God."

"Okay!"

THE TEMPTATION

As the holy man said this, he closed his eyes and let his mind drift with the devil. They arrived at a grand structure with a gold-painted dome covering vase tracts of land. Thousands of people poured into the structure: a church. The Devil took the holy man inside the grand church and placed him in the pulpit. The holy man preached a rousing sermon to the people and the congregation clung to his every word. Applauding the holy man's key words, their eyes were affixed on him in a deep stare, hypnotic and crazed. They called him a god and lifted him up in the image of their imaginations.

The holy man liked what he saw and wanted to see more. The big contributors in the church paid homage to him. It made him feel good. He was praised; he was important; he felt like a king. The church parishioners donated thousands of dollars to the holy man and pledged even more. In the middle of the holy man's perceived glory he heard a familiar voice that said "Avarice is an abomination onto the Lord." The holy man broke free of his mental journey with the devil.

"You tried to trick me with a mega-church."

The devil responded, "It's today's 'in' thing. I call it my 'holy man package.' You are not considered an important minister in the religious world unless you have one. It is my version of the multiplier effect. I influence you; you influence them and more souls come into the kingdom of evil. You know I love evil."

"The thought of loving evil is disgusting."

"Close your eyes again, I've got another one."

"I don't trust you enough to close my eyes twice."

"How else will you discover what you seek?"

The holy man thought about it and agreed.

This time the devil took the holy man to a swank nightclub where the party was swinging, the crowd dancing to lively retro and disco. The music was loud, sparsely dressed people danced with unrestricted movement, swaying to and fro entranced. The music grew louder; sweaty bodies touched and exchanged fluids, dancing the alluring dance of sexual fantasy. The lyric of the music suggested a tango of uninhibited lust. A beautiful woman danced enticingly while whispering in the holy man's ear 'shake your booty, groove and live, let go, let me make you feel good' as she brushed against him with provocative moves.

The devil stood next to the holy man on the dance floor.

"Take the plunge. I know you are thirsty and hungry. You only live once. I'll bet you have not been with a woman in a long time. She is yours; a gift from me."

That still small voice within the holy man spoke, "All good things meant to be should be asked for in Jesus' name. Is this your desire?" The holy man opened his eyes and said to the devil, "You enticed me with sex."

"You were about to take the plunge. I almost had you that time. I will get you next time. I have the best stable of them all. Write this in your book: the devil has the best and largest stable of them all, with exquisite women of alluring sexual appeal. Year after year my heart is broken by the players and pimps throughout the world. I suggest to them how they can be better players and not once have they elected me 'Player of the Year.' And I have out-pimped them all. Life is not fair."

"I think you talk a lot of stuff, but no, thanks, Devil. I seek answers, not brief moments of lustful pleasure. That is a stupid test. Why would I throw caution to the wind for a fleeting pleasure gone in seconds?"

"Okay, Holy Man, do you really want to engage me in straight talk? The two-fisted talk of transparency: let me be frank without being flippant in our discussion. This is mental roller derby where my language is not often kind, but my intentions are to puncture deep wounds. Okay, Holy Man, let's talk straight talk and don't cry if you can't stand the truth."

"I hardly expect the truth from you."

"You're full of manure, Holy Man."

"Remember, I said no foul language."

"Since when is manure so foul? You humans are all the same. Name me one human who does not bear residual manure in their underwear or on their person at one time or another. So you see, every one of you can be full of sh… okay I won't use that word. But you get my point."

THE BULLY

"I get your point; now tell me about your life. That is the best way to get to know someone."

"I have an interesting life, filled with many thrills, fun and so much evil. I meet a lot of people along the way. I know people very well; they are mostly the same. They are cute as babies, off limits to me by the other Spirit. But around seven months to a year when they develop a sense of fear and separation, I get my chance to haunt them. I am only allowed to make them cry though."

"That sounds like a bully making babies cry."

"I am a bully. I praise the hell out of people everyday then pimp slap them. I prosper because I perfected my talents and I love my job.

"At the toddler stage I emphasis self, you know, to make them selfish. The child attempts to master a simple task independent of the parent, that's when I move in. Just before it's time to start school I introduce them to their own body functions to prepare them for sex. There is a lot of sex at school. We have a saying in Hell that goes like this: 'School is just a sex pool.' At the same time I put a little guilt in their minds; by now they have been told by those directing them to stop doing this, don't do that, and no, no, no. They are told to stay away inside many boundaries and to limit themselves. I come along and tell them to break free from those restrictions and live. They like my proposal better and thus begins the making of the devil's child."

"That is evil."

"I told you I love evil. I am the devil, you know. Now let me finish; we are getting to the fun part. At age 6 through 12, I use school to teach the child about society and the environment through cognitive thinking, hoping the child becomes reliant on his primary senses. You know, only the things he can touch, see, smell and taste. I am attempting to make him conform, be dumb and break away from his sixth sense where he has direct contact with God, thus preventing him from discovering his most powerful invisible senses within his soul.

"Adolescence is my time, you see; when they are sexually driven. I have used sex since the beginning of time and it still works today. I recreate their surrounding world in their minds, whispering to them that they must be perfect in their social interactions. The goal is to create an impossible environment in which they will fail. It is during this stage that I create their identity crises and motivate them to find out who they are. I encourage them to learn about the things they care about. I engage them in the wonderment of being happy.

"By the time they have reached young adulthood I've got them. Now they are ready to place their happiness and future in the hands of others. Some of the people they place their happiness in are offspring from my seed. Some of my offspring are selfish people who don't know God. Others are self-righteous Christians who see only self. They work for me without knowing it. I try to match my new offspring up with one of my persuasive children. You know, keep it in the family. I monitor their behavior, charting the sins of both to see how they are progressing at evil.

"Do you ever wonder why most people's problems are rooted in their childhood? They can reach the age of 100 and still maintain an insecurity about something that happened in their childhood. You see, that's me; I did that; I get up early in the morning and go to work every day. I never took a vacation. I am proud of my perfect attendance and my efficient evil stewardship. You want evil, come see me."

WHEN JESUS COMES

"What about Jesus, what happens when Jesus comes into their lives?"

"See, that is the problem, this is where so many of my protégé go astray. When they encounter the ways and behavior of Jesus and it becomes deeply rooted in them, they disappoint me. If the seed is there but the roots are not deep, I can come and go in their lives by pushing their insecurity buttons. But the Jesus freaks are the worst. You can slap them upside the head and they swear it was Jesus. Some of them are not worth the effort; they're so fanatical they are of no good to anyone. They are what I call 'self-check.' You can leave them open in a game of basketball and they will never score because their minds are overzealous with a distorted image of themselves and God."

The holy man thought about his childhood and conceded that his improvised youth was the marker that had pointed him in the direction of poverty being better than being rich. His fears, though buried beneath years of religious study, were still there.

So he asked again, "What do you want from me, Belial?"

"I want you to give up this task; no good can come of it. The heavens are not yet prepared to handle an influx of the nouveau rich. Why? Here is the deal: if you add up all the wealth on

Earth, in both rich and poor countries, the total is so great that mankind has not yet conceived that number in his numerical system. Out of six billion people there are ten million millionaires and only one hundred thousand super rich with assets of over thirty million dollars. My figures are sound because I am the devil, and I know who is cheating and hiding money. This proves my point: the great majority of people have no idea they can share in the wealth of the world."

WARS IN THE HEAVENS

The holy man wanted to know more about the wars in the heavens the devil had spoken of and what he himself had uncovered in the Scriptures. He wanted to know about wars the Bible spoke of that had taken place before the creation of man.

"What really happened in the heavens before the creation of man?"

"I was accused of plotting to kill God's Son."

"I don't think that was a lie. You did arrange for others to kill Him. You are jealous of Jesus."

"That was the second time; the first time I wanted to replace Him; I never said I was going to kill Him."

"To replace Him who is by birth God's Son is to kill Him. How else do you replace the Son of God? The Bible says you seek to sit on the throne of God, to me that is enough evidence to expel you from God's Kingdom. Then what happened?"

"Another group of angels who were tired of all the emphasis on love and the rules of being nice and holy in God's Kingdom felt that I was being crucified. They joined me to form an army, and war ensued."

"Then what?"

"The battle went on without end. We were gaining ground when a general in my army made a strategic error and under the threat of annihilation we had to retreat. Since then the battle has taken place in the spirit world, for human souls: souls so weak I will prevail and claim the Kingdom of God as mine."

"But if you have human souls all neatly packaged and stored away for your use, how could this book I am writing stop you from your mission?"

FOR THE GLORY OF GOD

"It won't, it will just make things harder. There are many people who will make deals with me for the wealth I can give them. Some call it making a deal with the devil. I call it shrewd business. Some people deal with me because they are too proud or too greedy or too poor to wait on God. Talk about moving slow, Man, I move fast! The lustful won't read your book because they come to me for wealth as a means to sexual excess. The clueless don't have a clue as to what you are talking about. If I can't get you to stop writing, I will make sure only a few insignificant people read your book. Most people will not believe prosperity comes from God. Besides, you won't get rich writing books."

"I want to do it for the glory of God."

"Glory is overrated. So many people seek glory; little do they know I can convict them of sin. This 'glory to God' thing has come to the point where it's getting old. How much glory does one God need? Isn't it greedy to want and need more and more glory?"

"You really are evil; I think we should stop talking."

"I knew you could not stand the heat of straight talk, Holy Man."

"It not that I can't take any more. When you speak negatively of glory that God deserves, I don't want to talk to you anymore; I don't want to be corrupted by you."

"I corrupted you long ago just like the rest. In my spare time I provide humans with concoctions for the soul, sort of like a bartender. My favorite poisonous drink starts with of a dash of fear, then I stir in a little pride and top it off with vanity. When you asked God for wisdom I implanted the thoughts that you had it all together and that being poor leads to a better life. Of course that is not true and you are not exempt from error. I have been getting you drunk off your wisdom for a long time."

IN THE SPIRIT WORLD

"Let's talk about the spirit world. You mentioned earlier that things are going on in the spirit world."

"What about it?"

"Where is it?"

"All around you."

"Who are these spirits?"

"My demons."

"What are your demons?"

"Yours! Mine? Yes my armies consist of your demons. Demons are things that are within you."

"What kind of things, Belial?"

"The demons of the spirit world are your fears, your vanity, the lies you reinforce within you, your greed, your corruption, your excessive ego, your unreasonable stubbornness, your hate, your arrogance, your indifference, your selfishness, your negative intentions and self talks. All in all your demons are those ignorant things that separate you from Him. The messengers of God believe that not speaking of the devil lessen my power. The opposite is true. What you don't know can hurt you."

"What about angels of God?"

"They are there too."

"What else goes on in spirit world?"

"The inner workings of all that exist on this plane."

"The Bible first describes you as a serpent."

"Do I look like a serpent? Look at me; I have a body."

"Where did you get that body from? It is definitely not yours."

"I borrowed it!"

"You stole it!"

"Then charge me with identity theft!"

"It seems to me you were banished here on Earth."

"The earth is mine, I told you before. How can I be banished to something that belongs to me?"

"No, it is not yours. The world was created for human beings and the earth belongs to God."

"I got tired of worshiping someone else. I saw myself as god. Adam was a chump; he let his woman take him to a place he knew he should not go and so he is just as guilty. I could not see myself serving human beings and humbling myself to a status lower than humans. We (angels) spent most of our time praising, singing and carrying messages throughout the heavens. As time went on I became bored. So I decided to shake things up. You know, add some excitement to the place. You have to admit without me the world would surely die from boredom. I am the pepper of this world – and some like it hot.

"Before the creation of Earth and man there were wars going on in the heavens. When the Trinity of God conceived the idea to create new heavens on Earth, I was thrust from the bottomless pit that held me into the outer realm of the abyss between Earth's air and the wind. Sound was needed to speak this world into existence. So God, with the help of His Son Jesus and the Holy Spirit, used the wind for vibrations and motion. I had to be moved because the prison that held me was in the middle of their creation. I was cast down into the garden and confined to one area. The only way out was to enter the soul of God's created beings. I took what was meant for human beings and now it is mine."

"Why would God put you in the garden, a place so holy that all the inhabitants were expelled after you manipulated them to sin?"

"God has high-minded ideas regarding mankind. God thought free will was a wonderful gift to man; I saw it as a door opener to the weakness of mankind. It is the foundation of vanity, egoism, pride and murder. I exploited it again and again. And for the record I don't manipulate anyone to sin. I show them there is an alternative, and depending on the level of god-likeness in their ego, they choose. I then become the accuser just as I was accused."

AGAIN, WHAT DO YOU WANT?

"What is it you want from me? You are not revealing this to me without motive."

"Let's face it, my goal is to recruit, nurture and direct as many souls as possible the same as God. I have incorporated my evil. God and I are competitors; we are both in this game for market shares. A holy man like you can accomplish more in this mountain outpost than a congregation of thousands."

"You speak of God as if you know Him and yet you are so evil. What is your relationship with God?"

"We don't speak anymore; He stopped talking to me. But I encounter Him from time to time."

"It just occurred to me that you hate God. You do know there is no way you can win a war with God? You lost the war before the dawn of Earth and mankind. You lost the battle of death's permanency with Jesus and it is written that you will lose the final battle. You still did not answer my question: what do you want with me?"

"I want you to abandon your work. I cannot have too many poor folks leaving the ranks of poverty. Poverty places a permanent mark on those who experience it, especially in their childhood. The poor are blinded by their need for small things and cannot see the vast wealth of this world. It is among the poor that I do my best grassroots work. The rich are easy to control with the threat of losing their wealth. You would not want to put me out of a job, would you?

A DEAL WITH THE DEVIL

"When people come to me for wealth it is a matter of convenience. They choose their mate, friends, neighborhoods, church and God out of convenience. You can argue with me but the truth is plain: most human decisions have convenience factored in. They come to me out of convenience and impatience, especially when God is slow. They don't want to wait on a God who is constantly saying 'endure to the end; wait on Me.' No one wants to hear the same words over and over: 'hold on, I am coming.' It seems these days no one wants to be inconvenienced."

"I understand now that if more people accept that there is a connection between God and prosperity it would hamper your recruitment for human souls and put you out of business."

"I have never been unemployed. And I am too old to start a new career. Prosperity, like everything else of this world, comes from the essence of unseen darkness. Most people cannot understand what they cannot see, touch, taste or feel. Jesus was right 'you will always have the poor.' They lack the eyes to see or ears to hear. Even if they do obtain wealth I can still corrupt them, rich or poor."

"They will have a better chance if armed with godly wisdom and obedience."

"You rely too much on wisdom. The problem with wisdom is there will always be a new wisdom to replace the oldness of some thoughts. The poor wise man is only wise in spurts of knowledge for a period in time and then his wisdom becomes obsolete. He may go from fool to wisdom and back to fool again but what remains is: did he use his wisdom to change his impoverished condition?"

No Deal

"It just occurred to me that no conscientious, God-fearing person would make a deal with the devil when prosperity can be achieved through Jesus. Besides, the upside with Jesus is better. He offers and can deliver light burdens and eternal life. You can only offer wealth with heavy burdens and horrible death. Your whole agenda is to recruit, use, weigh down with grief and evil deeds, and inevitably dispose of their souls. In the end you dispose of all the souls you recruit; it would be contrary to your nature to love and hold on to them.

"You cannot grant eternal life because you don't have that power to give. You cannot grant peace because it is not within your nature. You cannot love because love is bigger than you.

You cannot grant entry into the Kingdom of God because you don't have access. In fact, you cannot claim omnipresence because you cannot be in more than one place at a time. You are limited by the boundaries of evil established by the blood of Jesus."

THIS IS MY POWER

"I have other powers: the power to influence those you seek to help, the power to convince them to turn on you. One thing I know about the rich and the poor: they will join forces against any perceived threats to their sorry existence. In this world it is the functionary who volunteers to bear the burdens of life: functionaries that ride with hate groups, join cults or carryout unjust laws with fever-pitched zeal. They are enlisted souls in my armies of the blind who do not see.

"If you show them what is good in vivid color, they ask: what is wrong with this picture? If you verbally proclaim good to them in thunderous sound they will say their hearing aid batteries are dead. If you write it down they claim they cannot read. How can they understand the vastness of it all when their minds are fixed on minding someone else's business and they will steadfastly refuse to see themselves as children of God endowed to receive God's enormous wealth? These are my people whose minds and ears I have on my Rolodex speed dial. I can direct them to attack you like a sea of critics determined to crucify you."

"If your people are so outstanding, why do you constantly recruit the people with the God's seed in them?"

"The people that deal with me are not of the best quality and they turned out the same in the end. They came to me and I helped them to power. As time passes, most of them think they are more evil than I. It's ironic that some of them think they could take my place and be the devil. It's a shame: you raise them, nurture them and show them how to overcome being good and still they turn on you. I know why God regretted creating these humans. I have no choice but to destroy those I recreate in my evil image. How dare they turn on me? What disturbs me the most is that once people discovered that I exist, I am accused of everything bad that happens."

THE VICTIM MENTALITY

"You really believe you are the victim?"

"I am! Name me a bad guy that did not see himself as the victim. I went to church the other day. Church is my favorite place, you know. When people come to church they are vulnerable. I also like toying with religious leaders; they tickle the manure out of me with their good old lies, and they always say how much *I* lie! If I lied as much as them I would burn in Hell! So what happened was the lights went out during the service; it was the electric company Edison. The preacher said the devil must be in the house of the Lord. It threw me off. I looked around, looking for him, and then I realized he was talking to me. It was true I was in the house but I had nothing to do with the electricity. I was there listening to the music and just being cool. I had had a blockbuster Saturday night. So on this Sunday I was resting.

"Later that day one of my disciples was at another church just chilling and scanning the minds of the congregation. While they were confessing my disciple was recording their evil deeds, sort of like bugging their souls. Suddenly the fire alarm went off and the minister said 'we won't let the devil stop us from having church, get back you devil!' My disciple had nothing to do with the alarm, it was a malfunction.

"That evening I had a meeting with my board of evil spirits and they all reported the same types of things occurred in all the lands on Earth. Every disaster that happened that day on Earth was blamed on me. It was all a lie because I do not have the power to be in more than one place at a time, only God does. I plan on putting a stop to these false allegations. I plan on taking control of the Internet, shoring up my army of evil and recruiting more religious zealots. We'll call them the moral something or the religious right. The name will throw people off.

"Just this morning a real psycho killed a bunch of people and he said, 'the devil made me do it.' I had never met this fool. It is my long-standing policy not to recruit psychos, especially without an interview first, because you never know what they are going to do. This one was too crazy for me to recruit so I passed and left him to be evil on his own.

IT'S THE MEDIA'S FAULT

"It occurred to me my image is suffering in this age of mass media; things are getting out of hand. The media is conspiring to smear my good name, but they are the evil ones. It is the media that is more evil than me."

"I cannot believe you are blaming the media and complaining about being accused of evil. For centuries you have done so much evil, all the while convincing the world you did not exist."

THESE ARE INTERESTING TIMES

"Those were the good old days. In today's world, mankind is evil unto himself. He is operating on automatic pilot. If I did an evil, I want the credit; put me down as the antagonist, and give me my Oscar, Baby! Hey, have you ever noticed the antagonist usually wins the Oscar? It makes you wonder about the folks on the selection committee. They never gave me an Oscar. If I did not do it, stop blaming me with adverse recognition that I don't deserve. We are living in some interesting times. There is a lot of sickness out there in the world. It is not safe these days to go out, even if you are the devil. I don't stay out long after dark these days."

"I cannot believe I am having this conversation with the devil."

"That is because you don't know me. You think you know me through movies portraying me as the bad guy: mystic writers and horror movie screenplays scandalizing my name, none of them ever thought they might be hurting my mother's feelings. A mother's love transcends her child's actions, even if her child turns out to be the devil. I have feelings, you know.

"Those people who come to me for help have got a lot of nerve, even the ones who privately say we are cool. They never introduce me to their family, friends or associates. When I come around they want me to come at their convenience through the back door. They never invite me to their parties unless they want me to knock off one of their competitors. They don't acknowledge me as a friend.

"They will swear allegiance to God yet never obey Him. But in my case they publicly refuse to swear allegiance or say we are friends or even acknowledge that they know me. And let's face it, I will not continue to lie; those who openly acknowledge me through worship are kind of crazy. I try to keep my distance from them. I see the hypocrisy of so many."

"I don't ever recall you being born. If you were never born there is no mother."

"That may be the reason I am the way I am; to be denied a mother is truly a curse. Better yet, put me in your book; say I have some good qualities. Say I have personality, a compelling character. If you must say something negative say I am evil only on Fridays and Saturday nights or on Halloween but like most people, angelic and repentant on Sundays."

"I respectfully decline to put you in my book. I can't believe you are crying."

A NEW STRATEGY

"See, that is my point. I shared with you missing pieces for your book and yet you refuse to include me. You extract knowledge from me then treat me like a plague. You act like you don't know me. You are insensitive to my curse of never having a mother, and yes I too cry. The more I think about it, you go ahead write your book. It will not change a thing. If God can change so can I. I will make a new covenant of evil."

"What are you going to do, attack me in my sleep or send demons to harm me?"

"No, I am going to hire the best public relations firm money can buy. I will hire the firm of Gog, Magog, Sodom and Gomorrah to change my image and show people that I am a really nice person."

"Is that your new strategy, to kill them with niceness?"

"People like you if you act nice. They don't care if you are the devil as long as you act nice. We are in an age of mass marketing and advertising. I need more hype; I need to become the 'in thing.' These are avenues that I will pursue to implement my new covenant of evil. It was nice talking to you. I must get back to work. I'll see you later, you know we don't say goodbye."

The stranger vanished.

The holy man thought about what had just happened. He questioned the validity of what he had seen and what was said. Was his mind playing tricks on him, was he dreaming or did he really have a long conversation with the devil?

He recalled the role he had played in grade school of Hamlet in William Shakespeare's play Hamlet, and he began reciting the words.

"The spirit that I have seen may be the devil: and the devil hath power to assume a pleasing shape; yea and perhaps out of my weakness and my melancholy, as he is very potent with such a spirit. Abuse me to damn me."

SCARRED FOR LIFE

The holy man dropped to his knees to pray but could not find the proper words, so he knelt in silence facing upward toward the sky. He asked God to clarify things; his mind was fuzzy and thoughts inside his head were experiencing shades of darkness. The holy man began to write: "There will be times we must go into the devil's house to get the prosperity God has decreed for us. By entering the devil's house you will be scarred for life. In the devil's house look for the cross that bears your name, it is the only way to rid yourself of generational curses that were not of your own making. Grab the cross bearing your name then exit the devil's house. God does not condemn us or convict us of our sins. It is the devil that reminds us then taunts us before convicting us of our sins."

The holy man smiled in acknowledgment of the fact that it is his birthright to share in the fruits of God's labor on this earth. "It is God's will that we enjoy freedom from scarcity. It is God's will that we experience happiness, good health and joy while practicing the application of His laws. It is our duty to discover the personal prosperity plan God has willed for each and every one of us.

OVERCOME AND PROSPER

"The secret to life is developing our seventh sense to the point where the sixth sense of ideas and intuition intersect with the divine mind. It is the most difficult of things to do. In the process we must battle the opposition that persuades us to give up or seek money from evil sources for evil purposes. We must wage other battles: the praise of men, passivity, trickery and self-doubt, and overcome the shortcomings of wisdom and positive thinking. We must set our mind on the path of constantly surrendering to the will of God. This is the point where success and light burdens are assured granting us prosperity and a good life.

"God loves us more than we love ourselves. He promises to never leave us. He is the source of comfort and guidance. He is our loving fortress that protects us from life's storms. He gives us angels and the Holy Spirit to watch over us and guide us in all our ways. He will not forsake us. He hears our prayers. We must trust Him, commit our ways to Him and wait patiently for Him. He shall give us the desires of our hearts.

"The only thing that separates us from living as God willed us to live is that we believe the Accuser (Satan) whose goal is to make us feel guilty, angry and doubtful. He wants us to feel unworthy, hopeless, ashamed, and finally, fearful."

A voice in a whirlwind said to the holy man, "Overcome and prosper, overcome and sit beside Me!"

CHAPTER FOUR

Sowing and Reaping

BENEFIT OF THE DOUBT

Man cannot create material things. In the mental and moral world he may produce new ideas, but when he is said to produce new material things, he really only produces utilities; or in other words his efforts and sacrifices result in changing the form or arrangement of matter to adapt it better for his satisfaction of wants.

Alfred Marshall, Economist

The atheist drives home his point with his declaration that he does not believe there is a God. He reasons that life came about through evolution and the progressive nature of things by random chance. He ends by saying he does not stand in the way or impose his beliefs on those who rely on God; in fact he gives believers the benefit of the doubt. Little does he know, in his self-talk he is actually praying to God.

I have heard the term "benefit of the doubt" used many times before, but this time it had a new meaning. Perhaps its meaning stood out because I was in the middle of writing this book or because I have had my own doubts from time to time, not that God exists, but whether He plays a prominent role in shaping our prosperity. I asked the question: is there a benefit to doubt or is this just a saying? Certainly doubt has its precautionary element. Doubt can sow seeds of confusion and reap the fruit of a double-minded person. It can also lead to over-precaution, which results in no action at all.

DOUBTING THE CLAIMS OF JESUS

I can imagine doubt surrounding some if not all the claims of Jesus. There was doubt surrounding His virgin birth. The priest Zechariah certainly had his doubts about his wife Elizabeth birthing a son at her age. Both Joseph and Mary surely held some doubts about their intimacy with God's Son. Jesus' disciples had their doubts every step of the way.

The Pharisee and Sadducees had their doubts about a number of things, including the decision to kill Jesus. To complicate matters even more, they knew the claims Jesus made about the Kingdom of God were true. It was a prophecy of the Messiah they had studied and knew.

Jesus' philosophy was not far from the philosophy of the religious leaders. It was truth abstracted from their Scriptures predicting the arrival of the Messiah. They had ample time to understand, but God in His variations caused doubt to cloud their minds.

Jesus recognized the doubt of all those around Him and addressed those doubts at various stages of His ministry.

LIMITED AND UNLIMITED

In that moment when we are at a higher consciousness acutely aware of God's presence, we are still limited to materialism down here on Earth. It is hard to fathom but there is a faint line between this world and the next. We have limited access to the next world and self-imposed limitations to a higher life here on Earth. One world directs the other and the other leads to the next. But through Jesus we can experience higher heights in both worlds.

How can we be limited and unlimited at the same time? Jesus knew the only way He could spread understanding of the coming Kingdom of God was to express it in terms of material things on Earth, most notably things of nature. The message was so important that it would have defeated the purpose to speak over the audience's head as I have seen many eloquent speakers do. Their message was lost in the audience's lack of ability to translate its meaning.

Toward the end of His ministry, Jesus said in John 13:7, NLT, *"You don't understand now what I am doing, but someday you will."* Is it possible that all that is now a mystery will one day be knowable?

FOUR SOILS

In three of the four Gospels, the book of John being the exception, Jesus relayed the parable where the farmer sowing grain in his field scattered seeds on various soils. Some seeds fell beside a beaten path and the birds ate them and they never had the opportunity to grow roots. Others fell on rocky soil where there was little depth, the plants sprang up quickly but the hot sun soon scorched them and they withered and died for they had so little roots.

Attacking weeds among the thorns choked others seeds and their growth, but some fell on good soil and produced a crop that was 30, 60 and 100 times as much as the farmer had planted.

Jesus disciples were not mentally slow or unable to analyze complex problems. To be successful at most things require knowing the techniques and being able to focus long enough to take home the prize. Yet the disciples did not understand what He meant by this parable. This fulfilled the prophecy of Isaiah "That I use these illustrations, so people will hear and see but not understand."

The true meaning of the parable is that doubt crept into the minds and hearts of each seedling except one. It is the words and ways of God that are the fertilizer that nurture seeds in our minds, creating good soil that brings forth an abundant crop. Anything less is putting the words of God on the back burner where the seed must settle for inferior soil. The parable ended with "He [she] who has an ear to hear, let him [her] hear!"

LISTEN!

To hear is an art, it requires concentration. It requires the listener to hear what is being said with their minds. A fair amount of mental analytical skills go into being a good listener.

It is a must that the listener be interested in what is being said, otherwise, the message is less likely to have merit. It also requires the absence of doubt. If doubt is present the message is lost, because doubt and belief are opposing thoughts. Our conscious minds are limited to one thought at a time. Doubt carries with it blind spots.

It is difficult to see others through the unbiased lenses of Jesus, where the vision is clear and doubt is replaced with faith. I am certain that doubt creeps into the belief that God is the creator of all wealth. I am also certain that doubt, along with the perception of injustice and inequality, plays a part in shaping the belief that God bestowed special blessings onto the poor and cursed the rich.

THE ROOT OF ALL EVIL?

It is easy to fall into the belief of money being the root of all evil when it is interpreted from the standpoint of not having enough while watching those with excess splurge in ways that seem unnatural. And no matter how pronounced the belief is, wealth is not of God but manmade. Know this, God's wealth is unbelievable. He gave us the option of taking in as much of God as we can stand. The will of man is a gift from God.

Money is not evil. Money was made for human beings, not the other way around. We have dominion over money because money was made for us. There are many other blessings from God that set us on a higher plane than money. We are capable of emulating Jesus. Money cannot emulate Jesus, because it has no soul or pulse, it does not breathe and it can never be connected to the heart of God.

Money's purpose is to serve us as a means of exchange and an instrument for measuring price on a unit basis. It serves us as a monitor for the value of wages. Money charts our progressive accumulation of time consumed. It provides an incentive for discovering, developing and enhancing our God given talent(s). Money's main purpose is to grant us a sense of freedom.

TIME ISN'T MONEY

In the world of finance and interest, there is a saying that time is money. This is a man-made concept based on the idea of usury and the forced submission into the material productive process where all efforts are motivated by money. The idea is programmed in the psyche of production: time is money and to waste time is to lose money.

There is a sneaky thought underlying this philosophy, a thought that God should not enter areas of finance. Further, if you spend too much time with God instead of keeping your hands on the buttons of productive finance it will lead you to ruin.

An angel raced across God's Kingdom bearing a message from Earth. He was a dutiful and determined angel. He did not know why the other angels claimed to have previous appointments when the call went out for a messenger of God. The message was urgent from the Trinity of God. Man had pushed a door on Earth to a close.

THE ANGEL OF TIME

Gossip spread throughout the Kingdom of God that man had just reduced time to money. This was a message of great importance because for man to narrow a door to the Kingdom by reducing time to money he had insulted God and must be dealt with by the dreaded angel of time, the most feared of all the angels, whose job it was to adjust and maintain the accuracy of the clock in God's Kingdom.

This angel had the power to dole out punishment to all those who messed with time. He loved his job. And he hated anyone who wasted time. He constantly noted in his book of time all the things he hated about human beings. He saw humans as disrespectful of time.

The other angels threw him a party on the day he finally admitted he did like people. But he never attended any party he was invited to by the other angels in God's Kingdom. He thought the other angels of the Kingdom were misusing time with all of their partying and small talk.

The angel of time was a strict fellow and often said to the Trinity "You are too flexible with time; if You are going to administer this 'time thing' the right way there is no bending. You cannot favor one situation or person over time; in one way or another we all have our time. God has His time, as does the Son and the Holy Spirit. I have my time," said the angel of time, "when I am free of my duties of being the timekeeper on Earth as I am in the heavens. At that time it will no longer be necessary for me to keep time. Not knowing what to do with my time when that time comes, I may do something foolish and act sociable."

The angel of time never left his mansion; he was grumpy and none too kind to those who knocked upon his door. All visitors were a waste of time to this angel. But the messenger angel mustered up enough courage and strength to push back the giant doorknocker on the angel of time's door.

ONLY A FOOL WOULD MESS WITH TIME

There was no answer until after the third knock. By now, the messenger angel was exhausted. A thundering voice echoed from behind the door, "Only a fool would mess with time: something so precious, when spent it can never be recycled. Don't mess with me. I am time and I believe in revenge. What kind of fool are you to knock on the door of time for nonsense?

"I bear a messenger from the Trinity of God; it is a message of great of importance. Man has used his power of thought to push doors closed on Earth by reducing the merit of time to a material thing called 'money.'"

"How dare they close the door of time on Earth as it is in Heaven? For money! I should call upon my henchmen and pass judgment upon them all. They are disrespecting me again. Respect the time! When are they going to learn to respect the time?"

Then he thought about his conditional entry into God's Kingdom and his anger was cooled. On a few occasions in biblical history the angel of time had reacted with anger at man and had acted without consulting the Trinity, pronouncing death sentences in time on rulers and sinners alike for disrespecting time. He had made the Trinity look bad on a few occasions. Once he had gotten so mad that he had passed a time death sentence on a war President.

The image of God in man's mind after the angel of time reacted with anger was that of a vengeful God, full of wrath and verbal put-downs. So the angel was still on probation: for his outbursts of anger, for cussing too much and for being unsociable with the other angels. The other angels had attempted on several occasions to be cool with the angel of time because he would be the first angel to know the date set by God announcing the entry into the new world of no more tears.

The saving grace of the angel of time was his love for God and his dedication to his work. At one point the Trinity of God had even discussed giving him time off. He was a workaholic and prone to abrupt interactions with everyone. His was an important job; no other angel understood the subtle intricacies of moving the levers of time at the appointed moment to open and close doors on Earth as they are in the heavens.

The angel of time, with the help of the messenger angel, was responsible for moving the giant lever on the clock in the Kingdom of God.

There was a moment of silence in God's Kingdom; the right thing to do in respect for the dead.

"What happened when we moved that lever?"

"Since man cracked to a close the door of time, he cut off the floodgate of time. The floodgate of any of God's blessings can only be achieved when the doors are set at open wide. Man has used the God-given power of his will to close doors on Earth through his mental and moral deeds. When a door is cracked open on Earth, a corresponding door in the heavens must be cracked so that time on Earth as it is in Heaven is synchronized."

"What happens when both doors are cracked?"

"Since man reduced his time to money, his understanding of his divinity has been slowed. He has placed his faith in money instead of God. His divinity is subjected to fluctuations between inflated egos and deflated dreams of money as his deity. It will take him longer to experience the wonderful things the Trinity of God has in store for him. The sad thing is now God cannot solve many of man's problems. God must crack open other doors where He can when man requests his help."

TIME MISUSED CAN NEVER BE RECOUPED

"Why would man limit his time and his blessings to a thing called money?"

"Because of his doubts about God, man thinks reducing time to money benefits him. However, to doubt God is to miss His lessons and blessings. There is no benefit to doubting the things of God. To do so is to worship limits."

"I have been enlightened on this day."

"I have also been enlightened. I thought man's thoughts would develop deep roots with God in time. I never believed man's faith would land on the shallow soil of money as their god. You should stick around when the light of Jesus returns to God's Kingdom at Calvary. On that day the consciousness of the Kingdom of Heaven will be open to man and a great celebration will take place. It seems like it is taking centuries to occur but when it happens it will seem like hours to me. That will be the last time I will pull these levers of time. What a glorious day that will be!"

"Wait until I tell the other angels that you are not so mean."

"You must be new around here. Certain things must remain as they are, just as man should not have cracked to a close the doors of time on Earth. I must be seen as a villain. You cannot say, based on one interaction regarding a sober moment of man's foolishness, that I have changed my ways. That is not to say I am always this nice.

"I remember when I first arrived in the Kingdom of God. It seems so long ago; I lost track of how long it has been. I did not take time for me. I started in the cafeteria serving others, and then moved to the mailroom. And I'll tell you a secret: if you want to be successful, you must work yourself out of the job you now have into the one you want by mastering the task involved.

"Now you go tell the other angels I am mean as Hell and not worthy of being this close to God. Tell them I am in need of prayer and blessings from God. And don't forget to tell them there may be hope for me in God's new world of no more tears."

"I shall tell them you are mean as Hell!"

"Good!"

How could something as important as time be reduced to the incremental measurements of money? And how could the love of money take the place of God? What is the true value of money compared to a higher form of life? If money is almighty then why does it lose its power at granting everlasting life?

We are subjected to the ideas of life, to the idea that we are more than our minds can conceive. It is through these ideas we were born and it is through these ideas that we will return to our Creator where an unbreakable circle exists.

The most profound ideas that greatly improved the quality of human life were inventions that saved time and made labor easier, improving our lot here on Earth. Money came into being over time as a reward for inventions that were of service to human beings. These inventions were conceived outside the conscious anxiety of man-made time; the outcome of seeds conceived in isolation or self-imposed exile, situations where time was not the dominating factor.

Do not worry about money. The less you worry, the more money will come. Money is easy, it requires us to just keep on living and it will somehow flow our way. But time misused can never be recouped.

WHO CAN UNDERSTAND?

When the disciples did not understand the parable of the farmer scattering the seeds, Jesus did not get angry. In fact He told His disciples the parable was intended for their understanding, not others. He could have scolded his disciples, lost patience with them, replaced them or, worse, traveled the path to His destiny alone.

In many ways, Jesus was alone like we all are, because each experience, feeling, inner thought or intimate moment with God cannot be fully expressed to another human being nor interpreted in the exact same way. Imagine Jesus' burden knowing He would die for our sins without anyone to really talk to who would understand or believe without some doubt regarding what He must do to save mankind.

Jesus took the high road, and said to His disciples "Many a prophet and godly man or woman has longed to see what you have seen, and hear what you have heard but couldn't."

THE SOIL OF A HEART

Jesus then went on to explain what sowing of the grain meant. The seeds that fell on the hard path represented the hearts of people who hear Good News about God's Kingdom, but doubt robs them of any real understanding, then Satan comes and snatches God's seed altogether. The only way this seed can survive is to stay grounded in the Word and ways of God. This is the only way our ideas can take root and prosper. It may take enormous concentration to comprehend God. By all means, intense frustration must be avoided and you must be determined, knowing that with God you always have a chance.

The seeds that fell on shallow, rocky soil represent those who hear God's message and temporarily receive it with intense joy, but their childhood blunders, family and friends do not provide the reinforcing depth to sustain a progressive walk with God. Doubt enters the picture and the seed of God's message does not develop any deep roots. So when trouble comes and this person is called to stand firm on God's Word they back down. In time, their enthusiasm wanes and they drop out. This seed becomes shaky when its belief in God is questioned, especially when asked tough questions such as: where is God, have you ever seen Him, how do you know He exists, can you show us a miracle?

The dictionary defines depth as the quality of being deep or the extent or dimension downward, backward or inward. So it makes sense that this person who is not inwardly deep would fall backward or down when faced with the test of faith in God.

You can counteract all negative things in this world by asking God specifically what you need. You can ask God to lift your doubt, develop deep roots in you, and stand firm in your belief in God. The only way out of shallow, rocky soil is to constantly worship God and ask Jesus to walk forward with you through life.

The seeds that fell on the soil covered with thistle (weedy plants) represent the hearts of those who hear the message of God but the concerns of this world and their striving for money choke out God's Word. Doubt sets in, and less and less is done for God. This personality is more interested in acquiring things. They are materially bent and interested in what is going on in the world. They will worship God for whatever reward He has to offer. However, if the reward is not immediately forthcoming or is denied they will stop seeking God. The seed of extreme selfishness lacks the inner substance to be like Christ and is a tough seed for cultivating prosperity. It is impossible to be like Christ when rejecting God for money. God has a place for you if you accept Him and love Him more than money and trust Him to change you.

The good soil represents the hearts of those who listen to the message, understand it, and more importantly, accept God's Word. They are unwilling to let doubt enter their minds. If doubt does appear, it is quickly extinguished. These seeds steadfastly continue to go out and bring other souls into the Kingdom.

ALL KINDS OF DOUBT

Doubt has three sides and one subtle moment. The most pronounced of all doubt is the doubt of steadfast refusal. In this mental state the individual's eyes and ears are closed thus closing the portal to the soul. This is doubt that refuse to believe in God, the Son or miracles. There is still hope for those in possession of the doubt of steadfast refusal because through God, all things are possible.

The doubt of material evidence is doubt grounded in what corresponds with the physical senses of touch, taste smell, etc. It is a materialistic doubt based on the physical. The spirit that backs all things material is difficult to comprehend, because it is invisible and cannot present its fullness through limited material expression.

The doubt of our purpose is reinforced when God is near but silenced. God does not constantly speak directly to us. There are times God does not talk to us either directly or indirectly; He does not talk to us at all. Even though His Spirit is constantly upon us otherwise we would perish, sometimes He has nothing to say. And it is not His nature to make constant conversation. When God does not speak to us, questions regarding our purpose creep in, in the form of doubt. We are not absolutely sure if our encounters with God are interpreted in the clear concise way of "God's intent." It is in those moments that doubt takes on the question: "is this my purpose, is this my destiny?" If we do not answer the question ourselves in the affirmative, apathy is sure to enter our world.

Lastly we experience momentary doubt that causes us to pause. Momentary doubt does not last long, it is more or less God's way of pruning us back for greater challenges that lie ahead.

Jesus experienced this kind of doubt on two occasions. Once in the garden of Gethsemane, and again at Calvary while on the cross. On both occasions, He quickly recovered, refocusing on God's will, determined to fulfill His mission.

Thomas experienced this doubt and the doubt of material evidence by refusing to believe Jesus returned to life unless He touched him. He, like other disciples, experienced the doubt of purpose, uncertain as to what their role would be after Jesus' death.

In the end, the disciples responded to their momentary doubt in the affirmative and went on to produce an abundant harvest.

THE HARVEST OF PROSPERITY

The parable of the scattering of the seeds is also about reaping and sowing. In other words, three separate events are part of the harvest. A seed is the perfect analogy for describing the interaction of God and human life, on Earth and in Heaven. The act of planting a seed is an act of faith. No one plants a seed without having faith that it will grow. The seed is an expectation of life and growth. It maturates in darkness, pushing forward toward the light. It requires water, as man does. It requires light, as does man, and it must catch hold of the rhythm of life, as must man.

The seed must be selected with great care. Some seeds call for a separation between the good, the bad and the ugly. Some seeds must ferment in water or be dried by the sun before planting. Cultivating seeds requires care.

Seeds come in many forms. There are material seeds as well as spiritual ones. In the seeding process, great preparation takes place, which is also required to reap the harvest of prosperity.

Jesus said the greatest commandments are to love God with all our heart and love our neighbor this in a nutshell is the simplicity of achieving prosperity and living a happy life. No matter what your faith is most people would agree with the first commandment. It is the second commandment where we must examine our motives. Too often, men and women of faith throw themselves into loving God to avoid loving their neighbor. By worshiping God through verbal and visible venues we can cover up a phony heart.

In Jeremiah 17:10, NIV, we get a clear understanding that God judges us by our motives.

I the Lord search the heart and examine the mind to reward a man according to his conduct, according to what his deeds deserve.

Prosperity is denied to many of us because we fail to understand and practice the commandment of "love thy neighbor." You cannot play God cheap and believe He does not know your motives.

He's Done No Wrong

The High priest was tired of hearing Nicodemus speak in defense of Jesus. Nicodemus hammered home the point of "how can we convict a man without a trial?" Caiaphas, the High Priest spoke: "If it is a trial you request we can certainly arrange that."

The chief priest and the other Pharisees asked, "What should we do, the whole nation will follow Him - and the Roman army will come and kill us and take over [our] government? You stupid idiots! Why should the whole nation perish for this one man? We will let this one man Jesus die for the people.

"Our forefathers faced tears and blood to set us on course to free us from this Roman reality. We are descendents of captivity and our souls know what it feels like to be shackled. The man we chose to die for the people is not one of us, although he has a keen knowledge of our ways. He speaks of intimacy with God but never attended our schools. He has mocked us and made us look like enemies of God. He called us names and what is most unforgivable is He cursed our forefathers, saying that we are in agreement with them. He is not of our social class.

"I sat here and listened to Nicodemus and Joseph of Arimathea argue on behalf of sparing the life of Jesus. To do so makes no sense, we have everything to gain by this man's death and stand to lose everything should this man live."

Nicodemus: "This man Jesus has done no wrong. None of us can actually identify His sin."

Joseph of Arimathea: "This man Jesus has healed the sick, fed the poor, uplifted the souls of the people and bought back to life the dead. These are miracles of good. What crime has this man committed?"

A group of Pharisees in agreement: "We cannot find any crime committed by this man Jesus."

Caiaphas: "He is charged with and convicted of threatening our position and our religion. He is guilty of coming between our comfort and the praise of men and we sentenced Him under the laws of capital punishment for messing with our money. If the whole nation should follow Him they will take their money with them. He is messing with our money."

Joseph of Arimathea: If Jesus had been taught in our system and been accepted as one of us we would not be doing this. His philosophy is not that different than ours. We are sentencing an innocent man to death because of money and His criticism of our contentment."

The Chief Priest: "Joseph of Arimathea and Nicodemus can live with the threat of Jesus to our way of life; God has blessed them richly while we walk among the people in filth, serving those who know not God and despise us.

[Silence]

The Chief Priest: "When Jesus threw the money changers out of the temple, we did not get our cut. How say you? Jesus is messing with our money!"

The other members convened at the meeting: "Yeah!"

Caiaphas: "Say it loud, Jesus is messing with our money."

The Chief Priest: "Say it loud and whip up the crowd."

The crowd chants: "Jesus is messing with our money. Don't let Jesus mess with our money."

Caiaphas: "It is the wish of this body that Jesus die for the people. Let His blood rest on the hands of the Romans; they crave and thirst for blood. We will justify our actions by acknowledging this is a blood sacrifice that will save the rest of us. And should Jesus come back to life as the prophecy predicts, we will do the same as we did to convict Him, pay witnesses to lie and say He did not come back to life."

Nicodemus: "How can we do such a thing that is contrary to our faith? We Jews were the first to embrace the one true God and the teachings of this man Jesus and accept Him as the Son of God. What will history say of us?"

Caiaphas: "History will say the Romans, Pharisees and other religious and political groups joined forces in unity. The records will say we were the forerunners for future religious political and business compromise - voices that seek to silence whatever is good. The bureaucracy of our decision will stand until the appointed hour when all other things of this world will pass away."

THE UNENDING DEBATE

There was a great debate that went on for years in our home between my mother and me. My mother firmly believed that people reaped what they sow. She also firmly believed that every person innately knows right from wrong. My position was and is we don't always reap what we sow and many individuals do not consciously know right from wrong.

Over the years, we would gather information as examples to support our position. There were times when the debate continued non-stop. There were times when my mother pulled rank and simply said she was right because she was my mother.

My position was and is that not all people who commit horrible acts against fellow human beings are punished here on Earth. My mother believed that people who willfully committed these acts suffered in bodily ailments, financial setbacks and suffered tragedies visited upon them or their families and significant others. I somewhat agreed with the "what goes around comes around" philosophy, but I have seen all too often sins that went unpunished. I steadfastly believe that we don't always reap what we sow.

REAPING THE BENEFITS

We reap the benefits of dreamers of old and take for granted significant inventions of the wheel, electricity and safe drinking water. The farmers sow select seeds combined with sweat equity, laboring so we can reap the benefit of convenient foodstuff at a minimal price. The civil rights marchers sowed seeds of justice and we reaped the benefit of their pain and a better nation. Manufacturers sowed the seeds of ideas, investing capital and solving problems as we reap the benefit of low-cost, time-saving goods.

We reap where we did not sow and sow where others will reap the benefit. We do not get paid for all the things we do and it is short sighted to believe we should be paid. God sowed the seeds of redemption for our sins through Jesus and we reap the benefit of God's grace.

There are times where what we reap is not what we expected. I sowed the seeds of beautiful flowers and got some strange weeds or nothing at all. I have planted seeds of friendship and gained new enemies. Many of us have sown the seed of love and reaped the venom of hate. And I have sown the seed of impatience and had to wait on God. Sowing the seed of concern reaped a call for me to mind my own business. And sowing seed of a helping hand reaped cold resentment.

On the other hand, I sowed the seed of cynicism and reaped the benefit of those who cared. I sowed the seeds of selfishness and reaped a community of people giving of themselves. I sowed the seed of politics and reaped the voice of Jesus. I sowed giving up on life and reaped a new life through Jesus. I sowed seeds of ill health and reaped the vigor of healing.

On the path to prosperity, you will sow seeds of success yet fail many times. Failure precedes success, growing pains precede understanding and understanding leads to acceptance of one God-given talent that opens the door to prosperity. You cannot fail if you live the life God has decreed for you. When we sow seeds that are in harmony with the life God has in store for us, we also reap the rewards He has set aside since the beginning of creation. It is in this arena of life that we really do reap what we sow.

LIVING THE PROMISES OF GOD

To live the life God wants for you requires first and foremost that you be teachable. Too many people are not teachable, because they know everything. Some people are not teachable because comprehension is a problem. Others are not teachable because God's promises seem too far-fetched, along the lines of fantasy. Some of us cannot reap because we spend too much time focusing on the world instead of God. If you want to be prosperous the ability to concentrate is paramount.

One of the things God does best is teach us. His teaching is not like our educational system where passing to the next level is a game of numbers: age, being cool with the teacher or at the discretion of the administration. If you fail at loving God and your neighbor, exercising forgiveness, letting go of negative thoughts; if you instead practice injustice and hate in God's classroom of life, you will repeat each lesson until you earn a passing grade. Ask God for a discerning mind and you will become teachable.

Give therefore thy servant an understanding heart...that
I may discern between good and bad.

(1 Kings 3:9, KJV)

Living the life God wants for you requires you give up worshiping idols. In today's world idol worship takes the form of materialism, thoughts and overbearing egotism.

THE TRAP OF MATERIALISM

Throughout the Scriptures, you will notice God used tangible items as contact points of faith. Genesis starts with the mist, then the fog, water, gold, pearls and onyx. We move downhill after encountering the tree of life. The point is: materialism has a two-dimensional meaning – one spiritual where God uses water, oil, wine, fire, trumpets, the images of the sword and seeds, and finally wood from a tree shaped in the form of a cross as instruments of faith, signaling answered prayers and blessings granted.

The other materialism is of this world: tangible accumulation with emotional attachment, as if inanimate objects have life and share love. This form of materialism is an abomination to God and a form of idol worshiping. The earth and all that is contained in it is God's to serve as a blessing and a gift to human beings. Materialism is not to be condemned unless it is detached from the recognition of its spiritual source. We need the material as well as the spiritual. We must acknowledge God as the source of all that is physical, as well as spiritual.

There is some good in the attainment of materialism, but it is secondary to worshiping God in spirit. This feverish desire for materialism in today's world is a form of idolatry.

I WAS THERE; WERE YOU THERE?

There is another fast growing form of idolatry taking place: worshiping 'being there.' Being there is so important these days that it has taken on religious overtones. I have witnessed people experience depression and pain because they missed an event and seen others spend most of their time, energy and money attempting to attend every event and party time-after-time. It appears that 'being there' is becoming an overriding important part of many peoples' lives. The theme is 'I was there; were you there?' He was there, she was there, and everyone was there. If the event was church-related, however, there is never a mention of God being there.

Some people fail at prosperity because they cannot find or mind their own business. It is sad to see individuals who cannot realize that God has prepared a life for them. On the road to prosperity you should learn from the mistakes of other people. You cannot be very successful at anything if you cannot first find and mind your own business.

THE LIFE GOD WANTS FOR YOU

In order to live the life God wants for you, you must deepen your hunger for God's Word. Fellowship with God is first experienced in the form of protection and guidance.

A friend who knew nothing of God found his hunger was deepened by two nearly-fatal automobile accidents within a short period of time. It was enough to motivate him to enter a house of worship; it was there that he experienced encouragement and enlightenment. He opened his mind and spoke to God in prayer. He sat silently reading Scriptures and let God speak to him. The lessons were hard and time consuming. There was no ceremony or certificate of merit but a changed man emerged. And the interaction between him and God remained a secret. *"I have opened my mouth unto the Lord, and I cannot go back"* (Judges 11:35, KJV).

In order to live the life God wants for you, you must make a commitment to yourself. Committing yourself to God is really a commitment to yourself. The commitment is simple; you are to find your God-given gifts. You must make a commitment to grow in knowledge and establish roots with God.

Sometimes in pursuit of spiritual growth we must go through many obstacles, hard knocks, dark nights and deep water. Since we are constantly evolving, this is often a prelude to growth. Commitment involves the choices you make which are within your control. Be committed to never quitting. Be committed to remaining focused. Be committed to opening your heart to the blessings of God and experiencing His joy, His power and His wisdom.

It takes just one seed to produce a new crop. One good idea is all you need to experience the conscious prosperity of the Kingdom of God. It is never too late; age will not hamper you.

Living the life God wants for you also requires you change your attitude. To open the doors to success you must look within. Within you is where God is. Once you connect with God within your soul, you will gradually change. If you pursue God with all your heart, your attitude toward your fellow humans will change. So will your attitude toward life in general, nature, your body-temple and the pursuit of happiness. In time you will live life joyously and cultivate a positive attitude. You will seek to understand the meaning of love. Negative things you once coveted with great zeal will dull in meaning. Eventually, you will give them up altogether and be certain not run to them as you once did. Your tolerance for strife will diminish.

Prosperity strives where there is harmony; prosperity flees where there is strife.

TAKE CONTROL OF TIME

When you live the life God wants for you, you will take control of your time. No matter how extensive your life resume may be, the only thing you have in this world is time. There will be times when subtle and not so subtle things will rob you of your time. Time robbers are everywhere.

I have heard people say that their prayers have not been answered. A close examination revealed an interesting pattern, many of us spend too much time at inaction (procrastination): dreaming, feeling sorry for ourselves and making excuses as to why we have not lived more and accomplished more. We forget that we must help our prayers to fruition by first being still in God's presence then going to work.

The saddest event in life is to have God bless us with ideas that will lead to a more fulfilling life and yet we do nothing. Years later when someone else acts upon what we conceived earlier, we experience a heaviness in the pit of our stomachs that makes us sick. Gian Carlo Menotti, the Pulitzer prize-winning composer, said it best: "Hell begins on the day when God grants us a clear vision of all that we might have achieved, of all the gifts we wasted, of all that we might have done that we did not do." This is where the living dead reside. Of all the wasted resources, lost opportunity is the greatest.

FOUR PHASES OF A NEW SEED

To live the life God wants for you, you must grow and develop a fresh approach to worship. It is fun when new people enter into the faith of God. There is excitement in the air as they experience the four phrases of a new seed:

New seeds are often uncultivated, raw and unstable. One of the most important parts of witnessing for God is acceptance. There is a difference between understanding and acceptance. Understanding alone is half of the equation. Notice the underlying essence of the parable of the scattered seeds: each seed heard the Word of God but only one kind of seed understood it. The difference between hearing and really listening is the key to understanding with a deeper meaning. The difference between understanding and acceptance is insightfulness with the mind's eye and humility of the heart. Accept God just as He is and He will raise you up faster. When the heart is moist and warm you can see God.

Eliminate the seeds of doubt. Doubt comes from losing focus; keep your mind stayed on God. God is your constant companion reminding you daily of His presence. Each day is a lesson in how near God's presence is, such as the near traffic miss. When you awake each day in good health, afforded another day to make a contribution to the betterment of self and this world, God is with you. Eliminate the seed of doubt and uncertainty about whether God loves you; He does love you. Eliminate the seed of doubt regarding whether you are worthy of God's special blessings; you are worthy. Eliminate the seed of uncertainty of God's capability to make the impossible possible; He can. *"I will trust and not be afraid"* (Isaiah 12:2, KJV).

Sow good seeds. The good seeds of this world are positive thoughts. Thoughts are things that carry weight in this world and the next. Your thoughts are your justification or condemnation for your actions. Thoughts have the ability to guide us in overcoming family curses that pass from one generation to the next. Sowing good mental thoughts speed the process of God declaring His approval of us. Let your thought seeds be of the fruit that produces an abundant crop. Plant thought seeds that are deeply rooted: caring for others, thinking of others, expecting good for others. The seeds you plant are a reflection of your life and effort. Your effort identifies the fruit you will bear. As Jesus said we are identified by the fruit we produce. Our fruits are not of the outer things of life. *The fruit of the spirit is love, joy, peace, patience* [enduring], *kindness, goodness, faithfulness"* (Galatians 5:22).

There are some strange religions out there, full of false interpretations. I suppose there is some benefit to doubting by exercising caution in the pursuit of man-made religious concepts. Many religions do not acknowledge Jesus as the Son of God and the Son of Man. Some say He did not exist. Others refuse to acknowledge the Trinity of God. Some say Jesus was just a prophet or a historical figure. There are religions that say Jesus did not die on the cross and return to life. Many religions treat women in ways that contradict the teaching of Jesus and deny them first class citizenship. There are religions that preach racial hatred. Some religions have strict interpretations of God's Word that makes them static, staid, rigidly unable to accept anything new that may help its followers grow. God, through the Holy Spirit, interjected Himself into the Old Testament, the New Testament, and any other doctrines or religious form, especially when that religion seeks to focus on the greater good for humanity. It does not matter which religion you choose if you interpret God with an open mind from a dynamic point of view, God will bless you. Your part is to let God do what He does best: teach you and bless you. God will make a way through your experiences and you will arrive at the truth. Scripture says it best: *"Eye has not seen, nor ear heard... the things which God has prepared for those who love Him..."* Jesus told us: You shall do greater things than the miracles you've seen. Only a dynamic, ever-progressive God would make such a claim.

THOUGHT-CHANGING BEHAVIOR

This leads us to the question: what are the good seeds that take root and multiply abundantly? Good thoughts are seeds that multiply and produce good fruit. Thoughts are things that transcend the physical and take root in the spiritual. So many self-help books and audio tapes stress visualization techniques and positive thinking through denial. Denial is a double-edged sword. Denying one thought and replacing it with another can aid us at overcoming bad habits but these thoughts may not be dealing with reality.

If you watch closely you will discover that most criminals or social misfits see themselves as victims not perpetrators. They have denied their negative immorality for a positive image along the lines of a martyr.

True thought-changing behavior can only come with spiritual backing. The seed of your thoughts must be centered on Jesus. It is your thoughts that grant you entry into the righteousness of God, but it is also your thoughts that can condemn you. Do you think of yourself as self-righteous apart from God's grace by way of the crucifixion and resurrection Jesus? Do you see yourself as the sole reason for the existence of the universe? Are your thoughts fit to be printed in children's books or religious texts?

Are your thoughts constantly focused on some form of vice? Do your thoughts include harming others physically, emotionally or mentally? Are your thoughts focused on gaining something without giving something in return? Do most of your thoughts contain fear or regret? Does Satan occupy your mind with thoughts of strife? Are your thoughts scrambled or disorderly, do they lack focus? The thought seeds you have planted will grow into the fruit of their kind. When you follow your own wrong inclinations your lives will produce these evil results: impure thoughts, eagerness for lustful pleasure, idolatry, spiritualism (that is, encouraging the activity of demons), hatred and fighting, jealousy and anger, constant effort to get the best for yourself, complaints and criticism, the feeling that everyone else is wrong except those in your own little group – and this includes wrong doctrines – envy, murder, drunkenness, wild parties and all that sort of thing. Let me tell you again as I have before, anyone living that sort of life will not inherit the Kingdom of God (Galatians 5:19-21).

TOTAL CONTROL

The mind is the one area in your life where you have total control of your thoughts. You can finesse them, caress them, change them, squash them and rest them. Jesus said, "As a man [or woman] thinks so he or she is [or does]."

There is hope. Ask God to grant you His thoughts. No matter what seeds you come from you always have a chance to reverse your fortune through God. Be ever mindful that His thoughts and His ways are far different from human thoughts and ways.

Prosperity is a byproduct of the enduring trials you will experience from family, friends, self and the world at large. It is your reward for giving God first place in your life, for making a conscious sacrifice to be obedient and practice God's laws. To pursue God is to pursue your treasure. To pursue God for the sake of receiving a reward is missing the point. Your return may not be in the form of money because that is not the reason we seek God. Money alone does not truly convey the essence of God.

Prosperity comes in many forms. Some seek justice, some good works, some peace, some love, some healing and some just want to see God. Jesus described what an insightful person would do once they discovered the location of God's treasure.

WHAT WOULD YOU TRADE?

He explained that the Kingdom of Heaven is like something precious buried in a field that a man [woman] found and hid again, then in his or her joy goes and sells all they have to buy the field – and get the treasure too (Mathew 13:44)! When you sell all that you have, you trade in your will, your desire to impress others, your soul, your motives, your pride, your sense of self, your ambition, your education, your beauty, your sexy body, your eloquent speech and manners and your career or job title in exchange for God's treasure.

So think noble thoughts and see God's light streaming into your mind. The divine is within you by way of the noble thoughts you implant. Ask God for wisdom, understanding, knowledge and acceptance; each is different but essential for a higher state of being. Let obtaining noble thoughts be your daily goal. Pursue noble thoughts in the silence of your daily sanctuary of unending prayers. Let noble thoughts guide your words and ways while pursuing God. So it is when you plant the seeds of noble thoughts you become noble and your thoughts shall multiply.

Whatever is true, whatever is honorable, whatever is right, whatever is pure, whatever is lovely, whatever is of good repute, if there is any excellence and if anything worthy of praise, dwell on these things...and the God of peace will be with you.

(Philippians 4:8-9, NAS)

CHAPTER FIVE

Faith in Action

Every living thing was endowed with faith at the creation of the world. Between the conception of life and the implementation, value was added by breathing the breath of life into all living things. Human beings were given an extra dose of faith through the abilities of senses, feelings, reasoning and intuition. Apart from the apparent senses, there is another faith. It is the faith born of the spirit called the soul. So when the Son of God comes in contact with us He can proclaim, "Your faith has made you well."

CONCENTRATE!

It was by faith that God conceived and created human beings. He made us physical beings endowed with the Spirit of God and faith. We all have faith. It is where we direct our faith that determines where our heart resides. The strength of our faith is perfectly correlated to our concentration. You cannot have a strong faith in God unless you are able to concentrate. Concentration is essential for developing enough faith to experience God's promise of prosperity. You must be able to concentrate with all your heart in order to give God first place in your life. One of the key elements of concentration is to make clear an image.

The image of God is that of the Father. The Father is wise and endowed with power and strength while dispensing kind discipline. The Father can correct error and handle situations with love. He is focused on our well-being with sincerity.

The Father has personality traits we seek to share. It is His image we seek to emulate. The Father is a perfect judge and teacher of things related to the soul. He is the seed of life that seeks to multiply. Our inheritance is decreed in the Father's will.

EXPLAINING AWAY THE MYSTERY

It is easier to place our faith, our beliefs, in horoscopes, palm reading, magic, witches and mediums such as tea leafs and lucky charms, than to believe in God. Mystic mediums support the innate longing for life's meaning by giving the unknown form that appeal to the senses. Mediums allow the believer latitude to interpret the spirit behind things with less complexity than God who cannot be categorized or given any form. Mediums do not need to be clarified or to possess any rhyme or reason of the law of things in the same way as a life-directing God. The mystery of life can be explained away through mediums with oversimplified pat answers to complex questions that appeal to the expectations of the believer.

As you encounter God's lessons, the Trinity of God may become confusing but with God's help it will become clear. The main thing to remember is your effort entails making constant readjustments to a blurred image of God while focusing on faith. Some of us have a blurred image of the Trinity of God. This is one of the hardest concepts for many Christians to comprehend. It implies God is all three entities, confusing some to the point of refocusing their faith altogether. Faith never vanishes, however. At times our attention is focused on symbols that are not backed by God's spirit producing roadblocks that cause us to bury our faith as the servant with one talent did.

NO SUBSTITUTIONS, PLEASE

Bars are one example of the symbols we give things that place barriers between us and God. It occurred to me while driving through the city that man-made bars are a good example of the barriers placed between material faith and real faith. I noticed many homes with bars on windows and doors. The rationale is bars allow us to feel safe, comfortable, protected and afford us peace of mind. Taken a step farther, bars can be categorized and seen as a substitute for several forms of faith.

When we put criminals behind bars we feel safe, protected, we experience peace of mind and feel that justice has been served.

Additionally, we go to bars to forget or at least to not face up to some of life's problems. A great number of individuals spend an enormous amount of time and money in bars drinking their problems away.

A person in possession of gold bars is considered well-off.

The law, music and codes that identify all use bars to add purpose to life.

The point is bars are symbols of faith in things we use as symbols of solutions to life's problems that appeal to expectations of faith. When we place faith in something other than God, our expectations of faith in God become distant from the source of where true faith was born. This is the substitute affect because faith in God is being replaced by man-made symbols.

THE IMAGE OF GOD

The image of God becomes blurred to many when the concept of a three-person Trinity is introduced. The concept was described clearly by a fellow educational seminar attendee as we shared conversation on the flight back from a university on the East Coast. The conversation segued into religion, particularly Christianity. I attempted to explain the concept of the Trinity. My fellow classmate did not understand until he related the concept to his world. He said God, the Father is the CEO and Chairman of the Board, Jesus is President and goodwill ambassador and the Holy Spirit is the Chief Operating Officer responsible for the administration of the universe. I laughed at his analogy because he was able to understand in the context of his environment.

This businessman who is now a friend went on to explain how God could split Himself into three distinct personages. He rationalized that the Father, Son and Holy Spirit are of one mind and one accord fused together by way of spiritual osmosis. All I could say was "something like that."

Another blurred image is that God is some kind of controlling "my way or the highway" deity ready, willing and able to punish us at the drop of a hat just for sport. This contradicts the whole concept of a loving God who would make the supreme sacrifice of giving His Son, and Himself for our sake, if He would then moments later in anger deliver a bolt of lightening to the buttocks of any man, woman or child that disobeys Him. How could the same God who pursues, entices, persuades, comforts, and makes constant overtures of love to us simultaneously engage in anger?

Faith starts with our thoughts; we were created with the ability to reason and formulate ideas with the additional gift to convey those ideas through language and deeds. The mind is where we can substitute one thought for another. It is in the mind where blurred, unclear images of God are to be cleared up.

When man first conceived the concept of a God he had to use his imagination. He imagined that there must be something greater than him after he encountered God through what first appeared to be phenomenon. God expelled our doubts of His existence with two simple words; "I am," placing man in hot pursuit from that moment on.

God's image is man's imagination. The secret is to not imagine too hard, just let go by accepting God and letting God be God.

WORTHY OF OUR ATTRACTION

The central theme of concentration is the point of attraction. What is attractive to you commands your attention thus tantalizing your thoughts. You become what you spend your time thinking about the most.

Just thinking about the life of Christ is enough to know His leadership can only be described as extraordinary and worthy of our attraction. Just observing closely how Jesus concentrated on the Father by never wavering should be worthy of our attention. Jesus' passion for our well being and spiritual betterment will never be duplicated, not by any prophets of old or new, any social reformer nor any politician or religious leader. His command for us to be perfect through Him is enough to arouse our interest to discover what He meant.

To grow in faith through concentration is the road to finding love and at the very least attempting to live the supernatural life and act like Christ. Christ is the creator of faith. Faith is Jesus' gift to us, created by the prophecy that one would come to bring us back into the fold of God. He is the finished product, the Son of Man and the Son of God, worthy of our attraction and, above all, our concentrated faith. Concentration is the key to achieving prosperity through faith. Concentration is necessary to understand and obey God; it is the only way of staying in His spirit.

POSITIVE REINFORCEMENT

A high school teacher and basketball coach once told me that today's youths have a difficult time concentrating and trouble focusing. I found that hard to believe, because I observed my sons playing video games with an iron-clad focus and concentration. If my wife or I called out to them while they were into their game-playing sessions they never seemed to hear us.

A short time later, however, I took a moment to watch my sons play video games, this time with the eyes of a researcher. Upon careful observation, I noticed my sons were not playing the games to hone their hand-eye coordination or to sharpen their mental concentration skills, but to score points and thus receive short-term positive reinforcement. They played to reinforcement their self esteem.

I learned by casual conversation that video games provide players with positive reinforcement at a rate of 90 per minute or 1.5 positive reinforcements per second. Video game players advance from one level to another knocking off an opponent then further advancing to the next level or conquest. There is presently no other vehicle that provides players with positive reinforcements at that rate of speed and at such a heightened stimuli.

After observing my sons I was left with the conclusion that we engage in selective concentration and focus based on whatever is the object of our affection.

We adjust our concentration and focus to fit our roaming interest. The problem is some of us are constantly changing our object of affection time and time again. This makes it difficult for God to bless us and gain a firm footing in our lives.

AVOIDING THE ALLURE
OF THE WORLD

My question is: how do we concentrate with our minds focused on God? It takes tremendous focus to find and obey God's laws. It takes enormous concentration to give God first place in your life. It takes ironclad concentration to resist the alluring temptations of the stimuli of this world.

The stimuli of this world are constantly attacking our attention and in many ways short circuiting our attention span. Every day of modern living is a day where our sensory perceptions are being attacked by sexual images: billboard ads, color-coded packaging, gadgetry, television, voice messages, email and suggestive symbols.

In the end, some of us will go crazy; others will become numb to any type of messages and thus dismiss God's message. Some individuals will numb their senses and lose their ability to recognize God's intuitive and counter-intuitive ideas. Many will become cynical and develop a posture that whatever is presented to them is a lie.

We are at a point in time where our technology has surpassed our functional intelligence. That is why we marvel at the latest gadgetry and must have it, but don't know how to operate them. It is a good thing that our children know how to operate the latest gadgetry, but practical knowledge and profound wisdom is a mystery to them. We are seeing very young gadget-literate children suffering from over-stimulated stress like misguided missiles.

MUSTARD SEED FAITH

To stay in an eternal state of grace requires a focused, concentrated state that no human besides Jesus could achieve. Jesus knew it was humanly impossible for us to maintain the undeterred level of concentration required to achieve a heavenly faith, so He informed us that all we needed was faith the size of a mustard seed and He would carry us the rest of the way.

A mustard seed is less than the size of one grain of rice. If so little faith is required, the question becomes: where is your faith being directed? It is not a question of "do you have faith" or "how much faith do you have"; you do have it, and you have enough. The beauty of petitioning Christ is you don't need much. You just have to concentrate your faith. It is as simple as it sounds. The key to concentration is to want to.

Faith, like all other positive attributes, can travel down misguided paths. So often the moment we conceive and believe that God has faith in us and blessings in store for us we began an active campaign to help fulfill those blessings. In pursuit of our blessings, we sometimes feel the need to help God out by solving our problems in a manner or avenue we think God should use. When we do this we are placing our faith in our own problem-solving abilities. When things do not work out as we envision them, we become frustrated and at times lose the focus of our faith.

FAITH IN THE RIGHT THINGS

We were endowed with the ability to lose our concentrated faith just as we have the ability to lose our lives. The more frustrated we become the more determined we are to direct God's blessings. Eventually fear grabs hold of us, creating more distance from the blessings of God that we once saw as near. From this point, we are one small step away from bitterness and despair. If we do not recognize how dark these negative traits can be and surrender our frustrations, fears, bitterness and despair to God, we are in danger of moving to the next phase: becoming angry at God.

The spirit of disappointment and fear has the ability to take our concentration away from God. Waiting patiently on the Lord is the most important yet also the most difficult component of faith. Our faith grows when we spend a lot of time with Him. It is imperative that we put our faith in the right things.

God is life. It is through faith that we can see the final goal God has in store for us. Keep your faith on the positive path: *"let not your heart be troubled; you believe in God, believe also in Me"* (John 14:1, NKJ). When impatience enters your mind, turn to Isaiah 40:31, *"...they that wait upon the Lord shall renew their strength..."*

THE PROCESS OF BLESSINGS

When Christians testify on their own eyewitness accounts of faith, they omit the punch line of success. It is God's faith in us that is the one and only faith; our faith is but a returned deposit. Our faith connects with His faith through prayer, reasoning, meditation and the spoken word, infused with a longing to add meaning to life. When people tell their version of how God blessed them, important parts of the story are sometimes omitted. They may say how they kept the faith or lost their faith or conclude that things "just happened." But things don't "just happen" as if by magic. Things happen through a process.

The process of blessings becoming a reality takes on so many twists and turns that hardly any blessing is just one story, but a combination of many stories. Where a series of events take place, paths are crossed, doors and windows are opened on Earth as they are in Heaven and God reveals to us He has a sense of humor in the process.

SUFFERING FOR THE GLORY OF GOD

What is important to most stories of God's blessings is that some suffering took place either externally or internally. Is suffering necessary for the fruition of God's blessings? The answer is no. We do not have to suffer to receive God's blessings; Jesus suffered for us. The reason some of us suffer is definitely for the glory of God.

Suffering brings out human trust in God and it has profound faith-restoring qualities. God, with all His faith and power, suffered greatly while creating the universe and suffers daily as He seeks to raise us up to higher heights. He suffered pain watching His Son's crucifixion.

> *Fear nothing that you are about to suffer. [Dismiss your dread and your fears!] Behold, the devil is indeed about to throw some of you into prison, that may be tested and proved and critically appraised, for ten days you will have affliction. Be loyally faithful unto death [even if you must die for it], and I will give you the crown of life.*
>
> (Revelation 2:10, AMP)

If you stay faithful to God your suffering will pass quickly.

RICH AND POOR ALIKE

For some odd reason some individuals think the rich do not suffer. However, the truth is the affluent or rich share the same fate as those with little material goods. They are really one and the same. Both want to be rich; both are susceptible to the same sins and lapses of faith and experience the same perils in life. Both cannot have a fulfilling life without God. And both will pass through this world unable to take their acquired possessions into the next world.

The sum total of a person's life, rich or poor, is: did they love God? Is their faith concentrated enough to submit their lives to Him? What good did they do for the betterment of life in God's name? Did their faith include their neighbor, the planet and all of God's creation?

Both the rich and poor are one and the same, especially if they worship money. Worshiping riches will keep both from entering the Kingdom of God. It does not matter if you are rich or poor the love of money makes you the rich person that cannot enter the Kingdom of God. To love and concentrate your faith on material gain is to hold on to a blurred image of God, a focus in futility; as a stand-alone concentration of faith, it is totally opposite of the thought process inherent in the Kingdom of God. One is totally material and the other is totally spiritual. This led Jesus to say you cannot worship (have faith) in both God and money.

THE MAIN POINT

The main point of faith is seeing God as our protector, director, teacher and creator of life. Our entitlement to the assets in the treasury of the Kingdom of God is a derivative granted to us by grace through the sacrifice of Jesus Christ. Although God decreed us an entitlement, the value of our entitlement is derived from another source: Jesus. We can tap into the source of prosperity by directing our faith with the utmost emotional and mental determination to receive it.

Just because you lack wealth today does not mean you will lack tomorrow, next week, next month and so on. The question is: do you believe God's promise that you are entitled to share in His wealth – a wealth that is far greater than money?

Some individuals believe that pursuing prosperity is not worth the effort and the underlying spirit of wealth is a curse not a blessing. It is easier to believe that the pursuit of prosperity is a game where the rich get richer and stay rich. But that would be settling for the narrow view that does not capture the whole story.

The difference between you, the evil rich and the thief who breaks into the Kingdom of Heaven's treasury is where their faith is directed. The evil rich and the thief believe the treasure in the Kingdom of Heaven is for their benefit. Their means of obtaining it are contrary to God's law but nonetheless they see themselves as entitled to it.

Have you ever thought that heaven's treasury was created for your use, if only you would ask with the right motives?

We teach best what we need to learn the most. Adam failed because his faith was redirected, which led him to bend his motives away from God. He became intrigued by the prospect of becoming a god himself.

FAILURE THEN SUCCESS

In today's churches we are constantly bombarded with stories of achievement that are so far removed from the experience of the people in the pews that many members of the congregation choose to leave church, convinced they are too far from God to even try. Many people come to church with pains so deep that God seems distant. From the pulpit come echoes of grand achievements, reinforcing those feelings that God does not make sense.

It is hard to conceive of being promoted to a vice president of an organization when in two days you are going to be evicted from your residence.

It is hard to conceive of being appointed to this or that board of directors or graduating with honors from graduate school or becoming a partner in a prestigious law firm when you or a loved one is facing terminal cancer and there is no medical insurance.

It is hard to see God at work when the clergy is stressing success and praising those who give the most money. The best sermons speak of failure and then more failure, followed by triumph. Most people have failed so much that failure has left a permanent impression. They can identify with failure *then* triumph.

FLEETING SUCCESS

Over the years I have heard the following reasons why some people feel success is fleeing in their minds:

Success is the by-product of having money to make money.

Success comes from having leverage over other people.

Success comes from knowing the right people. So in order to succeed you must get next to the right people.

Success is the result of being born into the right situation or marrying into the right family or circle of influence.

Success is the result of opportunity so it is best to wait on the right opportunity.

Success is happenstance and chance. If your luck is bad you won't achieve success.

Success is a secret rite locked away in hidden scrolls that the clergy and the rich reveal to those able to join their inner circle.

Success is the result of gaining entry into the clique. Better yet, it is granted to those who are accepted into the clique within the clique.

Success is impossible, it is best to get it out of your mind. Criticize those who appear to be successful, rage at God and call it "another day, another 50 cents" after taxes.

Successful ideas are elusive. Many ideas I've thought about left without a trace. I did not write them down and it is unkind for you to remind me. You still have to work after conceiving an idea.

Success is not for me, so it is best not think about it. I will just live for now and wait to die.

Success is not all it is cracked up to be. It is nothing but hard work.

My mother and father and all my other relatives were poor so why should I try to be better than them?

I tried success once and failed; why send myself through that pain again?

If you achieve success you gain false friends and everyone you meet wants to be associated with you because of your money and success. It is best to keep things as they are.

When you achieve success you lose yourself, becoming arrogant and contrite. Before you know it you are socializing with creeps and playing golf.

Success will go to your friends' and family's head. They will start expecting things from you until they use you up.

Success leads to being like the Pharisees and Sadducees and you won't get to Heaven.

Blessed are the poor; being poor is safer.

You cannot be successful, rich and saved.

I just want a roof over my head, shoes on my feet and food in the refrigerator. Anything more than that is too much of a burden.

I am lazy.

I am too old.

I am just average.

Success is hard work

PERFECTING YOUR TALENTS

I have to admit I was uncomfortable with the number negative responses people gave me over the years. Doubt seems to hold a special place in the minds of many people. Too many self-help books and motivational speakers exploit the doubts of many by preaching "you can do anything you put your mind to." So many people attempt to do things contrary to their God given talents, and fail.

It is difficult if not impractical to pursue being a scientist when your mathematical skills and scientific abilities are below average. It is impossible to run a large enterprise when your talents are more suited for manual labor or artistic endeavors. The point is: you can do many things in accordance with your God-given talents; therefore it is important that you find your talents as early as possible so life may afford you time to perfect them. The more time you spend perfecting your talents the more prosperous you will be.

THERE IS ALWAYS HOPE IN JESUS

Over the years I have found people fail for these seven main reasons:

Bad health and illness

Lack of insightful imagination beyond this physical world

Failure to mind or find their own business
Repulsive behavior
Inability to concentrate their faith on God
Incompetent stewardship (talent development)
Bad timing

Remember, there is always hope in Jesus. The Jesus effect can counteract these seven reasons for failure. He said that He is the vine and you are the branch; if you are connected to Him your request in His name will be granted. The power of God through Jesus can correct all ills.

When you appeal to God through prayer, your prayers will be answered, but in many cases not in the way you expect. I have found that prayer requests in the form of questions are responded to more rapidly: prayers with specific requests, asking God in Jesus' name to change my present situation. Ask Him: what shall I do that is pleasing to You? Question Him through your prayers, asking Him to show you what He desires of you, or what you must do to achieve His prosperity. Ask: what must I do to become acceptable to You? Tell me what I must do before You trust me with Your treasure.

These prayers work better than prayers such as: I am healthy, wealthy and wise and my prosperity is assured. Those sorts of prayers of an affirmative nature deny your present situation and do not project a true picture of where you are in Christ. You may *not* be healthy in body, mind and soul, certainly not wealthy, and wisdom may not have arrived yet.

Underlying some affirmative prayers are prayers with overtones of boasting wrapped in denial. Remember the parable whereas one worshipper entered the temple and proclaimed himself better than other sinners. He was in denial and he boasted of virtues he did not have; remember, he did not leave the temple blessed that day. The one who humbled himself did.

THE DOUBLE-EDGED SWORD

Denial is a double-edged sword. Both Adam and Cain went into denial mode when God questioned them, exemplifying denial of error. God asked Adam: "Why do [you] hide from me?" and Cain, "Where is your brother?" Both Adam and Cain placed the weight of their problems on extenuating circumstances. This type of denial is entrenched in the error of sin that deepens the committed wrong and prevents the person from coming clean, thus pushing them farther way from God's healing and correction.

The other side of denial is the denial of truth, whereas we deny that God will provide for us or feel we are too wretched for Him to make a way for us so dare not attempt to come into His presence. Jesus attempted to encourage those of low self-esteem and doubt when He reasoned to the crowd: If God clothes the lilies of the field and feeds the birds, your Father will certainly clothe and feed you (Matthew 6:28).

CONFRONTATION: A KEY COMPONENT

Many people fail in life because they cannot or will not confront life's problems. Confrontation is a key component to success. Some people have labeled confrontation as rebellion. I am not speaking of confrontation with a mindset of destruction or interfering with the happiness of others by causing strife or disobeying just laws. What I mean is confronting life's problems head-on instead of running from them. Running from your problems is a form of denial. Some people when faced with a problem go into imaginative modes whereas they refuse to admit the existence of the problem. You cannot run from your problems by using techniques of denial. The problems you run from will reoccur again and again until you deal with them. The act of confrontation is an act of faith.

Confrontation has a way of clearing up misunderstandings and letting others know where you stand. It also knocks down the tricks the mind sometimes plays on us through denial. Confrontation is a form of courage. In roles of leadership, confrontation is essential to establishing a vision toward a collective goal. You have to face your problems head-on and deal with them in order to achieve prosperity.

HANDLING THE TRUTH

Both denial of error and denial of truth must be overcome if you want to live peacefully in God's grace and enjoy the prosperity set aside for you at the beginning of creation. Learning to handle the truth will set you free. It clears the mind, calms the digestive system, quiets the nervous system and instills unshakable self-confidence. Keep your prayers in the specific request and questioning mode and God will surely provide you with an answer. Even if that answer is so truthful it hurts: "you are not able to handle abundant prosperity in your present state," this will let you know to keep trying.

SACRIFICING TO A LESSER GOD

Adam and Eve had it all. Yet the first son and daughter failed because their faith was redirected and their motives altered. Both Adam and Eve were intrigued by the prospect of becoming god. Their story may provide us with information regarding why some of us lose our faith and sacrifice our success and prosperity to a lesser god. Let us visit Adam and Eve in the latter years of their lives.

Eve: Adam, Adam, Adam, I need you to come and help me. Adam, don't you hear me calling you? I am tired of this! Adam, come here; I need you. Where were you when I was calling you?

Adam: I was over there.

Eve: You were over there at the stupid altar you made for God. When are you going to get it, Adam? It is up to us; God has abandoned us.

Adam: No Eve, God is still with us. We have to use our faith to get back into the Spirit that was present in the Garden.

Eve: Adam, the Garden is gone forever and God does not live here anymore. Right now I need you to help me harvest the grain. This food is for our survival: come winter the storm winds will ravage against our hut, the cold night air will penetrate our sheep-skin blankets and pain will grip our old bones that crackle like the sounds of the dry season. This is our lot in life, Adam. We move from place to place and toil for food as the land yields sparingly, then curse our efforts. This harvest will carry us through part of the winter and from there I do not know if we will survive. We must plan for the worst and hope for the best. Our plans must be based on circumstances, not dreams of yesterday that are no more.

Adam: Eve, we will survive the winter the same way we survived so many winters past. If we plan for future calamity, we invite it and when the storm winds finally blow we will still be ill-prepared. It is a lack of faith in God to fear the absence of our daily bread. When we look back on most of our fears, we see that those fears were without merit, rhyme or reason. Appearance is one thing, but things are not as bad as they seem. We have come this far with doubt and wavering faith and God has interceded and willed us through.

Eve: Adam, we could live better and acquire more if you did not spend most of your days worshipping God. He has turned His back on us and has not spoken to us in years.

Adam: I know He is still there, Eve. At times I can feel His presence.

Eve: How do you know He is there, Adam?

Adam: Look over here at this plot of grain. I prayed over this plot after planting the seeds, and dedicated the harvest to God. Look at the texture of this grain; see how much better and larger it grew in comparison with the other plots? We must give a portion of this grain to the needy in the new township down the road as a tribute to God.

Eve: Did you hear me, Adam? I said we do not have enough grain to last us through the winter. So why would we give the people of that God-forsaken township a portion of our scarcity? Tell me, Adam, how does that make sense? From my perspective it doesn't make sense to give what we don't have. I don't feel it, Adam. My hands are rough from working the land. My body aches; I am still not healed from birthing children. I spend years rearing children who grow up and leave when we need their help in our old age. Help me to understand. I do not feel God. All I see is land that yields less with each season. I grieve for Abel; he was a prophet the world will never know. It pains me to live with the uncertainty of not knowing if Cain is alive or dead. I worry about Seth and our other children: are they well? What are they doing? I wonder how many grandchildren we have now.

ONE DAY OUR SAVIOR WILL COME

Adam: Eve, please don't talk like that. God has prospered us by giving us our daily bread. That is all we need at this point in time, anything more will cause us problems. We must not let thoughts of poverty or prosperity destroy our generosity. If we are not careful both riches and poverty can harden our souls and we will give God less. If we keep our faith, one day our Savior will come.

Eve: Adam, what do you expect? Do you expect God to come down from His throne and feed us? And what will happen if you die before me?

Adam: Yes, Eve, many times God did just that. He provided for us in the Garden of Eden and He is still making a way for us. In the Garden we had all we would ever need. He placed gold, onyx, pearl and other precious metals in the Garden before creating us. We were prosperous and did not know it. It was in the Garden where we were in harmony with nature; more importantly, God lived with us. So yes, Eve, I do expect God to come down from His throne and feed us the foodstuff of His love.

Eve: Adam, it has been so long since God lived with us I can barely remember. I want to believe but I have to live in the here and now. The mystical world of God sounds good but it is over, Adam. We have sinned. God sees us as unholy and cannot bear to live with us. It is prudent to get over it, Adam, and accept that God does not live here anymore.

Adam: There is always hope, Eve. Think of the people in the new township; things may be different for them. I am excited for them. I invited them over for prayer and fellowship on the seventh day. We will praise God, sing songs of merriment and invite God's angels to attend our services.

Eve: Adam, what right do you have to preach the gospel of God? We were untested infants of faith and lost our steward-ship as toddlers do. Those people of the new township are igno-rant and evil, worshipping all sort of strange gods. We should be the last people on Earth to lift our heads in leading others to praise God. We hide our nakedness from the face of God; our shame will be shouted throughout all eternity. If you insist on preaching your sermon to the people of the township, this time ask them for a donation. At least get a she-goat for your reli-gious knowledge.

Adam: Why are you so bitter, Eve, so negative? God uses the flaws in us to bring others into His Kingdom. If we can over-come those flaws then we become powerful again, the way we were before we fell. We should praise God for another chance and invite Him to inhabit us.

DON'T BLAME ME

Eve: I am trying to forget, Adam, but time is a cruel reminder. I think about what you said when God confronted our sins. You said, "She gave me of the tree and I ate." You later blamed me by saying to God: "The woman whom You gave me caused me to sin." I have carried that hurt with me for many years, Adam. It pains me that at the first sign of trouble you abandoned me, and blamed me for your sins in the same breathe.

Adam: I admit, Eve, I was not a man at that moment; not the man God or my woman wanted me to be. My sins and my nakedness will be recorded throughout the ages and my name associated with being less than God's image. I tried to make amends by teaching the words God taught me to the people of the township; sometimes we teach best what we need to learn the most.

Eve: I fear I will go down in the book of time as the most hated woman ever borne by the hands of God. My legacy ignites my bitterness. The jury has already convicted me of my sins and the verdict of the spirit of evil is death. This could have been avoided had you spoke forthrightly about the things God whispered to you, instead of withholding those things from me. I asked time and time again: what did God say to you? And each time, Adam, you simply said, "things." If you had told me clearly what God had said about the forbidden fruit, I think the path we traveled may have evolved differently.

Adam: It was not our lack of faith that doomed us. We went down the wrong path, Eve, by misdirecting our faith. We are the only human beings who saw God and still let our contradictory behavior get the best of us. We saw His Spirit and we believed without a doubt. God gave us faith in the same breath He gave us free will. He trusted us by placing the spirit of evil near us in paradise. It was our mistake to think He made a mistake and to pursue alternative behavior. We assumed that God's intention for us was flawed. There was no danger or urgency to head in a direction away from God, we created our own danger out of fear. Our thoughts were confused and fear led us to believe there must be more to life than worshipping God and making Him the focal point of our lives. We turned our back on God, embracing our own souls with a declaration of independence. None of us can escape irony. But there is hope; while I prayed, I saw the One to come, the One who is a better Son of Man than I could ever achieve.

Eve: We fell from a higher consciousness down to a realization of our nakedness. In the future people of this world will use material things to redirect their faith away from God. Many will claim they need *more* faith than the faith that was implanted within us by God since the beginning of this world.

Adam: I feel guilt that I let you down, Eve; I spent an enormous amount of time with God and was still uncertain of His will. I failed to understand what he meant. I thought and pondered for years, still not sure if we were companions or servant and master. I spent more time with the animals and left you on your own, to be enticed, to face trickery alone, to be ravaged by pure evil. Here we are, trailblazers of stewardship, and our behavior turned out to be no more than human error. We made mistakes in the shadows that will light the paths of future generations. By comprehending one's mistakes and the mistakes of others we may come to a point of enlightenment. We may come to a point of discovering the whereabouts of God. Maybe others yet to be born will get it whereas we failed. I have made many mistakes, Eve. The most serious mistake was I never told you that despite all our flaws, I love you.

Eve: And I love you, Adam. How will those yet to be born perceive us, Adam?

THE FULL WEIGHT OF BLAME

Adam: Some will say we should bear the full weight of blame for allowing sin into this world.

Eve: Will there be none who see our innocence, Adam?

Adam: In time some rare individual will see the plight of our blind infancy and toss us some sympathy.

Eve: And will they call us names?

Adam: Yes, Eve; the worst of words not yet conceived.

Eve: Do you think we should still pray for those not yet born?

Adam: Yes, Eve, many won't have a prayer.

Eve: Adam, did you say you saw a man while praying to God?

Adam: Yes Eve.

Eve: How did he look, Adam?

Adam: He glowed with a commanding presence. He had a divine aura about Him. But He said nothing. He just wept with me.

Eve: Adam, I saw this man. He spoke to me and said, "Your sins are forgiven. I am the Son of God. Come to Me and I will give you rest – all of you who work so hard beneath a heavy yoke. Wear My yoke…I will give you light burdens." When He said that, I felt a sense of calmness I had not felt since before we were expelled from the Garden. Oh, Adam, it was not always as we see things now. We started as helpers, awkward and unsure of ourselves. Now in our old age, we are lovers and friends. Yes, God can forgive us our sins and restore our days of old. In those days we lived without shame. He may one day come back to live with us. If not, then we shall love God from a shielded distance and form a bond of first hope. It is through a leap of faith that we believe God will attend to our needs and we shall share the riches of His grace.

Adam: Eve, we messed up everything. How do you mess up a world where everything we would ever need is provided? All we had to do was be cool.

Eve: Are we going to make it, Adam?

Adam: Yes, all we need to do is look back on God's past blessings of love and say with renewed faith He will be there in the future.

Eve: Adam do you think His blessings will be a long time coming?

Adam: No! Eve, God blesses us each and every day. At times it appears that we have not worked out a very good timing schedule with God. Sometimes when we cry out in need, His timing is not our timing. If He is true to Himself, Eve, He will show up in the nick of time and soothe our racing hearts.

Eve: That is why my nerves are so bad! He comes in the nick of time and I cannot help thinking that one day He will be too busy to come to our aid. Adam should we continue our dreams?

Adam: Yes Eve until they become our faith.

Eve: Hold me Adam, as we think about all we could have been. Hold me in the grip of a utopia we once had. We can pretend to have never departed from paradise. Embrace the whole of me and I shall embrace the whole of you. Let us dance like the spiral of a whirlwind departing from the impossible, traveling in all directions simultaneously. For as long as we live, let us remain gripped in each other's arms, gliding into the heavens of our imagination, dipping our souls in a conscious embrace of God.

CHAPTER SIX

Links

THE SHOESHINE BOY

I remember seeing an old school movie shot in black and white, the title of which I never knew. In this movie a young shoeshine boy met a corporate executive outside a towering office-building daily. They would exchange ideas and wish one another well on their way. The learning experiences that took place through exchange were mutual.

One day the executive had a pressing work-related problem that the youth solved with ease. The executive, being a good administrator of ideas, recognized the validity of the youth's idea instantly. As the story unfolds the executive became attached to the young man's fortitude and the youth relied on the inspiration he received from the executive in search of a better life.

While attempting to put the idea he had received from the youth in motion the executive became embattled with opposing forces from within the ranks of corporate executives. Like most ideas and visions the conception stage is only one part of the process. The implementation stage is another and finally there is the fruition stage.

The shoeshine boy's home life was unstable; he lived in an orphanage administered by harsh nuns whose goal was to perpetuate the orphans' dependency. The executive lived a comfortable, charmed life but he was ambitious and dissatisfied, wanting more. As the story unfolds the executive needed the young shoeshine boy to solve an essential missing link to the idea.

Shining shoes was the boy's outlet from his harsh life. He daydreamed of a better life while shining shoes. His dreams were followed by dread as he thought about his home life. The shoeshine boy had never known what a stable home was like. He feared what laid ahead for a child on his own.

One day the shoeshine boy did not show up for work; he had run away. His absence was unusual; no one could recall him ever taking a day off.

MENTAL GYMNASTICS

The executive had planned on engaging the young man in a round of ideas: sessions they called "mental gymnastics." Worry crept into the mind of the executive when his newfound friend, his good luck charm of abundant ideas, was gone for several days. The executive's concern sent him looking for the shoeshine boy. It was then that the executive thoughtfully recalled his memorable interactions with his young entrepreneur.

The executive had seen himself in the lad. He knew, just like the shoeshine boy, he stood alone against the storms of this world. The closer he looked at the shoeshine boy's life, the more empathic he became, seeing his own childhood fears that had cut deeply into his soul. A child left alone, denied a childhood, is soon stripped of innocence, exposed to the beastly will to survive.

His thoughts were centered on the shoeshine boy to the point he forgot about the ideas he had wanted to bounce off of his friend. He said to himself: "A child infected with reduced roots, growing pains of an empty cup, faces many of life's perils. But this child is blessed with abundant ideas. Such a child is protected by the hands of God, sworn to provide extra care to those neglected and in need of tender, loving care."

ALL'S WELL THAT ENDS WELL

The tension of corporate infighting and the whereabouts of his friend started to wear on the executive's mind. He searched

New York, the city of millions, for the boy, following every lead as to the boy's whereabouts. Each lead painted a picture of the boy's short, bittersweet life. As fate would have it the executive eventually found the boy but discovered his living conditions were hardly suitable for any human being.

With the shoeshine boy's help the executive implemented his idea and pulled off a corporate coup that threw his rivals into a tailspin. The executive advanced from senior executive to company president. He secured a stable home for the shoeshine boy. He created an office job to keep the boy close. The story ended in typical Hollywood fashion leaving the impression that all is well that ends well. We don't know what happened to the executive or the shoeshine boy beyond where the story ended.

MORE QUESTIONS THAN ANSWERS

The human-interest side of the movie ended happily. But it left the viewer with more questions than answers. Did the shoeshine boy eventually lose his ability to contact the Spirit of God where ideas dwell? Did the executive forget the role the shoeshine boy played in his rise to the top? How long did the mixture of two distinctly different worlds between the shoeshine boy and the executive last? Did they reach a limit of interpersonal tolerance and end up unable to be in the same room with each other for any length of time? In time did the shoeshine boy see the older executive as a dinosaur and form an alliance with younger corporate lieutenants to unseat his friend, boss, mentor and father figure?

A real-life story in living color between a former shoeshine boy and a corporate executive may give us some insight into how the movie's story could have ended. This true story is not as flowery and the ending has yet to written because there is still work to be done.

The only similarity between the characters in the movie and the real-life characters is that both formed a bond from an idea that brought them together. God snuck into the picture and left before anyone knew He was there. A few times He showed up with an amazing sense of humor and profound irony.

The corporate rivalries and infighting were more vicious than in the movie and the social economic setting varied somewhat. Both the young man and the executive ran into ghosts from the past. Ethnicity and economic status separated their ideologies; trust sometimes took a black-eyed blow.

Some evil people arrived on the scene, one of them from Hell. Money blurred the minds of some of the players. The arrival of a presidential candidate changed their views, encouraging them to stay strong together because numerous fights were just around the corner. The price of oil and natural gas was the lure to a failed political commodity campaign. And in time both men went their separate ways to reunite ties that were never severed.

LESSONS IN THE JOURNEY

On the journey to finding God and prosperity, the different twists, turns and altered paths are often more exciting than carting away the treasure. What once seemed mysterious is really grounded in simplicity. The most profound thing that awaits you on the path to prosperity is the many life lessons you will encounter. The lessons will be hard and sometimes painful, but the journey is paved with interesting people encountered along the way. No one pulls themselves up by their bootstraps alone, as many success books would have you believe.

God's laws concerning prosperity are so exact that any request, asked without malice, which is not harmful to you and is for the greater good of others, is granted, time and time again. Years ago I asked a simple question, little did I know the answer was immediate and more than I bargained for. Jesus said: "God is willing to give more blessings than we can imagine." So why do we ask for little when God is prepared to give more if only we ask with the right motives in mind?

SEARCHING FOR MEANING

The bus ride was filled with excitement; travel not only crosses geographic lines and climates, but connects us with other social worlds as well. I was entering a world far different than what I had known. This was a world of old money and raw power wielded strategically, a world of social snobbery and one-upmanship. On rare occasions if you looked close you might see a touch of class.

I was 14 and a witness to most of the decrepit things the streets had to offer. This search for meaning all started from the cruel seed of a father dying at an early age in a child's life, leaving no memories. It was a silent portrait painted on a canvas of shattered hope; where get-rich-quick schemes were the norm. On occasion there was an unexpected visit from the Holy Spirit, where God would flash a smile on us.

ANOTHER WAY OF LIVING

The bus boy job came about unexpectedly through a dear friend who had departed this world violently and too soon. The job required traveling from the east side of Detroit to Grosse Pointe Farms, Michigan. I had no idea this pocket-money job would alter my entire perspective of wealth and provide me with a glimpse into another way of living.

Membership at the Country Club of Detroit was unique to a small group of people dancing, getting drunk and saying the wrong things; something that drunks seem to do. They had their cake and ate it too. However, they were not the beautiful party people we see in grand illusions of wealth and high society. Many were plain with the same problems as other people not so blessed with money. Yet they danced at grand banquets, consuming dinners made of delicious heart-stopping gourmet cuisines and drinking the best booze.

It was these people who controlled the city of Detroit. If you threw in the automotive executives and the characters that dealt in the shadows and their private companies, this group played a significant role in the U.S economy of the 1960's, 70's, 80's and 90's. If you factored in their network of worldwide connections you found you were in the room with men and women who controlled a nice-sized portion of the free market world.

As impressive as it seemed it was not what it was fashioned to be. There was always an undercurrent in the place. Those who reached the status of relative success rubbed elbows with an elite group of wealthy individuals. Those who wanted to be a part of the elite knew in the back of their minds they did not measure up. Some positioned themselves in hope of being invited to step up the social economic ladder. Some wives played dangerous games alluding to crossing scandalous lines to seal positions for their husbands. The person with the most money could and sometimes did sabotage the richest of his opponents. The bar was set: the one with the most money was awarded the highest seat at the table of discussion on how to gain more money. Getting more money was the only way to stay on top.

The worst of the bunch were the "yes men" (I once heard them called "functionaries"), who were willing to put their moral consciences in cold storage, willing to do anything in their desire to move up. The wealthy need these men and women, mostly from the poor and middle classes, so they were encouraged to strive with a resilient spirit, to be like the moneymen. The motivation was the same: "help me advance my wants of accumulating more wealth and thus help yourself."

UNRELENTING COMPETITION

The competition was and is between unrelenting men and women desiring to be like the super rich. As they compete, sport enters the game, keeping score to determine who won and who lost. Their willingness to put their faith in the wealth of man instead of faith in God's prosperity is never questioned.

It is the wealthy who usually carry the vision of the world, where the visionary always stands front and center in every frame. Is the visionary selfish or is this his perception? Can he share any or just a few frames with others and God?

So many people reject the notion that the Earth and all things within it, around it and beyond it belong to God. The wealthy are not exempt from entering the Kingdom of God. The only thing that gets in the way is the question of "how much shall I keep for myself and how much shall I use to store up treasure in the Kingdom of God?"

In time the sense of entitlement takes over. It is so easy to declare in tones of a mad man "it is all mine." It does not matter how you accumulate your wealth; that is the concern of God, although certain means of obtaining it are laced with evil.

Money is not the root of all evil, miss-education is. It profoundly matters that you give praise and thanksgiving to God where it rightfully belongs and stop seeking the praise of men. God has a way of letting us know we are poor when we cross paths with those without a material bent, who have no need for money nor social status, yet still possess happiness, joy, faith and peace of mind that can only come from God.

EXCITEMENT IN THE AIR

I thought the job sounded fun; it might have some possibilities. There was a sense of excitement in the air, in part because this was my first experience with those outside my race and my first eyewitness account that people of different ethnicity were the same. The elite and those pretending to be poured out insults on one another the same as the poor: insults fueled with resentful language and hurt that may or may not heal. They too engaged in slights, power struggles and downright meanness; the difference being they did not settle their disputes with violent language or street retributions. In this setting cursing a colleague out was done in pleasant tones that smelled of fresh-cut roses but lost its fragrance over time once they realized they were being put down in disguised prose delivered with a smile. In everyday terms they dogged each other out in a manner that was acceptable to maintaining club membership because it did not break the spoken and unspoken rules of a strict social code.

Those rules can be changed especially by the person with the most money and connections, until he or she loses their fortune or someone else surpasses their wealth. The moneymen loved the adrenaline rush of making money but hated the crushing affect that another man or women with more money could inflict upon him. There were no open threats of murder or assault, no vulgar language followed by threats of retribution.

Large sums of money changed hands but not much cash; members signed their names for club services (this was before the era of widespread credit card use). Cash was on the premises but not very visible. All the drama surrounding this place was not strong enough to distract my attention away from observing how deals were decided at club dinners, banquets, weddings and birthday bashes, with whispers and winks, especially on the tennis court and golf course. Credit should be given where credit is due, the Country Club of Detroit knew how to throw some fabulous parties, and party they did.

SCOUTING FOR INFORMATION

One night a group of businessmen and their wives gathered for dinner. Most of their conversations started out perfunctory and moved to never-ending talk of business. It was fun to hear bits and pieces of information on what this company or that company was doing. Most of time the members had no idea I was scouting for bits and pieces of information so that I could understand the art of the deal.

I thought it was odd when club members seated at tables in my section acknowledged me, the bus boy. This was during the era where African Americans seemed invisible in the eyes of Caucasians, especially in so-called polite society where many African Americans still worked in the domestic service sector. I thought it was odd because I knew my dark chocolate complexion was very visible and almost impossible to miss in a crowd of Caucasians, even with impaired vision.

An African American man caught my eye. In this arena he was a "bad dude." His name was Gregory; he wore a tuxedo every day and knew how to coordinate his accessories. In other words he knew how to dress. He was a waiter at the time. He was smooth as he glided across the room.

Gregory would engage businessmen and their wives in conversation on just about any subject. He understood business; he understood the thought process of the people he served. He understood that it was important to take care of business. Along with the conversations Gregory gave excellent service with a smile; his tips were consummate with his service.

WATCH ME

I learned from Gregory by watching him. On those occasions we worked the same table section he would say to me "do as I do and watch me." Being a superstar is not always possible in glamorous industries or sports, but you can be a superstar in any field consummate to your talent. Gregory's talents were well suited for this field; in this country club Gregory was a superstar. Watching him inspired me to also become well suited, especially as I noticed how good I looked in a suit once I began ditching the fashion of the streets.

Great preparation was required for Gregory to hone his social skills of meeting and greeting and serving people. I am sure he worked on his posture, his walk, his speech and his balance while serving members their food. Gregory had class. He was not serving food that he could not afford. He had honed his prosperity skills by getting paid fantastic tips. He went on to be promoted to headwaiter, receiving bigger tips, and finally to maitre d', where his tips grew more abundantly.

I watched Gregory and learned many things. On the path to prosperity it is wise to simply watch and listen. Don't say a word. You can learn more by just watching and listening.

On this occasion one of the businessmen seated at a table in my section spoke and acknowledged me every time I cleared the dishes or poured water. I remembered this man because I had looked at him: not the glance of a first meeting with no desire to ever meet again, but into his eyes, incuriously looking for the qualities of another human being. We smiled at each other; mine a smile of acknowledgment that very few people have class. Most people would swear they have class. Some would say they have a little, others will say they have a lot, some won't know what you are talking about and never admit to not having any class.

EVEN A BUM CAN HAVE CLASS

I once saw a permanent homeless man give half-bitten McDonald's hamburgers retrieved from the trash to a new member of the homeless ranks: a runaway child. The homeless man did not eat that day for the sake of the runaway child.

This went on for several days until the homeless man convinced the runaway to go home. He did not eat because he believed God would take care of him. He was homeless, some would say he was a bum; but even a bum can have class.

I know of many situations where homeless men emerged from alleys to stop young girls from being raped or to stop police brutality. In the scheme of things very few of our neighbors would give up their food or risk harm to themselves for our sakes. The point is: don't get too caught up in how much money or possessions people have or associate either with class. Class and money and possessions are things separated by spirit.

Think about how much money and class God has and how to go about getting your share from Him. Think about developing class first and you will be surprised when the money starts flowing your way.

TAKING THE HIGH ROAD

The businessman and his party departed for the evening, I had no idea we would meet again.

Several years later I was working in the mailroom of Michigan Consolidated Gas Company when one day a friend and I had lunch. During lunch, my friend, Theodore Hunt, told me he was departing from New Detroit Inc.: a civic- and community-based organization set up after the riot of 1967 to improve and assist in rebuilding Detroit. The organization was controlled, funded and macro-managed by some of the same folks I had met at the Country Club of Detroit in Grosse Pointe Farms.

Theodore (Ted) had served in the Navy then the Air Force. He had enlisted during the open-door call of Eleanor Roosevelt allowing entry of African Americans into military service during World War II. He was patriotic, yet he knew going in that criticism and racism would be rained down upon him, not only from people who wanted to keep him out but also from his own people.

Ted had taken the high road and had approached the situation positively. Through a love of music and entertainment he had achieved the rank of master sergeant assigned to the entertainment and recreation unit of the Air Force. He had then pursued higher education while honing his singing and speaking skills, and forged ahead with a God-centered determination to make a difference in this world.

His talent to entertain had gained him performances with notable entertainers in USO shows and other venues, and would eventually take him to the White House for a command performance in front of the President. His speaking skills would earn him a first place trophy in an orator's competition sponsored by the International Platform Speakers.

LENDING A HELPING HAND

Ted's relationship with me evolved into that of an ally, mentor, father figure and partner in an effort to help children. The one thing that we agreed on was that children are our future and they deserved a better future. Ted laid out a plan to get some corporation to sponsor a program he had developed to go into the Detroit Public School System and present positive motivational lectures to the entire student body to help eradicate the student drop-out rate, teen pregnancies, violence within the school system and drug abuse and last but not least to motivate students to choose success and achievement over bad choices that contributed to a life of despair.

I thought Ted had a good idea, and wanted to lend a helping hand to another brother, so I told him I would talk to someone at Michigan Consolidated Gas Company, but who that person was I did not know. I had only worked there a few weeks. I asked the receptionist, secretaries and staff personnel on my mail route: to whom should I speak in order to get things done around here? The one name mentioned most was that of Robert W. Stewart, a former Naval Commander whose background in science had opened the doors of opportunity for him to play a part in the development of the first atomic submarine while working under the command of Admiral Hyman Rickover.

At the time of our meeting Stewart had ascended to the corporate ranks of executive vice president. His Harvard education helped him reach the top. Connections linking him to other people also played a role. Each time his name was mentioned by the rank and file it came with a warning. The perception inside the company was he is a hatchet man, mean as hell; an overseer who was willing to punish any dissenting non-conformist or any perceived threat to the function or profitability of the company. In other words, he was strictly a company man.

NOTHING TO LOSE

Now I have known unsavory characters: the mentally deranged and sweet old ladies who drank too much while performing burlesque back in their day. I did not see any danger meeting with this man. He was not necessarily someone I would ever see again; I was just passing through. I had nothing to lose: this was a dead-end mailroom job in an environment of ruthless "good old boys" stuck in a minority-dominated community that hated the natural gas utility company.

There were urban legends circulating about the gas company's collectors, mostly Caucasians, kicking in customer's basement doors, removing gas meters after arrangements had been made to pay the bill or even after the bill was paid. There was never an apology.

The people felt they were being cheated because in the public utility business, finding financing for short-term operational needs was as simple as charging each customer an additional dollar or 2 or 4 or 6 or maybe 36 dollars. By the time the public service regulators corrected the error, often passed off as "oops," the customer was given a credit on future gas bills but no actual money was refunded. The public utility used these funds for short-term operating expenses; paying no interest on what was really a loan from the customer. The credit for over-charged customers was usually returned in the late spring or summer. The utility gained from the opportunity the cost of the customer's money during the height of seasonal demand. This method of internal financing is especially fruitful if you have a million or more customers as Michigan Consolidated Gas Company did.

SPEAKING FROM THE HEART

When I made the appointment with Robert W. Stewart his secretary wanted to know what it was about, so I said I wanted to help him run the company and I had an idea to improve the company's image in the community. It took several weeks and a great deal of persistence, but I finally got a confirmed date to meet the executive vice president. My friend, Ted, on whose behalf I had arranged this meeting did something he often did, he coached me on how to present the motivational program. Each time he coached me I did just the opposite because I felt that speaking from the heart was best.

Speaking from the heart is the guiding light of Jesus' ministry. On the path to finding God and prosperity you must learn to speak from the heart. People will have faith in you when they realize you speak sincerely without pretense or concealing your true intention. I was there for one reason: to help my friend and in the process help the company. It was a win-win situation; there was no need to engage in anything but straight talk.

I had asked God years earlier to send someone my way who would teach me business beyond the theory of text books, someone who would place me in the arena of experience and not let any harm come to me. I had a gut feeling that some good would come out of this situation. It is in those gut feelings where God and evil urge us on: the challenge is for us to discern the difference.

A DONE DEAL

When I walked into Stewart's office, I recognized the businessman I had met at the Country Club of Detroit. He did not seem as vicious as he had been described. The information I had received was wrong. Like most of us he had another side, a good side.

We talked; I laid-out my friend's plan for presenting motivational lectures to students in the Detroit public school system. I pointed out how a sponsorship by Michigan Consolidated Gas Company would benefit the company's image and improve the quality of potential future employees, convincing him that the educational skills of the community are directly related to the quality of future employees and customers. He wanted to meet my friend.

They met; the deal was done to sponsor the Theodore Hunt's motivational lectures to public school students.

In retrospect, placing myself in Robert Stewart's shoes, I would have understood if he had had security throw me out. My English was not elegant nor my presentation polished. Public speaking was not my strongest talent; it was my manners and strength of character (the way you carry yourself) that got me positive results at that meeting. That and the understanding that all I wanted from him was knowledge got me many extended invitations to return.

A TALE OF TWO CITIES

Years earlier on one particular bus ride to work at the Country Club of Detroit my level of first encounter perception had been raised by what I had seen. It was one of those moments where something touched you but you cannot say what it was or recapture the feeling of oneness while it is happening. After the bus had crossed Alter Road on Jefferson Avenue, the housing esthetics had changed from an average working-class neighborhood to manicured lawns with enough greenery to melt stress away. Harmony appeared to be commonplace as residents walked their dogs without fear.

There was another distinct difference: kids my age could sign for country club services with no money. And many spoke to their parents as if the parent were the unwanted child. Was this a tale of two cities or was this a border with different degrees of sin?

I saw on one side of the border people going about their business committing sins in the process of gathering their daily bread while those on the other side went about their business committing sins to gain more. All I could do is say "God why are these people on this side of Alter Road so poor and the people on the other side so rich?" In time God would answer my question; the answer was not pretty.

It took some time before the motivational program sponsorship moved from the idea stage to fruition. Ted Hunt began getting anxious; he thought it was taking too long to bear fruit. Since hands had been shaken and Robert Stewart had given the go-ahead, all that was needed was to speak the program into reality.

THE GIFT OF GAB

So many self-help books and articles these days advocate mental mapping and speaking success into reality. It is true God spoke much of the world into being, but before He spoke, an enormous amount of preparation went into the final product and He fought the devil in the details.

The most highlighted talent people crave these days is that of profound speech. Somehow intelligence has been equated with the gift of gab and much faith has been placed in the ability to speak, as if speech has the magical power to transform ideas into fruition, heal the sick, solve the problems of the world or even align human behavior with the speaker's point of view.

151

I have encountered many people associated with certain branches of Christianity that see speech as a cure all. A man said he was hungry and a group of Christians gave him a long speech but no food, and in their minds they had done the Lord's work.

History has taught us that the gift of gab in man's possession combined with the gift of profound implementation is dangerous to both God and man. In Matthew 6:7, AMP, Jesus said,

> *And when you pray, do not heap up phrases (multiply words, repeating the same ones over and over) as the Gentiles do, for they think they will be heard for their much speaking.*

In many cases if God gives you the gift of profound speech that is the only gift you will get in this world. Words are important to your prosperity journey; they serve as motivational tools to help bring you back to focus, back on track. Our words do have power but fall short of the power of God's words. Speech alone will not allow you to speak your way to God's prosperity but you can use your words to prepare for God's promises to you.

THE GIFT OF IMPLEMENTATION

Another significant talent is the gift of putting ideas on paper and lifting those ideas from their latent potential to their material realty. This is the gift Solomon used to build God a Temple. Solomon's father David conceived the building of the Temple because his was the blessing of vision. Solomon had the gift of implementation. This is the talent of many entrepreneurs who see a vision and have the talent of implementing it.

Many people are irresponsible with the administration of ideas. They are very good at conceiving ideas because the components of their mind and personality are plugged into the creative process, but they fall short at the implementation process. Being a visionary is a gift but in many cases the practical knowledge and skills necessary for implementation are somewhat hampered by the dominate forces of creativity.

Robert Stewart had the gift of intuition and implementation with the ability to see abstract pieces of ideas as they are being spoken, analyze the information, put the idea on paper and then lift those ideas from the paper into the material realm. He used a totally different set of communication skills that goes on at the executive level.

At the executive level you have to be very analytical without asking a whole lot of questions. Your lieutenants don't always convey the whole story or truth when speaking to you.

It was fun talking to Bob because we spoke a language that seemed vague to others but had deeper meaning to us. It is no different than a lawyer, doctor, engineer, philosopher, economist, religious leader, educator or any other specialized profession with its own set of language and clues that in many ways is also a form of speaking in tongues here on Earth.

PRACTICAL KNOWLEDGE

The administration of ideas is not a question of right brain or left-brain operation. Nor is it a question of common sense, which is a misnomer since certain knowledge is neither common to all the masses nor significant by geography, environments or lifestyle. The world of the materially visible realm operates on practical knowledge not common sense. Practical knowledge is limited and sometimes static in the dynamic world of the spirit. Common sense does not exist in either world; if it did what is common to one person would be common to all.

God created a world of diversity. It is this diversity that serves as the foundation for consciousness enabling us to distinguish a broad menu of variations. This is why I believe many people have trouble with the command to love their neighbor. Your neighbor comes with many different colors and behavioral customs. This disturbs many people because they assume their neighbors to be just like them. It is through diversity that God presents you with abundant living. Diversity is the essence through which prosperity flows; it is the choice of more and it is essential that you recognize and act on the ideas God gives you.

Bob and I came from diverse backgrounds: an unlikely pair. Most of the people around us spent hours scratching their heads trying to figure out what was behind our relationship. It took us a while to figure it out; we concluded God had something to do with it and He entered the picture with a profound sense of humor.

A MEANS TO AN END

Between the gaps of implementation Bob Stewart recruited the corporate players necessary to support the idea of sponsoring a motivational program for Detroit public school students. You would think with periodic horror stories in the media about school violence and the miss-education of American youths, this idea would garner widespread support. The truth is factions exist on all sides where good works are met with resistance simply because some individuals may not like the idea or you. I have seen good ideas killed because they did not come from a certain person or particular clique.

Recruiting yes votes for the program was necessary because many of the corporate players on the executive committee did not see Detroit as a viable city worth reviving.

The biggest obstacle was the Board of Education because internal reform is one of the hardest things to overcome. Detroit is a means to an end for many individuals in positions of authority in the corporations stationed there. There is still money to be made in this city. The question remains: is the city worth reviving, or does it have worth far greater than its water supply? This was the question Bob and I were asked again and again as we fought many obstacles to help improve the city's children against the enemy: the status quo, greed and miss-education.

SEEING IT THROUGH TO COMPLETION

My intent was to leave Michigan Consolidated Gas Company; I did not see a future there, especially working in the mailroom. Instead I focused on the job of seeing the idea of motivating school children through to its completion. Periodically I would visit Bob Stewart to reinforce why we were pursuing this program to help children and to offer new ideas on other ways we might want to approach it. On one such visit Bob Stewart introduced me to the president of the company, Charles Montgomery, who asked if I was going to stick around. I did not know what to say because the question caught me off guard so I said yes.

I would meet periodically with Theodore Hunt, the motivational speaker, to assure him that his program would be sponsored. I let Ted know that after having spent more and more time with Bob Stewart I trusted him and realized he was an honorable man.

Ted invited me to his church. Not being religious and certainly not in tune with the church I said I would go but it was a long time before I finally attended. I wanted to know more about God but was always turned off by what I had witnessed in the streets. The preachers I knew had one foot in the church and one foot in the streets. In fact, it took some effort to distinguish the true street players from those of the church disguised in sheep's clothing.

The vices of many preachers were satisfied in the dark byways of the streets. The people on the streets saw this and learned not to respect many of God's representatives.

UP AND RUNNING

Since I would not go to God, He came to me in the basement of corporate headquarters, in the mailroom. His messenger had music on his mind: gospel music.

One morning at our usual meeting place, the basement elevator adjacent to the executive underground parking, Bob informed me that the motivational program was approved and some minor details had to be worked out. The details turned out to be not so minor: Michigan Consolidated Gas Company was footing the bill of sponsorship but the Detroit Board of Education was still an obstacle.

The motivational program was up and running after Dr. Forrest Holman, Director of Community Affairs at Michigan Consolidated Gas Company verbally wrestled with the Detroit Board of Education during an epithet laced meeting. The program was a success and for the first time many Detroit residents looked favorably on Michigan Consolidated Gas Company.

When I heard of Bill Cosby's recent lectures to schoolchildren, there is a sense of deja vu because what he is saying is almost identical to what Ted Hunt presented to children in the early 1980's. Ted spoke to over a million children. Some of those children who heard Ted Hunt's motivational lectures now have children of their own and are imparting to them the values they learned from Ted Hunt. They called him the "Yes I Can" Man because he used that saying in his lectures. He was the pied piper of positive thinking, giving children a fresh perspective that life is good if you are willing to see it that way.

GOD WANTED TO TALK TO ME

Bob Stewart and I continued to talk from time to time about life, about success, about people and the future. Because of the motivational program's success and company policy of mandatory retirement at age 65, Charles Montgomery, the company president, retired and Bob Stewart was his hand-picked successor assuming the role of president. His job was to keep his hand on the pulse of the company, financial markets and government regulations. In order to do so he needed information.

I finally went to church, innately knowing that God wanted to talk to me. The church is a special place, especially the black church, where we prayed against the backdrop of a people who were once slaves. God at times seems non-exist or far, far away from the daily grind of life under the whip of despair and desire for hope. We held fast to a symbolic Jesus, a cavalry of freedom that was so long coming.

At Fellowship Chapel Church, Ted Hunt introduced me the pastor, Reverend James E. Wadsworth Jr. He was a six foot-two, blue-eyed, fair-complexioned pastor and one time school-teacher who had graduated from Virginia Union University with a degree in divinity. He held so many titles it was hard to keep track of. He was the deputy director of municipal parking, advisor to Mayor Coleman A. Young, chairman of the Democratic 13th Congressional District, former president of the Detroit branch of the NAACP, advocate for African American causes, father, friend and later mentor and political ally.

His reaction to me was to acknowledge what a fine job I had done getting Ted Hunt's program sponsored, and he asked me to join the church. I responded that I was not ready to join any church; I wanted to see what was out there before I committed to any religious organization. Rev. Wadsworth accepted my decision.

As an advisor to the mayor of Detroit, Reverend Wadsworth was entrusted with keeping his hands on the pulse of the city. In order to do so he need information. I was not comfortable with a minister who was deep in politics. The justification was when Jesus took on the political faction of His day, He was political. My Bible must have been different because the Jesus I was beginning to know was not political in the man-made sense of politics. In my Bible Jesus was not in or of politics; His mission was not political but spiritual.

The mixture of religion and politics seems to blend when both parties seek to advance their own agenda. If politics were the answer by now we as a people would have lifted ourselves up from the root cause of despair. What politics does is lift up a few in favor of using many.

DOING WRONG WITH NO END

I begin visiting other churches. The first thing I noticed was each church enforced their own way of worshipping God by their own set rules. This turned me off and prompted me to question the controlling tendencies of religion. I noticed the old-ness of some religions that are deeply entrenched at keeping things the way they are and insisting on labeling others as heathens if they do not agree. I have seen church members do worse things to others than the folks at the Country Club of Detroit and at times surpassing street people.

The Bible says forgive your brother 70 times 70. I know some church folks that purposely continue to do harm to others and have no problem taking advantage of the 70 times 70 rule, constantly seeking forgiveness in accordance with biblical multiplication and constantly doing wrong with no end.

CORRECTING PAST SINS

Over time Reverend Wadsworth and I developed a friendship. He, being a fisherman of souls, knew how to cast his net to pull people into seeking God instead of pushing people into the curiosity of God; the difference being to pull people is gentler and resistance is not as forceful.

One topic that stayed on his mind was the past sins of Michigan Consolidated Gas Company. We had lunch one day and I said, "Okay why don't you meet Bob Stewart and you can tell him how you feel? If one person can and will correct those past sins it would be him." The original plan was I would set up the meeting, introduce each man to the other and leave. But both sides insisted that I stay at this meeting.

Bob Stewart knew the Reverend was an advisor to Mayor Coleman Young; the relationship between the company and the city was cool at best. Bob's position was to bridge the gap between the company and the city. Rev. Wadsworth's position was to remind Bob of the company's past sins. I sat there with an eerie feeling that something bad was going to happen as a result of this meeting.

For the first time I understood that Michigan Consolidated Gas Company had a long-standing history of racism. The company's racism was different from other companies' racism; theirs was overt and clearly spoken. The meeting ended with Bob Stewart acknowledging that the company's past was not pretty, and he assured Rev. Wadsworth that things would change. Bob and I talked after the meeting. We thought it was a good idea to hire more African Americans. He was sincere in his promise to change things; I believed him.

But before Bob Stewart could implement his promised changes, Rev. Wadsworth went into action. He and another minister on the Detroit City Council convinced the council to impose a moratorium on paying utility bills for all city residents. This was a form of political extortion designed to make Michigan Consolidated's management sweat. It was a move that no court would honor because no sane judge would declare utility payments void for goods and services received under legitimate circumstances.

It was a dumb move that hurt a mostly-poor community. The worst thing a political leader can do is to tell his or her poorer constituents they don't have to pay their utility bills. The results will always be the same; those with the least resources struggling to balance monthly expenses are the ones that can least afford to fall one month behind in their utility payments. It is almost impossible to catch up when expenses exceed income. And that is exactly what happened. It was the most ill-conceived plan to "stick it to the man" city leaders could have come up with.

Bob went into action to correct the error. The company came up with the idea of budget payment plans and energy assistance programs to put low-income residents back on track. He did something that would change my view of city politics. Bob gave the current administration several million dollars to help residents with energy assistance. Before he gave the money Bob requested that the state's public service commission endorse his action that way the company could pass the cost onto its customers through one or more rate hike requests. When I asked him if this a payoff, he responded that it was energy assistance. We both knew the money would never reach those who needed it.

BEING THE MIDDLEMAN IS NEVER EASY

Bob Stewart never criticized me for setting up the meeting between he and Reverend Wadsworth, all he said was "see!"

I said, "Yeah, I see." I learned from that experience that being the middleman is never easy. When things go wrong the man in the middle gets it from both sides. As a result of that experience I started to play by my own rules. When Reverend Wadsworth asked what kind of things Bob and I talked about, I would respond "We talked about a lot of stuff." When Ted Hunt asked what Bob and I discussed I said the same thing. If I was put in a situation where someone inside the utility company wanted to know what the reverend and I talked about, again I responded the same way. Each time I responded in that manner I was telling the truth.

I was fortunate to be linked with three mentors and father figures of noteworthy accomplishments in the persons of Ted Hunt, Reverend James Wadsworth and Bob Stewart. They were all close to the same age, they all shared similar traits, having changed the course of their lives from humble beginnings through education and desire. They were all successful in their chosen field and they all talked "a lot of stuff."

THE RIGHT THING TO DO

Bob went to work to change the past sins of Michigan Consolidated Gas Company. The first thing he did was hire several qualified African Americans for management positions. He personally hired future NFL, hall of fame cornerback Lem Barney. A year later he hired a second round of African American managers that included Jim Thrower, another former professional football player. By the time he finished there was no other company in America of comparable size with as many African Americans managers, department heads and vice presidents. Better yet, every appointee was educationally qualified with tangible experience. Each knew they had to whether the storms of a deep-seated belief that blacks could not manage complex systems and that they had gotten their jobs under affirmative action programs.

At the time a few suburban politicians spoke frankly, saying African Americans lacked the ability to manage city affairs, especially the Detroit City Council. However, I had the opportunity to witness how most of the African Americans Bob hired performed admirably under pressure. He not only hired African American managers and vice presidents, but under the radar, without fanfare or publicity, he also helped one African American acquire an auto dealership and others gain contracts to do business with Michigan Consolidated Gas Company. Bob helped me understand that we are to do certain things not because they are popular or for any reward but simply because they are the right things to do.

UNCLE TOM

Ironically, some of the company good old boys saw Bob Stewart as a lover of another ethnic group. The more African American managers, directors and vice presidents Bob hired the more convinced the good old boy network perception of him as a lover of another ethnic group. It stood to reason that he would be perceived this way giving Michigan's southern roots. The lure of auto industry jobs lured not only poor blacks but poor whites. Their migration did not shed their beliefs. Factor in the times where high school dropouts and nepotism provided a steady stream of high wage factory and other blue collar workers jobs. With their beliefs in tack any influx of African American employment was seen as a threat. Add in racism and plain old hate and their economics was colored with fear and the green of envy. This was a sure fire sign that company sabotage was on the horizon.

Some of the African American managers who held an unprecedented place in corporate history, part of a corporate executive revolution, the ones whose hiring I had applauded, saw me as an Uncle Tom.

It was funny because this was a period of my life where I was inundated with black radicalism. I was in search of meaning and this race thing was constantly at the forefront of every move made in the city of Detroit. Mayor Coleman Young played the race card to get what he wanted.

During this search for meaning I walked a tight rope through two different worlds. In one world there was Bob Stewart and other people I met from different ethnic backgrounds. In the other world I was listening to the Muslim faith through *Muhammad Speaks* newspapers and listening to lectures by Minister Louis Farrakhan. Church on Sundays was a constant reminder of our blackness, mixed with God's hand at freeing us from slavery. I spent many Saturdays listening to lectures about significant contributions black people had given to the world by Dr. Benjamin Johanna, professor of anthropology at Cornell University.

I also heard lessons of racial hate told to me by Reverend Wadsworth and Ted Hunt and others. Secretly I spent hours reading every book, article and pamphlet I could get my hands on regarding the subject of slavery because I knew in my soul that there was something terribly wrong with it. It was the horror of slavery that led me to seek higher meaning from God that no human being could satisfy.

WE HAVE A PLAN

Scenarios come and go but the racism of many ethnic groups remains the same. The Arab store owners arrived in town with their plan, so did the Indians from India. The Koreans had a plan to lift themselves up out of the hardships of those poorer than them. The Asians, who came here long ago, held on to their plan of action in silence and claims to speak no English when confronted. The Eastern Europeans were on the way with suitcases in hand and a plan packed within their hearts.

All had a plan to lift themselves up by the bootstraps, over the poor black people who did not have a plan and were trapped by their weariness and miss-education. Some of the poor decided to pretend to be rich and fake it before they made it; whereas in the backs of their minds they were awaiting for their fabled "ship to come in" with a pot of gold in tow.

BRIDGING THE GAP

Bob and I spoke on occasion on the subject of racism; it was a start toward bridging the gap between a hate more powerful than the threat of civil war. It was an unusual discussion because most men in high positions become silent, silence dissenting voices, or change the subject when the discussion moves toward racism. This was a role now assumed by real Uncle Toms who counter-attacked whenever racism was mentioned and were more condescending than Caucasians ever were.

A true Uncle Tom is willing to accept his or her lot in life based on the will of his master. The true Uncle Tom sees his people as not fitting into his or her version of what constitutes a good African American, more so along the lines of an embarrassment.

Parents were horrified when their children came home from school and reported that they were being taught by African American teachers who said they hated black people. You really have to hate yourself to believe other races are more significant than yours.

A true Uncle Tom reasoning says, "So goes the fate of the dominant race, so goes me" – a thought process that was never a part of my thinking then or now. In a rare conversation on the subject of the Uncle Tom I was told that a person with such a perception is not respected by the dominant race, nor trusted. How can a person who is more than willing to turn on their own race be trusted? They may achieve relative success but sooner or later the dominant race will discard them when their usefulness is gone.

The fact that Bob was willing to confront racism proved to me he was trying to be bigger in character than speech or deeds. That is success and should be the goal of anyone seeking prosperity.

WE ARE ALL GOD'S CHILDREN

Through it all, the need to know God overruled my tightrope-walking between the two worlds: one black and one

163

white. I came to a decision: there are racists in all groups and I would not contribute to an ignorance that was here before I was born. I truly believe we are all God's children; some of us know it to a greater degree than others. Once everything is said and done He loves us all the same. When Jesus spoke of hope and equality for all under the same God, He shook the foundation of the ruling class of His day and caused an uproar that lives on today.

This race thing, especially when God is used in the debate, is a clue to how far away we are from His understanding. If we understood the spirit God placed in us greatly exceeds any skin color, we would stop engaging in nonsense that disconnects us from God. It is very important that we understand that racism can and will put a chokehold on prosperity. And in many cases prosperity will flee where there is racism, because racism strikes at the heart of God's diversity, which is a vast menu of abundant living.

THE MISSING PIECES

A fellow worker in the mailroom at Michigan Consolidated Gas Company spent most of his days singing gospel songs and thinking about God's work, who would in time supply me with the missing pieces as to why many religions fashioned the Word of God to fit their agendas. This fellow employee spent most of his days with his mind on God. He gave the mailroom supervisor fits by constantly disappearing at various times during the workday; it was amusing to watch the supervisor inquire into his whereabouts. When he did work, he was constantly singing. When he was not working he was singing and visiting other employees. The whole sitcom of where he was and what he was doing was a never-ending source of comedy.

Of course management did not think this employee's behavior was funny. I saw this employee as sincere about the business of God. Sometimes people who are constantly focused on God appear strange. Upon closer examination, however, I find they are not strange at all; they are focused on being and grow-ing into the image of Christ.

My co-worker was Marvin L. Winans, the one and only per-son I trusted at that point in my life with inquiries about God. On your path to prosperity you will encounter those with whom you can share true thoughts and feelings: people you can trust to discuss your walk with God.

Marvin and I talked about the different man-made laws inserted in various religions. I shared with him my doubts about religion and asked: how could God be so all-powerful and allow all the bad things I had seen in this world? He told me there are many ways of expressing God.

We shared another common bond: our jobs would soon end at approximately the same time. He would finally put his once comically unorganized family singing group together, motivat-ed by his love of God and advice from others. The Winans would change the rhythm of the beat of gospel music: *"And [now] they sing a new song"* (Revelation 5:9, AMP); in the process they won several Grammy Awards.

Bob saw something in me that I had not yet discovered and said it was time for me to go. Our lives by now had become linked.

BAD FOR BUSINESS

In 1980 the Republican National Convention came to town and local businessmen were called upon to support the Repub-lican Party. George H. Bush, the former CIA Director, arrived at the convention hoping for the nomination, but it was clear Ronald Reagan would represent the Republican Party's bid for the Presidency. George Bush had crossed paths with Bob Stew-art in the Navy, so it was natural for him to seek Bob's support. Some of Bob's subordinates within the company urged him to support the Republican ticket with money and influence.

Not only did Bob not support the ticket while being enor-mously pressured, in his usual epithetic vocabulary he strongly disagreed with the Republican Party's agenda. He later told me the party's agenda was bad for business.

His intuition was right on target: during the 12 years of the Reagan-Bush era the economy experienced multiple lows, one after another. And the auto industry should have learned by now that they are hammered in most years the Republicans hold the White House.

I had a feeling that Bob either knew the Republican energy policy was bad for the country from inside information or his intuition was at its best. The bigger fight would ensue after this administration was firmly in office. Bob Stewart would soon gear up for political and legal fights on several fronts.

CHAPTER SEVEN

The Desire to Fight for Prosperity

Bob, on more than one occasion, spoke of desire being the key to success. But he never said that desire means you must be willing to fight for prosperity. Fights have been known to occur where there is no money involved. Add the fuel of billions of dollars and there are those who would physically punch their mother in the eye and maybe even kill her. On the path to prosperity you will have to develop a desire to fight for prosperity.

TRANSFORMATION

I noticed Bob was different after the election of the Reagan-Bush ticket. We both knew the country had changed course. One day I came to congratulate him on being named president of the company by presenting him with his favorite cigar. He had said his promotion would not change him, but I knew that the pressure of being responsible for hundreds of millions of dollars in assets and the livelihoods of thousands of people made the risk of change higher as he advanced in rank. No matter how hard you try to stay the same, as your prosperity increases, you will change.

Bob did change. He talked to me more persuasively about going to college. I did not like school because I hated the power instructors held through the grading system and because of past experiences where unfair teachers had attempted to reform me. My other excuse for not going to school was I read just about everything I could get my hands on in the mailroom.

In the mailroom an industrious clerk has access to many important inter-office memos, reports and periodicals. Between reading and one-on-one sessions with Bob I had a workable understanding of the oil and natural gas industry. I reasoned there was no better education than the one I was receiving from Bob.

I never had a Monopoly board game so God entered the picture with His sense of humor and allowed me to watch Bob play monopoly with real money, real people and real property; he was a slick player with a Missouri swagger. He had tried on other occasions to get me to consider going to college, but his roundabout approach had not worked. So one day he gave me his best sales pitch.

LIFE IS NOT FAIR

Bob had honed his sales skills as the manager of marketing with American Natural Resources. He told me desire was the key to success and being special was a good thing but we all need help along the way. He went on to say that being intelligent is fine but that does not mean the prize is assured. He ended with a zinger: "life is not fair."

You have to be careful when mentors, friends or associates say to you over and over that life is not fair. In some cases this is a set-up whereas the person conveying this message may have plans to do you in. Some mentors hold their protégés back when they start to advance too quickly so the statement "life is not fair" is designed to implant acceptance of the fate they have in mind for you.

So on every occasion when Bob said "life is not fair," I said "yes it is."

Finally he said "You will see." I refused to believe life is not fair because I knew the multiplying spirit of Jesus is the equalizer.

Freedom was the one thing that I pursued with the most passion; he knew this and said, "Doing whatever you want to do won't last for long." That statement punched me in the eye with persuasive reality.

SHOW ME ANOTHER WAY

So I went off to school with a list of subjects supplied by Bob that I should study to become a well-educated person. Fate had a hand in my decision to enroll in college that fall. I had injured myself while performing manual labor in the mailroom. In retrospect I remembered while being tutored by the future Reverend Winans, I had asked God to show me another way of life.

When you seek God He will present you with an opportunity, encouraged by that inner voice, to take a calculated risk. In other words you will be urged to step out of character and your comfort zone to get the prize.

Bob Stewart was presented with an uncharacteristic risk. He would initiate a divestiture of Michigan Consolidated Gas Company from American Natural Resources. The process involved purchasing the assets of Michigan Consolidated Gas Company from American Natural Resources, thereby moving assets between holding companies. The new holding company would be called Primark Corporation. The theory I was studying in school could not have come close to witnessing the process first hand and listening to the problems and strategy.

STRAIGHT TALK

Around the time of Bob's divestiture, Ted Hunt had developed a friendship with an administrator at the Marygrove College reading clinic. Ted conceived the idea of establishing a scholarship program for children ages 6 through 14 that would raise money for their admission into the college reading clinic. Research had revealed that a large number of inner-city youths experienced difficulty reading in their early years of development, which helped create a large pool of adults who could not read or found reading difficult. If the reading disorders persisted, eventually frustration would set in and contribute to behavior problems, thus adding to the high school dropout rate, which at that time was at an all time high.

Legal papers to incorporate the charity were obtained. Ted Hunt wanted Bob Stewart on board as one of the founding members of the charity, and I was to be fourth and final founding member. Ted Hunt and his newfound friend approached me between classes. I was a full-time student with a heavy class load; I had no idea that my becoming a founding member of the charity would soon change the dynamics of my tranquil college life.

Ted Hunt had already spoken to Bob Stewart about becoming a founding member of the scholarship fund. The reading clinic administrator's strategy was to meet with Bob, give him a razzle-dazzle sales pitch, and then manipulate him into signing the incorporation papers. I knew better, however. Bob was proficient in straight talk and transparent management, a subject hailed today as the way to go in self-help management books.

The meeting went like this: we are starting a charity to help kids read. We have the incorporation papers right here. Bob responded by asking if the final signature spot on the papers was for his signature. When we replied affirmatively, he took the papers to the company's legal department and returned them with a signature.

What the reading clinic administrator did not know was that Bob Stewart was a protégé of Admiral Hymen Rickover, a man feared and revered by U.S. Presidents and Pentagon brass. He was a straight-talking powder keg of abrupt mannerism with a legendary no-nonsense temperament; some said he was embarrassing, some said he was a man who got things done. Bob saw him as his mentor and regretted that the real story of Admiral Rickover was yet to be fully told.

HIT THE GROUND RUNNING

The charity hit the ground running with Bob as chairman; he helped raise money quickly and gave the organization creditability. Although I was attending college full-time I was appointed administrator of the scholarship fund for children.

We immediately planned a high-profile dinner to attract money and publicity to the fund. At the time Marva Collins, a schoolteacher from Chicago, was featured in a made-for-TV movie. She became our primary choice as a keynote speaker at the fundraising dinner. I wrote Mrs. Collins a letter. She did not respond but her agent did. We went back and forth, finally reaching agreeable terms.

The date and place for the dinner was set. Behind the scene fences had to be mended. The main obstacle we had to overcome was Mrs. Collins' rebellious characterization in the movie. The second obstacle was there was a small faction of people who did not want us to succeed. The third obstacle was we had to make sure no one was slighted. It never ceases to amaze me how people jockey for name recognition, the honored seat at publicized events or how important "being there" is to some people.

PAY ATTENTION!

We had the most difficult time pleasing those who thought themselves to be important. Some people fail to achieve the prosperity God has in store for them or fail to perfect their talents because they spend too much of their lives striving to be there or jockeying for the best seat at parties, sporting events and social events. Another group cannot achieve prosperity because they spend too much time strategizing to gain the attention of others. Don't ever underestimate what some people will do for attention.

No one knew my experience as a bus boy at the Country Club of Detroit had played a significant role at setting up the fundraiser dinner. The dinner was a success as it achieved our goal of raising money for children. Implementing the dinner was the first of many future experiences at taking ideas off paper and turning them into material reality. Along the way I ran into some shady characters. Bob discovered their interest in me and thought it was best that I stay close.

FIGHTING THE GOOD OLD BOYS

I accepted Bob's summer job offer to help run the newly created MichCon Foundation, a corporate charity funded with five million dollars providing grants to other non-profit organizations such as churches and community groups in the Detroit metropolitan area. It was a two-person operation coordinated by Harold Edwards, a nut and bolts manager from customer service. He was a six foot three ex-college football player whose family had migrated here from the Virgin Islands. He wore corporate wingtip shoes that fueled many jokes from me and others.

Harold was a seasoned manager who spent a significant amount of time fighting injustices imposed by the corporate network of good old boys. He and other managers such as Haywood Dortch fought constant battles against many injustices imposed against defenseless African American clerks, staff personnel and customer services representatives.

Every day in many corporations throughout America there are people like Harold and Haywood who wage corporate battles that never cause a blimp on the radar of life. If nothing else these brave individuals let the network of corporate good old boys know you cannot do evil deeds without someone speaking out.

Harold managed the foundation's program by the book and worried too much. His biggest asset was his heart, which was as big as his body frame. Harold and I became fast friends. It was a good working relationship of balance: I was as much a risk taker as he was cautious.

The programs sponsored by the foundation were recognized as a unique model of private sector initiative by President Reagan at a ceremony in the rose garden of the White House. Bob refused to go so Harold Edwards went representing Michigan Consolidated Gas Company.

THROWN TO THE WOLVES

My return to Michigan Consolidated Gas Company was different in that I had left as a mail-clerk and came back as an administrator of the corporation's foundation. Resentment was in the air, not only because there was a significant upgrade in job title, responsibilities and a private office, but because of my relationship with Bob. I learned that on the road to prosperity is it best to assume a low-keyed posture, the more low-keyed the better. It helps to throw off the keen-smelling ability of wolves. The theory is if they don't smell you, just maybe they won't attack you. But the instincts of wolves and wolves dressed in sheep's clothing operate on more than just the instinct of smell. They found me and attacked.

Bob was also being attacked, on several fronts. The democratic Michigan state attorney general, Frank Kelly, stayed in office over 20 years by calling attention to public utilities as the villain of all villains. If ever there was a candidate who hammered home one issue to gain re-election, this guy was it.

There was very little sympathy for regional monopolies because there was sentiment that public utilities were giant monsters that forced you to do business with them out of necessity, with no competition. The utilities provided politicians like the attorney general with scenarios being played out in the consumer's mind that they were being charged whatever the utilities wanted to charge. He would periodically call for an end to the tyranny of utilities companies.

Bob would return to his office on many occasions mad as hell after a public service commission hearing where the state attorney general had lied under oath. Since I was there to listen, the conversation would drift into, "that blankety-blank blank is a blank, blank lie."

The attorney general wanted to limit the utility companies' requests for rate hikes to once a year, in place of the current rules that allowed utilities to request rate hikes as fluctuations in costs occurred.

A DISASTER IN THE MAKING

Critics were attacking Ted Hunt's motivational program as being too repetitive, and one educator had gone into a frenzy when Ted had mentioned God in his lectures. Ted did not know that within the ranks of Michigan Consolidated Gas Company his program was also being questioned and criticized. Some ranking officers repeatedly asked Bob to eliminate the program. Some African American managers and vice presidents requested that his program be eliminated.

There was pressure on Ted as president of the Scholarship Fund for Children to lift the organization from its infancy. His friend from the Marygrove College reading clinic was named Executive Director. This decision was a disaster in the making. Little did we know she was undermining Ted and in the end would deceive us all, especially me, because she had me believing she was the saint in the storm.

The criticism accelerated when Ted was selected by a local newspaper as an example of outstanding achievement as a member of the exclusive "Michiganian of the Year" Club.

WHAT'S YOUR MOTIVE?

The seed was planted in Detroit politics proposing the legalization of casino gambling. It was hailed as a cure for falling tax revenue and structural unemployment. Reverend Wadsworth was one of the first ministers to publicly come out in favor of casino gambling. His motives were questioned because of his political cronyism with Mayor Coleman Young and the allegation that a street numbers banker stood in the shadows of the issue.

Reverend Wadsworth was also attacked on the health front; he was secretly battling for his life against the dreaded disease cancer. Because of his position as chairman of the 13th congressional district his illness was kept a secret.

At the same time, I was fighting many obstacles to change my condition and put to rest demons from the past.

174

A TAILSPIN OF LEGISLATION

The country went into a tailspin of legislation after the 1978 OPEC oil embargo. Although the embargo was first announced as a shortage of oil there was never a shortage of legislative proposals regarding the price of oil or natural gas. The problems are the same problems we face today. The question is: what is a fair profit margin producers should receive as compensation for their risk of extracting the world's number one commodity from the earth?

On the national front the Carter administration successfully pushed and passed a deregulated natural gas bill, which outlined a schedule for gradually removing price controls on most categories of natural gas by 1985. The law had its flaws if allowed to stand as it was passed. It meant a multimillion-dollar increase in gas prices for industrial users that used natural gas in the manufacturing process and lower gas bills for residential customers. The Carter administration then proposed deregulating domestic oil prices.

The proposed oil deregulation bill had a rider attached to it that imposed a tax on the oil industry under the theory that the industry would reap windfall profits from deregulation. The tax would go into the federal government's general revenue fund where the funds would be used to pay for energy assistance programs for the poor and to fund research and development for alternative sources of energy.

Under the Carter proposal, pipeline companies, utilities companies and consumer groups feared consumers would switch to other sources of energy should prices double. One of President Reagan's first acts after taking office was to repay the support his ticket had received from the oil industry by immediately deregulating oil prices and supplies without attaching any additional taxes to the legislation. As a footnote the country experienced one economic downturn after another at the height of the push for deregulation of fossil fuels.

WAGING WAR

On the state level, the Attorney General waged a fight that would leave no one un-bruised, especially me. The state Attorney General, along with a group called the Michigan Citizen Lobby and certain media outlets, advocated a freeze on utility bill increases whereby if long-term costs abruptly increased, utilities seeking to recover increasing operational costs had to do so all at once, annually. By law utilities were granted a profit percentage return on investment.

The Attorney General and the citizen lobbying group were successful at getting their proposal on the state ballot. Proposition D was communicated as a way to correct wasteful mismanagement and slow down the rate increases of utility bills. This could be done by eliminating automatic rate increase clauses in Michigan's law and creating a new law whereby utilities could recover their additional operational costs only after a full and complete hearing before the Public Service Commission, once a year.

The utilities, under a group calling themselves the Michigan Jobs and Energy Coalition, countered with Proposition H. They argued that one rate hike per year would affect their financial stability. They communicated Proposition D "was dumb" and would hamper their ability to borrow operating funds because lenders would become skeptical of their ability to repay loans. The utilities also cited their bond rating would be downgraded, jobs would be lost and suppliers would adjust input prices according to the utility's ability to pay. They even threw in that energy shortages could occur if this proposal passed. The utility company's proposal would allow gas, electric and telephone utilities to recover reasonably prudent costs as they arose and not be restricted to once-a-year rate hikes.

PAY NOW OR PAY LATER

Another Proposition was slipped onto the ballot which would prevent utilities from paying off public service commissioners by requiring them to run as elected officials instead of being appointed by the governor. The counter argument put out by the utility coalition was that elected commissioners would be candidates subjected to the influence of campaign money and organizations.

The Attorney General accused Citizens for Michigan Jobs and Energy and the utilities of confusing the ballot issues in an attempt to raise utility prices. The real issue was how much consumers would pay for utilities services over time. It was a "pay us now or pay us later" ballot issue, with the one side wanting to delay payment and the other side saying "Pay us now and spread the impact. Time is money. It is in our best interest to get our money now."

I knew I could help Bob win so I asked to participate. He had me contact an executive within the company ranks who was coordinating the project in-house and let him know I was to be part of the campaign. The executive stonewalled me and never returned my telephone calls.

So I went to the Citizens for Michigan Jobs and Energy, which was a shadow group funded by the utility companies. It was a coalition of Detroit Edison, Michigan Bell Telephone, Consumer Powers and Michigan Consolidated Gas Company. There I was assigned a low-level clerical position so I did what any self-respecting rebel would do. I struck out on my own. The first order of business was to develop a team.

A RAGTAG OPERATION

My team consisted of college students from local colleges and universities. We saw ourselves as a ragtag military operation without a clue as to how we would pull it off. We distributed a fair amount of campaign literature in comparison to other groups funded by the coalition.

Students majoring in communications and theater had more fun than anyone else. They were supplied with quarters to make telephone calls from pay phones posing as senior citizens and public officials. They posed as public officials when contacting senior citizens and pretended to be mad-as-Hell senior citizens when contacting media outlets. I had no idea we were breaking the law by posing as people we were not. Only the Lord knows some of the things that were said over the telephone.

I would meet with centers of influence to gain their support. If any official refused support he or she would get a telephone call from one of our aspiring actors or actresses posing as someone else. The second time I approached these centers of influence they were very helpful.

In the end the one issue won, one lost and the third was defeated. The decision of how frequently utilities could hike prices went to the court system, where the utilities would surely come out favorably. The utility companies were fined by the state of Michigan for breaking state campaign finance laws. I never told Bob we might have broken some laws in addition to the ones his coalition broke.

DEMAND WHAT YOU EARN

The utility companies were so afraid of losing Proposition D they were willing to spend enormous sums of money without question, so the political consulting firm they hired felt compelled to charge them through the roof. The utility company's shell organization, Citizens for Michigan Jobs and Energy, ignored my invoice as it disbanded its operation. I had promised my small band of college students compensation for their effort. I approached Bob for the money because I owed those hardworking students who had contributed more to the campaign than the highly paid entities that had done less. Bob surrendered the money but he questioned the way I had gone about conducting business. I became defensive because the students who had helped me deserved every penny.

On the path to prosperity there will be times you must demand what you earned; in a sense you must take what is yours. I am not speaking of taking by criminal force, flimflam or bribery, or by selling things of no value. Rather, you must take your prosperity by claiming it in Jesus' name and make a living pursuing prosperity through avenues of the spirit and character of Jesus.

I am also saying that there are times when close friends and associates may underestimate your value.

JUST EFFORT DESERVES JUST REWARD

On the path to prosperity you must see yourself as worthy of compensation; not in the sense of an inflated ego but in all fairness where just effort deserves just reward. This is important because many people miss out on prosperity because they do not see themselves as worthy of reward. Some people work so hard yet never get what is due them because when it comes to their reward they downplay themselves, asking for less than they deserve or believing they are exercising one of God commands by charging less.

I know of two best friends who were partners in an artesian business. One partner worked harder than the other but never got paid in money. He would end up with clothing, alcohol or some electronic gadget but rarely money. I call him the hustler that never got paid. You must develop a burning desire that you are worthy of prosperity if you really want it.

However, there are times you should charge less, especially to those who have little or no money.

SETTING THE TONE

In the process of working on the ballot propositions I realized that ballot issues set the tone for a living democracy. Those with a vested interest in making money and keeping money are ever busy shaping laws in accordance with their self-interest. It is not the charisma of the candidate or which party he or she is affiliated with but where the candidate's self-interest stands on the issues that should determine your support.

179

I realized early in life that political issues shape the type of society we live in. I am thankful for the opportunity to be a witness to the political process first hand. In the political arena, party affiliations shape positions on issues based on how the party views the world.

BURNING DESIRE

To have that burning desire you must overcome fear. The sad thing about many of our decisions is they hinge on fear. We vote our fears, live in fear and ground our hopes in fear. Many people worship God not because they love or know him but out of fear of distancing themselves from Him. Most of our decisions in the area of prosperity and how much to keep are buried in our fears. Some people strive because they fear failure, while others refuse to pursue prosperity because they fear success.

Buried in political issues is the amount of prosperity you can achieve through barriers to entry, and how much you get to keep for God's work. Don't be fooled by slick tax breaks or increased benefits to social welfare programs that are not what they seem. Two thirds of this country's economic engine is factored into the cost of interest rates and energy costs. These are issues that politicians you elect have a voice in. They too are issues that are usually grounded in our fears. Issues we usually do not pay much attention to have a way of becoming dangerous laws that can chip away at the soul and wealth of the people and the nation.

RUNNING INTO JESUS

I entered politics and ran into Jesus. I returned to school in search of why and immersed myself in the self–taught subjects of moral philosophy, religion and ethics while seeking my degree in economics. I engaged nuns and fathers at Marygrove College and the University of Detroit and others on the subject of virtue. The seriousness of my purpose caused many educators to flee my scrutiny. I was searching for answers about God, and the more I learned about God, morality and ethics, the more questions I had. What better place to extract knowledge than these two Catholic liberal arts institutions with their archives of ancient books, scrolls and canon law?

After working on the campaign ballot issue I realized politics is a convenient vehicle some use to justify lies and conniving motives. I saw the bad and the ugly in myself and set out to find the good. I was on a mission of self-reform, the only place where true reform begins. I was in the spring of my Christianity searching for knowledge with a thirst that only God could satisfy. My zeal and self-righteousness turned people off and justified my position of them versus me.

AN ALL-TIME LOW

The beginning of summer meant returning to Michigan Consolidated Gas Company. But this summer was different; employee morale was at an all-time low. By now Bob had completed his divestiture from American Natural Resources and the new holding company, Primark, was up and running. He had become Chairman and CEO of Primark Corporation.

In the process of taking the divestiture from conception stage to realty, Bob had had to make deals with other executives. Some executives and their families held large blocks of company stock that represented votes Bob needed to complete the spin-off. Some of the deals he had made shifted control and authority away from Bob into the hands of other executives and the executive committee of the newly-formed company.

The Bob I originally met had worked so hard because one of his darkest fears was losing his job. He had witnessed the perils of the Great Depression as a child where only the fortunate few had a job. He was God-centered through Bible teaching and through his grandmother, who was a door-to-door evangelist in accordance with the Jehovah's Witness faith. He had gone to Southeast Missouri State College on a football scholarship and studied enough science during the war to merit being selected to work on the first atomic submarine. Because of Bob's humble beginnings he lacked the snobbery of some Ivy League MBA's. But some of the deals Bob made to share corporate authority would come back to haunt him.

YOU'RE OUT OF HERE

A consultant convinced Bob and other executives to rid the company of certain employees, specifically high-paid, white-collar employees with years of seniority. The prescribed method was to send appointed hatchet men along with security personnel to the targeted employee's desk or office, fire the employee on the spot and escort them from the building without allowing the employee time to gather personal items, make a telephone call or say good bye to co-workers they had known for years. Just in case an employee might experience a heart attack or faint from extreme stress, ambulances were stationed outside company headquarters for first aid purposes; in extreme cases they could rush victims to the hospital.

The strategy behind the move did have merit and it gained the attention of the Public Service Commission to seriously consider pending and future rate hike requests. Fired employees were entitled to unemployment benefits after a waiting period. The company saved money by removing that employee's salary immediately from the payroll. The employee's medical benefits were also cut off, and in some cases retirement benefits under old pension plans could be reduced. A new, younger employee could be hired for less money.

The strategy of immediately escorting the employee from the building did not allow the employee time to take with them valuable company information or to commit an act of corporate sabotage. If some of the fired employees applied to the court system for justice, citing wrongful discharge and age discrimination, the company still saved money because if the court ruled in favor of the employee, settlement could be reached for pennies on the dollar by threatening to drag it out in court for years with one legal maneuver after another.

TEACHER-PUPIL IRONY

Some employees who knew of my relationship with Bob said, "I told you he was a hatchet man." I stuck by Bob under enormous criticism out of loyalty and because he had shown his loyalty to me on several occasions. However, I felt Bob could have done more to push for attrition by offering early retirement packages. He knew there was more than one way to institute an idea.

I cooled towards Bob and thought for a moment he needed his butt whipped. Here was another one of those teacher-pupil ironies; a year earlier Bob had insisted that I be fair when I had requested temporary suspension of a Hispanic group from the summer youth employment program because I had seen the same names appear on several different payroll registers. I thought about what Jesus had said: that a pupil would share the same fate as his teacher.

As fate would have it a national fight was brewing and the corporation's performance would eventually set the stage for Bob to get his butt whipped. On the other hand I was not always on my best behavior either and just maybe life would issue us both a butt whipping. God was changing my mentors and me in subtle ways we could not see at the time.

KNOCKING AT THE DOOR

My past came knocking at the door in the form of two childhood friends. My best friends had been raised in the church and knew more about God than I did.

Every day many once-loyal followers of God reject His ways for reasons of lifestyle, money, sex, anger, frustration and busyness. Many of the people who go to church are not helped by being exposed to the Word of God. At the same time, people who have felt the pain of life realize God is the answer and gravitate to His words. The doors to God swing to and fro like a pendulum.

My two best friends believed they no longer needed God; their lifestyle would eventually take them to a gangland-style end. Though I had not been raised in the church, I needed God more than ever.

The word on the street was my two friends who had traveled through the age of innocence with me were involved in the sale of drugs. The profit margin for street-level drug sales had declined as more and more sellers entered the market and wholesale prices increased. Many dealers doubled as informants and drug cowboys that ripped off unsuspecting sellers in the market or had them jailed to reduce competition. Many of my friends chose the career path of drug dealing out of frustration and the difficulty finding decent jobs during the 12 years of the Reagan and Bush administrations which were especially difficult for African American males.

My friends planned to use the cover of a college campus dormitory as a center for distributing their drugs. It is difficult to dissolve a lifelong friendship under the heartbreaking moment of a brief scuffle. My actions were in defense of my evolving principles: my people had been devastated by the drug trade and I knew what was right in the eyes of God.

GOING ALONG TO GET ALONG

Friendship is a positive thing. I truly believe that God intended for us to be social beings. We are to be social in the sense of encouraging one another in good times and bad, in worshiping God and searching for the positive meaning of life. The whole business of the drug trade comes between blood and God's social mandates.

Positive thinking is a wonderful thing. It has the potential to plant seeds of hope and to paint a vision in the mind that allows sustaining faith to take root. It allows us to focus on thoughts of the goodness of life.

On the flip side, positive thinking not grounded in the things that are of God is a trap. This business of turning a blind eye to actions and deeds that are wrong has brought us nothing but grief. There is no upside to "going along to get along" by ignoring wrongful acts that bring down the community and bring hardship to people's lives.

In my positive mind's eye I saw a city with many possibilities, but when I looked again without blinders my positive thoughts bore false witness to what I wanted it to be. I saw a city that looked like a bombed-out Beirut: the three main contributing factors were self-destruction by riot, self-destruction through corruption and self-destruction through drugs.

Isn't It Ironic?

The eeriness of the era was whenever anyone outside the circle of cronyism attempted to help save the city they were soon labeled an enemy of the people, while drug dealers and unscrupulous characters were considered friends. Things got to the point where police officers, who had taken an oath to uphold the law no matter who the criminal was, would examine whoever they stopped to see if they were related to or a supporter or friend of the mayor. To arrest or issue a ticket to such a person meant reprimand or demotion, so out of frustration some police officers starting committing crimes that added to the city's crime rate. It was the beginning of a new era where the abnormal was becoming normal and we were evolving into a new normal that had once been considered sick.

Staying in the Public Eye

A person from Bob's past entered the picture. The Scholarship Fund for Children needed to stay in the public eye to raise money and compete with other charities in the competitive arena of charitable giving. We had made a big splash with our fundraising dinner but afterwards funding started to dry up. Our other main fund-raiser was a three-mile fitness run through the streets of downtown Detroit. We partnered with the Detroit Pistons Basketball Company as sponsors of the annual event. The Detroit Pistons were attempting to reconnect with the city; in the early 1980's the team had endured years of losing but things were about to change. Oscar Feldman, the Pistons' General Counsel and part owner of the team would bring their newly drafted franchise player Isaiah Thomas to speak to the kids at the annual fitness run.

The Board of Directors of the Scholarship Fund for Children decided to elect two additional directors who could help with fundraising efforts. One new member was a U.S. Navy Rear Admiral. During the selection committee interview process the admiral acknowledged he had crossed paths with Bob in the past. He provided us with a surface brief of his past interactions with Bob Stewart.

GOING OUT TO SEA

At the admiral's first board meeting Bob arrived late, which was natural given his schedule that started early and ended late. When Bob entered the room we could see both surprise and disappointment on his face.

As the meeting moved along, the admiral played his hand. During a report I was in the middle of completing the Admiral said, while looking directly at me and speaking to Bob, "When we needed to talk in the old days we would go out to sea." I knew this to be coded language. If you listen close to the history of political rhetoric you will hear phrases such as "we need to restore this country to its place of prominence," or "this country needs to reinvigorate its conservative roots."

In this case, "going out to sea" meant in accordance with maritime law the captain of the ship was accuser, judge, jury and executioner. During the U.S. Navy's days of deep division, blacks were "put in their place" with disciplinary actions at sea. It was dangerous to venture onto certain parts of the ship earmarked "us" or "white only." The risk of venturing onto unwelcome parts of the ship was enormous. You could end up missing in action by strange accident or falling overboard at sea.

Bob immediately went into action and confronted the admiral. He told the admiral he was telling on himself by what he had said. The admiral stood down because he may have out-ranked Bob in the Navy and at Harvard as a part of an elite clique, but in civilian life Bob was much too powerful to fight.

THE MESSAGE WAS CLEAR

The entire board was swayed Bob's way that day; the message was clear that sort of mentality would not be tolerated. He pointed out to the admiral that I was with him. It was clear to me that Bob would fight to defend against all attackers.

I was never cool towards Bob again. I had asked God to send someone my way to enlighten me with knowledge, prepare me with understanding and point me in the direction of wisdom. Naturally I had thought it would be someone of my own race like John Johnson, publisher of *Ebony* and *Jet* magazines, Bill Cosby, or a Martin Luther King-type figure, but God had sent Bob Stewart, Ted Hunt and Reverend James E. Wadsworth. I realized that God had answered my prayers by sending help from three sources instead of the one I had asked for. To further highlight the abundance of God: in time he would send a fourth mentor.

A good mentor is like a good coach. He watches players practice and displays a keen eye during the warm ups just before the game. When the game is on the line, the mentor (coach) pulls an unusual move; he may insert into the game the most unlikely player. It could be the last man or woman on the totem pole. When the player comes through in heroic fashion, the mentor (coach) looks like a genius. In actuality the mentor (coach) understood that the least can end up being the cornerstone by transcending their potential, motivated by faith.

Ask and you will be given what you ask for. Seek and you will find. Knock and the door will be opened. For everyone who asks, receives. Anyone who seeks finds, if only you will knock the door will open (Matthew 7:7-8). It is your responsibility to accept help from the sources that God sends. I understood at that moment why every time I had attempted to flee from Bob,

Ted or Reverend Wadsworth, God would instruct me to go back. My reason for wanting to flee was there was no way I could follow in their footsteps. I need to find my own footsteps.

YOUR ENEMIES ARE MY ENEMIES

Being affiliated with Bob, Ted and Reverend Wadsworth, I racked up some enemies. When self-help books suggest you find a mentor, they neglect to say the enemies of your mentor become your enemies. I knew Bob was not the kind of guy you would want to mess with at that board meeting. I understood how fierce he would fight at the drop of a hat, especially if you attempted to move in on him or someone he cared about.

On your path to prosperity you will have to swallow your pride and accept help from those whom God sends your way. There is a saying that it is lonely at the top. It is lonely because most people have no idea what it takes to get there or stay there. The stewardship and decision-making process at the top of a multi-billion dollar holding company is far different than the everyday decisions most of us make. It is especially difficult when you are responsible for the lives of thousands of people and their families.

On that day in the boardroom Bob did not realize it but he separated me from the rest of the board in several ways. It was a separation that would add fuel to the fire of my desire and future on the board of the Scholarship Fund for Children.

PROBLEMS ON THE HORIZON

At the urging of some Senators, Congressman and Pentagon Officials, President Ronald Reagan fired Admiral Hymen Rickover. I could tell his firing saddened Bob Stewart. However, there were bigger problems on the horizon that would force Bob to join forces with others to combat a new threat.

Oil prices declined from the market mechanism of deregulation, but natural gas prices rose. This defied all the rules of economics because natural gas is a byproduct of oil-producing wells. Supplies of natural gas were at surplus levels but prices rose in spite of a glut. At that time natural gas warmed 55 million homes and supplied 27 percent of the nation's energy needs.

In a properly functioning market a surplus of natural gas should force its price downward. The rapid rise in natural gas prices created a groundswell of complaints to members of Congress. Congress responded with approximately 16 legislative proposals but no real answers.

The Reagan Administration blamed the liberal Democrats, believing the problem was due to the gradual deregulation legislation of the Carter Administration contained in the Natural Gas Policy Act of 1978, and called for immediate deregulation of gas from old wells instead of waiting until 1985.

The real problem, however, was that federal regulation had enabled pipeline companies to pass on their increasing cost of natural gas to consumers. Long-term contracts between natural gas producers and pipeline companies contained "take or pay" provisions which allowed gas to be sold at whatever price purchasers were willing to pay. Under the current system pipeline companies bought gas from producers and sold it to users such as utilities at monopoly prices.

Gas from old existing wells sold at one price whereas gas from new, more expensive wells sold at a higher price. The stepladder pricing was intended to encourage new oil well discovery and extraction of new gas from new supplies. The trick was to introduce legislation that would allow old gas to rise to market levels through immediate deregulation and presumably the price of new gas from newly discovered wells would fall. But there was no way of knowing what mix of old or new gas flowed through pipeline companies' pipelines.

PHILOSOPHICALLY OPPOSED

Some pipeline companies and natural gas producers were not enthusiastic about deregulating natural gas prices immediately: it would have upset their windfall profits. The opposing group, called the Citizens/Labor Energy Coalition (CLEC), consisted of 300 organizations of labor unions, senior citizens, farm groups and other citizen groups that put together a grass-roots door-to-door campaign to put the pressure on Congress.

On most issues regarding price controls Republicans are philosophically opposed, but in this case the fear of not being reelected took precedence. A number of Republican senators and congressman broke rank with the Reagan Administration and opposed deregulation. The oddest members of this mixed bag of advocacy groups were local utilities joining forces with consumer groups. For years these two groups had waged battles against one another but now they were strange political bedfellows on the same team. Utility companies feared the deregulated price of old gas could mean higher gas prices for them and their customers. The producers and pipeline operators wanted to continue their record profits.

Bob Stewart was chosen to lead the consumer groups opposed to deregulating the price of old gas. He was a natural choice at this point in his life: he was chairman of New Detroit Incorporated, the civic organization mentioned earlier established to help rebuild and restore Detroit. He was elected Chairman of the Detroit Renaissance Club, a civic group founded by real estate developer Albert Taubaman, Jewish philanthropist and political fundraiser Max Fisher and Henry Ford II, who influenced the direction of Detroit from behind the scenes. Bob Stewart held seats on the board of directors of Primark Corporation, Michigan Consolidated Gas Company, and National Bank of Detroit, the Ford Motor Company and the Stryker Corporation. He had a significant amount of influence over the Detroit Economic Club, the Chamber of Commerce and several other companies and organizations.

This was a period when leaders in Detroit played a significant role in national affairs through characters such as Lee Iacocca, Max Fisher, Henry Ford II, Roger Smith, Albert Taubaman, William Clay Ford, Tom Monahan and many others, and Bob was at the top of his game. He talked more "stuff" than ever in colorful language. After all, he was a sailor.

A No-win Battle

We talked about the issue. I offered my opinion but I did not want to appear negative so did not tell him the issue he was fighting was a no-win battle. I felt that way because one of first things President Reagan did when he took office was attend a meeting of a southern coalition at the urging of Senator Trent Lott of Mississippi. At this meeting white southern men and women formed a pact to take back the country and put non-whites and liberals in their place. It was a shot fired signaling a campaign of conservatism using fear to disguise a new order where a religious shadow group called the Moral Majority would cloud the real issues with issues of morality.

The purpose of the religious shadow group was to attack and label those opposed to the party's agenda and views as ungodly sinners. It worked the same way as using a woman in an all-male debate. At strategic points in the debate the woman can allude to sexism or say the way she is being treated is chauvinistic. The male dissenter is thrown off guard and the real issues become clouded by name calling.

The second reason I felt Bob would lose was because his opponents were Shell Oil, Exxon, Mobile, Phillips Petroleum, Conoco and other major oil and natural gas producers.

Switching Sides

The fight over immediate deregulation of natural gas pricing took another turn and escalated into a fight pitting southern and western states against other regions of the country. The states with an interest in the production, distribution or inter-related industries sided with pro-deregulation forces.

It was hilarious witnessing senators and congressmen switch sides again when the issue took on regional flavors or when those with vested interest showed up with more money. When the rhetoric faded the congressional committee vote tally of those for and against immediate deregulation of natural gas prices was similar to the division of the country that was labeled red and blue states of the 2004 presidential election. Another religious shadow group called evangelicals or the religious right appeared on the scene in 2004 using the morality of sex and fear to detract from the issues of humanity.

There is really no loyalty among politicians, only self-interest. That is why politics are not the answer. The self-interest of politicians is often not in the best interest of the people who elect them.

Billions of dollars were at stake; even Bob's point man in Congress, Congressman John Dingell, began to experience headaches on this issue. Should the energy bill come out of committee and be subject to a full congressional vote, Bob assured himself of at least one more vote from Michigan by hiring a congressman's wife.

Bob was a workaholic but hid this fact because of the negative connotation surrounding the label. I was sure he did not have time to sleep nor eat because in his real-life game of monopoly he was too busy playing all the angles.

A LESSON IN FUTILITY

Whenever lawmakers investigate huge profit and wide price fluctuations of oil and natural gas, the time and effort expended turns into a lesson in futility. The reason these investigations never uncover any irregularities is because there are different qualities and grades of the commodity and different ways of accounting for cost and expense. Add to the mix that there is no way of knowing what unit price of oil or natural gas is flowing through various pipelines at any given time. Low-cost-per-barrel oil or low-cost British Thermal Units of natural gas could be flowing in the pipeline, but as soon as the prevailing price increases those same low-cost-per-unit prices go up as it exits the pipeline.

Wide swings in price between the entrance and exit of fossil fuels in the pipeline is one way of creating windfall profits whereas producers can charge more for units of oil and natural gas they paid less for. Then there is the problem of capping or rendered supply wells non-operable in order to decrease supply and raise prices. When the price is right the well becomes operable.

Another problem is the commodity has been politicized: politicians and oil executives had contingency plans and secret deals with hostile governments to acquire the commodity. If the public cornered oil executives with questions on why the price was high, they would blame the high prices on the Arabs or those Nigerian hoodlums or South Americans and other communists or lastly divine decree: blaming it on the weather as an act of God.

Over time the market mechanism of the commodities became so intertwined with the dark, shadowy world of covert intelligence that after OPEC cut production in 1978, any investigation would automatically be redirected to innocent reasons for the increase in price and not reveal any evidence of collusion.

Bob was opposed to Vice President Bush's two-faced role as a member of the executive branch and the saying in the industry "once an oil man always an oil man."

BLOOD FROM THE PAST REQUIRES BLOOD FROM THE PRESENT

It is ironic that the key ingredient of fossil fuels is the sedimentary remains of human beings, animals and plant life. The blood of living things is especially important to the incubation process for fossil fuels. It stands to reason in the Middle East where millions of human beings have been slaughtered for ideological reasons that the land is rich in fossil fuels.

It is also interesting that blood from the past requires more blood from the present to keep the wheels of industrialization churning. The circle of positive events states that if one throws his life away and never thrives by harnessing his God-given talent, his dead carcass was designed by God to be a dynamic force even in death. God created us in His image with enough internal energy to power machinery in our physical afterlife. Jesus said it best when He said, "What a wonderful thing God has done."

GETTING CLOSE TO THE ACTION

As the issue dragged on for several months in legislative committees, Bob decided he needed to be close to the action so he moved Primark Corporation to Mclean, Virginia, where his lobbyist and Pentagon friends and other business connections he had developed while managing acquisitions for the U S Navy's supply's department were. This move also helped Bob keep an eye on Congress and keep abreast of moves inside the Reagan Administration through informants inside the administration.

Bob had made many friends managing navel supplies; there was never a shortage of companies or contractors beating a path to Bob's door in hope of securing a lucrative military contract. He had served during the era when the Navy's policy dictated that you had to spend all the money allotted to you or Congress would cut the next year's budget. So department heads thought of creative ways to spend or hide the money. The results had proved disastrous; history recorded payments of $800 for toilet seats that could have been purchased on the open market for less than $100.

Bob's spies began sending him reports of what was going on within the administration. His colorful epithets and jokes steamrolled with lively momentum once he confirmed President Reagan used mediums (horoscopes, psychics, tea leafs etc.) to aid him in making decisions of national importance. Bob joked on several occasions that during the height of the day when the stock market was in full swing and things were happening in the Middle East and other parts of the world, President Reagan took a ritualistic nap and Nancy Reagan ran the country while he slept. He would say America elected its first woman President without knowing it. Bob and his intelligence network did not know the President was in the early stages of an illness.

THE REAL WAR BEGAN

I had my own battles with a group of priests and nuns. I had gotten tired of the fathers and nuns at school imposing their self-righteous morality and convenient ethical Catholicism on us while pitching their belief that some ethnic groups were inferior to Caucasians. So I engaged them on the subject of slavery and the role the Catholic Church had played by first advocating it and then supporting it: looking the other way and issuing coded messages of approval. There were books near the library stacks that contained detailed accounts of the Catholic Church's role in the slave trade. I stumbled on books that talked about the church's role in preserving Rome and its role in Nazi, Germany during World War II.

But the real war started when Bob Stewart joined the Trustee Board of the college. I do not know why he decided to join the board. He thought he was helping but again it separated me and gained me more enemies. When we talked about the nuns, Bob's colorful comments regarding nuns are not appropriate for print in this book about God. I did not help matters by firing the first shot and calling the Pope a pimp.

THE PLOT THICKENS

What I feared came upon me; some of my schoolwork was downgraded. There was a plot to fail me but on one occasion a priest's conscience got the best of him and he informed me of the plot. Over time that Jesuit priest and I became friends.

To counter the plot of the nuns I supported a certain candidate for president of student government. When he won, he appointed me to the students' grade appeals committee which consisted of two professors from the college and two students. That way I could control not only any unfair grades I may receive but also bring fairness to the grades other students were receiving.

The students on campus who realized what I had done gave me the nickname "Clever Cal"; the nuns labeled me "Slick."

Now that kicking me out of school for unsatisfactory grades was not an option, the nuns attacked me on the financial front by demanding that I immediately settle my unpaid tuition balance or face not returning to school. They made their move in my last semester before graduation.

Reverend James Wadsworth got wind of what was going on and raised the money I needed to graduate. He later told me he did not know what I would be, but he believed one day I would make a special contribution to the betterment of my people.

On the road to prosperity people will start believing in you, having faith in you and trusting in you. It is your responsibility to live up to their faith and trust, and by all means don't lose it.

ANOTHER FIGHT BREWING

Another fight was brewing. Ted Hunt's friend from the Marygrove College reading clinic decided she wanted control of the Scholarship Fund for Children. I must admit, for a moment she had me fooled. The experience left all of us with a bad taste in our mouths but the consensus is she was masterful at playing us against one another. Bob was not fooled for a moment; he told us from the start that she was trouble. What made us not take Bob seriously was there were times we thought Bob was old fashioned regarding women and this was a new day.

When Bob moved to Virginia he resigned as Chairman of the Scholarship Fund for Children. The chairmanship of the fund was entrusted to Federal Judge Damon Keith of the 6th District of Appeals.

With Bob out of the way, the Executive Director of the Scholarship Fund for Children seized control of day-to-day operations and the minds of some members of the board. She went into action, attempting to get rid of me by accusing me with trumped-up charges of inappropriate behavior. She recruited the support of a small faction of board members under her control. A hearing was scheduled to determine if I was fit to continue serving on the board. I made it easy by pointing out step-by-step in an open letter to the board how I felt about her charges. I revealed her grand plan and questioned the complacency and competency of the board. Of course this further infuriated the board. I then resigned with a warning that the board should take a closer look at the financial dealing of this lady holding the Fund's money.

WE BLEW IT

In time the Scholarship Fund for Children's Board of Trustees did look closely at the finances, but by then it was too late. The Fund was insolvent and disbanded. In fairness to Federal Judge Damon Keith: with his duties of the court, he was not abreast of what was going on and played no role in the demise of the Scholarship Fund for Children.

Every now and then I run into former board members with the look in their eye that says "we blew it." A wealthy Michigan family attempted to recreate our idea of the Scholarship Fund for Children. The name of their fund was so close to the one we had created most people hardly knew the difference. The difference was we did it with a style, a flair and controversy that could never be duplicated. But our plan was flawed because we let the devil's little sister on our board.

On the road to prosperity you will get burned by someone so slick you cannot believe you were so stupid. Take heart and do not get down on yourself. When it comes to prosperity through gaining something for nothing there are those who are far cleverer than God's children.

CONCEALING MORE THAN REVEALING

Bob embarked on a public relations campaign with well-placed articles in publications such as the *Wall Street Journal* and *Financial Times*, calling attention to his maverick spirit. These articles, developed by media consultants, painted Bob in the image of a crusader.

When we consciously set out to establish an image for the express purpose of accomplishing a goal, that image conceals more than it reveals: namely our shortcomings and true motives. The media campaign created new enemies for Bob. At one point Bob had many friends at the American Gas Association who favor immediate deregulation, now those friends were not speaking to him at all.

The truth is Bob and my other father figure mentors had their flaws as did I. If I had not known better I would have thought Bob was flawless judging from the articles written about him. In actuality there were times when Bob was moody and in his own words mean, evil and ornery. In spite of our flaws we supported one another in an effort to obey the teachings of Jesus and help people, especially the children.

STRATEGY OF THE GAME

The deregulation issue began to age Bob's point man in Congress, Congressman John Dingell. The pipeline companies found creative ways to break long-term "take or pay" clauses in their contracts with producers, without the help of Congressional interference.

There is a strategy in business game theory, politics, chess and life where you box your opponent in with the appearance that their next move was thought out in advance. Once your opponent makes their move you make a counter move to victory. At a fork in the road where the signs read "Hell" or "Bull" a wise player counters by using the drop-dead technique: refusing to participate in the game. You simply do the opposite or nothing at all. This is a way out especially when any move you make will result in a no-win situation.

That is exactly what Congressman Dingell did. I laughed at the congressman's cleverness. Bob was mad as Hell and did not think it was funny. The Congressional Energy Committee agenda simply scratched the issue of immediate deregulation of natural gas prices off the agenda allowing it to die on the vine. In other words, after months of debate it just disappeared. Who won? The lobbyists collected fat fees and the legislators benefited from the lobbyist's gifts. Big oil would win in the future because this experience helped them hone their skills at offering simplified answers to complex questions regarding price.

THE REAL LOSERS

The players in this fight, namely big oil, labor unions, local utilities and other businessmen simply passed the enormous cost of attempting to influence legislation on to their customers and members. The American people were the real losers in this battle. We had a golden opportunity to create alternative sources of energy without the urgency of oil and natural gas shortages. The 1980's presented us with the opportunity to solve our heavy reliance on foreign oil and natural gas and we blew it. Greed got in the way.

A groundswell of ideas had emerged for solving our energy dependence from 1978 until we killed legislation for exploring other possibilities in 1984. In 1984 we abandoned or cut back on research to develop alternative sources of energy such as synthetic fuels made from vegetation, shale oil, hydrogen, solar and nuclear power. Most notably the Reagan Administration dismantled the Department of Energy.

CONSPIRACY THEORY

Of course conspiracy theorists screamed loud, attempting to pass on their beliefs. The problem with conspiracy is it is difficult to gain the consensus of large groups of people without some members breaking rank from the plan. On a smaller scale we will always have conspiring individuals because that is the nature of greed and those who seek something for little in return.

Was it a conspiracy? No, it was more incompetence on the part of lawmakers than anything else. The same incompetence came into play when Congress approved the merger of several oil companies that reduced competition and contributed to raising prices. It is the same incompetence that will eventually kill democracy.

This occurred because we let people with vested interest run the show. There is no greater loss of resources than lost opportunity. The extent of how badly we blew it in the 1980's is evident today and far reaching into the future.

The more I understand God the more I realize that incompetence runs rampant in every sector of our life. This mass incompetence is no more than human folly and further proof that God must constantly lend a hand to compensate for our shortcomings and our incompetence. This whole wide world and every function therein, including our pursuit of prosperity, only works because of the grace of God.

KILLING THE IDEA

What the players in this drama did is reminiscent of the strategy too many corporations and citizens employ these days. It is the strategy of petitioning government for legislative entitlements, comfort and profit. Since the Chrysler Corporation bailout a host of other industries have used the same tacit of petitioning government for relief or favoritism.

The real danger in this constant petitioning strikes at the heart of killing the idea. If the ideas take on the attribute of positioning oneself to get someone to give you something then your God-given talent will die from lack of use. Sadly, we have no problem petitioning government for something we should be petitioning God for. Even a just God will not give us what he has implanted in our talents to get for ourselves.

When you appeal to a perceived almighty government this is a form of idol worshipping. You will definitely miss the prosperity that God has set aside for you if you rely on the government instead of God. If you spend enormous amounts of time and effort attempting to get the government to give you something or take care of you, you deserve whatever stipend that is thrown your way. You should not complain when you miss

God's abundance. Barring any uncontrollable misfortune such as bad health we generally get out of life what we put into it.

BITING THE HAND THAT FEEDS YOU

Bob decided Michigan Consolidated Gas Company was dragging down the profit of Primark Corporation so he proposed selling the utility company to the current management team through another holding company divestiture. There was another reason for selling off the gas distribution business. His leading the charge to stop the pending deregulation of commodities prices had pissed off many members of the energy community. The energy community felt he had bit the hand that fed him; some members of the community promised that there would be repercussions.

Bob asked for a handsome severance package from Michigan Consolidated Gas Company. Some executive and stockholders barked at his request. Bob got his money but saw more money on the table as a member of the Board of Directors and as a paid consultant. When Bob took the paid consultant position I begin to wonder when enough money was enough.

Some Wall Street analyst wrote that the company would have faired better had operating expenses been put into a savings account; remember this was the 1980's when bank accounts paid handsome returns. Morale at Michigan Consolidated Gas had gone into the dumps after the dramatic firing of white-collar employees and had never really recovered.

The utility company had operated independently for several years until things turned around financially, only to be destroyed by missteps, a slick con game and greed.

FINAL DEMISE

Michigan Consolidated Gas Company's final demise as a stand-alone company was at the hands of a top level executive from India who had the ear and trust of the chairman succeeding Bob. The executive convinced the chairman that natural gas could be acquired at a good price from a reliable supply in his homeland.

After several million dollars were sent to India over the protest of the new president and no natural gas was delivered, it was clear that the company had been conned by an elaborate scheme. The financial damage was so severe no top-level executive wanted to talk about it. This time the Indians had won.

I chided my sources who relayed the story to me. I was willing to bet that the amount of money the company had lost was equal to the amount the company had cheated customers out of over the years, plus interest. When the Spirit of God requires a payback there is usually an interest payment attached.

Michigan Consolidated Gas Company could no longer stand on its own and was acquired by Detroit Edison. Events truly came full circle when the highly regarded IHM economist nun who was my instructor and the seed behind my journey to find the connection between God and prosperity-she put a substantial sum of the college's money in her purse. She might have gotten away with it had it not been for forensic accounting and God's ever-seeing eye. When confronted about the missing funds, she wrote a check for most of the money with a promise to repay the balance and said what youths today do when committing ops, "my bad."

CUTTHROAT TERMINATION

Many ironic twists occurred on my journey to find the connection between worshipping God and prosperity. Some lessons are things we should do and things we should not do. The one lesson that stands out the most, from a moral standpoint is the firing of employees in a cutthroat manner. The after-effect (spirit) remains long after the act.

Just recently Ford Motor Company utilized the same method of firing white-collar employees. Ford Motor Company bears watching closely; I believe morale at that company will be in the gutter for a long time, which will affect the company's performance. In the Michigan Consolidated Gas Company case it took many of the terminated white-collar employees three to five years to find jobs remotely compatible to their previous positions. Some employees never did fully recover.

Eventually Bob revealed to me why he had fired those employees. I know it was business but it could have been handled differently. Bob's actions had put us both in an uncomfortable situation because he was the person who insisted I be fair and refrain from being a scoundrel.

I realized God places mentors in our path to teach us the things we need to learn. God also places mentors in our lives to show us things we ought not to do. Bob did exactly as the street hustlers did who were conscious of their shortcomings. They were self-conscious individuals who sought to place younger people on the right path. Bob said to me: "don't be like me."

God loves us all. He wants us to learn from other people, but ultimately He wants us to be taught by Him.

DOUBLE-CROSSING SELF-INTEREST

Bob fought a gallant fight for the common person based on his own self-interest. But he miscalculated the double-crossing self-interest of the political system and how money speaks. On the surface it appeared he had lost.

Bob spoke to me on several occasions about how the fear of failure stopped people from succeeding. If you really want to succeed you must lose your fear of failure.

Bob sat quietly in Virginia with no more major battles to fight. His battle scars took their toll on his body; in time he would have to battle health issues. With all the confrontations and fights fading along with his steadfast philosophy of letting people know where he stood, it seemed that the ghost of Admiral Hyman Rickover had finally released him. He did what a true Chief Executive Officer would do; he turned his attention to cashing out by exercising his stock options, playing golf, smoking cigars and talking more "stuff" than ever while he waited to retire.

Bob had one smart move up his sleeve; he acquired Disclosures Inc., a financial reporting company where publicly traded companies submitted their financial statements for public access for a fee. I laughed after getting wind of what he had done. Bob had a knack for knowing what was going on in the stock market and he prospered. He had spent too much time on crusades for ordinary people and Primark's Corporation earnings were far from expected.

In the past Bob had made money for stockholders, investment bankers, bond holders and bankers, especially during the divestiture. The thing about making money for others is they expect you to keep making money for them again and again to no end. In addition, the company stockholders and Wall Street analysts were giving Bob the blues, calling for his head on a platter.

NEVER LOOK BACK

When you see others prosper, be happy for them. Don't worry about how they got their prosperity. Look at it this way: since God took care of the prosperity of people around you, picture in your mind that you are next. Be happy when you encounter those with great wealth; they are just trying to make it through a life filled with the same problems you have. The truth is they have more problems than you have.

I finished college and could not fully understand why my mother, Reverend Wadsworth, Bob and Ted were so happy. After graduation Bob put a plan in place for me to rise within the corporation. Bob's handpicked successors had other plans and dismantled just about every good corporate citizen program Bob put in place, including eliminating Ted Hunt's motivational program. Bob's successors went farther and one by one eliminated the African American managers, directors and vice presidents he had hired. I left the company because once again my true worth and talent were underestimated. I learned to never look back.

A NEW MENTOR

Reverend Wadsworth died from colon cancer. A local newspaper set in motion an article to smear him politically and morally after his death. Some community leaders thought the newspaper's actions were a vendetta for past actions of the Reverend when he led a successful boycott against the newspaper for its negative portrayal of African Americans. Community leaders united to stop the newspapers smear campaign. Before he died he introduced me to William R. Marshall, chairman of the church trustee board. What he did was turn his mentorship of me over to his friend. I guess God felt I needed a grandfather figure because my new mentor was nearly eighty years old.

William R. Marshall was a former local United Auto Workers (UAW) secretary who had honed his skills of management and negotiation by coming up through the ranks of the union. He was also a high ranking member of the Free Masons Fraternal Order. He had participated in the progress of African Americans during the 1940's and 50's by owning a piece of the rock in Idlewild, Michigan at a time when blacks had to create their own resort towns because they were not allowed to frequent the resorts of mainstream America.

It was William (Bill) Marshall's job to teach me church management, church finance, the subtle politics of the church through delicate interpersonal relationships, and last but not least the art of negotiation. His best talent was that of a negotiator: a skill he had developed at the local and national level by participating in negotiations with the Big Three automakers.

We were cool toward one another at first. In many ways we were feeling each other out. Bill liked to play mind games with people. He threw most people off with his examination: when were you born? Where were you born and why were you born? When that did not move you, as in my case, he showed me his gun.

I HAVE JESUS WITH ME

I told Bill I had Jesus with me and I packed a bigger gun. I must have passed his test of inquiry because we became fast friends and he became my new mentor. He would put any representative of church auxiliaries under the microscope when they requested funds from the church. Although it was done in a good-natured manner it frustrated most members and advanced the negotiating skill of those who endured.

We talked every day up until the day he fell dead in the bathroom of his home and I stood by helpless unable to revive him. He and Reverend Wadsworth had a rule on the subject of stewardship. Their rule was; "Do not let anyone who had never acquired money on their own handle church money."

NUTS AND BOLTS OPERATION

I realized it is one thing to conceptualize the enterprise of complex billion dollar corporations like the one Bob dealt with but it is a whole new ballgame to roll up your sleeves and deal with the nuts and bolts operation of a multi-million dollar church. Looking back in retrospect on what I learned from Bill Marshall, it seems as if I went backward to go forward.

Sometimes on the path to prosperity in order to go forward you must go backward to relearn the things you think you know. In time I understood that one of the key components of prosperity is stewardship. And in the talents and experiences of stewardship you must learn to negotiate your way through the prosperity process.

Bill also taught me many valuable lessons about church members and how they operated on a different plane and how the business of administering God's house is all about God.

SELF-IMPOSED EXILE

My mother died one month and a few days after Reverend Wadsworth's death: two good friends departed within a short time period. Bob, Ted and Bill tried to lessen the pain; they asked what I wanted them to do. I said nothing. I wanted to be alone. I went into a self-imposed exile for a few years.

My most opinionated friends felt I was running from the responsibility of leadership. It was a one-in-a-million occurrence for a streetwise youth to be taken in by a corporate executive, an international award-winning platform speaker, a big-shot minister and later a UAW officer and taught so many things. Some said I was the wrong choice in the first place. A very close friend I had met in college who was to be my future wife knew I was looking for God.

LOST IN THE SHUFFLE

I went to work for an insurance company and waited on God to reveal to me the meaning of the many lessons and fights I had experienced. I had trouble hearing God in church because He sometimes got lost in the showboating noise there. I begin to understand the meaning of the saying "go into your secret room, shut the door and summon God in silence."

While I was in exile it became clear to me that many churches are composed of busyness, entertainment and comedy. On the road to prosperity you must go to a place of solitude where it's just you and God. Every great work in the name of God was preceded by a period of forced or self-imposed exile.

I got married, served on my church Board of Trustees for 15 years, and then split with the church over its desire to become a corporation. I founded an insurance marketing firm and years later became a business consultant.

On a consulting assignment, a company CEO asked me if I knew of any cost-saving strategies for purging employees with several years of experience or of any techniques for ruthlessly cutting employee benefits. I answered no. He had no idea to what extent I had been exposed to such maneuvers.

WORDS HAVE MERIT

I still lean on the sayings Bob, Reverend Wadsworth, Ted, Bill Marshall and I used over the years to motivate us and keep us focused. We used these sayings to keep our spirits up and propel us forward when obstacles got in the way. Words do have merit; they just don't have the same power as God's words. You can use our words or create your own:

When people attempted to come between us or distract us, we would say, "Our business is better business."

When we were under attack and fear entered the picture, we would say "There are very few things in this world that can hurt us."

When our spirits were down, we would refocus, saying "Desire is the key to success."

"Don't associate with those who have nothing to lose and don't care."

"Don't entrust money to those that never had any money."

"Humility will carry you farther than arrogance and pride."

"If your mind can conceive it you can achieve it."

When asked how we were doing, we would respond: "Hanging tough."

When we reached an impasse or new heights while brainstorming. We would say "Keep playing the movie."

When we were pressed to step out on our convictions, we would say, "Let them know where we stand."

The response to anything positive was "You're damn right."

When departing from one another and committing to be there for one another we would say; "We don't say good bye."

And last but not least: "Treasure what is dear while it is near and not when it is far away."

A STORY OF CHARACTERS

Bob retired from Primark Corporation, collected another severance package of cash and generous stock options. Then he did what most sailors do: moved to seaport communities where he could reminisce on his adventures by the sea. He spent his days with his wife and grandchildren and having long talks with God.

Before his departure Bob asked one more thing of me to help my people. I said to myself: I not sure my people want help.

After some time passed, we started corresponding again.

Ted Hunt and I stayed in contact. Our relationship had changed. On several occasions Ted would replace me with people that entered the picture with impressive titles or educational degrees. Sadly most of those new faces burned him in one way or another. One new face with impressive credentials gain his confidence took a book Ted Hunt wrote, changed the tone and wording, copyrighted the book overseas and did well financially off Ted's ideas. Another fellow motivational speaker borrowed some of Ted's presentation materials without his permission and became famous. I suppose it was justice that the people that stole from Ted prospered. Ted had a habit of claiming the ideas of others as his. When confronted he would say that ideas come from the universe to be used by us. I got tired of the familiarity syndrome that drives a wedge between protégé and mentor or friends and family and put some distance between Ted and I. The familiarity syndrome is the chief reason some people venture from church to church and people to people searching for the next in thing.

Bob and I renewed our contact, staying in touch periodically over the years. I went back to school twice for advanced degrees and post graduate studies, back east mainly because Bob and Reverend Wadsworth had planted such strong seeds in favor of education.

Our story is one of characters from totally different backgrounds with the desire to change our condition by changing our thinking. All of us were in search of God, having felt His presence in our youth.

Intertwined in my story there are seven reasons why people achieve prosperity. They are:

1. The ability to focus your faith (concentration)
2. Insightful consciousness (vision) to see beyond the physical world

3. The ability to find and mind your own business
4. Developing well-integrated behavioral clues (people skills)
5. Developing sound stewardship skills (talents, work ethic, thrift and management)
6. Possessing a keen sense of timing
7. Possessing a willingness to give (monetary giving or service)

LIVING BY CONVICTION

Along the way Reverend James E. Wadworth, Theodore Hunt, Robert W. Stewart, William Marshall and I discovered who we were, our talents, our shortcomings and most of all we recognized the presence of God and understood that He has a sense of humor. Every day we had to recognize what was wrong and had to fight to do the right thing. We stepped out of our comfort zones and lived by our convictions. We made a lot of mistakes and we were controversial as Hell. We endured enormous pressure by learning to trust God.

Fighting leaves scars in the form of guilt. It seems that life is a series of fights so why should the pursuit of prosperity be any different? You will not be victorious in life unless you put on the whole armor of God every day. Our prosperity grew in proportion to our knowledge of God. Through it all we believed the slogan used often by Ted Hunt, "Yes you can!"

CHAPTER EIGHT

Where Is the Love?

TO KNOW HIM IS TO LOVE HIM

When Jesus put forth the question: which is the greatest of all the commandments? The answer was "Love God with all your heart and love thy neighbor." To love God and our neighbors is the only way to buy gold purified by fire – only then will you truly be rich.

The command to love one another was so important that Jesus gave it special emphasis. Would Jesus ask us to give love if we had none to give? No; rather, He knows we are blessed with innate love: a love we can draw upon whenever we experience a heightened state of desire to release our spirits. A desire of affection is at the forefront of our secret yearning for God and understanding.

To know Jesus, be it real or superficially, is to acknowledge Him. To acknowledge Him is to love Him. How can we love God and His Son sight unseen and not love our neighbors? Why in moments of fear do we run from God's love?

It is easier to love God inwardly because we feel His attachment to our souls. We can see our life in the rear view mirror, looking back on situations where problems were solved under our helpless watch. We feel soothing hands rubbing away our distress. There is no other way of explaining or rationalizing the positive outcome of our distress; our positive instinct tells us an invisible hand entered the picture. So we love with an inner knowledge: this is the only way to live.

THREE WAYS OF THINKING

When we acknowledge God, we experience Him with three ways. First, we see God as the creator of life. Secondly we acknowledge that He is directing life. Thirdly we see God as a higher source of daily bread, love and comfort guiding us through this world into the next. But even in those moments of heightened out-of-body consciousness we still see life through filtered lenses from the standpoint of "self."

In the process of rationalizing God, He becomes personal. The disconnection occurs when we attempt to rationalize the personal relationship that others have with God. It is hard to fathom that other living beings and all living things seek the same thing: to form common spiritual bonds with God. It hard to imagine every other living thing knows Him and acknowledges Him personally. But His love is vastly universal and available to all in equal measure. All we have to do is let God love us.

How can our relationship with God be personal but yet be a very small piece of God's grand plan? Why does God love and need us, although to fulfill His grand plan He really does *not* need us? This is a paradox: a smaller picture of connecting factors grounded in our jobs, our image of God, our method of worship, our intimate friends and family.

Still, how can God and other living things need me, then shift their attention in another direction when I am no longer among the living? Life goes on as if I had never existed. Could it be the confusion of our common bonds and our sense of self that lead to us to this paradox? Does this explain why we find it difficult if not impossible to love our neighbors?

LOVING YOUR NEIGHBOR

Love takes on a different meaning when the subject is our neighbors. Loving our neighbors is where our religion and worshipping God fall apart. How can this be?

In 1 Corinthians 13:4, Paul's description of the attributes of love falls into the category of the reverse of an idea under the same legality as Mosaic laws. The introduction of "thou shall not" is negative. The attributes of love put forth under the "thou shall not" laws outnumber Paul's positive descriptions of what love is. He starts with: love does not envy, love does not parade itself, is not puffed up; does not behave rudely, does not seek its own way, is not provoked, thinks no evil, does not rejoice in iniquity.

Paul wrote the letter in 1 Corinthians to bring the church together under the banner of a single flock united with one mind and one heart under the spirit of Christian harmony. The undercurrent of fighting played a significant role in the direction and tone of the letter. When Paul delivered his letter of love under the negative banner of the law, he took the essence of love from the spirit of good and placed love under the spirit of human differences.

With all the poems, books, pamphlets and songs written on the subject of love we should by now have a better picture of what love is. Jesus gave love new meaning when He said; "For God so loved the world that He gave His only begotten Son, that whoever believes in Him should not perish but have everlasting life" (John 3:16, NKJ). Does love include sacrifice? Can we love God and not believe or obey Jesus' command to love our neighbors?

There are many religions that do not believe in Jesus. To truly believe in Jesus is to believe He was both spirit and a human in the highest form. To believe in Jesus is a reminder that we fall short of the divine.

When Jesus exclaimed there is no greater love than to lay down one's life for another human being, suddenly we assess the worthiness of our neighbors by counting their flaws and proclaiming them unworthy of such a sacrifice. What further disturbs us is that to love our neighbor according to Christ's teachings is unsettling. In Luke 6:27, Jesus said, "Listen all of you. Love your enemies, do good to those who hate you. Pray for the happiness of those who curse you: implore God's blessings on those who hurt you." But loving our neighbor seems impossible; who would want to love someone that hurt us badly?

SUFFERING OPENS THE DOOR

In the past religious leaders taught that long-suffering was part of God's plan leading to greater appreciation and humility of any blessings received after the suffering ended. It is true that suffering opens the doors to God's love and comfort. Some religious leaders concluded that suffering is for our own good. So suffering was thought to be a natural offspring of love.

The truth is God does not require us to suffer nor does He want us to suffer. The thought of suffering originate from the way we view ourselves in relationship to the world. Suffering is a form of attitude malfunction derived from pain that can be physical or emotional. When suffering reaches its lowest depths of reasoning it becomes fatalism. There is no need to suffer. Jesus suffered in order to end our suffering. Rather, it is the negative aspects of life that cause suffering. When we attempt to legislate love, justice and decency we miss the mark of the true meaning of love. Forced love, as a component of behavior controlled through laws of decency and religion will always fall short of loving our neighbor. When people are forced to do something there is a tendency to comply irresponsibly. That is why laws legislating terms of endearment fail and the pleas of parents for one child to love another go unfulfilled.

LOVE IN ACTION

True prosperity is clothed in love. Love in action is serving the needs of our neighbors and the needs of other living things by sacrificing ourselves. Any attempt to achieve prosperity without loving God and loving our neighbors is what Jesus described as breaking into the Kingdom of Heaven.

It is possible to break into the Kingdom of Heaven under God's grace without attributing our accomplishments to God, or loving our neighbors, or treating others with respect, or practicing forgiveness or having any positive feelings for human life. Prosperity is available to those that do not acknowledge God as well as those who love God with all their heart. It is possible to achieve prosperity and still practice the negative attributes of "thou shall not" in Paul's letter. Then why should we give God first place in our lives for the sake of a promise? If we read further, Paul goes on to say that things not grounded in love will one day vanish.

Men and women through the ages have come into fast fortunes only to lose them just as quickly. There are many instances where those who broke into the Kingdom found their wealth lasted for one generation then vanished. Some families achieved long-standing wealth without love but they have experienced one tragedy after another from generation to generation, while others enjoyed long-standing wealth, health and a relative measure of happiness and were never punished for their sins here on Earth.

But one curious note: the wealth of those who were not punished for their sins here on Earth ended up serving God's purpose sooner or later. Their wealth was redistributed into the hands of the needy through charities, trust and benevolent funds. Their wealth was accumulated by means contrary to God's goodness but God is the master of turning the tide of things. He used His prosperity on loan to the thief for the good of others. Watch closely, you will see this occur time after time.

Remember it is by God's grace that we have life, and His ways are not our ways. Did the person accumulating the wealth intend for this to happen? No! Take note: some people's love of money motivate them to spend a lot of time trying to figure out how to take their money with them. This is clear evidence that the love and worship of money is extremely flawed thinking.

LOVE EQUALS MATERIAL THINGS

One Christmas I tried an interesting little experiment that brought home what I suspected. I suspected that a significant number of people equate love with material things. I gave approximately 20 copies of a book called *Love* by Leo Buscaglia to my friends and relatives and a few associates. The author states in the book what I suspected but I wanted to take it a step further.

After presenting friends and relatives with the book I noticed their faces. A book about love is not a common Christmas gift; though it may have more value than common Christmas gifts. Just like many people who cannot see God, there are those who cannot see value in a book called *Love*. Christmas is a celebration of the birth of Christ: the central focus of the holiday. Christmas is a reminder of His commandment to love one another. In fact, every aspect of His birth and life is a love story.

The mouth of each and every recipient of the book flew open as he or she unwrapped the gift. Some questioned the choice of the gift. A toaster, a necktie, perfume or electronic gadgets would have been more loving in their minds. Others thought I was saying they needed love or I needed love. I am sure some recipients thought I was gay, reasoning no straight man would give such a gift.

Most of the people who received this gift never read the book even months later. A few were downright angry. Remember, I purposely gave this book to get a reaction. Of course I laughed at the variety of reactions; only one person read the book and responded positively. All the other recipients reacted negatively.

DON'T RUN FROM LOVE

Love is something too many of us avoid. When you wake up in the morning, have you ever stopped to think that God put love in you? Can you conceive that God loved you when you went to bed last night and loved you while you slept through the night? The only sacrifice God requires of you is that you fall asleep in love with life, cry to God for more understanding and awake to a new, better day. Why would anyone run from love or God?

To experience a continuous flow of prosperity today, tomorrow and everyday you must take the ideas God gives you, saturate them with love and wrap them in sincere heartfelt intentions to be of service to the betterment of your neighbors. There is a profound reason why Jesus encouraged us to love God and our neighbors. The fruition of the ideas, visions and longings of your heart are all tied to your neighbors. Your hopes and dreams and the hopes and dreams of your neighbors are intertwined under God's spirit of love.

In other words, your prosperity is dependent upon your neighbors and your neighbor's prosperity is dependent upon you.

On your first attempts to find prosperity through God you will experience up and down feelings of detachment and attachment to a higher Spirit. This is natural because to seeking prosperity through God is a process. As your ability to trust and acknowledge God grows, so will the flow of your prosperity. God will reveal to you His nature that you once thought was a secret. It was withheld from you in the past because you were not ready to catch hold of His love.

Some of the things God reveals to you may be shared with others. Many other things He shares with you He will request that you keep secret. It is important that you understand you must acquire certain wisdom to handle prosperity so that money or the things of this world will not overtake you.

It is true that you are to use your prosperity blessings to be a blessing to others. But not all of your blessings are intended to be blessings to others. God wants to teach people around you individually, one on one. If all of your blessings become their blessings there is no need for them to go to God.

Prosperity and the things of this world were made for you, not the other way around. God did not create you to be used by the inanimate objects of this world. Worshipping money is crossing the line. Paul stated that money itself is not evil but the love and worship of money is.

MOUNTAINS OF ERROR

It is a contradiction to believe that a loving God who is overjoyed to fulfill our daily needs at the same time is willing to dole out punishment unmercifully. The two poles of thought are opposite and contradictory.

The thought of punishment is derived from scorn, whereas when God grants us our daily bread, His actions are derived from the love of goodwill blessings. Sin is denial of God's presence: a state where we reject God and all His good. The punishment is clear; how can we reject God's good and walk away clean? We are cited for our sins under a divine rule of law just as we are punished under human rule of law designed to regulate the greater good of many. God's laws have the same affect as the laws of man; the difference is God's judgment is accurate while human judgment has piled up mountains of error.

The laws of God are not really laws in the same sense as man's laws. His laws are more or less curtains of separation where on one side there is love and on the other side of the curtain there is separation and confusion. Love resides in the heavenly realm of spirits. Sin is contradictory to the spirit of goodness; it is first recorded in the mind creating a chemical imbalance in the weakest parts of the body. The weakest organs in the body are genetic weaknesses, an Achilles heels so to speak.

ON A DEEPER LEVEL

God is constantly preparing us for His good by prodding us to go this way and not that way. He calls upon us on many occasions saying: listen, hear Me, those who hath ears to hear, let them hear. He is trying so hard to show us the right way and only asks that we thank Him on a much deeper level than our words because the love He has for us is in the unknowable parts of the soul.

There can be no love without forgiveness. None of us are exempt from committing acts that are contrary to God's love. At best we can limit our sinful acts in preparation to live a life of greater good.

It is no mystery that some of the best people do not run for political office or step forward and take command of endeavors of the heart. Their past sins are too great for the public forum so they remain in the background. In so many cases great sins from the past hold us back, but God can prune our souls for enormous growth and deeds that propel our talents to higher heights. The good news is God loves you in this world and the next, from life to life; no object or money can do that. In Him we have redemption (deliverance and salvation) through the blood and the remission of sins, in accordance with the riches and the generosity of His gracious favor (Ephesians 1:7).

THE PUNISHMENT FITS THE CRIME

Many of us have witnessed justice served immediately upon those who willfully broke into the Kingdom of Heaven by breathing life into the inanimate object of money. We saw from beginning to end the horrible acts they committed to obtain money and felt that the punishment fit the crime. Our beliefs are reinforced, so we see it as a contradiction to God's good when willful sin goes unpunished. However, what we are seeing is not God handing out punishment but the laws of His spiritual heart that were established before time began: a Spirit so deeply rooted in the attributes of good that by its very nature it repels what is not good.

It is God's nature that good will triumph over evil. Love is God's law that is written in our souls. That is why we all must love something. I know of people who love their dog or cat better than they love people. One fellow did not think too highly of people but he loved his flowers and plants. A gentle old lady secretly could not stand people but she loved animals. Another fellow hated people but he loved birds and another cared not for people but loved spaghetti. The emotion of love placed on inanimate objects is not the same as loving another human being or God Who is a spirit. Nevertheless we all love something.

WHY IS THERE SUFFERING?

Many people are puzzled by those who suffer after trying by all means to live in accordance with God's moral and ethnical standards. Why do people who love God with all their hearts, minds and behavior still experience tragedy? What should we make of their suffering?

Some may say that God punished this man or that woman or that child, so they must have committed some dark sin, maybe on the subconscious level. The difference is willfully committed acts and acts unknowingly committed are judged by God differently. What we are speaking of are sinful acts that were committed consciously and the believer suffers.

There are times in human reasoning when God does not make sense. Some things happen for the glory of God in accordance to His grand plan. Take for instance the story told by one minister about the demise of the gladiator games in ancient Rome.

Gladiators in ancient Rome were held in high esteem, equivalent to the professional football players that some of us worship today. The story goes that a godly man traveled to Rome from the rural lands. He followed the crowd to see what the excitement of the games was about. He was horrified by what he saw: men killing one another while the crowd cheered as those who delight in the suffering of others do. The godly man came out of the stands of the coliseum, stood in the middle of the arena and yelled "stop this madness!"

Amidst the excitement of the games, one gladiator thrust his weapon into the godly man's heart. The crowds stood in silence, watching the old man take his final breath. The crowd became silent; one by one the fans exited the arena. This event marked the end of the Roman gladiator games. Did the godly man die because he had committed some unholy act or did he die for the glory of God? The answer is he died for the glory of God. It is situations like these when the laws of fatal or unintended consequences apply. These are economic laws that were bought to our attention by Nassau Senior and Edwin Chadwick and later expanded on by John Stuart Mill.

WITNESSING TRUE LOVE

We should hold dear those moments when we witness true love; there is no guarantee it will last long or have a happy ending.

The wedding had a magical air, the bride possessed that fairytale glow: the glow that love novelists describe so succinctly, creating a tantalizing moment. The groom beamed with smiles of humility and cordial harmony. From all appearances there was no doubt this union would conquer life's trials, the killer of most marriages. One would have to be blind both in sight and the mind's eye to not have noticed that this couple genuinely loved each other.

The wedding continued without a hitch, followed by a gala reception where the only sign of trouble was a dirty old man putting his hand on the rear end of one of the bridesmaids. Alcohol is the standard excuse for such behavior and a scolding from his wife put him out of action for the remainder of the evening. The bride and groom danced across the floor with flawless grace. Their dance reaffirmed the goodness of marriage and why God had joined this man and woman together.

Two years passed and their marriage was still intact. Four years later a child was born: a daughter blessed with good looks and a spirit of future blessings to come. In five years the couple purchased their first home: a place to put down roots, a place they could call their own.

Six years later a second child was born: another daughter, a difficult birth. Minor medical complications forced the couple into dangerous stress. The bride had to return to work sooner than she had with the first child. Childcare and money fears came knocking at the door and anger entered their home, the anger Jesus warned us about because anger plants seeds of false premises.

UNCHECKED FEAR

Fear has the ability to take on a life of its own if allowed to run free, unchecked. Many of us know that God has brought us thus far by faith. But fears start to diminish our view, convincing us that the water in the glass is getting low. Yet there is ample supply if only we would turn the faucet on. But the voice of fear says there may not be any more.

Some false premises come from the pulpits of churches. When Jesus said, "Give and it shall be given to you," the church ministry twisted it and advocated that the more you give the more you will be blessed, creating the false premise that the more you give the more favored you become in the eyes of God and certainly within the church. One minister went so far as to incorporate "no finance, no romance" into the biblical text.

The once bubbly bride left church that day feeling less than a child of God and thinking God must be punishing her because her substance was low. On that day faith had taken another blow at the hand of a religious messenger in the pulpit.

RELIGION COOLS LOVE

The church and so many ministers engage in nonsense that turn more people away from God more than anything else. Religion is responsible for cooling the love of many and contributing to the break-up of numerous marriages. The message from the pulpit has inflicted much pain and killed the self esteem of others.

I recall a situation where a lady came to church with a very heavy heart. She prayed and cried then went to church and prayed until the most calming voice she had ever heard said "I will bless you; all is well."

However, the next voice she heard was that of the pastor who said, "God sees your raggedy hard heart." After experiencing oneness with Jesus through total release and then hearing the voice of this wayward preacher she immediately went into an emotional tailspin.

After church she spoke to me, still distressed. I told her the first voice was the voice of Jesus: the only true voice representing God but the second voice was the evil voice of the pastor. I told her to listen and take heed to the first voice. She left church that day feeling both good and deeply disturbed. This lady left church that day blessed, though I am certain the pastor was not a blessing that day.

That was a day like so many other days where the messenger's actions were in direct opposition to Christ. The lady has never returned to that church again and I cannot blame her. This is the reason God does not condemn atheists or people angry with God. He knows that the atheists and the angry have come in contact with a human representation who imparted the knowledge of a false God.

ANGRY WORDS SPOKEN

Things degenerated in the marriage. Money problems had persisted since the birth of the couple's second child. By year eight the usually easy-going, happy-go-lucky groom had lost his job to corporate downsizing. The once happy couple home became inflamed with daily arguments, angry words spoken that hurt so bad they could never be forgotten.

The bride attended church more often but her mind was not really on God but on her problems. The groom spent more time away from home doing odd jobs to help support his family. At church the wife met a doctor that knew there were problems in the marriage. This doctor had learned as a pre-med student that pretty women thought of medicine men as men of means and pursued them as lovers and husbands. It was for this reason he had gone into the profession.

It is easy to mistake the allure of material trappings as a romantic prelude to fairytale love. Romance is the setting where the mind may not decipher the difference between real love and the outer trappings assigned to love. The rescuer with money has been mistaken for love ever since the story of the prince in shining armor was first told and retold. But it is merely a false premise of love.

An affair developed between the wife and the doctor. For months the wife lived in two different worlds. With her doctor lover she spent most of her time on shopping sprees and secret rendezvous. With her husband and children she spent most of her time arguing and complaining that she was imprisoned and not really living.

One day she confronted the husband with her affair and the announcement that she was leaving him and the children. Her lover doctor was divorced from a previous marriage. His ex-wife had custody of their children, so he emphasized that he was accustomed to no children.

The once-happy bride thought the shopping sprees and lack of money worries were a worthwhile trade-off for her marriage and family; she left both. The once-happy groom lost himself in not caring anymore, lowering his dreams and aspirations, and fading into the status quo.

As fate would have it the doctor eventually got tired of her constant need for romance and spending sprees. To him the malice behind the "sneaking around" sex had lost its luster. Once the sneaking was removed the thrill of the rendezvous was gone. The doctor began to show more interest in a younger, prettier woman and in time put the other man's wife out. The story ended with destruction that was established in their views of God and their differences.

LOVE BEGINS IN THE HEART

When we speak of things of the heart we are really saying the heart is part of the soul which is directly connected to God, Who is a spirit. Love begins in the heart. The consciousness of our feelings is filtered through the mind where we become aware of variations in our interior and exterior perceptions. In the spirit world of the heart and mind other emotions are also present such as hate, disease, fear and separation. Just as love develops in the heart so does divorce and other physical manifestations.

More importantly, our heart is where we develop our concept of God as His intravenous teachings touch our minds then in the fullness of spiritual incubation collide with the resources from invisible substances to grant us our requests.

The former bride and groom had everything they needed to live an abundant life. But their fears and perception of money got in the way. Like most people they could not equate God with money so they never thought to ask Him for it. They started out with the main ingredient: they had love in their hearts. Their religious beliefs became stagnant in the thoughts that God and money should remain separate in the same manner as church and state.

This loving couple missed the point that combining the essential ingredient of love with faith was the key to solving most of their problems. It is a sad day in the life of loving couples when they depart from love because of money. The statistics are staggering: too many couples and families part ways because of money. Money is at the top of the list of reasons people divorce. Most of our prayers are not answered because we pray amiss and ask not in the spirit of love and faith.

DECIDING WHOM TO LOVE

The decisions we make determine our love, the kind of life we will live and our prosperity. It is strange witnessing how some people decide whom to love. I am saddened when I witness people base their decision to love on the false premise of money and the appearance of power.

One woman I know loves men that dress well and speak nicely to her. They must have good grade of hair and have an important-sounding job title. She thinks men in possession of these attributes according to her criterion are good persons. She fails to understand that men with evil intent also possess these things.

Another person I know bases his love on fair skin, a good grade of hair and the height of the person. I have seen others love only those affiliated with their religion. And so many can only love those of the same social status and thought process.

The truth is many of us love out of convenience and crazy idiosyncrasies that have little if anything to do with love.

It is funny observing potential lovers going through the motions of getting to know each other. Their inquiries are along the lines of the superficial. Instead, they should ask the two best questions put forth to any potential lover. The first question should be: how warm is your heart? The second: how is your luck?

Of course there is no such thing as luck. All good fortunes are blessings. But every person you meet comes with their blessings or curses based on what is in their hearts. If the person has no idea what you are talking about, that is a telltale sign that your potential lover does not get it. Too many of us are love poor because we make bad decisions based on false premises.

RELEASE IT ALL TO GOD

When you become mature at dealing with spiritual things, you should ask God to change you into whatever His will is for you. As you advance in prayer you will learn to release all your concerns, your will and your life to God.

Even the prayers of some are in the wrong spirit or in total opposition to God's ways. I remember children praying that God kill their parent(s) because they were disciplined. I had friends who prayed to God for sex with a certain person. I know people who prayed to God for money to gamble, to buy drugs or to have power over others. I have another friend that prayed for God to make a certain woman love him. I told my friend God got out of the matchmaking business after the Adam and Eve debacle, so he was on his own. The woman never did give him the time of day. A businessman prayed for God to eliminate his competition. In a beauty pageant one contestant prayed for another contestant to slip and fall while walking down the runway.

It is no wonder most of our prayers are not answered. I believe God's response to many of our prayers is: "You must be kidding."

On your prosperity walk, as you advance in prayer and meditation, you will learn to release all your concerns to God. When you become spiritually mature, you will ask God without fear to change you into whatever His will is for you.

THE PRICE TAG OF LOVE

What is the real price tag of love, or is love free? I ask this question every time I see people putting a price tag on love. In shopping centers I witness parents being blackmailed by their children threatening to withhold love if the parents do not buy them this or that. I have seen on many occasions one partner in a relationship imply that love will be diminished or withheld if they did not receive this item or that item. I witnessed a situation where a man was told if he did not come home with a diamond cocktail ring with a specific carat weight he shouldn't bother coming home at all because "love don't live here anymore." I have a friend who on more than one occasion stated that sex is love. And he is constantly praying to God for some love.

Another friend's main goal in life is to bag a peacock: a glamorous female that some men call a showpiece. I told him peacocks have their vanity; they are mean and scornful birds. Few noteworthy chefs attempt to make fine cuisine from a peacock. Not wanting to be totally negative I mentioned that peacocks do have pretty feathers that garnish a table nicely.

When love is condensed to the thought process that "love cannot exist where there is no finance" or "what money cannot buy I cannot use" we reduce the love of God and Jesus to a lower denomination.

To kill or betray love for money is an indication of how much we love ourselves. To reduce love to money by using another person, exchanging sex for money and calling it love, is not love at all. Jesus loved Judas but Judas rejected Jesus' love and betrayed Him for money. Judas' actions were in part ideological differences and in part greed – the end results were devastating.

The lesson is: our differences are the main reason we cannot love our neighbors. Every time we engage in the false premises of love and willfully harm our neighbors, it is the equivalent of becoming a Roman soldier, hammering the spikes into Jesus' flesh and crucifying Him all over again.

THROUGH FORGIVENESS WE CAN OVERCOME

When we reject God's plan for our good, we reject the forgiving love of Jesus. There can be no love without forgiveness. And God's promise of prosperity is a by-product of His forgiving love.

Through forgiveness we can overcome all wrongful acts. The desire to forgive sin is an act of faith. With faith comes release that leads to trust, and with trust comes love of self and others. If we truly want to experience the consciousness of the Kingdom of Heaven here on Earth we must use our gifts and talents in the spirit of love. We must step outside our lives and get into the lives of others.

I stepped outside my life and into my sister's life in her time of need. It was God's way of pruning me back for His grand plan. The experience was an act of love that knocked me off my feet.

It is no mystery that we find it difficult to love our neighbors. It is our differences that keep my neighbor and me from loving one another. My neighbor and I travel on different paths. My neighbor and I have differences in the colors of our skin, our interests, our views of what life and prosperity is, our unspoken class system, our political views, our fears, in what we view as important. My neighbor and I see ourselves differently and our views of God are different. My neighbor and I express love differently, we worship God differently. My neighbor and I cannot come to terms of endearment because of our differences. However, true love can take place between me and my neighbor in spite of our differences if only we can overcome them.

GOD IN EVERY TWIST AND TURN

My sister was healed years ago but I remember it as if it were yesterday. God was present at every twist and turn of her story. We had to overcome many differences. She lived her life one way while I felt life should be lived in another way.

On a cold November night with Thanksgiving near, I received a telephone call from my sister. She said "Something is wrong. I have not worked in weeks. I went to the doctor and he could not find what ails me. I am home alone and I feel terrible." I went over to my sister's house, looked at her and knew she was ill. I took her to the hospital emergency room. The hospital admitted her for medical tests and evaluation. A few days later we received the news. Her diagnosis was cancer. When the cancer originates in the stomach and advances to the liver then the rate of survival is greatly reduced.

My sister would need medical treatment and someone to care for her daily. The doctors described the extent of care my sister needed at a family meeting. One-by-one family members offered feeble and coldhearted excuses why they could not care for their sister, aunt, and mother. My wife and I were expecting our second child in two months. By default we took my sister into our home, not knowing how we would manage or if we had the physical or emotional strength to deal with a life coming into the world and a life scheduled for departure. My wife's doctor had put her on medical leave a month earlier because the progression of her pregnancy was difficult.

UNCHARTED TERRITORY

Attending to the needs of my sister was un-charted territory for me because I had a difficult time dealing with illness, mine or anyone else's. I constantly petitioned God unsure if I could continue. The circumstances required me to go from our bedroom upstairs to my sister's bedroom downstairs attending to the needs of both my sister and my wife. My duties also included running a full service insurance agency and juggling taking my sister to chemotherapy treatments and my wife to her doctor for prenatal care. It also involved taking my eldest son to the babysitter, making sure my sister's adolescent son's needs were taken care of, performing my church trustee duties, and last but not least working through the obstacles of my sister's medical HMO.

What the insurance company and her doctors did not know was I sold and managed employee benefits packages to area businesses. This gave me an advantage at overcoming every obstacle put before us by the insurance company. I was the cook, the maid and the chauffeur, and I learned to be a good listener during this stressful time. I had to drop out of graduate school and delay pursuing a degree in finance. I did not sleep because I was too afraid that either my wife or my sister would wake up in the middle of the night with a medical emergency.

At night my sister and I would watch movies, pop popcorn and talk about things that had happened in our childhood. She told me about things that happened before I was born, since I was the youngest sibling. In these heartfelt interactions God touched our souls. We did not realize God was changing both of us until we finally released all the love we had inside us for one another. There was no need to hide anything; she was dying a physical death and I was dying the death of self, watching her die.

MONEY POURING IN

My sister had had money problems her entire life, but in the months following the announcement of her death sentence money ceased to matter and it flowed into her hands from many sources. In the past she had spent every dime she had, even mastering the art of deficit spending in ways that would make the federal government take note. In her short life she had not missed many parties, social events, retail sales on fine clothing or trips to other cities and countries, and she gave generously to all with money she did not have.

Money began to pour in from her postal worker friends who took up numerous collections. Additionally, they donated sick days into her sick day bank to keep her payroll checks coming. When she was healthy her payroll checks had been cashed immediately and gathered no moss but the illness took precedence and un-cashed checks piled up in her night stand drawer. She belonged to several bowling leagues where more donations flowed her way. For the first time in her life she had accumulated more money than ever. When other situations are more serious and the mind is not focused on money, it will flow to you from several sources.

UNANSWERED PRAYER?

More importantly she had family, many friends and several churches praying for her healing. Months later, after completing the scheduled numbered of chemotherapy treatments the doctor informed both of us that the treatments had failed and she had little time left. The doctor asked her if she would like to die at home or in the hospital. My sister selected the hospital under hospice care.

After receiving this devastating news my sister began a compassionate discussion about how senior citizens often lose their balance and hurt themselves in a fall. She spoke of ideas that could be accomplished to stop senior citizens from falling. My first reaction to this discussion was that my sister was in denial. Denial, when used properly, can change bad habits, discriminate between positive and negative behavior and reject the ills of this world. However, denial can also be used to usher in illusions.

I later realized that my sister was engaging in the power of release: a form of healing whereby you totally place in God's hands the outcome of your desires. She was at peace in the midst of her own troubles, so she focused on the problems of others and counteracted her own sober situation. Within a few minutes she was laughing as if the doctor had not delivered a death sentence. I went into the bathroom and cried.

It seemed all the prayers on behalf of my sister went unanswered. When the moment for her departure arrived it was as Paul described in his vision of the third heaven. Her face glowed in her comatose state with brightness like the sun shining through a window of sheer curtains. There was no pain, partly because she was in a transitional state and partly because medication had been provided for pain management. Family and friends gathered around her.

Finally she awoke from her coma and whispered, "I am ready." Within the hour she died with a peacefulness of spirit and a touching love I have never experienced before. How do you explain such a peace at death? How do you describe a love so profound at death? I will never forget. I saw life that day, not death.

HEALING IN MIND AND SOUL

The many prayers on my sister's behalf *were* answered. My sister needed healing in her mind and her soul. Her body was too far gone for the renewal of healing and it had fulfilled its purpose. She lived months longer than most people with the same cancer. The soul that housed her body was scheduled for a new home in the third heaven with Jesus. God was with my sister from the beginning to the end. At her moment of transition I saw Him.

My sister displayed what love is all about. Apparently she had listened to me rant and rave on how selfish life insurance prospects were and the creative excuses they used to get out of buying life insurance and leaving their loved ones better off. Years earlier my sister had purchased additional life insurance, and she did something I am still working on. She left equal shares of her life insurance proceeds to each of her relatives: the same relatives who had blatantly said mean things and abandoned her in her time of illness and great need. She forgave them.

My sister was rich in life and became wealthy at death. The differences was she embraced life while alive and departed from this world cradled in the loving arms of God, the origin of all wealth.

When people ask what the best thing I have ever done is, I would have to say it was caring for my sister during her scheduled transition from this world to the next.

THE BOOTSTRAPS OF JESUS' RESURRECTING LOVE

The road to prosperity is not a mystical secret controlled by ministers, holy men, the wealthy or self-help gurus – although some would have you believe otherwise. The same Holy Spirit that ministered to Jesus is the same Holy Spirit that you and I can tap into by way of prayer and meditation. We must be willing to recognize and accept God's love. If you fail to demonstrate God's prosperity it is your own doing because you failed to pull yourself up by the bootstraps of Jesus' resurrecting love: a love so pure, so receptive to God's blessings. God loves you very much *"How great is the love the Father has lavished on us, that we should be called children of God! And that is what we are"* (1 John 3:1, NIV)!

THE ESSENCE OF LOVE

The public service announcement read:
**PRESS CONFERENCE AT THE UNIVERSITY
WEDNESDAY AT 2:00 PM
THE BRILLIANT PROFESSOR TINKLE, WINNER
OF NUMEROUS SCIENTIFIC AWARDS, WORLD-
RENOWNED SCHOLAR, WILL ANNOUNCE HIS
BREAKTHROUGH DISCOVERY ON THE ESSENCE
OF LOVE.**

Reporters David Allen and Stephen Cato were assigned to cover the press conference by *The Examiner* newspaper.

David: Why are we here? Why would the newspaper send both of us to cover this crackpot professor? The guy is absent minded, his lectures never make sense, plus no one really knows what love is.

Stephen: Look at the bright side; it got us out of the office and back to the university. We are returning to the scene of our many crimes. We could not wait to get out of here, but this was the best part of life: chicks, parties and fun, no worries. Why were we in a hurry to get out? I liked the professor; he would come up with the zaniest theories and attempt to connect them to the meaning of life.

David: It's true. The editor hates me. Why else would he send both of us to a minor story such as this?

Stephen: I would not go so far as to say he hates you. He may not trust you since you created that last story. It was a lapse of journalistic integrity to name news sources that did not exist and report a story that happened completely differently from the way you reported it. It was an embarrassment for the newspaper.

David: I did what most reporters do: I gave the readers news, interesting news, news with pizzazz, news that holds the reader's attention and takes them away from their sorry, boring lives. I gave them news with spunk.

Stephen: Be quiet! The news conference is starting.

Professor Tinkle: Ladies and Gentlemen, the university has requested your presence to share in a landmark discovery based on years of research. Before we get started I want to introduce to you Dr. Glass, President of the University.

Dr. Glass: Good evening, Ladies and Gentlemen. We are grateful that you came here today. With all the newsworthy things going on, we know your time is valuable. Over the past several years the university has received foundational grants and gifts from our alumni, friends and corporate partners to explore life's possibilities; to seek and find new avenues for the betterment of life and in the process heal the sick and bring clarity to the dark crevices of the soul. Today we will share with you a breakthrough in a research project Professor Tinkle has been working on for several years, a breakthrough that would not have been possible had it not been for your support.

David, whispering to Stephen: I wish he would hurry up.

Stephen: Shhh!

Dr. Glass: Professor Tinkle's will be the next voice you hear; but I want to put something on your hearts. As you know my last name is Glass and with a name like that it would be foolish of me not to be transparent. I say to you in the spirit of transparency the university's endowment fund is low and we need your money. So on your way out the door the university and certainly I would appreciate if you would leave behind those men of founding qualities by dropping some Hamiltons and of course old Ben Franklins in this collection plate right here on this table. Again, thank you, Ladies and Gentlemen. I know you will find this press conference interesting; refreshments will be served at the conclusion of the conference. Please drive safely on your way to your respective destinations and remember to leave your money. Thank you!

Professor Tinkle: Thank you, President Glass. Ladies and Gentlemen, today is a special day here at the university. For some time now we have experimented with an elusive entity called "love." This is big. As many of you know I have tinkered with many things the world over, high and low. As a young man I tinkered with biochemistry and discovered a link between chemicals in the brain and behavior. I climbed Mount Everest and tinkered on high. I tinkered in the depths of the sea and got bitten by a shark. I tinkered with the stock market and did well with IBM. I tinkered with marriage and lost half my wealth. I tinkered with the effects of marijuana and I can't remember a thing. And now, Ladies and Gentlemen, I have tinkered with love.

David: I told you this press conference was a joke.

Professor Tinkle: Who said that? I heard that! You, Young Man, I heard that. I cannot remember a thing but I invented a super duper hearing aid and I hear very well. What is your name and what media outlet are you from?

David: Who, me?

Professor Tinkle: Yes, you.

David: My name is David Allen and I am from *The Examiner*.

Professor Tinkle: Well, Mr. Allen that was rude of you to speak when others are speaking. You said something about a joke. Do you know a good joke? If you do, please share it with all of us.

David: Not at the moment.

Professor Tinkle: Since you don't have a good joke, please refrain from making comments, Mr. Allen. I will take questions at the end of this news conference; until then, please behave. Now where was I? Oh yes, I was tinkering. I tinkered with love and found its meaning.

David (whispering to Stephen): This guy is a fool.

Professor Tinkle: Young Man, not only do you insult me but you continue to interrupt me. If you don't want to be here, Young Man, you can leave.

David: Professor I would be honored if you would explain to us the meaning of love.

Professor Tinkle: I was getting to that. People in love have chemically-altered brains. The brains of people in love experience excitement and calmness simultaneously. This, Ladies and Gentlemen, is a contradiction. How can the brain of lovers be both calm and over-excited?

David: Boring!

Professor Tinkle: Mr. Allen, I would greatly appreciate it if you would leave this press conference.

Stephen: Professor Tinkle, if you would be so kind and forgiving and allow Mr. Allen to stay I assure you his behavior from this point on will be acceptable to you. I would be grateful and so will our employer, *The Examiner*.

Professor Tinkle: So you both work for the same paper?

Stephen: Yes, Professor.

Professor Tinkle: Isn't it unusual for a newspaper to send two reporters to cover the same news conference? Oh, I get it; Mr. Allen is a screw-up. I see what is going on here. Mr. Allen should go into the corner and put the dunce cap on. Whatever happened to putting students in the corner with the dunce cap on? I guess education, like everything else, discards ideas that still have merit.

David: Stephen, I don't need you to speak up for me. I have been kicked out of better places.

Stephen: The next step for you at the newspaper is out the door. I would mellow out if I were you.

Professor Tinkle: What was I talking about?

Another reporter, from his notes: You ended with the question: how can the chemical reactions in the brain produce both excitement and calm?

Professor Tinkle: Yes, Yes, the chemical reactions in the brains of lovers produce both excitement and calmness. This contradicts the nature of things. We can compare this chemical reaction to that of fear. When fear is present our heart rate increases and our blood flows to the heart and skeletal system, causing groups of muscles to tighten and our pupils to dilate, producing mental clarity. Our bodies are alerted to stand guard for a flight or fight response. These are all responses of the sympathetic division of our nervous system. In this state our pulse, blood pressure and respiration are all increased in function.

David: Professor what does this have to do with love?

Professor Tinkle: I am getting to that, Young Man. Hold your questions until I finish. Where was I? Oh yes. On the other hand, other physical reactions are taking place within lovers at the same time. The calming affect in the brain is opposite to the fear response. The blood flows to the heart and skeletal muscular system and conserves energy as an operational response of the parasympathetic division of the nervous system. The lover's pupils are constricted, mental clarity is not as keen and the organs return to normal. The sympathetic and parasympathetic divisions of the nervous system counteract one another and thus balance is achieved.

David: So what is the point?

Professor: You wouldn't understand if I told you, Young Man, but here it is. The point is this: how can love cast out fear when both love and fear contain the very same elements? The reaction of love and fear on the nervous system and emotional behavior is the same. This makes it impossible for love to cast out fear. Since their traits are identical they cancel out one another and equal zero. So the logic is if you are too fearful you cannot experience love and if you experience love you are just a fearful individual.

Silence.

Professor Tinkle: No reaction. Hmm. This is a tough group I see. When I make statements like that I wait to hear trumpets sound or a thunderous voice from the sky that says "This is my main man, listen to him," but no such luck.

Anyway, the components of love are counter-intuitive and contradictory to all reasoning. Love contains all the components of fear; both love and fear have the same behavior factors, as does depression. There is a loss of energy, poor appetite and difficulty sleeping. We see in both depression and love the feeling of guilt and the decreased ability to think that hampers concentration and the ability to make sound decisions. Lovers are talkative as are those experiencing upswings in their depression. Both the depressed and lovers share a characteristic trait of declining social activities.

There are also similarities between love and anxiety. The similarities are rapid heartbeat, clinging dependency, and the inability to listen, maintain attentiveness and remember. This is proof that Mr. Allen and I suffer from anxiety, I cannot remember and he doesn't listen.

Laughter.

Professor Tinkle: Where was I? Oh yes. The drop in blood pressure is a component of the parasympathetic division of the nervous system, and depravation of oxygen to the brain is a product of the sympathetic division of the nervous system. Both components of sympathetic and parasympathetic divisions of the nervous system are operational in the bodily function of love. The same components are present in mental shock and stress. Both the lover and people suffering from mental shock and stress experience increased dreaming, sleep and mood swings. Lovers, the stressed and people suffering from mental shock experience fantasies and delusions of grandeur, something that has been noted in schizophrenia. The brains of lovers and schizophrenics produce a chemical similar to an addictive opiate that insulates against pain, thus producing a feeling of all is well.

Silence.

A Reporter: Professor, Professor!

Professor Tinkle: Wow, I must have zoomed somewhere else. As you can see I am an old man. The 1960's were my days of refuge. There are times when I go blank. Sometimes it is a senior moment. This time the word "opiate" sparked memories: a marijuana moment.

Laughter.

Professor Tinkle: Where was I?

A Reporter: Speaking on the irrational components of love.

Professor Tinkle: Yes. Lastly, sex shares similar traits. Sex produces a feeling of warmth and contentment; that is, if it is enjoyable. Sex, like love, has the ability to influence both the sympathetic and parasympathetic divisions of the nervous system. Sex raises and lowers blood pressure, increases and decreases pulse, causes muscles to contract and then return to their normal state, increases and restores respiration back to normal and lastly increases and decreases the heart rate. It is for these reasons that love is confused with sex and fear.

In conclusion, Ladies and Gentlemen, it is impossible for love to both cause fear and cast out fear. Of course, magnetic attraction is always present in the universe, therefore the negative and positive elements of spirits, behavior and bodily function are attracted to love and in many cases resemble love.

In conclusion; it is the light of Jesus that separates the negative aspects from the positive and only by His light can love cast out fear. This is a question only God can answer. Can I get an Amen?

The Reporters: Amen!

David: I knew it! This crackpot wasted my time.

Professor Tinkle: On the contrary, I may have saved your career, Mr. Allen. It seems to me you are on your way out the door at *The Examiner*. I hope you did not think the answer to something so deep as love could be solved by science. It would be naive of you to think that science can explain the essence of love.

David: Then you misled us, Professor, because that is what the press release said.

Professor Tinkle: Forgive me, Mr. Allen; we did not do anything the media does not do on a daily basis.

David: This is bull!

Professor Tinkle: Love is never bull!

David: Come on Stephen, we are out of here.

Professor Tinkle: Before you go, Mr. Allen, you need to hear this. And let all those with ears to hear listen. Love is something that is dying in the world today. The love of many is cooled. Love is not accessible to someone like Mr. Allen with his large ego and his self-absorbed narcissism. Too many people equate sex with love, like Mr. Allen did during his college days when Amy, his secret lover, showed him love. Mr. Allen lied to his college buddies thus disguising Amy's love as merely the affection of a study partner. She adored him but he could not get past her weight or the fact that her looks were not on the level of his fantasies. There was a moment when she cooked him a meal and gave him love, a rare moment when he was in the moment and thought he loved her but his rational mind took over and he rejected her and broke her heart.

Our idiosyncrasies get in the way and we reject love. This person is too fat; this person is not on our social economic level, this person's feet stink. We then rationalize: this person does not conform to my behavior code, this person smokes cigarettes and this person's appearance doesn't fit my idealized standards, so we reject true love for something superficial.

David (whispering to Stephen): You must have told him about Amy. I am going to kill you!

Stephen: No I did not.

Professor Tinkle: No, Mr. Allen, he did not inform me of your relationship with Amy. I cannot remember much but I have a keen sense of hearing. What I hear from you, Mr. Allen, tells me you are a self-absorbed person who places a low priority on relationships. You are a person who has a hard time respecting or trying to understand others. Your friendship comes with strings attached; I don't know why Stephen would be bothered with you. You cannot be responsible with love because you avoid love by playing the blame game. Scientifically, it is true love cannot cast out fear, but it takes courage to love and Mr. Allen lacks courage; therefore he has no love.

David storms out of the press conference.

Professor Tinkle: This concludes our press conference. We thank you for your attendance. Before you leave let me remind you to leave us some money. We pride ourselves on being part of one of the finest research universities in the world. Since I do most of the tinkering around here I appeal to you for your support of my next research project on human wants. Have you noticed these days that successful individuals continually want to be something else? We see successful businessmen wanting to be golf professionals. We have professional basketball players wanting to be hip-hop music rappers. We know of a highly successful male lawyer who wants to be a woman. We are witnessing successful preachers wanting to be businessmen and politicians. We are seeing successful politicians wanting to be a little bit of everything.

There are successful movie stars wanting to be singers. Nowadays we see beautiful, successful high-fashion models wanting to be movie stars, kept women or drug and plastic surgery addicts. I met a successful heart surgeon the other day who wants to be a hockey player. I met an astronaut who really wanted to be a male stripper and float across the stage.

You get my point; I don't know why we ask the kids what they want to be. Maybe we should ask the adults what they want to be when they grow up. I shall call my new research project the "Dissatisfaction of Human Wants."

I have my hypocrisies just like every one else. I am not ashamed to request that you leave your fifties and hundred dollar bills on the offering tray as you exit. Show us some love by filling our coffers.

If you have not learned anything here today, know this. My name is Professor Tinkle, and I have tinkered with many things in this world because it is so vast that I cannot stop learning. In my heart I believe the Spirit that upholds the universe is busy tinkering too. Don't be a scatterbrain like me, find your one true passion, focus on the things you do best and love doing what you do. Don't be incompetent and try to be the best at all things.

Now let us conclude with a prayer. Of course I tinkered with spirituality and I still cannot figure God out.

Dear Lord, we come in prayer to exalt Your holy presence. We seek forgiveness for our unholy ways. We ask that Your will be done something we fear saying in prayer because we think we will lose our free will. We thank You for not weighting us down with many laws. We now know through Your Son Jesus that there is only one law, the law of love. God is love. Teach us to prosper by returning the love Jesus gave us and in the process learn to love our neighbors, and abound in love to one another. We ask a special prayer for Mr. David Allen and those of his persuasion who have not the faith or the courage to love. Amen!

CHAPTER NINE

Giving Away Prosperity

Establishing the Scholarship Fund for Children was a mission to help kids learn to read. It was our intent to eliminate the frustration of reading without comprehension. It was an endeavor to help build self-esteem in children through reading. We hoped if the child learned to read, life may not beat the child down too much in the future and we might help move the child away from poverty to living a decent life through education. The beauty of our motives was they were pure at first, with the exception of one among us who in the end bought the whole organization down.

WHY GIVE?

Why does God demand that we give when all that exists is His? What does God get out of our giving? Are all the gifts we give blessed? How do we know if we are giving to wrong endeavors? Are the motives of the givers always pure? Are the motives of the recipients always pure?

I asked myself many questions while thinking about the subject of giving. The answers are both enlightening and sad. But like most things that cause us to pause for a sober moment, with God's help joy never fails to show up in the morning.

God does not need our sacrificial material gifts; what He does require from us is obedience, respect, honor and friendship. When we give, we are giving back to God what He has given to us, like a father that gives his children funds to buy him a Father's Day gift. The experience can be compared to a father that demonstrates to his children acts of compassion and empathy through giving, and in time his children catch hold of the practice and do as the father does. We gain spiritual rewards by giving and God appreciates that we acknowledge Him and consider Him with our gifts.

In Luke 21:1, when the poor, old widow dropped two small coins into the Temple collection box, Jesus was so impressed that she gave all she had, that He commented that her small gift was more than the others who had given a portion of their excess. The mandate of giving ten percent was in place at the time. Ten percent was the amount established hundreds of years earlier by Jacob in his vision where he saw angels ascending and descending the ladders of Heaven.

The significance of the widow's gift was she trusted God to provide for her, and in so trusting she gave all that she had. The gift of ten percent is the minimum asked of us by God. To give all requires an enormous belief that God is directing us to greater blessings. Most of us cannot imagine giving all we have to a good cause. To do so is preparing us for greater blessings that may not be forthcoming immediately. In the interim we may even suffer want. Jesus informed us that the measure we use to give is the measure that will be used in the invisible world of the spirit where sincerity is sincerely returned.

THE POWER OF GIVING

God rewards the enormity of our hearts, not necessarily the size of the gift. Of course the widow received an enormous reward, and she will remain forever linked with Jesus to the end of all eternity. There is no greater blessing than to have Jesus acknowledge us for our unwavering faith; such an acknowledgement is eternal.

Giving evolved into a life of its own when Abraham was willing to offer his son as a sacrifice out of obedience to God. Abraham's act of supreme trust and sacrifice was a prelude to what God would do in the future by giving us the ultimate gift: His Son, Jesus. Through Jesus, God would give the soul of His soul, the flesh of His flesh, the blood of His blood, the love of His love and more importantly the holiness of His Spirit. It was God's greatest act of giving and the last necessary act to complete the Trinity of God. It opened the doors and windows of the heavens, granting us the ability to transcend this world by way of our giving.

The act of giving has added power. Giving has the energy to heal, the power to inspire, the power to connect us with God and our neighbors, and it has the power to bring faith to the forefront. Jesus is the ultimate example of giving back to God what God has given us. He gave God everything He had. He did it without money or earthly possessions that at times distract our attention away from God.

When Jesus gave to the multitude the food of hope – a new way of thinking that led to healing – He not only took away power and energy from the religious-political leaders of the day, He also put to rest the power of death. The real opposition to Jesus' giving had nothing to do with the food He gave or the healing or the criticism He spoke openly, but more to do with the spiritual knowledge of equality He imparted: in God's loving arms we are equally blessed, equally loved and equally entitled to a life of abundant living.

Jesus spoke of a conscious heaven now and God's gift of more abundant heavens in a life to come. His adversary's only defense against such greatness was to use the laws of the Sabbath and blasphemy as an excuse to convict him. He was really put on trial and convicted of giving the world hope through a more clarified God.

GIVE CAREFULLY

I asked God: is all of our giving blessed? And should we give to all who ask or express a need? Not only did God return an answer, but being true to His nature He went beyond the parameters of the question. You must be very careful who and what you support by giving. We need to note decades of giving to very poor countries as our guide. Most of the aid sent never reached those in dire need. Much of the aid was stolen or plundered by the governments of poorer countries, soldiers in the military or rebel factions. Whatever aid remained after the initial looting found its way into the black market and was exchanged for weapons or used as bribes or enticements for sexual favors. The sad thing is the poor we intended to help still suffered from the ravages of tragedy, famine, genocide, pestilence or disease.

In the case of giving to Africa, corruption and ignorance has caused many in the developed world not to give at all. Some of the organizations we supported with our money and trusted to deliver the badly needed aid either did not spend all the funds raised or eventually the funds disappeared.

We do not have to look far to see how our funds were misappropriated. The 911 World Trade Center tragedy and Hurricane Katrina are perfect examples of how we relied on relief organizations for logistical planning but their plans were ill-conceived from the start and money was wasted or stolen at various stages of the operation.

GIVE THANKS

Thanksgiving is a very important part of giving. Much of the reoccurring tragedy, famine, pestilence and disease we have witnessed in poorer countries and regions could have been adverted or at least minimized through thanksgiving. There are many countries, communities, small towns, cities, nations, friends and family members who have experienced decade after decade of poverty. One of the main reasons for this entrenched poverty is no education or miss-education on the customs that promote prosperity through thanksgiving.

In the spiritual realm of things, the frequency or severity of the storms of the poor are interrelated to the lack of acknowledging God through thanksgiving. There are several poverty-stricken nations and communities that do not have a word in their language that translates to "thanksgiving." If they do have a word it is not used often enough to avoid reoccurring tragedies.

Sometimes poverty has a way of causing depression and we neglect to be thankful for what little we have. Thanksgiving and giving are not at opposite poles in the giving process, in fact they are the same from different points of view. It is through thanksgiving that we truly give back to God by honoring Him as the source of our blessings. Thanksgiving is praising God, and praising God has the power to prosper.

In your prosperity walk learn to give God praise through thanksgiving. Be thankful for small things as well as large; this is the most important aspect of giving. Don't worry about anything; tell God your needs and don't forget to thank Him for His answer (Philippians 4:6).

PROFESSIONAL RECEIVERS

There is an army of people in this world that use the good-hearted nature of givers to create a charitable living. I call them professional receivers or takers because they have mastered the art of persuading others to give them what they need, in most cases while they spend what they earn on what they want. We sometimes call these people "moochers" but the problem goes deeper than that. It is a misnomer to say they do not have faith in themselves because faith is sewn into the fabric of our being. Instead their faith is placed in their conniving and they find it difficult to trust God.

I have been hoodwinked into a false sympathy regarding a dire need that did not exist and paid dearly for being fooled. I know of a woman that paid her niece's first year of college tuition until another family member mentioned they were paying the same bill. I know of non-profit organizations where little if any of the funds raised goes to help people in need. You really are poor when you spend an enormous amount of time playing on the sympathy of others in an attempt to get them to take care of you.

Life is reciprocal: we get out of life what we put into it. That is the beauty and fairness of life. If we play God cheap with small-portioned giving, we reap cheap blessings. But when we give in a spirit of sincere motives, value is added to our gifts and the multiplier effect acts as an accelerant propelling our blessing forward with compound interest.

THE MULTIPLIER EFFECT

Even from a standpoint of practicality it makes no sense to receive back exactly what we gave. Without the multiplier effect it would be like exchanging a paper dollar for another paper dollar in return. It does not make sense because I could keep my dollar and you could keep yours because there is no incentive to exchange. Giving is a form of exchange. I exchange my blessings for the needs of others and in so doing I satisfy my need to walk with God. As I give, God is my witness, the redeemer of my exchange…and to the distress of many He is our judge.

Not all giving is in the form of money. Many people give of themselves as much or more than those who give large sums of money. I had to step back and take notes one summer while watching Luther Campbell, former NFL football player and personal trainer to several professional track and field, NFL and NBA athletes, working with a group of high school and junior high school students. He coached them on the importance of the development of their bodies, their speed and endurance. He stressed giving extra effort, but the most important thing he was developing was their minds by encouraging them to think. He spoke frankly, telling the youths that not all of them would become professional athletes but if they listened all of them would become leaders.

Some of the professional athletes who were in training with the youth reinforced the things "Big Lu" was teaching them. I could not help noticing how my youngest son blossomed into a young man concerned with his eating habits and his overall health. He still takes care of his body. The punch line was when he started volunteering to do things around the house.

That summer I witnessed both of my sons mature each day they spent with "Big Lu." Ted Hunt spoke to the youths and personally encouraged "Big Lu" to continue giving of himself because so many have stopped sincerely serving the children with extra effort. The message hit home because the one thing I enjoyed doing was giving to children, my own and others, but in my busyness I had stopped. Luther Campbell sensed what was happening and began sending youth participants to me for direction. I had a ball!

TAKERS HAVE NOTHING TO GIVE

Unfortunately there are takers in the world. Those who attempt to go through life without giving at all or, at the very least, relish getting whatever they can without giving up a thing. If you would recall the story of the widow that gave all she had, she had faith within her to commit to such an act. A taker trusts no one and it is this lack of trust that leads him to not trust that God will provide.

It is safe to say that too many of us develop clever ways and rational excuses not to give, in fear that if we give there will be less for us. In many cases people who take with the attitude "it is better to receive than give" are practicing a form of hoarding and avarice. Giving maintains a balance within the soul – the souls of those who take without giving dry up, making them unbalanced and causing all those around them to experience misery.

The overriding goal during our prosperity walk is to achieve balance: the one thing so many religious and non-religious people lack. It is difficult if not impossible to be a giver without being truly thankful. So takers are not happy or thankful, even if they have success in accumulating enormous wealth. A true understanding of God is missing, the true meaning of thanksgiving is missing, the growth of the soul is stagnate, and they live in a strained conscience where thieves break in and moths eventually consume their treasure.

I learned first hand as a child that takers have nothing to give. An old junk man gave my friends and me a football he had found in the trash while searching for treasure. He gave the football to me and in our excitement we ran off to play without thanking him. We did the exact same thing as the ten lepers who Jesus healed; only one returned to thank Him. In our case no one thanked the old junk man.

A few days later I ran into the old junk man and he said, "When someone gives you something you should at least say thank you. There are people in this world who will not give you the time of day."

Years later I asked a friend what time it was. My friend of many years told me his battery was low and refused to give me the time of day. I immediately remembered what the old junk man had said to me years earlier and understood there are people in this world who will not give you the time of day and for those who will, I am truly thankful for small things.

THE CHURCH IS A BEAUTIFUL THING

Our giving to the church should be closely examined. The church is a beautiful thing; it is one of the largest employers in the United States and the number one employer of African Americans. It is the place where we can meet openly and discuss issues that held us in confinement especially during the Jim Crow era. It is the place where the Quaker faithful and others prayed and planned the abolishment of slavery. The church is a place where the faithful spent their days and nights praying to God to send the Messiah.

The church is also a place where many people were given the opportunity to learn marketing and especially speaking skills. It provided many of us the opportunity to develop musical and managerial skills and helped us hone our interpersonal skills. The church is where we can seek refuge from the slings and arrows of life, where the gospel is preached to the poor, the brokenhearted healed, the blind made to see and emotional captives and the oppressed freed from bondage. The church is where God is prepared to give blessings to all who come to Him. But the church's present state is not living up to its God-given charter; therefore, our giving to the church requires us to use the discerning mind God gave us.

DECLINING EFFECTIVENESS

The church is not a cure-all because if it was there should be less crime, less corruption, less hate and less deception. There is a lot of sickness in the world and it is debatable whether the church can play a significant role at changing things in our lifetime. You would think with so many churches on so many urban corners and rural fields a great healing would have taken place by now. If the church was at least 50 percent effective, a great number of sincere, repentant hearts would open up and sinful acts, poverty and crimes should decline on average year after year.

But the effectiveness of the church is declining as the buildings and revenues increase in size. We should give to the church but we should make sure our giving is used wisely to help the poor, heal the sick, free the captives and the oppressed; and that the overriding direction of the church is enabling the multitude to go directly to God.

In our giving to the church or any other organization or person in need we should be mindful that our gifts are intended to be blessings and if the motives of the receivers are in accordance with the spirit of the nine lepers, the gifts cannot catch hold of the multiplier effect and will vanish. For this reason the spirit and the motive behind the giver and receiver have a profound affect on whether the gift is blessed.

JUST DOING WHAT YOU SHOULD

By the discretion of God not all of our giving is worthy of returning as a blessing, as children of God there are times we are merely doing what we are suppose to do. No matter what our version of God is or if we believe in no God at all, we have an urging desire to give – call it innate; whatever you call it, it is undeniable. It is impossible for any person to go through life without giving. We have certain duties that come with being human, and sharing life with others through giving is a major part of our duties. The problem is some of us seek to give less. A liberal heart seeks to give more.

POSITIONING THROUGH POLITICS

We are seeing churches today return to the old days when the church and the ruling class joined forces to form a so-called nobility class. There is nothing noble today about church and its leaders positioning themselves through politics in an attempt to gain something from the prevailing political party in power.

The goal of each party, no matter which party it is, is to gain control of the wealth of the land and redistribute it to their advantage. In the end money will be siphoned off to friends of the party in power at the taxpayer's expense.

The church's assignment in the deal is to deliver the votes of the congregation so the desired party can win. It does not matter if the church is slanted in its thinking to the religious left or right they are all pawns in this political game. The leaders of the church and ministers think they are interjecting their moral code onto the legislative political agenda.

The argument on the part of church leaders or ministers is that change can best be influenced by positioning yourself to sit at the table of power. So these church leaders, pastors, ministers, etc. accept or manipulate invitations with the Mayor, Governor or even the White House, leaving with a promise that their agenda will be studied, or simply basking in the thrill of having been in the company of greatness.

It is similar to my trips to the executive suites to visit Bob Stewart. After leaving I returned to the mailroom in the basement and interacted with those on my level. Those brief moments of grand feelings of being on a higher plane were illusions because I had not truly arrived at that plateau.

So the church leaders or ministers return to their congregations to deal with the problems of the people, problems they really don't want to deal with, somewhat deflated that he or she went to the mythical mountaintop but ended up down here below in the trenches of life where Jesus would be.

CLOSE, BUT NOT TOO CLOSE

I am speaking from many years of experience of being close to ministers who were deeply involved in politics. I have also been in private meetings with politicians who spoke frankly. What the church leaders and ministers do not fully understand is that any smart politician knows it is best to appear close to religious leaders yet keep a calculated distance. The fanaticism of religion at times is too much to bear.

If there is some monetary gain realized, clever politicians and businessmen will encourage church leaders and ministers to take the money for themselves. When the political parties and businessmen abandon their promises to the religious right or left, church leaders or ministers go away in silence or threaten boycotts or to sit out the next election. After church leaders and ministers accept the money they can no longer speak to power on certain issues and in essence they have become whores.

FAIR COMPENSATION

Another problem with giving to the church today is the top-heaviness of the church's operational expenses. I believe pastors, ministers, bishops or deliverers of the word by any other name should be compensated for their energy and effort. The compensation should be fair.

What I disagree with is the increasing number of individuals who go into the ministry specifically for the money and other ulterior motives. Some people would say that God calls flawed individuals because they have a story to tell. It is true that God can turn the tide on any insincere motives. But many of these individuals we see entering the ministry today go beyond being repentantly flawed. Their motives are more along the lines of calculated chaos with retorts such as "who, us?"

My people are destroyed because they don't know Me, and it is all your fault, priests, for you yourselves refuse to know Me; therefore I refuse to recognize you as My priests...

(Hosea 4:6, TLB)

Jesus would say they are the blind leading the blind. So many people entering the ministry today are not sincere nor called and certainly not chosen.

I have listened to many church members from different denominations speak of interviews with potential ministers whose sole motives were money, benefits, housing allowances, vacation and retirement packages. And many had only a vague idea why they were there. There are a number of ministers raking in salaries that are examples of extreme greed. In the end greed will kill prosperity and any good thing it comes in contact with.

A FEW BAD APPLES

Of course any self-respecting church would want their minister to earn a decent living, wear festive clothing and be presentable at any social or religious gathering. But in our worship of God, we must be realistic and cognizant of the fact that there is a faction in many congregations that insist on worshipping the deliverer of the Word on a plane equal to Jesus. The ministers who are being worshipped by members of the congregation get caught up in the attention and refuse to stop it. What they are doing is lifting themselves up before God. When this happens, the power behind giving to that church loses its steam and returned blessings are denied.

Sadly, there are some noble and conscientious ministers dedicated to preaching the Word of God who get lost in the shuffle or categorized with the bad apples even though they do not deserved to be placed in the same room as those disciples of deception.

What we are seeing today are ministers who opt out of visiting the sick in hospitals, nursing homes and jails. We see ministers passing the buck to associate ministers to perform weddings and funerals and refusing to counsel families in crisis unless there is something to gain from media attention or political mileage. Others check to see how much the person in need tithes before considering rendering any assistance. This is miss-discipleship and the primary criticism Jesus directed at the Pharisees and other religious leaders over 2000 years ago.

The very things ministers are opting out of are the things that exemplify what the ministry is about. Some ministers think too highly of themselves and have what I call a "Jesus complex" where they project themselves into the red print words of the New Testament – the gospels of Jesus. Sadly, when their Jesus complex is in high gear any constructive criticism of their ministry is met with defense mechanisms such as "they are just jealous" or "God forgive them for they know not what they do."

The church is a place designed to give, not take, least of all from Jesus. You must keep in mind that some ministers, like some schoolteachers and politicians, went into their respective professions not as their first choice but after failing at every other attempted endeavor. The amount of money a minister raises is not a good measurement of how godly he or she is. It could be that the minister who brings home the money is a good beggar or slick marketer. Everyone who sounds godly isn't.

GOOD STEWARDSHIP

We should give to the church just as we should give to other good causes. We should be mindful that there are numerous good causes that need and appreciate our thoughtful giving, which would put our gifts to good use. It is the mandate of our stewardship that we make sure our giving is used to help the poor, heal the sick, free the captives and the oppressed. We must be sure that church and other charitable operational expenses are reasonable and not excessive. More importantly, we should not compensate ministers and administrators like rock stars, movie stars or heads of state.

There are moral and ethical responsibilities that must be adhered to when administering the church's charitable assets. Those entrusted with this responsibility should get their directions from God, not the pastor or some entrenched group or clique within the organization. There are many churches today that are top-heavy on the expense side; most of the money is used for church operations, a mortgage or the pastor's salaries and expenses.

A WELL-MANAGED CHURCH

A well-managed church should spend the majority of collected donations on benevolence. You can tell when a church is well-managed because it is able to bury those with no money at the drop of a hat. The church has funds available for human needs instead of parties, celebrations, rallies and special days that praise themselves.

A well-managed church is able to find housing for the homeless. A well-managed church is able to encourage families to stay together, send youth away to college and stop people from being evicted from their homes. A well-managed church gains the respect and trust of street people, many of whom are very cynical. A well-managed church visits the sick and the jailed and feeds the hungry. A well-managed church exercises the virtue of thrift as a key component of stewardship, which weights heavily on the prosperity process. It is very important that thrift be used when administering church funds.

IMPLODING FROM WITHIN

Some churches embark on ambitious building programs to the point where the focus on the mortgage becomes a financial trap that by far exceeds the accumulation of spiritual capital that is the mandate of God. The church becomes straddled between imparting straight-talking sermons and feel-good sermons designed to not offend parishioners but to get their money.

I have this reoccurring nightmare that has awakened me on numerous nights; I see churches imploding from within. When I asked God the meaning of the nightmare, the response was "tell them to stop playing with My house."

Listen, you priests, to this warning from the Lord of Hosts: "If you don't change your ways and give glory to My name, then I will send terrible punishment upon you, and instead of giving you blessings as I would like to, I will turn on you with curses. Indeed, I have cursed you already because you haven't taken seriously the things that are most important to Me.

(Malachi 2:1-2, TLB)

It is not how large the church is or the amount of money the church has accumulated in its coffers that determines the viability of the church. It is the collective giving hearts and minds of the congregation that are a true measure of the church's worth. Some churches are dead because they cannot relinquish their stubbornness or find their way back from a wrong turn or sex scandal cover-up. Stubbornness and ignorance go hand-in-hand; where one is present, the other is also present.

Some of the characters in the Bible were unable to follow Jesus, not because they did not believe He was sent from God but because of their stubbornness. In Luke 9:59-60, KJV, Jesus said, *"Follow Me,"* and for those that cannot, *"let the dead bury their dead: but go thou and preach the Kingdom of God."* In the physical world it is impossible for the dead to bury the dead. In the spiritual world dead spirits can bury their dead beliefs about life and real living by following Jesus.

Large Is Not the Answer

Very large churches are not the answer; they were tried long ago by the Catholic faith and other denominations. Today the

Catholic Church is abandoning the idea of largeness and is downsizing. In order not to offend, many large churches present God's image as a feel-good, happy-go-lucky God, in non-threatening tones that are more appropriate for motivational seminars. These churches are dressed in esthetic buildings of huge dimensions holding large numbers of worshipers whose prayers sometimes go up to heaven, but their thoughts remain below, because the mortgage is due every 30 days. Making money and making ends meet are overly emphasized, which sometimes blurs the congregation's focus on God.

Large churches, due to their shear size, are more susceptible to drowning themselves in politics than any other house of worship. The large church is more susceptible to losing many of its members in the shuffle of largesse.

God is a respecter of persons because He loves each and every one of us through the personal attention He showers on us. In some cases the personal development of some members will be hampered by the corporate-style operation of large churches. And the mega church is more likely to commit suicide through incompetence like many organizations that are too large to manage.

I have listened to many people in search of God say they entered this or that mega-church and left, feeling God is too difficult to serve or they were too small to swim in a sea of so many personalities.

My question is: why would a church use the blueprint of the corporation as a model for developing faith in God? The corporation was never designed to develop its employees. In fact, the corporation has borrowed many of its attributes from the church, once the realization was made that human capital is the fuel behind all human endeavors. At the end of the day it is people that are the backbone of any organization.

The main focus of the church is to develop its members and employees, thus enabling them to become the brothers, sisters, mothers, fathers, friends and disciples of Christ.

Priests' lips should flow with the knowledge of God so the people will learn God's laws.

(Malachi 2:7, TLB)

A CHURCH WITHOUT SALT

You can tell when a church has lost it salt. In a church that has lost its salt, the pastor refuses to preach sermons on prosperity. You can also tell when a church has lost its way when the church emphasizes giving at the expense of your parents or loved ones who happen to be in dire need. Jesus challenged the religious leaders of His day, advocating that satisfying parents' needs is just as blessed as giving to the church.

The church has lost its salt when it is divided between wealthy members and poor members or the beautiful people versus the ordinary. Its salt is gone when a sex sandal is covered up. It has no salt at all when members are berated by the pastor for not giving more when they are giving all they can afford. When you see a pastor or worship leader bless members that gave and refuse to bless those that did not have money to give, that church has lost its salt.

When you see employees and long-standing members of the church that are not gradually prospering, something is wrong. Look closely to see if former church secretaries, janitors or associate pastors move into higher, more prosperous positions at their next assignments. If the prosperity of the people associated with the church is declining, something is amiss.

When you give to a church that has lost its salt you have violated a cardinal rule of giving which is a component of stewardship. When you realize you are giving to a cause that has lost its salt, stop giving and find another church or another cause to give to. If the alternate loses its salt, keep searching until you find another good cause. Don't stop giving; simply stop giving to causes that have lost their salt.

EXPANSION AND GROWTH

This is very important because "mega" means abundance and "prosperity" is another word for increase and growth. Whenever you are in a situation where the pastors refuse to preach sermons on prosperity you will see a church in decline. It makes sense that if the church is to grow, so must the prosperity level of the membership.

Jesus preached expansion and growth, a growth He said would expand like unrestricted yeast until all the world knew His name. His story is a story of unimaginable blessings constantly multiplying because He released His spirit into the world at Calvary; the church should do the same.

NOTHING TO GIVE BUT EVERYTHING TO GAIN

There is power in giving; power attracts negativity. In Genesis 3:4-5 the serpent had nothing to give so he cleverly twisted human reasoning by getting the first man and woman to believe evil is good and disobedience to God is the way to be like a god. The serpent was clearly a taker; he had nothing to give but everything to gain by knocking human beings off their higher pedestal.

Pretending to disconnect us from God in exchange for sin is as close as you can get to giving nothing. What the serpent gained was access to human consciousness and all that was endowed to us by God. He actually stole man's birthright.

It is no mystery that the central focus of the Old Testament is idol worshipping, negative thinking, birthrights and the promise of prosperity by going to God to make things right again. It is your birthright to be prosperous; the serpent stole your money. You can get it back through giving in the spirit of love; the very same spirit that is the substance of God.

Jesus gave us a parable on how clever takers operate in this world. In Luke 16:1-14, Jesus tells the story of the rich man who discovered his steward (business manager) stealing from him.

The rich man demanded the steward put his books in order before being fired. The steward hatched a plan to reduce the amount of money each debtor owed his boss. His plan was to make new friends that he would rely on to take care of him when he became unemployed.

The steward was again stealing from his employer by reducing the debt of each person that owed the rich man, taking money away from the rich man and transferring it to those that owed him. This steward did not give anything of his own to the rich man's debtors. More importantly, he caused the rich man's debtors to participate in his sins. The question is: were his actions blessed? No!

LOSING THE BLESSING

I know of two childhood friends that are not speaking to each other today because one held a job as a cashier and gave hundreds of dollars of merchandise to the other. When her friend came into the store where she worked, she would ring up sales for small amounts, though the value of the items removed from the store were worth hundreds of dollars. When the cashier lost her job she felt the person she gave hundreds of dollars of merchandise to should take care of her, or at least return the favor. The problem is they were both stealing, which nullified the blessing behind the giving.

I heard a drug dealer of notorious reputation speaking proudly of the free drugs he had given away at swinging parties during his heyday. He is now financially and morally broke but honestly believes the drugs he gave away were gifts that were blessed by God. The sad thing is no one had the heart to tell him he was passing out poison; how is that blessed?

A panhandler taught me the best lesson on giving that does not return blessed. One morning when I was exiting the employee parking deck in downtown Detroit, I ran into a panhandler who I was familiar with and on previous occasions had given money. He again asked for money, so I gave to him, thinking my gift was in accordance with my Christian faith. However, this time I asked, "Don't you think it is time to get off the streets? This is no way to live."

The panhandler, who obviously had some emotional issues, retorted, "I don't have to do a thing. I don't have to get up in the morning if I don't want to. I don't have to wash if I don't want to. I don't have to go to the bathroom if I don't want to. I don't have to change clothing if I don't want to. I don't have to breathe if don't want to. I don't have to live if I don't want to. I don't have to do a damn thing that I don't want to do."

THE THINKING OF A PROSPEROUS MIND

It was a lesson that would stay with me the rest of my life. What the panhandler said is true: we don't have to do anything if we don't want to. Everything in this world is permissible but everything is not beneficial. The panhandler helped me clearly understand that we should use discretion when giving.

To those that think along the lines of the panhandler we should give a cup of coffee and enough for a sandwich; on some occasions nothing at all. They are children of God just like the rest of us but their way of thinking is disconnected from God. On the other hand, to those who believe we should do things for the betterment of others, we should open our checkbook and whatever doors that need opening. This is the thinking of prosperous mind.

Jesus said, "Don't give pearls to swine," which translated means: "do not give to those who will not do for themselves what you are willing to do for them." It is not of matter of whether they can afford to do for themselves what you are willing to do. The question is: are they *willing* to do for themselves what you are willing to do for them.

There are some people who will not buy themselves underwear no matter how much money they are in possession of. Why should you give them underwear? That is why your feelings are hurt when you see a gift from the heart treated in a non-appreciative way: thrown on the floor or given to someone else because they did not want it.

Your blessings are not necessarily the blessings of all those around you. Some of the people around you do not like you. Some of the people around you actually hate you. This is the meaning of "Don't give pearls to swine." No matter how you dress up some pigs they will still wallow in the mud in the fine clothing you purchased for them. It is not because it is the nature of the pig to wallow in the mud. The pig has been *trained* to do so. There are house pigs with discerning minds that would not dare wallow in the mud.

So it is with prosperity, if you are willing to use the discerning mind God gave you, you would not dare to be poor.

GIVING OUT OF GUILT

There is another personality who gives because of wrong motives. I know some people that give to the point of poverty. They understand the giving act of the poor widow in Luke 21:1, and feel their giving falls short. So they give more and more out of guilt.

God does not want you to overextend your giving to the point of debt or poverty, especially when the gift is given in the negative spirit of guilt. I have seen people with a socialist philosophy describe poverty as a blessing or at least a safer route to God's Kingdom. Their corresponding actions are to give their material blessings away and then experience poverty. Poverty is not a blessing, however, because if you are too poor you are more susceptible to being enticed into activities that lead to sin. Poverty is the reason many people entered the world of thievery, prostitution or drug dealing, or becoming con artists, contract killers and other criminal categories.

Poverty is the stuff insurrections, race riots, looting and destruction of property are made of. Poverty creates debt and debt creates poverty; the two are intertwined and in some cases one and the same.

Some people give away all their possessions because they see themselves as giving away money they consider the root of all evil. They also believe giving away their possessions will gain them entry into God's Kingdom. It will, but your motives must be right.

Jesus knew we would always have the poor among us because the mindset where poverty is entrenched will always remain.

GAINING FRIENDS AND INFLUENCING PEOPLE

There is another personality that gives to the point of want. Their motives behind giving are aimed at gaining friends. Subconsciously they believe purchasing friends is a form of having a tender heart; some call it being kind-hearted. However, this form of giving is not real living or wholesome, because when there is no more to give the fake friends flee.

I have seen this type of personality steal when there is nothing else to give. The real cure for those who give to gain friends is to teach them that Jesus is their best friend. Jesus' friendship does not require you to buy Him material trappings to maintain the relationship. People that engage in attempting to buy friendship have a disease and need to know that God has blessed them with prosperity so that they can live.

You are to share some, save some and give some away...but not all. Sometimes people who give all their money away and then wallow in poverty secretly see themselves as martyrs. This form of religious thinking is so far from the truth. You should work hard to dispel this denial of the truth, which is no more than false teaching and a false belief. God wants you to be prosperous. Being fruitful and multiplying means give some of your resources away and keep some for yourself.

STAGNANT GIFTS

Not all the gifts you give will return to you as blessings. Furthermore, not all the people receiving your gifts are blessed.

Stagnant gifts benefit one entity on a short-term material basis then vanish under the boundaries of goodness set forth by God. We see this sort of stagnation when giving to hate groups and groups that advocate oppressing one group over another. The gift cannot multiply because the sacrifice of Jesus limited the boundaries of hate and death by overcoming these ills with love and everlasting life.

Behavioral attributes that cause prosperity to flee from us are:

1. Arrogance – study arrogance closely and you will under-stand that thanklessness and arrogance are partners. They both see no need to apologize or to be introspective. One is necessary for the other to exist and both are potent forces that kill prosperity.

2. Blatant corruption and thievery - these two are twins where one exists the other surely follows. Both kill the spir-it of harmony that is required for anything to flourish. Cor-ruption is very deadly because it kills efforts and takes pros-perity to the underground.

3. Ignorance and stubbornness – where you see one, the other is attached. Ignorance is not what we don't know; we all experience things we are not familiar with. The differ-ence is the willfulness in which we choose not to learn or experience anything other than the limited things we have incorporated in our world. Poverty and many other ills of this world are rooted in these two brothers.

4. Greed - greed cuts off the flow of prosperity by damming avenues God uses to prosper the people. Greed is a close cousin to jealousy. I know of some very greedy people and I have watched their reactions when other people receive a blessing: they experience a furiousness that will not cease unless they are included in the blessings. Greed and jealousy occupy the same space. Both will cause prosperity to flee. It is a lie to believe greed is good; that is like saying evil is good.

THE TRUE PROSPERITY MULTIPLIER

Giving with love in the spirit of a joyful heart is the true prosperity multiplier. The Scholarship Fund for Children failed because those entrusted to govern the charity were more interested in their own agenda, and one founding member had a lust for control. The organization became stagnant and died.

Some organizations have a naturally stagnant character because the sole reason for their existence is selfish. This whole thing called *life* is about giving, loving and belonging, and the legacy we leave behind has a lot to do with how we worship God. In the process we can experience peace, harmony, joy and wonderment, and be comforted by the love of Jesus and the Holy Spirit.

Giving from the heart is also receiving. The giver receives the spirit of an uplifted heart where the mind resides in the realm of the divine. Giving is contagious; it encourages others to do the same. It is through giving that we expand our capacity to help and care for others. Giving opens up the mind, refocusing our attention on compassion and empathy, thus enlarging the heart.

Giving broadens the soul which allows us to dream of a better world and to practice mercy in an attempt to replicate God's grace. Giving helps wipe away sober tears of hardship, quelling our fears and exciting the possibilities of hope. Giving answers "yes" to the question: "Am I my brothers keeper?"

Ultimately giving is essential to human endurance and survival, serving as the portal through which we must travel in Jesus' name to reach the end of this time. God gave us a gift that cleanses our souls and soothes our minds, promoting health, wealth, happiness and joy at Calvary. If you will do as Jesus did and truly give from the heart, you will prosper.

CHAPTER TEN

Invisible Substance

"Our legions are brim-full, our cause is ripe…There is a tide in the affairs of men, which, taken at the flood, leads on to fortune…And we must take the current when it serves, or lose our ventures." William Shakespeare

PERFECT TIMING

The timing of Jesus' birth was perfect… the pleas of the masses gathered momentum at the breaking point of the eternal circle where the Holy Spirit could stand in and reinforce the gap by entering the affairs of men. Human life expectancy had declined each year, and the prayers of the people had reached the point of being sincerely focused on God. A great number of people had lost their will to live, seeing the pain of those who had lost lives through barbaric killing methods.

The people faced threats of war and insurrection; famine, captivity, murder, disease and injustice were commonplace. To reach the age of 30 was considered a blessing of long life. Corruption was rampant and a normal part of life, as was widespread insanity – which is why Jesus had to cure so many demon-possessed people.

There was absence of hope among the multitude; God was thought to be the only answer. The masses clung to their hope that He would send the Messiah, fulfilling His promise to change things. The groundswell of prayers ascended upward into the heavenly throne where God released His promise:

I will bind you to Me forever with chains of righteousness and justice and love and mercy. I will betroth you to Me

*in faithfulness and love and you will really know Me then
as you never have before.*

(Hosea 2:19-20, TLB)

THE RIGHT PLACE AT THE RIGHT TIME

It is difficult if not impossible to achieve prosperity if the timing is out of whack. In the scheme of things timing is everything. A number of legendary figures and everyday people experience instances where prosperity found them instead of them finding prosperity. They prospered not because they were smart, but simply because they were in the right place at the right time.

It is a lesson in the unexplainable when these people are invited into classrooms to lecture children on how to achieve success. So many of them describe the secret of their success in old clichés such as "plan your work and work your plan," or "visualize your success and speak success into reality and it will be yours." A few found by prosperity will say things like "think positive thoughts and in time you will succeed." Other will give you a list of habits highly effective people may or may not possess. A majority will provide pat answers to questions to which they do not have a concrete answer because they really don't know exactly how it happened. Only the rare honest individual will tell you that they stumbled and bumbled upon prosperity or success and they really don't know how it happened. Some would say it was by the grace of God. That is the truth.

I have met some very prosperous and successful people who are real-life examples of prosperity finding them by being in the right place at the right time. They certainly were not brilliant or astute at all. How did they do it? Many of them do not have a clue as to why it happened to them. There were people around them who were more talented, better looking and smarter, and who possessed more personality, but these people did not make it. Meanwhile the clueless individuals did achieve prosperity and the prognosticators reasoned it was luck. However, there is no such thing as luck; all good fortunes are blessings.

DON'T SPEAK TO STRANGERS

I knew of a wino who was a perfect example of being in the right place at the right time. This man was a drunk who harassed the children on their way to school. Most mornings when the children reached a certain spot on the path to school, this wino would impart some philosophical drunken gibberish. The children did not pay much attention to the wino because their parents had taught them to not speak to strangers and had told the children the wino was a bum.

The wino would say things like: "A broke man with a negative attitude is doomed. I am a broke, happy man with a positive outlook so I've got a chance because every dog has its day." The children were taught to respect the wino, though on occasion they ran from him. This wino served dual roles in the community: he imparted knowledge to the children who listened in rhymes such as "Don't you be no fool, go to school." In his other role he watched over the children because perverts have a history of lurking around kids as they walk to school. He once saved a young girl from being raped by rising up in a drunken stupor from behind a garbage can, a garbage can that would one day prove to be his blessing.

KEEP SMILING

So the wino would say to the children "keep on smiling, it will take you far." The older people in the neighborhood thought the wino was an embarrassment and they were relieved when he purposely committed a minor crime to go to jail for the cold winter months. They saw him as an eyesore in a neighborhood with too many other social ills. The wino would often stand in front of the liquor store and beg for money.

One day my mother and I passed the wino while he was begging for money. My mother gave him a dollar I said to her, "You know he is going to buy some wine." She responded that it was not my concern. So I gave him the dollar and told him to buy him something to eat. I thought: it is not what he does with the money; what is important is that I did what God told me to do.

People would laugh at the wino, but the children missed him during those winter months when he was in jail. He called his jail terms "winter vacation." The wino had another saying when he saw us walking slowly: "Be on time, timing is everything. The early bird gets the worm, so put some pep in your step and get that ed-u-mu-cation!"

When the wino disappeared for longer than usual the people in the neighborhood began to suspect that something bad had happened to him. The last person to see him was a lady that ran a flophouse for the indigent. She said he had come to her flophouse and given her back rent money plus extra, out of appreciation.

A few years later a man got out of jail and repeated what his cellmate had told him. His cellmate said he was running from the police with a bag of loot, proceeds from illegal activities, and he dumped the money in a garbage can while in stride. The wino slept behind that same garbage can, usually knocked-out drunk.

It seems this wino was right: everyone has his or her day and timing is everything. Several years' later word reached a former member of the neighborhood that the wino was alive and well, living as a successful businessman in a southern community. He no longer drank and he looked good.

The point is this you don't have to kill, steal, cheat or knock off others to achieve material prosperity. This is the perception of those that see the world as a pot of limited resources. If you keep on living happily when you are without a dime, money will come to you. Even a drunken wino knocked out cold in an alley with perfect timing can achieve prosperity.

WITHOUT REGARD FOR TIME OR SPACE

In the early 1980s my college roommate conceived the idea that bottled water would be the wave of the future. At the time the most popular brand of bottled water was a French brand that we believed did not appeal to the common people. We discussed my roommate's idea to exhaustion, brainstorming in our minds. We discussed packaging and distribution; we targeted our market.

It was one of the best ideas we conceived, but we failed to follow through because we discussed it with other people: people who could not conceive of bottled water as something consumers would buy. We were labeled as weirdoes and were the brunt of campus jokes.

Less than ten years later bottled water was a worldwide industry. I regret to this day that we dropped our idea because we listened to the crowd; crowds are sometimes fickle. The crowd did not kill our idea, however, we did. We lacked a steadfast belief. Our timing was off; we were not in sync with the times but nevertheless it was a very good idea.

Ideas flow without any regard for time or space. They are not confined to the same laws of time and space that we are. Many ideas need time and space to help them become realities in the physical world.

God uses ideas to enrich us. Since ideas come from universal intelligence or intelligent design they do not exhibit the same logical traits as sciences or mathematics do. Logic works in sequential steps, ideas do not. God's ways are not our ways when it comes to ideas, in fact, logic often gets thrown out.

INFINITE IDEAS

Ideas operate under mechanisms that are illogical, intuitive and counter-intuitive. For example, an idea may start at step five then proceed to step one then present to you the finished idea or vision. Some ideas and visions come in the form of the finished products or services with no other steps in between. The missing pieces to the ideas God presents to you are to be solved by your God-given talents and persistence. Both your talents and the ability to persist are gifts that God blessed you with before you were born. Your job is to be persistent at finding your talents, the sooner the better.

The Holy Spirit acts as the administrator of universal intelligence and does its work by connecting you with infinite ideas contained in the universe. The most harmonious way to connect with the spirit of universal ideas is through prayer, meditation and contemplation. I would be lying by omission if I neglected to say that you can also tap into the invisible stream of ideas with the help of drugs. Drugs enhance receptors in the mind and play a role at extracting ideas from the universe in the short run. In the long run, drugs destroy the very same receptors that once helped you tap into genius.

The best way is what others have done: tapping into the flow of ideas through prayer, meditation, perfecting talents, hard work, persistence, positive thinking and then falling asleep where dreams take over and supply the missing piece(s) to the idea.

INVISIBLE WAVES FROM THE SPIRIT WORLD

The flow of ideas has also been known to respond to insanity. The insane mind is receptive to extracting invisible waves from the spirit world. This is why insanely possessed characters in the Bible were able to recognize Jesus in many cases before the rationally sane recognized Him.

When we petition God, the spiritual side of things emits vibratory waves dipped in faith and crowned with love. If our motives are sincere on the side of doing good, ideas are immediately released to us.

We may not recognize the idea until we go into a silent place where nerves are calmed. Ideas are best recognized under a state of calmness. Jesus understood how the Holy Spirit worked, so He said to His disciples *"...come away by yourselves to a deserted place and rest a while..."* (Mark 6:31, AMP).

If you do this you will experience God's peace, which is far more wonderful than the human mind can understand. His peace will keep your thoughts and your hearts quiet and at rest as you trust in Christ Jesus.

(Philippians 4:7, TLB)

THE PATH OF CREATIVITY

The Holy Spirit travels the path of creativity, traveling from individual to individual in leaps that seem random but make sense to the Trinity of God. The same ideas are put on the minds of individuals in Asia, Africa and America simultaneously. It is for this reason many are led to believe that God is not a respecter of persons, when in fact this phenomenon of the Holy Spirit is God's omnipresence at work. His Spirit can overcome time and space, being all-encompassing in all places at the same time.

The belief that God is no respecter of persons has led many people to develop dogmatic views that discount the value of human capital and worth. In a constantly evolving creative universe God cannot leave to chance that we will use our talents. So He spreads His abundant ideas into the minds of many.

The Holy Spirit will guide you through the process; it is up to you to pursue your ideas. The Holy Spirit will open up windows and doors and place circumstances before you that were once closed to you. Your part is to develop that burning desire while pursuing your ideas.

IT MUST BE A MIRACLE!

A series of events that will open up to you that seem like miracles. Heaven and Earth will move in ways that seem like both were designed just for you and you alone. People you do not know will come into you life and have faith in you: some are angels; some are every day people that see you differently. They will have faith in you and what you are about to do, although they are not sure what it is.

Some people who did not like you in the past will now be willing to help; these characters are the scary ones because you are not sure if they are friend or foe. This is where God's sense of humor comes into play. It could be that He has recruited them to help you because they did not like you in the past or that He is using them on your behalf for the success of His plan.

Some of these people will go back to disliking you once their role in your success is completed. They will spend the rest of their lives wondering why in the world they helped you, especially since they never liked you in the first place. They may never understand that God was in the plan.

SPECIFICALLY DESIGNED FOR YOU

The events that were opened up to you by the Holy Spirit were specifically designed for you. I can say this is true because the events that take place are in your time and space based on your emotional state of being and available resources at that time. Some of the people that enter your life during the implementation stage of your ideas are people you will cross paths with at that exact moment. These doors and windows that open and the series of events that occur will close as soon as your ideas reach the point of fruition, and remain sealed so that they cannot occur again in the exact same way.

Once the Spirit of God comes upon you things will happen to you that may seem like hardship. Pay close attention to the success stories of others, you will notice that what seemed like hardship in truth played a profound role in their development. Being laid off or losing a job is a common occurrence of the Holy Spirit at work; it is part of the preparation process that God must send you through to connect you to other doors, windows and events that He will open to you.

Beware of the waiting period between what seems like hardship and God's transitional period at work in your life. This is where we often try to help God along with foolish moves that hamper the Holy Spirit's goal of guiding us to a better way of life. The hardships and problems are there to alter your life story to give you the life God planned for you from the foundation of the world.

It is not our problems or hardships that keep us from the richness of life God established for us. The Holy Spirit is holy and cannot engage in anything unholy. It is our strong attachment to material things and behavior traits contrary to God, such as disobedience, fears, stubbornness and pride that cut us off from the flow of blessing administered by the Holy Spirit. In those states of mind the Holy Spirit will still provide us with protection until we come back to the harmonious state of mind where He can come in and touch us.

Your prosperity may not be where you are today. It may be in another city, state, or country. It may come in old age or come to your heirs who will reap the benefits of where you sowed. Your flow may not be in your present career or with your present employer, it may just be the hobby that is dear to you or the positive things that excite your mind. It may be a heartfelt endeavor to make this world a better place to live or some method or product that heals or makes life easier.

POVERTY VERSUS PROSPERITY

Poverty travels in the same spiritual realm as prosperity, but in reverse. There are two kinds of poverty, the poverty of no flow and the poverty of flow. In the poverty of no flow few if any people in that country, state or region experience prosperity. Prosperity has been sectioned off into the hands of a few who are intent on keeping things the way they are. We see the poverty of no flow in environments with limited industries, dying industries and corruption.

The state of West Virginia comes to mind; at one time coal mines were the dominant industry and primary source of prosperity in the state. When alternative sources of energy came into play the coal mines experienced financial setbacks and unemployment skyrocketed. In the 1990's when the rest of the nation benefited from the harvest of prosperity, the people of the Appalachian states still wallowed in poverty, but not because they are godless people; in fact it is just the opposite. West Virginia has some of the most spiritually principled people in the country when it comes to the subject of God.

Their poverty is the poverty of no flow and it will not get any better until the state and the people develop new flows of prosperity through new ideas, and tear down the concentration of wealth in the hands of a few and put that wealth in the hands of many. The poverty of no flow is the most pervasive form of poverty because great ideas cannot flourish in a state where the flow of wealth is blocked.

You may have noticed that extremely impoverished environments seem to experience continuous tragedies. The mindset of soberness has a way of attracting one tragedy after another. In extremely impoverished environments, ideas are hampered by resistance and an undercurrent perception that "hardship is realty." Ideas still flow in this environment because the Holy Spirit can penetrate any situation where at least one spirit is focused on God.

The penetration of the Holy Spirit is needed more so in impoverished environments where prosperity cannot flow. The problem is many ideas conceived in extremely impoverished environments are discarded because of a lack of open-mindedness and follow through or extra effort necessary for implementation.

ENDURING EXTREME POVERTY

Extreme poverty does horrible things to the soul and thwarts the desire level; two major items that make up invisible substance. It causes the impoverished who escape to strive on the strength of a vow or oath that says, "I will never be poor again." Their strength at times is not really strength; they strive under the umbrella of shame where fears often remain within their souls their entire lives. In many cases their striving may fuel a criminal aura or a cutthroat mentality.

A number of people who have experienced poverty with no prosperity flow are hoarders with a miserly disposition, practicing greedy accumulation of things and food. Some have a propensity to engage in pretentious spending described by Aristotle as "niggardly" under the banner "the magnificence man." The black communities call it "ghetto fabulous"; some call it "bling-bling." The end result is the over- accumulation of things with an extremely flawed sense of self worth.

The most sobering trait of those that grew up too poor is their boasting and large egos. As they strive under the vow to never be poor again, they will let you know "I am the first to do this" or "I am the only person to do this" or "I lifted myself up from poverty by the bootstraps of my effort and look at me now." When you look closely at these people, you will see a trail of irreparably hurt or misused people in their past. However, the striver is unaware they have left behind such a large trail of destruction.

What people who have experienced dirt-poor poverty need most is healing through understanding: an understanding that Jesus went through extreme hardship so we do not have to.

Do You Really Want to Be Healed?

They also need to go back and understand what Jesus meant when He warned us against making vows. A vow is a seed that independently exercises our will and not God's will. It is a seed wrapped in strong emotions with the ability to summon others spirits from the spirit world.

What happened to you was not your fault. Here again when things don't make sense, economic law applies to life. It is the law called "The law of fatal or unintended consequence." It is a law contrary to God's intent; a law that is activated by the deeds of men, not God. When you experience extreme poverty, it is not what God intended for you. God can heal you but you must first take a good look at what Jesus asked of the man that lay at the mythical healing pool for 38 years. His problems were so deeply rooted that his depressed psychology froze at the thought of attempting any effort to help himself. The question Jesus asked of the man at the pool, and of you, is, "Do you [really] want to be healed?"

ESCAPING POVERTY

In Detroit's heyday money flowed into and stayed in the black community at a rate that helped many of us escape poverty. On the eastside near downtown in and around the famous "black bottom" section of the city, money flowed from the paychecks of factory workers to black-owned businesses, and from visitors outside the community searching for soul food restaurants, gambling, drugs and prostitution. Domestic workers rode buses to affluent addresses, cleaning homes for low wages and imparting moral values to white children raised with little affection but plenty of money.

When an associate talked about how he and other children in his native southern town exterminated rats using sticks, bricks, rocks and bottles on pesky rodents, I knew immediately he had experienced the poverty of no flow. We performed the same community service for fun, but we had baseball bats handed out by the Detroit Tiger Baseball Club where local businesses paid for children to attend free bat day. We used our Louisville sluggers, firecrackers and air guns on the rats, gifts from local businesses, numbers bankers or pool hall owners, or money we earned from running errands for old ladies and street hustlers. The only thing that people in the neighborhood and street hustlers asked of us was that our lives not turn out like theirs.

We went to school in decent clothing and ate some of the better foods whenever family members or members of our extended family were blessed with windfalls that occurred often. Some of us found bags of money, the product of ill-gotten gain, in alleys and garbage cans stashed away or hidden from corrupt police. Even the little kids had money because soul singers such as Marvin Gaye and Jackie Wilson would throw hundreds and hundreds of quarters in the air and get a kick out of watching us scramble for the money. We knew our prosperity was near when those Cadillacs rolled in. If you were quick and aware of what was about to happen you went home with jingles in your pockets.

THE CONSPIRACY

We lived well because life yielded its windfalls to us from the flow of prosperity under the spirit of caring for one another. Some said the neighborhood's prosperity was the result of unity, but that was not entirely true. The unity was out of necessity. Outside forces perceived as the enemy evolved into a sincere concern for the well-being of others, soon to be destroyed by envy and jealousy that cooled the appearance of a unified front.

It was not pretty, but people lived well under circumstances not of their own making. This was the ghetto, set up to displace and confine a people in deprived conditions; instead the people had a resilient spirit that turned the tables and created a middleclass life in an environment that was supposed to be impoverished.

We lived decent lives through good times and bad because someone in a large extended family "hit a lick," so to speak, by receiving a taste of prosperity. In spite of all ills God was definitely in the neighborhood. There was a spirit of banding together that allowed God to create avenues where doors opened to a few, thus multiplying into the blessings of many. Prosperity flowed with the rhythm of the beat of a vibrant neighborhood of sharing. The conspiracy was this: no one told us, so many of us did know we were poor.

CUTTING OFF YOUR BLESSINGS

By virtue of free will you have the ability to cut off your prosperity flow, and thus your blessings. One surefire way to cut off your blessings is through covetousness, in other words, greed. Greed will kill you in the end if it doesn't kill you physically; it is certain to embarrass you, rob you of your credibility and put you to shame. Greed is selfishness, though in some Christian communities greedy behavior is passed off as God's abundant living. There is a distinct line, however, between God's abundant living and greed.

At one point I was greedy in that I spent an enormous amount of time learning about God, never sharing what I learned. Even this will run its course under God's spiritual laws: too much study without works can produce religious intellectualism. Like too much of most things religious intellectualism will eventually fall under the law of diminishing return. God wants us to go out into the world so that we may enable a multitude of mature worshippers to come to Him.

The flow of prosperity is eventually cut off from the sex-mad man or woman who strives for riches in order to trade the allure of their accomplishments for sex. This is one of the lowest forms of human interaction because neither the sex-mad individual nor the willing participants being used are living up to their fullest potential. The sex-mad man or woman has cut off the Spirit of God because their goal defiles God's decree of spiritual intimacy. Sexual madness strikes a blow at the intimacy of harmonious bonding and nurturing passion presented in God's idea of fleshly union.

We were created to seek a sense of belonging through relationships and obedient reunion of the souls. The sex-mad man or woman's only motive is to engage in sexual brokenness where secrecy, shame, sorrows and misuse resides. To use another person only for sex is the most degrading form of downplaying human worth. The true nature of spiritual intimacy involves honesty through loving disclosure. The best sexual brokenness can produce is resentment and a degrading spirit against God's temple in the human body.

FULFILLING SEXUAL DESIRES

Sexual madness and freakiness are forms of greed. When one partner is sexually promiscuous, the spouse feels it necessary to prevent close contact with others. Oftentimes this results in the couple's inability to connect with other couples, even those having many things in common. In a few cases had sexual promiscuity not stood in the way these couples could have prospered together; perhaps one couple had an idea and the other had a missing piece and together the pieces could have formed the whole of prosperity.

Sexual greed will cut you off from the flow of prosperity because your motives for seeking entry into God's Kingdom are wrong.

Too many people strive for success in order to fulfill their sexual desires. Some buy sexy sports cars and sexy clothing and spend enormous sums of money to look and feel sexy in order to attract and gain sexual favor.

Those who pursue prosperity for the sake of sex, however, eventually experience pain and illness in the body. It is interesting to watch these people pursue God's forgiveness and healing after their bodies become ill. They do not seek God out of true reform from their old sex-mad ways but rather to reinvigorate the body for the purpose of engaging in the same behavior. Under these types of motives the Holy Spirit cannot help because He cannot enter into the unholy places of the thoughts.

Sex-mad man and woman exhibit the same behavior as heroin addicts. In fact a large number of drug addictions started out as sexual addictions. They are drawn to their addiction again and again, all the while in denial. They will lie, cheat, steal and in highly-charged situations even kill and risk it all just to temporarily satisfy their two-second addiction: the duration of an orgasm and the equivalent of a rush from a fix.

SLEEPING WITH THE ENEMY

Mrs. Flowers is the busy-body church lady familiar to many churches. She is a long-standing member of the church and part of just about every church committee. She spends a lot of time with the youths of the church because her grown children did not accomplish all that she had hoped for them. She had disciplined her children, sometimes for things she did not see them do but what they might have done when she was not around. As a result her children grew up learning to conform and be content. They lived relatively normal lives with no exceptions.

Mrs. Flowers sought to do a better job with the children of the church. The church setting was her second chance. She entered the life of a young lady blessed with the voluminous Spirit of God upon her. This young lady deeply loved God. Her gracious ways and natural beauty were a gift from God, so was her loving heart.

As the young lady grew older so did her interest in men... not the boys her own age, but men. Though she made no move to satisfy her curiosity, her thoughts gave her away to a man of ill intent. He sniffed her out. He was slick, cunning and polished, accomplished at overcoming all objections to an invitation to ravaging sex. The beautiful young lady was attracted to his dark edge. She could see he was indifferent to the goodness of life. She was aware he had a dark side, but the tingling desires of her body overruled the discerning mind God had given her and she thought she could get away with it untouched.

So when the busy-body Mrs. Flowers saw what was to come, she informed the young lady. "If you sleep with the devil, your act of love is not the best sex he ever had. He does not feel. His goal is to place his evil seed in your soul. He has no interest in you, your body or your love. He will use you to get to your soul."

Mrs. Flowers asked the young lady a question: "When the devil has sex is it with the body or the soul, and is love present?"

The young lady answered "probably with the body."

Mrs. Flowers corrected her, explaining that the act of sex or making love or whatever you want to call it enters the mind, body and the soul. When bodies join in sexual union the act is recorded in the Book of Life. In the spirit world it is recorded in the annals of time. The soul is sensitive and receptive to good and evil. If you have sex with another it does not matter the number of years that pass; the act is recorded in the infinity of time. It is placed on the bulletin board of your eternal résumé. The young woman realized the truth of what Mrs. Flowers said and lost interest in the man to whom she had been about to lose her virginity.

On your path to finding God and prosperity you must understand that those with a spirit of evil intent will recognize the significance of your talents and gifts before you do. Those with evil motives possess keen radar at spotting the good in you to exploit. They only want to use you and dim your light before it reaches the launching pad and shines brightly. You are probably endowed with more talents and gifts than you might think. Why is it that people with evil motives recognize from a distance what you have trouble seeing up close?

GOD'S POWER IS UNLIMITED

In the flow of prosperity healing must come before the blessing is granted. It is the healing process that prepares us for maturity. We need to stay in constant contact with the Holy Spirit. A wise God would not give His children a fortune to buy video games and electronic gadgets, a maturity process is necessary for God to grant you prosperity.

God's power is unlimited whereas new fortunes come into being whether the economy is in the midst of a trough or a recession. Prosperity flows in the wake of depression and stream rolls into livelihoods in environments of hopelessness and unemployment. Prosperity can and will flow where money is scarce and greed seems to dam the circulation of God's will.

In God's will, flowing rivers contain abundant food, and soils lay ripe for impregnation from the seed. Over-fished oceans and seas regenerate rich eggs with golden nuclei, while the angels sing "Life cannot die. It is biased on the side of good. To resurrect life requires merely a faint pulse here and a resuscitating breath there. You cannot kill this life, this flow, this God."

The rhythm of life swirls as free as the wind, roaming in all directions. The rhythm of life has a simple beat: there is always hope, there is always love, there is always abundance, there is always a way.

A carpenter rubbed his hand over wood and marveled at its fine texture. The Father rubbed His hand over the rough-splintered tree shaped to form a cross at Calvary and marveled at the fine texture of his Son's soul. It was wood that held His Son pronounced dead. Yet both the wood the carpenter sees as a possibility and the rough tree symbolic of the cross of God's sacrifice are dead. The molecules in the carpenter wood and the wood of the cross multiplied by transformation becoming stronger in death than in life the same as our Lord. This is no illusion; there is nothing else to see. God has decreed for us abundant prosperity.

CHAPTER ELEVEN

Forgive Us Our Debts

In the spiritual realm our only debts in life are to love the Lord with all our heart and soul, love our neighbors and love ourselves. In Matthew 18:23-33, the parable on debt contains a lesson of forgiveness and unforgiveness. A servant owed the king over ten million dollars and the king asked for the entire amount. When the king realized the servant could not repay the debt he ordered him sold along with his wife and children as payment for the debt. The servant fell on his knees and worshipped the king, saying "Lord, have patience with me and I will repay you."

The king was moved with compassion, freed him from his servitude and forgave his material debt. The servant went out and located a fellow servant who owed him a 100 pence (about 2000 dollars) and beat him and demanded that he be paid in full. The fellow servant fell down on his knees saying "Have patience with me and I will repay you."

But the servant would not have patience or forgive his fellow servant, and had him put in prison until the debt was paid in full. When other servants witnessed what was done they felt sorrow and went and told the king what had happened.

So the king called in the servant whose debt he had forgiven and said "you wicked servant, I forgave and cancelled all your debt because you begged me to. Should you not have pity on your fellow servant as I had pity and mercy on you?" In his wrath the king turned the servant over to the torturer (jailer) until he had paid all that he owed.

Jesus ended the parable with "So will my heavenly Father

deal with every one of you if you do not from your heart freely forgive your brother of his offense.

Defining Debt

Forgiveness is not only essential to love but also a necessary act for relinquishing debt. The definition of debt is something owed; a liability or obligation to pay or render; trespass; an offense requiring reparation. If debt is all these things it becomes obvious to the discerning mind that debt has negative consequences. If most of the characteristics of debt are negative I ask the question: why are so many people opposed to getting out of debt?

Debt is an anchor that holds us down, adding to our anxiety and stress. It contributes to sickness and creates anger and abuse in the home. It has been known to be the root cause of suicide and worry, motivating some to throw good money at bad by borrowing money from loan sharks or predatory lenders. It drives some to drink, consume drugs and gamble. It places many people under the drudgery of heavy burdens. It causes rashes on the skin and drives a wedge between friends and kin. It causes us to make mistakes and produces much heartache. So why do we ignore and even fight to keep our debts?

Debt is such a concern that the United States government recently imposed stricter repayment laws on credit card companies, increasing the minimum payment on unpaid balances to reduce the country's debt level. The national debt has been a problem for some time now and an issue of concern for those who understand that it can change the dynamics of the economy and democracy. It causes some of us alarm when we see many of the country's leaders refusing to address the national debt.

So why then do we refuse to retire our debts? Maybe I have been asking the wrong question. The question should be rephrased to ask: can we forgive ourselves our debts and forgive our neighbors their debts? As I said earlier, when we ask with sincere hearts God will surely answer our questions, provided we ask the right one.

ACCUMULATING DEBT

What causes us to wait at putting our debts to rest? There are many reasons we accumulate debt. The main reason for accumulating debt is our desire for things we do not have: either needs or wants. The positive quality of debt is it allows us to afford high-priced things and spread repayment over time in smaller increments.

The compound interest attached to debt is the multiplier effect of a nation, firms or individuals. Debt can be a positive vehicle for raising capital to use in the production process that contributes to the wealth of a nation. Of all the reasons for accumulating debt the most negative reason is the need to "keep up with the Joneses." God knows our every need, but in the process of receiving God's blessings, from prayer to understanding, we sometimes attempt to circumvent His plan with our incompetence.

Most of us measure ourselves by the accomplishments and possessions of our neighbors, friends, family and those within our social class. We spend in conjunction to our social group. The majority of the spending behavior in western society is tied to our wants. We spend an enormous amount of time chasing the feeling of contentment by accumulating things and then adding more things to what we already have. The definition of wealth is being redefined as lifestyle as opposed to assets.

We are under assault from the art of marketing and advertisers but the main culprit is our inability to distinguish between a need and a want. We were created to need God, food, clothing, shelter, sex and through self-discovery develop a sense of belonging through relationships. Beyond that all other pursuits fall under the category of wants. In too many cases the debt that we cannot forgive is our impatient wants.

When debt takes root many people spend out of frustration, in an effort to feel good about themselves. Some of us give in to the temptation of skipping payments; by doing so we go farther into debt. I have seen clients, friends and family engage this scenario again and again.

THE PERPETUATION OF POVERTY

As an insurance agent I had the opportunity to see first hand how poverty is perpetuated. I watched people buy cars they did not really qualify for credit-wise or income-wise. The idea of special financing has good and bad qualities in that it helps those with poor credit restore their credit, but places others deeper in debt with exorbitant interest rates; this is called predatory lending.

I have seen automobile salesmen coach prospective buyers into excluding items such as childcare from their credit applications, instead stating the child is being cared for by the prospect's parents. Another area where prospects are coached is the exclusion of rent expense, instead listing their parents' address as their place of residence. These maneuvers increased disposable income on paper but in reality the prospects' disposable funds did not match their ability to repay the car note.

In one instance the prospect borrowed money for the automobile down payment or insurance down payment from a grandmother on a fixed income. Sadly, the grandmother was never repaid because 30 days later the purchaser could barely pay the first car payment or the first insurance premium due.

As a consequence of poor judgment and wanting what is not affordable the car ends up repossessed or worse yet, stolen without recovery. This type of transaction, misrepresented loans that eventually crash and turn into bad debt, increases the automotive industry's sales revenues.

THE BURDEN OF HEAVY DEBT

The burden of being under stress and anxiety due to heavy debt motivates some purchasers to go from monetary debt to sin by manipulating fraudulent insurance claims and other crimes.

The truth is those with the least spend too much money on transportation and over consume on many other things, putting a million dollar front on annual salaries ranging from $12,000 to $30,000. Many people fall into the temptation of the easy-payment plan and entertain loans from payday lenders with interest rates that are on the level of loan sharks. If you carefully unravel the language and benefit of loans you may discover that the repayment is not so easy.

On a visit to a prospective client's liquor store to review his building, contents and liability insurance coverage, I noticed a middle-aged gentleman enter the store and cash his auto industry payroll check. He paid a check-cashing fee of three percent. He then purchased 20 dollars worth of lottery tickets, a bottle of cognac for 18 dollars, a carton of cigarettes, a sandwich, some beer and cigarette papers (which I assumed were for the marijuana he had or would buy later, because few people buy cigarettes and cigarette papers these days at the same time). My financial mind took over. I had just witnessed this gentleman, who should know better because he had lived on this earth at least 45 years, spend eight percent of his take-home pay excluding the marijuana. He had spent this amount before paying any essential bills for food, clothing and shelter. I don't know this gentleman but by observation I can say with certainty he is in debt.

I could take this case study further by assuming the cognac and marijuana would serve an auxiliary function to a sexual rendezvous later in the evening. If so, more funds should be factored into the equation. If we project the cost of marijuana at 20 dollars, the percentage increases to nine percent of his take home pay.

BANKING FROM OUR POCKETS

It is no mystery that expenditures taken off the top of your wages before you pay yourself or take care of your essential needs are a prelude to depleting your wealth. You are automatically operating from a deficit when a significant percentage of your money from wages is spent on things that are wants instead of needs. Obviously the middle-aged gentleman did not have a bank or credit union account; if he did, why would he pay three percent to cash a check when a bank or credit union would cash his check without a fee?

When we bank from our pockets, money has a way of getting away from us without a record of where it went. It is hard to stick to a realistic budget when banking from our pockets. The truth is our decisions are directly related to the quality of life we live, our debt and our prosperity.

The thought of debt falls under the thought pattern of denial of error. The thought of debt is really a thought citing scarcity or lack. The one accepting the liability (debt) feels deprived of satisfying his or her immediate needs or wants. The lender (debtor) feels a sense of want from forgoing their needs or wants for the sake of someone else.

If asked, both parties will deny they were operating on a mental mechanism that focuses on what they don't have before making the transaction. Both are looking for something to be gained, because each feels they lack something they want or need. One wants it now, the other is willing to forgo his or her wants and needs now for an increased return later. What is really going on is the one assuming the debt is placing two liens on themselves. The first lien is a form of self-imposed enslavement to what is received at the close of consummating the agreement. The second lien is on future earnings with a risk premium factored in. So there is an immediate obligation and a future obligation incurred.

IMPATIENCE IS AT THE CENTER

In the parable Jesus pointed out that forgiveness of debt is a form of patience. Remember the first servant's debt was forgiven when he fell down and asked the king to be patient. Impatience is at the center of accumulating debt. If we were patient and willing to wait on God for the things we need first, we would ask God two things; (1) can I have the thing I am requesting? (2) Is my request in accordance with Your will? If we asked God for the things we need or want with an obedient heart, the accumulation of debt would not be an issue and we would avoid the pains that accompany debt.

Notice the king in the parable was not accustomed to forgiving debt because the first thing he did was order the man sold, along with his wife and children. The king was not a forgiving man but in this case he was influenced by God, the giver of compassion. The king's compassion went farther than just forgiving the debt, however. He freed the servant from his servitude, forgoing the price the slave would command on the open market. So not only did the king forgive the debt, he gave the servant his freedom. Similarly, when our debts are retired and thus forgiven we gain our freedom.

FREEDOM FROM CAPTIVITY

When Jesus first came into His ministry, He read from the book of Isaiah saying that He had come to fulfill His mission by freeing us from the captivity of our oppressor. Debt acts as a torturer that holds us captive, eating away at our psyche, causing mental aguish, fear and headaches. The heartaches of debt produce stress and anxiety that interfere with our bodily functions.

When the servant's debt was forgiven by the king, the servant immediately went out and beat another servant who owed him money he could not pay. He was acting as an oppressor. He acted without compassion because God could not break through the hardness of his heart. So the servant had his fellow servant, who was still under the laws of enslavement, jailed, thus adding to his burden.

The servant's behavior is not unusual. The oppressed generally becomes the oppressor when freed from bondage. Immediate freedom does not mean an immediate behavior change; it takes at the very least about 100 years for an enslaved people to begin to break the psychological chains of slavery. The time spent breaking those chains is a pruning process; many will die a physical death and hopefully in the process take their slave mentalities with them.

That does not take into account the 100 years of Jim Crow laws that were barriers of entry into a decent life and extended the idea of true inner freedom for additional centuries. It took several thousand years for the Jews to make a round trip from Egypt back to Israel again after World War II. And the Jewish settlement still faces many problems and divisions today.

In the process of breaking the psychological chains of slavery the oppressed usually become the oppressor, acting out behavior learned while enslaved. The servant in the parable still possessed the feeling of indebtedness within himself although the king had forgiven his debt and freed him from enslavement. The servant could not forgive his own debt so he pursued relief by demanding the debt owed to him by another be paid in full.

COPING WITH ABUSE

Heavy debt can lead to neglect and abuse. People cope with debt in a variety of ways. Some people become so distressed by their debt load they cope by walking away.

One situation that stands out in my mind was the case of a young lady with too many children whom she could not afford to take care of. At the top of list of things that contribute to debt and poverty are having too many children at an early age. We hear from time to time how the accumulation of debt from having too many children has caused some to abandon them, and in extreme cases has provoked some to kill their children because the burden of the debt overruled all sense and sensibility.

In this case the young lady was drowning in debt from having children too young, too rapidly and raising them alone. As her debts mounted, she was on the verge of being evicted from her rented house. Her best friend solicited funds to stop the eviction. A few people pitched in because of the children.

Once she got her hands on the money, she lied to her best friend, telling her she had raised a surplus of what was needed to stop the eviction and now it was time for her to enjoy some of life's pleasures. She convinced her friend to go on a cruise with her.

This young lady and her girlfriend went on a Caribbean cruise sponsored by a foundation that helps students enrolled in black colleges stay in school. What this foundation does is a very good thing. I was one of those students that ran out of money in the last semester of my senior year of college had it not been for the heartfelt goodness of members of my church I may not have completed my degree.

The young lady's decision to spend all the money raised plus some on a cruise is a perfect example of how people faced with insurmountable debt engages in neglect mentally if not physically fleeing the situation; she did both. She left her three kids, the oldest eight years old, with a few dollars and a meager amount of food. The kids, being children, ate most of the food in two days, because each child cooked different items for each meal – a sure-fire way of depleting the food supply fast. A neighbor realized the kids were alone but decided not to call the authorities because to do so would cause more problems.

ESCAPISM

A good friend of mine has been advocating for years that prospective parents should be required to take a parents' test to see if they should be allowed to become parents. Each time he says it we laugh and then think about the merit of his idea. The idea contains elements of reform; forced reforms have residual affects that often create more problems then they solve.

True reform begins within the mind and soul of the person, not by legal decree or force. There is no test that will make people responsible or make them love a life that is a part of them. Children will always represent debt with compound interest in the scheme of things here on Earth. But it is loving them that is the greatest of all investments. To love them is to keep them out of harm's way, even if that means forgoing your needs and wants.

The best friend of the young lady scheduled for eviction had no idea her friend had left her children home alone with little food and no supervision, and had spent all the money on the cruise. The best friend was visibly upset when she discovered what had happened, especially after watching her friend act on the cruise ship as if she had no children, wearing the finest clothing, sporting several bathing suits and splurging like the rich and the famous as if she had come into a fortune.

This is a classic case of coping with debt though escapism. As fine a job as this foundation does keeping African American students in black colleges; in this case a parent used the cause to misuse much younger children left home alone. These children experience neglect because their mother's priorities defied sound judgment.

COME ON IN

The best friend went into action again, just like the fellow servants in the parable who informed the king of what had happened. Upon returning from the cruise a week later the friend felt sorrow for the children and the conditions they were living in. She again recruited help for the sake of her friend's children. She was able to stop the family from being evicted again.

Debt is deceptive in that it persuades us in subtle ways to "come on in." It is like the pied piper who promised ease and comfort but neglected to say at what price. Debt dances in exuberant delight when releasing its direct and unshakeable bite. It is passion encamped with uncompromising terms, terms of imprisonment and despair.

The debt God paid was enormous, so was the sacrifice: He gave His Son's life to pay our sinful balance plus interest. God, forgive us our debts as we forgive those who are indebted to us.

THE SUBTLETY OF DEBT

When we put off paying a debt we delay our prosperity. Say you owed a 50 dollar debt last month and delayed paying the bill. Next month you still have the 50 dollar debt plus other bills that have come due. So now more of your money is required to pay the current month's bills plus the bills you did not pay last month. The more you delay paying bills from months past, the farther you go into debt. Each month more of your money is needed to bring your debt to current status. This is how debt subtly accumulates; before you realize it you will not have enough money to cover past due bills and your current bills.

Another subtle side to debt is in the pursuit of acquiring things cheaply. I know a man who buys automobiles from auction. The problem is he bids on vehicles with low ground-floor opening bids, vehicles that have some mechanical problems or are considered close to salvage status. The vehicles he buys are vehicles that have been passed over by brokers and used car lot buyers. This man banks on finding diamonds in the rough. What happens, however, is the vehicles require too much additional investment to bring them up to speed and he puts more and more money into them. There have been many times when a vehicle broke down permanently after he went into debt to restore it.

What this man does not understand is he is spending more money for junk cars than if he simply purchased a good used vehicle. I have witness many do-it-yourself home improvements that were supposed to cost little but ended up accumulating debt more so than if the person had hired a contractor in the first place.

Debt is so subtle that in many instances "cheap" is not really "cheap" and you put yourself in debt by buying the same things over and over, especially if you continually purchase durable goods. I watched a family buy television sets over and over. The first set was destroyed because one of the children poured milk into the circuitry. A physical fight between family members destroyed the next television. The third's circuits blew out because it was never turned off.

THE MOST PRECIOUS OF GIFTS

It is a fact that buying the same thing over and over will put you in debt. You must learn to appreciate every possession given to you as a blessing from God, and take care of it as if it is the most precious of gifts. True prosperity works in reverse: instead of continuously buying the same things God will give you the human capital attributes to perfect an idea so that consumers continuously buy or upgrade your goods or service.

I know of several people who continuously refinance their homes. What they are doing is extracting cash from their home but in the process exchanging less time for more time thus postponing paying off their debt. If you have 15 years left on a mortgage and exchange those years for an equity cash out that increases the pay-off years back to 30 years, did you really save money? Even if the interest rate is lower, remember, most of the money owed on the 15 year mortgage is or soon will be accredited to the principle. When you refinanced you gave up 15 years of payments that would have been applied to the principle. Instead you now have a lower interest rate while increasing the years to pay-off by 15 thus accumulating more interest payments. In essence you postponed paying off your debt by accumulating more debt through interest.

If you refinance too many times, when you or your heirs sell the property you may be surprised that you are what is known in the industry as "upside down" on the mortgage, meaning the amount of your mortgage is more than the market value of the property. So if you sell the property you still owe additional funds to pay off the mortgage.

CHEAP IS NOT ALWAYS
FINANCIALLY PRUDENT

I witnessed several people purchase fixer-up homes and end up spending more on repairs to make the house livable than they would have if they had bought a home for more money that needed little or no repairs. One person spent so much the home ended up in foreclosure. It was then they realized cheap is not always financially prudent.

In too many cases we get what we put into material things and what we put into our spiritual growth. We pay more when we attempt to upsurge God by circumventing His plan. The price we pay is high here on Earth as it is in Heaven (spirit world) when we are impatient.

It took many years of studying the behavioral aspects behind economics and finance to understand why we will always have the poor. We will always have debt as it is associated with poor thinking.

Over the last 20 years I have witnessed many people refuse to act prudently to materially improve their wealth and the wealth of their families by purchasing life insurance. The trade-off between satisfying a present need or want consistently overruled the need to increase or least maintain the family's wealth in case of death. I have offered low-cost, affordable life insurance to families only to see them very cleverly delay consummating the deal, avoid me or flat out refuse to buy it.

It did not matter to these families that life insurance is one of the few vehicles through which money can be transferred from one person to the next without income tax or uncertainty. It is the one vehicle where a small dollar amount (discount dollars) can be exchanged for a larger amount guaranteed under the provisions of the contract. I have seen the same people who dodged me or came up with very creative excuses die and leave their family in more debt because they refused to buy life insurance.

Today we are seeing relatives refuse to claim their loved one's bodies so as not to accumulate any of the deceased's debt if there was no insurance. The bodies of the deceased remain unclaimed in county or hospital morgues. There is a saying that some people buy what they want and beg for what they need. One of the most heart-wrenching and embarrassing moments is to see families beg for the cost of a funeral when I had practically begged them not to plunge their family into unnecessary debt by simply purchasing some life insurance.

FORGIVING THE DEBTS OF OTHERS

Do we really forgive the debts of others and thus forgive our own debt? In the parable the king forgave the servant's debt then changed his mind when the servant refused to forgive the debt of a fellow servant. The king could have reinstated his original sentence of selling the servant and his wife and children, but he did not. He sentenced the servant to the same jail term as that servant had given to his servant. The king kept his compassion and his blessing by not imposing his original sentence.

This is significant. Slavery in western civilization persisted so long because slave owners could not imagine themselves releasing their property without compensation. For centuries, western civilizations such as the British, Portuguese, Spanish and American colonies along with the Arab and African collaborators reasoned slavery was a form of economic trade. It was also reasoned that the splitting of families, the sexual abuse, the psychological scarring, the cruelty and neglect were considered mere by-products of the human cargo business.

As time went on slave traders, owners and their families left church with the words of God on their hearts, knowing that what they were doing was wrong. It was the thought of debt and loss that drove them on, ignoring God's urging as they hardened their hearts.

When we write off a debt do we really forgive that debt or do we pretend to forget and hold on to our residual resentment? When someone borrows from me and never repays the debt I would say "I don't have to worry about them ever coming back again." I wrote it off as a bad debt but I never really forgave the debt. I recently learned of a rock band leader who successfully advocated that western capitalist countries should write-off the debt of poorer third world countries. I thought about this and must admit it was a God-sent act of compassion. I still wonder:

did those countries really forgive the poorer countries' debt, or the next time those countries apply for aid or consideration for restructuring future debt, will we remember the debt we said we forgave? I think we will remember, so did we really forgive the debt?

WHAT STANDS IN THE WAY

Pride and a sense of loss often stand in the way of forgiving debt. It was pride that prompted some slave owners to allow their slaves to buy their freedom, that being more acceptable than the feeling of guilt resulting from simply freeing them in humanitarian weakness.

In many well-documented cases slave owners still felt short-changed after selling slaves their freedom. Some slave owners reneged on the agreed sale of freedom and had slaves recaptured. They reasoned the price paid for freedom did not match the cost of labor lost and a debt still existed. Other slave owners forgave the debt on their deathbeds (over their dead bodies) after realizing they could not take their possessions with them… and that they would not be around to suffer the public humiliation or the appearance of being weak by freeing their slaves.

The sad thing is the holdover feelings of debt from abolished slavery have accumulated compound interest through Jim Crow laws which imprisoned former slaves and profited from prison labor and chain gangs; now the debt is enormous.

INDEBTED TO GOD

I have witnessed a number of people hiding behind the mask of business as justification for ignoring God. However, if these people were serious about building a successful and purpose-driven business they would dedicate that business to God. More businesses would prosper if more directors, managers and owners would put God first in their goals and operation, entrusting God with what truly belongs to Him.

In essence we are merely stewards of God's Kingdom here on Earth. When we depart from this world we still owe God a debt of judgment. We will have to answer to Him: did we forgive others their debt, did we treat people right? The questioning will be intense: were we noble in the one area where we had total dominion: were our thoughts, our behavior Christ-like?

Our debt to God will not involve money but rather love, compassion, empathy and obedience, and whether we followed the example of Jesus. If our debt is too large, if we did not forgive others their debt, if we showed no mercy while we were alive, will the King banish us to where the torturer resides and the jailer rejoices in our pain?

THE KEY TO OUR PROSPERITY

People asked why I was happy when Bob Stewart retired as Chairman and CEO of Primark Corporation. They asked this question because many people believe it is whom you know and their position that is the key to your prosperity. The truth is: knowing God is the key to our prosperity. Being a CEO is not all it is portrayed to be: eventually boredom sets in from the every day grind of drudgery.

To run a natural gas distribution company and a billon dollar holding company mean capital must be constantly raised for operational purposes, especially during the summer months when revenues drop off significantly and commitments must be secured for natural gas supplies for the coming season. What many people do not understand, is the gas distribution business is seasonal.

Bob was always concerned about how bond-rating agencies viewed his company's debt. He was also weary of investors who saw their investments as loans instead of as true investments and so expected returns above and beyond their initial investments through dividends and capital gains. I knew when stockholders were giving Bob the blues or when Wall Street was on his butt to improve earnings: he got a certain look on his face; it was obvious he was pained by some of those encounters. He did not always get the "good old boy" interest rate or favorable terms that would benefit the company and his million plus customer base.

In the 1980's when interest rates were very high, Bob paid dearly. Banks and other lenders loaned the company money in the first place because the company had the ability to repay and there was profit to be made from interest on huge sums of money. Bob made it through the day behind his macho facade because he knew God and got on his knees at night consulting Him about the tough decisions he made.

There was another reason I was glad when Bob retired. Employee ineptitude had seemed to rise: people had even died from natural gas explosions after service workers severed pipelines while performing repairs. As the lawsuits mounted, creating more debt, so did moral debts as Bob had no choice but to prosecute some ministers for stealing natural gas to heat their churches. He hit rock bottom when he paid one minister a handsome sum for a vague research study that was really a pay off.

So I learned from Bob's experiences and others when dealing in debt you cannot always trust some of the people that loan you money. I tried with a mighty effort, but to no avail, to get a church with mega dreams to understand that people who loan you money are not necessarily your friends.

THE GREATEST DEBT

The tax collectors in the New Testament represented material debt *and* spiritual debt: they placing heavy burdens on the people. Most importantly, the tax collector is symbolic of one who brings prosperity into the treasury storehouse.

It was important that Jesus interacted with the tax collectors because they were both debt collectors and most indebted to God. The tax collector represented the duality of debt. They had the ability to act humane in the collection process or to at least lighten the debt load by being creative and coming up with favorable terms for the poor and disenfranchised. The tax collectors represent the thoughts of those dealing in debt on a daily basis. Furthermore, when the tax collector came to his senses he would naturally go to God with forgiveness in his heart and receive God's blessings.

The tax collectors were despised among the people with the greatest debt to God. The tax collectors' trustworthiness with small things represents positive or negative fiduciary stewardship. When we are trustworthy with small things, materially or spiritually, consideration is given to us. If we relinquish our earthly indebtedness in a spirit of forgiveness, God will respond in kind by canceling our spiritual debt without remembering the past. We are then invited to join in the righteousness of Jesus where we become responsible for larger spiritual things and are given shelter in one of God's many mansions.

THE SUBJECT OF MONEY

Credit is a good thing if it is approached with great care and responsibility. Credit is an indispensable need for large and small enterprise. However, it should be well thought out, with a plan for sufficient cash flows to retire debt on time without delay. Under these circumstances credit can increase prosperity. Credit, when used correctly, can build a nation, keep a nation's citizens employed and enhance the flow of goods and services that contribute to a better quality of life that benefits all. The use of credit and wisdom go hand in hand. If wisdom is used in handling of credit, it will not bring misery.

The subject of money is one area many people do not understand. Financial planners have told me, "It is difficult to get people to talk about money." Many people feel uncomfortable discussing money with family, friends, associates and spouses. If you cannot talk to others about money, talk to God. The uniqueness of seeing Him as the source of prosperity will help you develop a comfort level for discussing money with Him. If you are apprehensive about speaking with a financial planner, let God be your financial planner. When you consult God about financial matters, you are getting advice from the very best. See God as you financial partner; you will make fewer mistakes, feel good about the subject of money and be on your way to a happy life.

THE BURDEN OF DEBT

The burden of debt belongs to Caesar. When Jesus was asked if He should pay taxes, He asked the Pharisees to show Him a coin and then asked, "Whose face is on the coin?" The Pharisees replied that it was Caesar's and Jesus responded, "Then render onto Caesar what is his and render onto God what is His." The point was this: Caesar's face was on the coin. The undercurrent was this: all Caesar can render unto you is pennies compared to God's abundant wealth. Jesus later instructed Peter to pay the taxes from the mouth of the fish and He declared that free citizens (God's children) are not taxed. It is the foreigners (debt) that are taxed.

Debt is foreign to what God has in mind for us, which is freedom. We are to live *without* the burden of debt. If you want to truly experience prosperity you should be ready, willing and able to retire debt as it comes due. Realistically weigh your ability to pay on time without delay before you sign on the dotted line. Your freedom is at stake.

TAKE CARE OF YOUR PENNIES

I have a friend who is the godfather of my sons. I have watched James over the years. I marvel at his ability to assess and act on complex financial situations with no formal training. James has a nice house in a nice neighborhood and a luxury car, and he purchased a new SUV with the shrewdness of a MBA. He retired from Ford Motor Company, taking advantage of his employee discount plan and a special cash-back rebate available to those who qualified under a special finance program.

Financing anything is difficult for James because he does not believe in credit. What he did was finance the car, pay a few monthly payments until his rebate check arrived, then used the rebate to pay off the balance of the vehicle. He used the financing offer to get the cash rebate; overall he paid less for the vehicle because he waited and did his homework.

James' favorite philosophy is: take care of your pennies and the dollars will take care of themselves. When I first met James I thought he was cheap. He is far from cheap. What he does is wait for the right price to buy what he wants. He goes on vacations often and buys big-ticket items at his target price by doing his homework while he waits. James still manages to put money away for a rainy day and investment purposes although at this point in his life it is not necessary. He saves out of habits developed over the years.

UNFAIR ADVANTAGE

Another friend of mine commented that James had an advantage because he had access to free financial planning advice through his association with me. This is far from the truth; James used his practical knowledge of handling a dollar long before I was born. The problem with what my friend said is that in truth those most in need of financial planning advice, mostly the poor and disenfranchised, do not or will not interact with those who are blessed with this knowledge by way of education or years of trial and error.

A debt exists between those who are blessed with financial knowledge and those whose circumstances did not permit them to learn to handle money. The underlying debt becomes shame on the part of those who were blessed, as many refuse to reach back and help those who are less fortunate. Others have tried to reach back but are promptly rejected.

There is the debt of resentment on the part of both: one expects a return for helping the less fortunate with recognition and fees, the other expects many things for free with hypercritical glee thrown in. As you can see the debt of expectations is twofold – both the indebted and the debtor have it. The way things stand, both are at an impasse.

MOM, I NEED YOUR HELP

Note the following telephone conversation between a mother and daughter:

Daughter: I need your help again this month. I paid most of my bills and I am still short.

Mother: What are you doing with your money?

Daughter: I spend it all on essentials and each month there is a gap between what comes in and what goes out.

Mother: What about that husband of yours; what is he doing?

Daughter: He helps as best he can. He does not make much money and he has his own household to take care of.

Mother: Then why don't you divorce him? I told you long ago not to marry him; he is just an auto mechanic. You should have married that other young man, the one that is an engineer.

Daughter: Do we have to relive this again? I will say it for the thousandth time: I married for love, not money.

Mother: But look what it got you, you are separated from your husband. He never could provide for you and your children. By the way, how are my grandbabies doing?

Daughter: They are not babies anymore. My husband and I did not separate because we stop loving one another; he simply could not take it anymore. He worked so hard, at two jobs, and so did I, but we could never keep our heads above water. We went without and still were drowning in debt. The older the children got the more they needed. He sacrificed himself for his family and still never seemed to get ahead. One day he snapped and wanted to end his life. He thought he would be worth more to his family dead. When he recovered from his attempted suicide, he said he had to leave us. I accepted his decision, Mama.

Mother: Well I say divorce the bum and get another man. Next time get a man with some money.

Daughter: Some women raise their daughters to be prostitutes. I remember my best friend's grandmother would say to her: "milk that cow until it is dry." She was speaking in reference to the granddaughter's boyfriend who cared dearly for her and volunteered to shower her with gifts. The advice was stupid because in our lifetime we need milk today, tomorrow, next month, next year and so on.

I looked at your life, how you married for money four times and sucked each husband dry. I still see you as destitute in many ways. With each marriage you preached wiping away the stain of each husband instantly; cleaning the slate as if human feelings and emotions are eliminated with soap and water. I don't recall you ever being happy. I do recall the husbands you married for money; they hated your guts before they divorced you. One said on his deathbed that he wanted to spit on your heart. You may have money but your debt is piled so high. How can God wipe away your sins when you cannot see your wrong?

Mother: You are certainly not helping your request for support, Young Lady. If you live to be 100 years old I am still your mother. Wisdom comes with age. If it were not for me you would not have been born and certainly you would be on public assistance if not for my help.

Daughter: God is too powerful to depend on you to bring my life into this world. I would have been born into another situation with different parents. We are all conduits for God's grand plan. Being my mother does not make you right. You have been wrong about so many things.

Mother: I don't want to have this conversation with you. Remember you called me asking for money.

Daughter: Yes I did call you and it hurts me to do so. There was no one else to call. I called my husband and he gave me all he had. He gives more freely than he would if I filed for divorce. I knew I would have to hear a lecture and put downs from you before you would throw me some pennies. I knew you would bring up how indebted I am to you; I knew you would attempt to make me feel ashamed and inferior because I am in debt and did not marry for money. It is a shame when our need for money interferes with our need to worship God.

Mother: You never answered my question: how are my grandchildren?

Daughter: Your granddaughter is at odds with me the same way you and I are. She is a deviant, on the verge of having sex with the first boy that suits her convenience. As for your grandson, he joined a gang and is into sex.

Mother: How could you allow this to happen? What kind of mother are you?

Daughter: I am a mother that cares, a mother from a different era than yours. I taught my children ethics and morality; I taught them about compassion and God. Kids learn many things these days apart from their parents. They will not accept the old ways of parents that said: "do as I say not as I do." They see their parents' flaws and take note of our hypocritical behavior. They learn from television, the Internet and schools: a parent's nightmare of wrong teaching.

I admit I wanted to distance my children from the way you raised us. My brother and I are damaged goods. Every time I think about him I cry. I wanted to raise my children by talking to them and treating them with respect like human beings. We did not beat our children like you beat us. Worse yet, you allowed your husbands, men who were not our fathers, to beat the hell out of us. My brother, your son, was beaten so often and so severely I now realize you prepared him for a life behind bars. I asked him once why he keeps going in and out of jail and he said jail feels right at home.

One of our childhood friends' parents would beat him and say it was better that they beat him than for him to be beaten by the police. The irony is his parents beat him to death one day. Another childhood friend was hit by his father with a stick in the back of his head and now he is blind. Can this be another one of the old folk's justifications for misrepresenting God?

Can your generation say we fulfilled the false belief of no mercy by not sparing the rod?

Had it not been for God I would not have known compassion and self-love because my mother taught me coldness and kept me indebted to her through dependency. So what did I do? I married someone that made me more dependent. I thought it was love but it was really a love of dependency.

Mother: Don't blame me for the way your life turned out. I never interfered in your marital affairs. In fact I stayed away purposely. I knew your marriage would not work; marriage is so overrated. It is the money that counts. In my generation if a man could not take care of you, then what good is he? Get another one!

Daughter: In your generation a family survived on one income and now two incomes require juggling debt. I reject the notion that your generation had it right. There are no "good old days." There is no generation more favored or stronger than the next. The young children are violent because the old folks of past generations were extremely violent.

I remember those days: when parents told their children if they did not fight to beat other kids the parent would beat the child. The "good old days" were filled with sex, lies, cheating, violence and manipulation, just as they are today. Most of the hate today is actually hate of old that traveled from generation to generation and just won't die. The debt is this: every generation financed their wants and needs off previous generations. And the debtor and the indebted are dependent on one another. The debt is piled high because we cannot forgive the debt of one generation to the next. You owe my brother and me and God a debt, a debt for messing up our hearts and heads. It is a debt that will never be repaid and in the end spiritual poverty will pursue us all.

Mother: I don't understand a word of what you are saying. It is all nonsense to me. There is no debt for those of us that got paid. It does not matter how I got it. You are the one in debt. I say: when in debt you either have to get more money or cut expenses. The ideal situation is to do both. Your criticism of me means nothing to me because I got mine and you need to get yours. Then you would not have to call me, begging.

Daughter: Thank you for your advice, Mother. I will take it a step farther and ask God in Jesus' name to forgive my debt as I forgive yours. I have dishonored God by being dependent on you and my husband instead of God. I will ask God to forgive me for going to my mother first instead of Him. I now know why God wants us to give Him first place and not put our faith in the folly of human error. Goodbye mother!

The daughter hung up the telephone.

USE CREDIT WISELY

If you want to experience the prosperity God has in store for you, you must learn not to spend every penny you earn. It is a must that you learn to use credit wisely. It is a good idea to retire most of your debt as quickly as possible. Look at saving as a bill that you are paying yourself. Allow savings and investments to become the backbone of your prosperity walk and watch how quickly your blessings grow.

A just and loving God will give prosperity to His children who are captives to debt so that they may be free from their oppressor and all the negative consequences that come with debt. God will give prosperity to His children who learn not to let money master them and instead learn to master money. If you really want to be free, you must freely forgive others their debt and thus forgive your debt.

Do you really want to make contact with the right people to help you understand and obtain prosperity? You need to get to know God the Father, Jesus the Son and the Holy Spirit. Give your heart to God and wait on His direction. Ask God for what you need and want and resist all attempts to circumvent His process. God really does love you and want to give you the right desires of you heart. Expand your heart, making it as big as possible. Jesus put it this way: "for where your treasure is, there your heart will be also" (Matthew 6:21, KJV). The bigger your heart the bigger your account will be in the treasury of God's Kingdom.

FORGIVENESS IS KEY

Just remember the key passage in the parable of the king and the servant regarding debt is forgiveness. If you really want to be prosperous, you must learn to forgive your debts by retiring them. When God makes a way for you to pay off your debts, resist the temptation of skimping on the amount or timeliness of payments. Skimping implies a lack of faith that God will give you more.

Learn to be patient at waiting on the Lord. Do not allow yourself to become frustrated. When you forgive others their debt by releasing all the negative thoughts and consequences of debt, God will forgive you your debt. Gather all of your debts (bills), hold them in your hands and pray:

> God of the most high, I come to You in debt, acknowledging Your power to make a way for me to pay my debt. My impatient wants separated me from You and placed me in this predicament. I ask that You send the Holy Spirit in Jesus' name so that I may breathe the breath of life and not be suffocated in debt. I give thanks that You hear my prayers. I ask in the name of Jesus Christ that You remain with me after You fulfill my prayer request and keep me out of debt. Be my financial adviser in matters dealing with money so that I avoid the burden of debt in the future. Amen!

CHAPTER TWELVE

Money: a Liar and a Cheat

Ho! Everyone who thirsts, come to the waters; and you who have no money, come buy and eat. Yes, come, buy wine and milk without money and without price. Why do you spend money for what is not bread, and your wages for what does not satisfy? Listen carefully to Me, and eat what is good, and let your soul delight itself in abundance.

(Isaiah 55:1-2, NKJ)

THE ROOT OF ALL EVIL

Money is not the root of all evil; it is a good thing when used properly. It is not an evil we should rid ourselves of as quickly as possible in an effort to cleanse our souls. Money should not be worshipped as an idol; it is not a cure all. If it was we could buy our way out of soul, mental or bodily sickness and we would not need the healing power and guidance of God.

Money is a component of the ideas of God's prosperity. It is a symbol of prosperity that you are entitled to by God's decree. Money is the physical manifestation of God's abundance. It is our material dimension of living: we need *things* that confirm the senses to help us determine what is real. Money is just one component of prosperity in physical form. The entire prosperity process encompasses walking and talking with and feeling God.

It is essential that we keep prosperity in its proper perspective if we want to maintain its flow. God must teach us how to handle prosperity or it will destroy us. It is God's promise that you shall have prosperity; just as Jacob did there are times we should remind God of His promise.

AN OUTER EXPRESSION OF THE INNER MIND

I truly believe little children of all ages should have money; so should the old folks and all those in between. I had an interesting debate with a friend of mine. He thought what I said was preposterous. He asked how in the world I could believe such a thing, that everyone should have some money. I told him God does not deceive us when He makes promises to us; it is our thoughts that deceive us. If every man, woman and child were rich it would not make God any poorer nor would it diminish Earth's overall wealth. There would still be millions of acres of untapped land and enough natural resources yet to be discovered to accommodate us all.

There are vast amounts of untapped land in the Arctic region filled with untold oil reserves. Man is now developing seafood farms that will produce an abundance of new sea life in order to eventually replenish the oceans. Wealth is a conceptualized occurrence in the minds of men. There is never a shortage of ideas therefore there is never a shortage of wealth. Wealth is an outer expression of the inner mind.

In our point and counter point discussion my friend countered with: if the poor became rich it would upset the order of things and cause a sort of worldwide ghetto anarchy. I pointed out to him in that most cases anarchy occurs as the aftermath of uprising whereas the poor and the victims of unjust treatment become enraged at their poverty and injustice and act out of frustration, turning their anger into destructive behavior and lawlessness.

My friend's argument is the same argument used the world over. It is the argument used by the rich to protect their vested interest and keep the poor, poor. Their rationale is like the cartoon image of the king atop the pyramid throwing rocks down on those who attempt to ascend. Do I believe that all of us will be rich in the physical world? No, because like most things, barriers of entry to wealth exist. In today's world ideas of merit are constantly being blocked by those who have a vested interest in seeing those ideas fail. Realistically some people are not equipped to handle wealth. However, I do believe that we are rich in the spirit world of rich ideas, where true wealth is available to all.

GOD'S IN THE DRIVER'S SEAT

Fear is one of the main culprits, inspiring some to create illusions in their minds that motivate in the opposite direction – inaction. Fear kills God's promise in the mind before we even attempt to ascend the pyramid, and causes some of us to hide our talents through lack of faith. It causes many to aspire to a lesser degree: willing to hurt more and conjure up myths in the mind that cryogenically freeze the soul, waiting for some future happening we hope will occur when the time is right for us to succeed.

God wants us to ride in the driver's seat with the assurance that He will serve as our protector, counselor and co-pilot. Some of us feel comfortable being back-seat drivers, criticizing the vehicle chosen by God and complaining about the road because we believe it is better or at least safer to close our eyes in the back seat and not see ahead. If we miss an exit, entrance or make a wrong turn we can declare, "I am not driving."

This journey with God at times seems so uncertain it causes us to think it is better to cling to our fears than to get crucified like our Lord. On the road to prosperity you will constantly face your fears and come face to face with many tough decisions. At one point money will be the problem; at another point there will be something else. There will always be something that causes you concern. You cannot go wrong if you ask God to guide you and remain by your side on the path of your prosperity pursuit.

WRITTEN IN OUR HEARTS

This book is very clear in its position that the love of money above all else is a form of idol worshipping and that greed for money is the forerunner to committing other sinful acts. We take for granted that everyone knows what a sin is. Sins are thoughts or actions that disconnect us from life's power source, which is God. The Ten Commandments give us some direction at figuring out moral sin, so does the Bible. But real answers to what is right and wrong are written in our hearts.

Much caution is required when relying on other people's interpretations. To place your faith in the hands of others regarding the interpretation of what God is saying to you may be a grave mistake. There are many false teachers in the world who sound so polished, so good. A prudent person learns to understand God in one-on-one situations, with some help from others to process, gauge, verify and clarify God's pattern before declaring with certainty God's meaning. The study process is arduous and long; you must ask God to open up the windows and doors of your mind so that you may grasp the creativeness of His Word and thus see that truth really is beauty.

This book goes on to state that prosperity exists in a variety of forms, including health, physical wealth, forgiveness, joy, peace, social interactions and human service. We believe that all prosperity comes from God. If we forget the Source of our prosperity, we cut ourselves off from its flow. We acknowledge that prosperity is achieved by keeping our minds focused on God and His Word, in the process learning to love our neighbors. By refining our souls and training our thoughts to stay focused on things that are noble and godly, we have a better chance to stay in the flow of prosperity.

AN ATTACHED RIDER

This book strongly believes that God endowed us with the power to have dominion over the earth through the power of our will, especially when our will is in accord with God's will.

314

Because the will is endowed with automatic power it enables us to break into the treasury of God and steal physical wealth without giving Him first place in our lives, but the real treasure which is spiritual in nature is denied to the thief.

When the thief successful breaks into God's treasury an ironic twist is set into motion, a rider is attached to the treasure. None of us can escape irony. No matter how close we are to God we will encounter irony of the spoken word, irony of events and irony of things spiritual. The thief who attempts to rob God will experience all three in the same measure he or she uses to plot and scheme, plus interest.

God proclaims His laws are biased on the side of good. He will sentence the thief to a punishment of humiliation, sickness, death or suffering and then reclaim His stolen treasure. In extreme cases you can experience the dilemma of Judas, whereas it would have been better had you never been born.

To attempt to rob God seems preposterous but it happens every day. The Bible provides us with a glimpse into Satan's constant attempts to rob God's Kingdom through wars in Heaven before the beginning of time and today. The devil will tempt you with money and then rob you of something more valuable: your soul. The nature of the devil cannot change. It is his nature to destroy all souls he uses.

Many people reject the notion that there is a connection between prosperity in the form of money and worshipping God. Yet many people acknowledge that Jesus' ministry was supported with money and He acknowledged that wealth is in God's plan.

A BACKDROP OF MATERIALISM

The old idea of money being the root of all evil is still prevalent today. The belief did not diminish during the life and times of Jesus nor will it ever vanish. The clergy played a big role in initiating and reinforcing the idea of money being evil. It made sense for the church to pursue its own self-interest by suggesting to its members to rid themselves of their evil money and offering to help cleanse their souls by laundering their money for the coming Heaven.

By the time Jesus arrived on Earth, materialism was so entrenched in the minds of the people that the only way He could get them to understand God's plan was to convey each and every parable against the backdrop of materialism. The writers of the New Testament differ in their accounts of events surrounding the life of Jesus. The one thing that is consistent in Matthew, Mark, Luke and John is Jesus spoke extensively on the subject of prosperity as it relates to real living and healing.

Money and wealth are not everything but it would have been difficult to get people to listen to Jesus at the time when life in the Middle East was entrenched with thoughts of material reward. The people could not overcome their dependency on materialism. Toward the end of Jesus' ministry the people asked for more food and more physical miracles and missed the real spiritual food and miracles, causing our Lord disappointment to the point of tears because He knew their faith hinged on material reward.

THE LOVE OF MONEY

The Pharisees loved their money; a fact that Jesus pointed out. The poor who aspired to be like the rich wanted money as the cure for all their problems. The robbers flanking Jesus on the cross robbed for money. Jesus' disciples, who were mostly fisherman, fished not for the enjoyment of fishing but for money. Some of the women supporting Jesus' ministry were part of the money class. Joseph in, whose tomb Jesus' body was buried, was a member of the money class. The Roman soldiers fought in part for country and in part for the spoils of war. We do not have to look back far to see that war was an opportunity for plundering and looting. As recently as 2003, the Iraq invasion was the largest bank heist to date, which took place under the cover of war.

Jesus arrived on Earth with perfect timing as the people's prayers and meditations cracked opened doors and windows on Earth as in Heaven, calling forth God to come forward. Man had also cracked open the doors and windows on Earth as it is in Heaven by proclaiming money his god. And the reliance on money throughout his past and future will always remain the same. The issues between the "haves" and "have nots" have not disappeared and never will, without help from God.

THE PROPER PERSPECTIVE

Jesus knew we would need money; for that reason He cautioned us to view it in its proper perspective by rendering "unto Caesar what is Caesar's and to God what is His." There is a connection between prosperity and God, but at the same time a separation. If you love money too much you will abandon God. If you love God and give Him first place in your lives He will grant you prosperity in the form of money accompanied by harmony. In the latter state, money is not that important to you. Your heart will reside in God's and so will your treasure.

Money is a gift from God, given to you to be used for living, for merriment, for nation and community building and for helping God fulfill His grand plan. The flow of money is consummate with your obedience and willingness to serve without expecting reward, and your focus while knowing you are entitled to God's wealth. All you have to do is ask God in Jesus' name with an open heart of honest sincerity.

WINE AND MILK

Isaiah 55:1-2 is an invitation to abundant living. Yet if read at face value, it could be interpreted as hyperbole, exaggerated speech or flat-out rhetoric, skirting the fine line between socialism and a handout. In a materialistic world, how do you buy wine or milk without money? It would be simply a matter of time before people would see you as a bum or a free loader. And how do you buy wine and milk with no money and *without price*, unless you trade? However, even if something is traded, a price must be established by expectation and mutual consent.

If you isolate the underlying meaning, you understand that the passage is truly about Jesus. Jesus is the wine; it is symbolic of His blood sacrificed on our behalf in payment for our sins. When grapes are being made into wine, during the fermentation stage an expansive moment takes place in the same way as the universe is expanding without ceasing. In other words, a multiplier effect takes place. When the wine reaches maturity it is ready to be used as communion in remembrance of Jesus the Christ.

The milk represents nourishment and growth, especially after a new birth. It is used to feed the young and to sustain us through the rest of our lives, symbolic of Jesus' nurturing and sustaining Word.

BREAD AND WATER

The bread is food, also regarded as necessary for sustaining life, and made with the expansive ingredient yeast which is able to rise above its beginning and exceed its origin as far as the measured input will allow. The bread is the communion of the Body of Christ, symbolic of the call to abundant living, a gift from Heaven like no other. We are told if we eat of the bread that came down from Heaven, we shall live forever (John 6:29-38; 48-51).

The waters contain all forms of abundant edible life. The sea stretches as far as the eye can see and beyond. The water is the Spirit of Christ that quenches every thirst and sustains God's state of grace. He is the water of everlasting life that satisfies our thirst for the spiritual life. The profound question is: why do we spend money for what is not bread, and wages for what does not satisfy? We should not be concerned about perishable things like food. Instead, we should spend our energy seeking the eternal life that the Messiah can give us. For God the Father sent Him for this very purpose (John 6:27).

THE PRODIGAL SON

Jesus gave us more clarity on the subject of prosperity in the parable of the prodigal son. The parable is rich with subtle nuances that weave through a multitude of lessons all pointing to our ability to fall from God's prospering grace and be welcomed back with open arms.

The parable starts with a man with two sons. The younger son said to his father. "Father, give me the inheritance set aside for me." So the father gave the youngest son his inheritance and soon the son departed from his father's house and journeyed to a far-away country. There he wasted his inheritance with prodigal living. According to Aristotle's interpretation of prodigal, it means self-indulgent spending, wasting one's substance, accomplishing ruin by one's own fault. Aristotle goes on to say that prodigal behavior is a form of meanness and a character defect as it relates to wealth.

After he dissipated his inheritance, the youngest son experienced poverty in a foreign country. Poverty attracts other calamities; as luck would have it, a severe famine (economic depression) occurred. In a state of economic depression the mass psychosis of the people produces lower expectations and lowered consumer confidence that cuts off the flow of prosperity. First there is depression in the mind followed by behavior that is depressive to the productive forces which create wealth.

The young man was hungry and without money or friends so he joined in with other citizens working the fields and feeding swine. He was so hungry he would have gladly eaten the feed given to the pigs that was unfit for human consumption. He was in a foreign land, separated from his father, and no one would give him any food.

When the prodigal son came to himself (his senses) and realized that the hired hands at his father's house ate better food, had better accommodations and made a better wage than he, he left the foreign country and returned to his father's house. The father, seeing his youngest son coming from a distance, had compassion and ran out to meet him. The youngest son said to his father, "I have sinned against Heaven and you and I am no longer worthy to be called your son. Make me one of your servants."

But the father said to his servants, "Bring the best robe and put it on him, put a ring on his finger and sandals on his feet. And bring the fatted calf and kill it, and let us eat and be merry, for my son was lost and now he is found."

The older of the two sons was in the field and as he approached he heard music and saw dancing. So he asked one of the servants what was going on. The servant said, "Your brother has returned safe and sound so your father killed the fatted calf and declared a feast." The oldest son became angry and would not join the festivities. So the father came out and pleaded with him. He answered his father: "all these years I have been serving you and never transgressed your wishes at any time, yet you never gave me a young goat that I might have a party with my friends. But as soon as this son of yours returns who wasted your money with harlots, you kill the fatted calf for him."

The father said to the oldest son, "You are always with me and all that I have is yours. It was right that we celebrate and be glad for your brother who was dead and is alive again and was lost and now is found."

THINGS THAT DO NOT SATISFY

The direct link between the prophecy of Isaiah and the parable of Jesus in Luke 15:11-32 is the prodigal son spent his inheritance on things that do not satisfy. We also have an inheritance that God has set aside for our use. Some of us, like the prodigal son, may become lost if God gives us our inheritance without first educating us on how to use it properly. If God gave us our inheritance without the corresponding wisdom it may even kill some of us.

The good news is when we come to our senses after engaging in riotous living, we can return to the Father's house, where the wine of merriment is free through grace because Jesus is the vine that nurtured the grapes and became the choice wine. The milk is purified by the mammary glands in mammals and purified again by the second spiritual birth through Jesus so we may experience both earthly growth and heavenly growth.

The prodigal son spent his inheritance on things not in accordance with the Spirit of Christ. When we spend our money on sex, drunkenness, gambling and splurging on material things that are wants, our thinking is clouded. During those moments it has not dawned on us that our cash will soon be depleted at the rate we are spending.

THE DANGER OF RIOTOUS LIVING

There were no banks at the time so the prodigal son banked out of his pocket; this usually leads to spending outside a budget. In days of old as it is today there are prostitutes who specialize in "rolling" customers (slipping them a knock-out drug and robbing them when they fall asleep). Wild spending of one's money on sex will put you in a situation to get rolled by a prostitute if you fall asleep in possession of a lot of cash.

The parable does not go into every detail but another part of riotous living is going into drinking establishments and buying drinks for everyone in the place. In those days there were liquid drug concoctions extracted from certain roots and plants, so it is possible the prodigal son may even have gotten high. It became obvious his riotous living could not satisfy his soul. After his resources were gone, he came to his senses realizing he was worst off than the hired hands at his father's house.

Returning to his father's house meant the prodigal son returned to God. He was greeted with true merriment. Here is the irony: when we engage in riotous living we waste our substance by attempting to satisfy our wants. After the party is over and our resources are gone, we find our behavior has created greater needs that we neglected while living riotously.

During the course of our riotous living, God cannot touch us until our willfulness runs it course. The place where God dwells is holy; the place where we dwell during our riotous living is unholy.

THE REAL PARTY

The prodigal son did not understand what a real party was until he returned home to the Father's house. None of us can put on a party like the parties in the Kingdom of God. He will put a robe on your back, sandals on your feet and a ring on your finger. You will hear music in the air: the angel's notes of a heavenly choir, sweet hymns of joy. And He will prepare a magnificent feast because you and I were once lost and now we are found; we were dead and now alive. The prophecy of Isaiah ends with this message

...Listen carefully to Me, and eat what is good, and let your soul delight itself in abundance.

(Isaiah 55:2, NKJ)

What happened to the oldest son who stayed with the father and remained devoted is just as important as the prodigal son's return. It is true the older, more devoted son had his moment of resentment, envy and jealousy. What is missing is this: the father told the oldest son that he should have compassion for his brother because he was one of the lost ones. What the father said next is very important: "When I am gone all this will be yours."

The father was wise because he knew the oldest son was more stable and more likely to stay the course and continue the legacy. We do not know if the prodigal son took off again in the future after tasting riotous living. There is nothing that indicated his boredom with farm living and impatience was rooted out of his life upon his return home. His decision to return was more rational than spiritual. To often people leave the word of God out of boredom with religious ritual and impatience. The taste of riotous living is like a drug addict that says, "I will quit" but the mind and body is weak and the only way to stay in the new life of God is to stay in his words. So many return to the Father's house to be healed and comforted then voices call them from the dark and they go back to the same riotous living that put them in the lower depths of Hell.

LONG-TERM GOALS

God is a God of eternity, so why is most of our planning in business and finance short-term? All your prosperity and financial planning should be long-term. Impatience is the root cause of most of our errors. After making errors, we attempt to pull ourselves out of a hole of our own making without God's help, but instead simply compound our problems.

The compounding effect of trouble works the same way as compound blessings, only in reverse. God will not continue to restore your prosperity again and again if you repeatedly waste His blessings by continually repenting and continually going back to riotous living. The one thing about God is He does not deceive you with social promotions like public educational systems and corporate "good old boy" networks. If you fail one of God's life lessons you will repeat that lesson again and again and again until you get it right.

A wise God will do the same as the father in the parable of the prodigal son: choose the more stable and predictable son who is bound to stay the course as the one who will inherit more than those who secretly desire to live a riotous life. There are no secrets with God; He judges us by our motives.

THE HISTORY OF MONEY

The history of money is unique. Money as a means of exchange took shape in different forms. Man placed value on physical items based on his mental evolution. Animals once served as a form of money. At one point in time rocks served as money, so did a variety of metals, some precious some not. Salt once served as money and of course a variety of cash crops as well.

There were problems using animals as a means of exchange. The process proved to be cumbersome and unreliable for establishing uniform pricing. Sometimes the quality and value of an oxen, sheep or she-goat was suspect, as dishonest men traded sick animals to unsuspecting herdsman who were left holding the bag of worthless goods. Man reached his lowest point, disconnected from God, when he resorted to using human slaves as a means of monetary exchange. At one point the Portuguese, British and American slave trades were all about nation building. In time it evolved into a must-have sweetener in the form of sugar to sweeten English teas and make rum, promoting drunkenness.

In the colonies cotton, tobacco and other cash crops were backed by slavery that was in essence money because Great Britain went to great extremes to keep money out of the hands of the rebellious colonists. What truly backed inanimate objects called money was the idea of money as wealth. The object was simply an object; it required man to use his imagination to add value to it. The idea of man imagining his faith onto an object and giving it value that invoked men to move, to die, to kill, to steal and to engage in back-breaking endeavors is the powerful gift of perception granted by God.

THE MONEY CLASS

At times it is difficult to assess what is really on the minds of the money class. Most of our conversations are centered on recent business articles in financial publications or on ideas that may gain an advantage in the equity market. Our conversations are peppered with tax shelters and tax-credit strategies that weigh heavily on the minds of the money class. We talk about business trends in western civilization and the world.

Occasionally the subject of sports enters the picture, but we usually refocus on the competitiveness of sports and project that into the arena of making more money. On those rare moments when an impasse exists and the power of money falls short of fulfilling all of life's promises, the money class is willing to engage in frank conversations about money. It is then you get a clearer picture. Money is a lying, cheating, double-crossing illusion, but they would still rather be rich than poor.

THE BACKLASH OF MONEY

The former shoeshine boy, now a 20-something, ran into an old friend he had not seen in many years. They had discussed money matters in the old days when the shoeshine boy was just a child. In the 1960's, the shoeshine boy's friend had stumbled into the heroin business and had made so much money he had not known what to do with it. He had a secret that his street associates did not know: he was illiterate and had trouble reading and counting his money, so he had children help him. When the shoeshine boy asked him where all the money had come from, he told him he was a vending machine operator. On several occasions the shoeshine boy was sure he was in the street numbers business but the boy was wrong.

This story is about the backlash of money. Although the old friend quit the drug business before most of the people involved with him went to jail or died, he was hit especially hard by money's backlash. At the height of his operation he supplied his loose-knit consortium of drug dealers with ever-increasing amounts of drugs. He grossed large and rapid sums of money in the mid-to-late 1960's when a dollar was actually worth a dollar.

One by one each member of his consortium was arrested, jailed or died violently. Two died from paranoia-caused heart attacks. Two other members were driven to see life through the eyes of insanity. Near the downfall of the entire operation, several members of the crew locked themselves in hideout prisons by choice and would not speak because they thought their hideouts were bugged with listening devices. One guy was so paranoid that he told everyone there were listening devices in his food; he thought the Feds were listening to his stomach.

The shoeshine boy's friend occupied his time gambling, losing most days. Meanwhile, paranoia spread to every member of his crew; many turned witness for the prosecution and informed on each other. One guy imagined hearing sounds all over the house and would shoot bullets through walls and doors when no one was there. Another guy heard the Feds used bugs to listen to conversations so he called an insect exterminator at least twice a week to debug the place.

The shoeshine boy's friend was finally indicted. By this time he was broke and at the mercy of a public defender. He was convicted of income tax evasion and conspiracy for operating a criminal enterprise. He was sent to federal prison and fined, and died a short time after his release. The shoeshine boy ran into the old friend on his way to jail. The old friend told the boy about the trial and all the evidence the Feds had against him. His parting words were "if I could turn back the hands of time, I would have stuck with working in the factory, instead of selling this poison. This drug thing is poison. The Feds knew exactly how much I made and the amount of drugs that passed through my operation. Tell other young men 'don't fool yourself, every kilo is counted and tracked before it enters this country.' In this game you are working for people you don't know. Why do we have to be a pawn in someone else's game?'"

IF I DON'T DO IT, SOMEONE ELSE WILL

Over the years I have seen acquaintances become the perpetrators and the victims of the drug trade. There is no shortage of people who believe selling drugs is a positive opportunity to change their condition and improve their lives. The prevailing rationale is: "if I don't do it, someone else will." That sort of thinking is just an excuse. People who use this excuse have no problem lifting themselves up off the degradation of other people.

It is a shame at family reunions and other gatherings, including church functions, to see drug dealers treated like celebrities and given the honored seats and exalted. It is the same "bowing down" that the Israelis experienced when they sent spies into the land of Canaan: some exclaimed the people were giants too strong to overcome. We too often bow down to the money men and drug dealers in the same way, believing they are too large to overcome. We must not forget all things are possible through God and the moneymen are probably weaker than we are when separated from their money.

If you break down each and every chemical in heroin and cocaine there is no doubt that it is poison. I have seen drug dealers read their daily devotional booklets, attend church and pray that God would bless their way of life. The truth is they are selling poison; how in the world do they honestly believe God can bless that?

THE DRUG TRADE

The drug trade has devastated many communities and threatens to alter the course of a people. The trade took on new meaning with the switch from heroin to cocaine. Cocaine is derived from the cash crop of countries indebted to the world's financial markets. Drugs have altered the landscape of many minds, especially with the innovation of crack cocaine. Crack has very little cocaine in it; the dominate ingredients are mostly household additives to give it a boost.

Unfortunately, under the 1990's crime bill and sentencing guidelines too many people have been given jail sentences that do not fit the crime. Federal and state judges are now complaining and protesting their inability to exercise some flexibility at sentencing minor drug offenders under laws that impose stiffer penalties for crack cocaine as opposed to cocaine. Many judges are calling for reforms in the crime bill laws.

Why is it that drug dealers, ignorant athletes, gangster rappers and white collar and violent criminals fascinate our minds and take on hero status? All too many people ignore the negative and glamorize the lifestyle of these characters by rationalizing that they are getting paid. We need to stop seeing other people as that fabled rescuer riding on a white horse coming to save us. We need to stop worshipping people and spend more time worshipping God. It is very important that we stop being pawns in someone else's game. Above all we need to give God our minds, our bodies and our souls and know that He will make a way for us, and that no force on Earth but us can stop us from achieving the good God has in store for us.

THE VOICE OF MONEY

Money is a lying, cheating, double-crossing illusionary thing when it gets in the way of worshipping God. The voice of money boasts that it will provide you with security but actually leaves you feeling insecure. The voice of money brags like cancer: "I am bigger than life" yet it cannot save your life when your time is up here on Earth. Money whispers in your ear saying, "Worship me and you shall have influence," but then you realize that the people around you actually resent you. Money sings "come to me and I will set you free" and then puts you in a jail of dependency, limiting where you can and cannot go.

It seems that many people love you when you have some money, but only a few remain when it is gone. You thought your money would stay around and comfort you, but money is like a two-timing woman or man: it leaves you for another. You dreamt that money would grant you safety, but you soon learned that it is not safe to let people know you have money because robbers, kidnappers and moochers will seek you out.

You once had a loving family, but when the money arrived their love cooled and their materialism flourished. Old friends with whom you once shared fond memories don't interact with you since your money arrived. You thought people would respect you by granting you the honored seat, but deep down inside they envy you and hope you fall on your face one day. You hoped that your money would allow you to become a member of the beautiful people and the finest country clubs, but after being strung along you discovered that they would not accept you because of their belief that your new money does not mix with their old money. Your siblings and your parents think you have lost your mind and abandoned them because of your money; they truly believe that you should take care of them.

The material things you buy with your money bring temporary satisfaction, but then you fight depression. Money is not what is seems. You have heard people with large sums of money say if they could turn back the hands of time they would have taken a different path. You've also heard people say if they had millions of dollars life would be better. But life would not be better unless they developed a money consciousness through preparation before the money arrived, and even then there will be problems.

MONEY CONSCIOUSNESS

Is there such a thing as a money consciousness: a consciousness that distinguishes between variations of what it takes to be rich and not poor? The answer is yes, and unless you develop that money consciousness before your prosperity arrives there will be big trouble.

People who come into large sums of money often experience hardship and despair. On the one hand, some of those who have had money all their lives lose their fortunes and regain them again within a short period of time. On the other hand, I recently read a list of lottery winners with brief descriptions of what had happened to them after they had won. In too many cases the win was a blessing followed by a curse. I was stunned at how many winners lost all their money within a few years and ended up in extreme debt. One winner's tragedy was so horrible I could not help but weep...for a millionaire.

This story touched my heart because I still cannot believe what happened. Their real names will not be mentioned because it is best for those family members still living. We will call the first person "J"; the second person is "T." J was hurt in an accident; he struggled through rehabilitation and experienced poverty for several years until he received a settlement from the insurance company for his accident...which leads to the question: are those who receive a windfall after years of poverty well off or merely catching up from a deep deficit?

J cashed his settlement check and asked T to join him at a motel room to eat, drink and get high. Both men were using drugs with alcohol. This went on for three days until it appeared J had had enough and went to sleep. T partied the rest of night away by himself until he too fell asleep. In the morning T could not awaken J. J was dead from a drug overdose.

Several years later, T also received a settlement from a lawsuit. He too engaged in riotous living and after several days was found dead. Both men had been getting high for years under different circumstances with limited funds and therefore notably diluted drugs. The moment both men got their hands on thousands of dollars they were able to buy larger and better-quality drugs.

The moral is: money can and will contribute to our death if we do not develop a money consciousness before the money arrives. Sometimes God will not give us large sums of money although we desire such because He knows to do so would end up being the death of some of us. This may sound harsh to some readers but I have seen this time and time again. It is best that some people not experience abundant prosperity. There is a mental preparation that must come first before you can handle large sums of money. If you do not master the money consciousness of handling money and instead allow money to master you, it will become the death of you.

WHAT'S YOURS IS MINE

Money has a tendency to rob us of our innocence. It is a joy to see siblings share everything they have as children without any regard to "yours" and "mine." But it pains many parents to see those same children ready to do extreme harm to one another as the time approaches for those parents to depart from this world. I have talked to many parents in this situation: they know one child will do more with the money than the other but they want to split their assets equally because as parents they have a sense of equality when it comes to their children. Other influences come into play when grandchildren and spouses serve as the wedge of division between siblings.

Then there is the dilemma of the child "in waiting." This child is waiting for the parent(s) to die, so they can use the inheritance to pursue their plans. This is the child or children that cause parents the most grief because this child may love their parents to a degree but the future inheritance consumes the child thoughts and actions.

There is one case that comes to mind that truly broke a father's heart. This father suffered illness for many years with no improvement in sight. His health declined to the point where a ramp needed to be installed at the father's house so he could enter and exit the home in his wheelchair. The son "in waiting" protested vehemently. Without realizing what he was saying, he complained that a ramp would lower the marketable value of the home that the son intended to sale as soon as his father died. The father cried because his son was counting his inheritance before his father was in the grave. Jesus was confronted with a similar issue in Luke 12:10-13.

BEWARE OF COVETOUSNESS

Jesus was speaking to the crowd, telling them: anyone who speaks a word against the Son of Man, it will be forgiven; but to speak ill against the Holy Spirit will not be forgiven. When you are brought before the court and authorities do not worry about what you should say. The Holy Spirit will teach you in that very hour what you ought to say."

Then one from the crowd said to Him, "Teacher, tell my brother to divide the inheritance with me."

Jesus said to him, "Man, who made Me a judge or an arbitrator between you?" Then he said to the crowd, "Take heed and beware of covetousness, (desiring things that belong to others, envy). For one's life does not consist in the abundance of the things he possesses."

Then Jesus spoke to the crowd using this parable:

Then He spoke a parable to them, saying: "The ground of a certain rich man yielded plentifully. And he thought within himself, saying, 'What shall I do, since I have no room to store my crops?' So he said, 'I will do this: I will pull down my barns and build greater, and there I will store all my crops and my goods. And I will say to my soul, "Soul, you have many goods laid up for many years; take your ease; eat, drink, and be merry."'

But God said to him, 'Fool! This night your soul will be required of you; then whose will those things be which you have provided?'

So is he who lays up treasure for himself, and is not rich toward God.

I have seen people worry about money when they had little: as their money increased so did their worries. Now they worried they might lose their money and go back to being poor. So with money there is worry whether you have or have not. Money by itself really is a lying, cheating, double-crossing illusion. You have to answer this question: do you really want to place your faith in money or God?

WILLIE WANTS

We conclude with the story of one of the most colorful moneymen in the history of mankind. He lived in the Stone Age in the land of Gent, once a part of the continent we now call the Americas when it was connected to Africa before the Ice Age separated the continents.

This man's name was Willie Wants. No one knew where he had come from when he settled in the village of Gent. One morning the villagers woke up and there he was. No one trusted the stranger.

The men of the village were skilled hunters. Willie attempted to learn the skills of hunting but he was so inept the male villagers forbade him from hunting in the same territory they were hunting. Willie tried hunting alone but many of the animals sensed he was more fearful than them and chased him away.

No one in the village gave Willie any food or clothing or offered him lodging, so he slept in the village square where the wild dogs circled him repeatedly, contemplating the day Willie would be their food. He experienced many hungry days. One day some men of village returned from a day of hunting, and resenting Willie's lurking around the village with their women while they hunted, they beat him and questioned his manhood.

Willie left the village dejected and defeated. He wandered for miles, finally heading into a cave. In the cave he noticed a rock-like substance hanging from the cave walls and ceiling. Out of curiosity he gathered some of the rocks to take with him. The rocks tantalized Willie's imagination and his senses when sunlight caused them to display a rainbow of color.

Willie arrived back in the village at the same time the men of the village returned with their food for the day. Willie showed the men of the village his rocks. They were fascinated by the rocks' ability to sparkle and change colors when exposed to sunlight. The men of the village offered to trade their food for Willie's rocks. This was Willie's first chance to eat in a long time and he jumped at the opportunity.

The men of the village returned the next day wanting to trade more food for Willie's rocks but he did not have any more rocks in his possession. He told the men of the village that when they returned from hunting the next day he would have more rocks.

The next day Willie gathered and traded his rocks for food but not all the men of the village were able to trade for the rocks. So Willie told them to come back the next day. The next day Willie traded his rocks for more food...more food than he could eat. Soon the men of the village began to spread word of Willie's rocks to other villages and other hunters wanted to trade for the rocks as well.

Willie was soon trading his rocks for food, weapons and animal skins, and eventually the services of the men of the village. On each trip to the cave Willie would bring back more and more rocks. When it got to the point where he could no longer keep up with demand, he decided to mass-produce his rocks using an animal-powered conveyor system to mine more rocks. He established a division-of-labor system that paid the strongest men in the surrounding villages to mine his rocks and the toughest men of war to guard his rocks and watch those working in the caves. Paranoid thoughts entered Willie's mind where he envisioned everyone attempting to steal his rocks; he trusted no one.

The more rocks Willie extracted from the caves the wealthier he became. Soon the masses accepted the rocks as a means of exchange and a standard for assessing human worth. There were a few incidences where employees were caught stealing rocks in the mines. The punishment was always brutal. For the sake of continued wealth and rule of law Willie established a tiered punishment program for the crime of stealing his rocks: hands were cut off for the first offense and immediate death for the second offense.

WILLIE RULES

Willie used his wealth to establish a council of justice to further his push for rule of law under his control. He funded and controlled the judges of each village and established a regional council to govern the province; he called them "parliament." Since his wealth paid their salaries, these men were merely window dressing for Willie's wants. Willie called all the shots and the rule of law was based on his perception. When his perception changed so did the laws.

As Willie's business interest grew he needed and hired an administrator to coordinate his enterprise, which now consisted of wholesale manufacturing and distribution of animal skins, weapons, food, seeds for planting, tools for farming and imported crafts from other villages. He also sold licenses (government) to others wanting to establish businesses or favorable regulatory rulings.

Willie wanted to establish a more fluent market so he created a commodities exchange to regulate prices and terms of value. His new administrator asked where the mine was located, so Willie said the cave was located on the bank. Actually the cave was located on the riverbank but Willie skipped the first part and adopted the last. He felt it had a certain jingle.

The years went by and Willie started lending his rocks to the citizens of surrounding villages and charging them interest on what they borrowed from him for the purpose of trade. The women of the villages who had once gravitated to the best hunters left their huts to become part of Willie's harem. Willie's administrator convinced him to maximize his profit by imposing taxes on goods being traded and on all the citizens of every village under Willie's financial control. He hired the toughest men in all the villages to collect the tax. Those who could not pay were sentenced to work in the mines under a sentence of free labor.

In time a new metal was discovered called "gold" and coal was found to be useful for keeping the fire burning. Working in the mines was dangerous because cave-ins were numerous and many men died. Willie did not care about the dead; only that their body debris was cleared away and more workers put in place to replace those who perished. Willie shouted at his administrator: "Time is rocks! I want the mines reopened."

WILLIEVILLE

The philosophers of Willie's day wrote their philosophy on stone tablets, stating that human beings were born to worship a higher being. They agreed the only way to evolve to a higher state was through worshipping one deity. Since Willie funded the philosopher's think tank he insisted that the philosophers include a clause in their findings that this deity of higher heights appoint a man to act as liaison between He and men, and that Willie was appointed this liaison by divine decree. If any man attempted to bypass the liaison, the deity would become angry and put the scoundrel and his entire family to death. The philosophers agreed because Willie threatened them with direct and veiled threats.

After Willie consolidated all surrounding villages into his province he named it Willieville. He then decreed that his name and seal be put on all legal documents regarding tangible goods. He also decreed it proper to acknowledge the deity of higher heights one day a week, and he erected a statue of himself that was to be worshipped the remaining six days of the week. A daily tribute of one-tenth of the citizen's wages was to accompany the worship of Willie. The daily worship ceremonies were called "Willie's anniversary offering." Any citizen caught shirking their tributary responsibilities would be banished from the lands protected by Willie's military and hopefully eaten by prehistoric animals.

THE HOLY MAN

One day a holy man was sent by the God of higher heights. He entered the Willieville province and condemned the people for worshipping Willie's statue; he hammered at the statue with his staff. Willie had his guards detain the holy man and said, "By whose authority do you come into my land and disrespect my statue, the beloved deity of the people?"

The holy man said to Willie "I am a prophet sent by the God of higher heights. I say to you God has lost patience with your evil ways; if you do not change and bow down and worship God, you will die a horrible death." What the prophet said angered Willie. He tore off his animal skin robe and yelled at the prophet, saying, "How dare you lecture me on what God said? No self-respecting god would speak to someone as lowly as you." Willie then had his guards chop off the prophet's head and immediately hang his body in front of the entrance of the mine as an example to all who might think of opposing him.

God then spoke to an honorable member of parliament, who began to speak out against Willie. He said to other members of parliament: "What kind of men have we become, rejoicing in the misery and suffering of others? If there is a God, He is ashamed of us for delighting in the pain of others. So I ask the question, are we men of God when we rejoice in the suffering and hardship of others?"

Willie was oblivious to the suffering and hardship of the people. He imposed longer workdays and more taxes. This particular member of parliament set out to expose Willie for what he was. He had once seen Willie in the bushes coveting another man's wife. He saw Willie as a tyrant and a fraud.

IMPENDING DOOM

A mosquito bit Willie on the butt and gave him malaria. He felt ill but dismissed his affliction. He reacted by imposing more suffering on the people. He ignored the increased frequency of bad dreams. God was smiting his mind so that all the decisions he thought were correct would lead to his doom.

At an important meeting of parliament Willie bragged to those seeking public office that their blessings: "come from me. And all who seek higher office call on me for favor. If I wish something done I merely wave my hand and it shall be done. If I wanted to run for king of the world, I would win. I am not being egotistical; I am just stating a fact. You all come to me because of my position. I am the biggest thing to hit this part of the world since the discovery of fire. I am the deity put in this honored seat to give the world a sense of direction and to lead people out of the bondage of their minds. The world is going to remember my name!"

The honorable member of parliament who was opposed to Willie could not stand it anymore and said, "You are just a country boy with country ways who could never make the transition to nobility. I am tired of this governing body following lesser leadership knowing full well that it will not get any better. We will not advance our race of people until we get rid of yes men and jive. It is hard to separate the yes men from the jive because they are intertwined and often one in the same. It will take an act of God to kill this disease of yes men and jive." He walked out of the meeting in resignation and Willie joked that the man's wife must not have rubbed his tummy that day. The rest of the members of parliament broke into loud laughter.

Many of the members of Willie's parliament knew and understood what the resigning member of parliament had said but they could not or would not side with him. They stayed and said nothing to protect whatever reward or favor they could get from Willie. Most of the members of parliament owed him favors. Some remained unopposed to him because they wanted something from him. They did not necessarily like Willie but they tolerated him. Willie plotted to have the resigning member of parliament discredited and banished from the province.

It was clear by now that Willie exhibited the behavior patterns of one who had grown up too poor. He hoarded food in excess to the point of obesity. His lust for coveting things of others increased and he secretly held contempt for those who had grown up with most of their needs satisfied. He missed the mark of being considered handsome but women called on Willie because he was wealthy and powerful.

IF THEY COULD SEE HIM NOW

As Willie grew older he attempted to make up for his lack of good looks and insecurities with numerous sexual conquests by granting women who hoped for a life of ease a favored place in his harem. Willie's thoughts were actively engaged in his previous life where people had laughed at him. He often bragged "if they could only see me now, I have arrived."

Willie lacked class and style both are hard to manufacture no matter how much money or position one has. He was what he was: just Willie stripped bear, psychologically scarred and too sick to seek help, too proud to be clearly aware of himself and too stubborn to be touched by anything but ignorance.

As time passed Willie's illness became full blown. One of Willie's women had given him a venereal disease. One day his administrator asked him what his rocks should be called. At that moment Willie was itching uncontrollably from his vene-real disease and he yelled out "Mony!" The word caught on and is still with us today.

Willie finally realized that he had a disease and recruited the help of the provincial herbalist. The herbalist tried every mixture of herbs and roots known to him and none of them cured the disease. Willie's health deteriorated further until he was no longer able to care for himself, at which point he hired servants to care for him. The servants remembered how badly he had treated them when he was healthy. Some took pleasure in spitting in his water and food. Some took pleasure by pre-tending not to notice when Willie fell down and taking their time coming to his aid to pick him up.

On Willie's deathbed he stubbornly dictated his last will and testament to his administrator. It was his wish that his wives and children would not receive any of his "mony." He signed a parliamentary decree devaluing his rocks and declaring they were no longer the currency of the province. He installed new rocks called "gold" as the new official currency. He had been stockpiling gold since it was discovered. He left the bulk of his gold mony to medical research to search for a cure for his dis-ease. He funded a think-tank foundation to conduct research on more efficient ways of exploiting wealth and techniques to keep the poor, poor and make the rich, richer.

In his final hour Willie saw the future. He prophesized "other men will catch my disease. It does not matter whether you break into God's Kingdom or not, wealth is followed by per-secution. My mony is not the root of all evil. It is the wants of Willie that caused my disease. I tricked these foolish people into worshipping my rocks. God knows I will kill anyone who steals from me. When I am gone these fools will get their hands on my mony. The nerve of future generations: they will teach my busi-ness techniques in centers of learning for a fee and never give me credit or my cut. I will not be around to collect royalties for my contributions to the world. They will call me a primitive cave man and dismiss the sophistication of Willie Wants. I used rocks to replace God in their minds. I was a poor man with a tyrant's disposition, a man who broke into God' treasury. Such a man is detached from God and doomed to cause more destruction than good. All is lost when the idea of physical gain takes the place of God. Ignorance has lived before the realization of my rocks. And woe to man, who can escape ignorance, the root of all evil."

By now the men of the province were experiencing extreme anxiety. Willie owned all the women and there were no other natural outlets for release. Before Willie died he pumped more rocks into the economy with the goal of devaluing them. There were more rocks than goods and services, causing inflation. With their worthless rocks and the absence of women the men of the province began to go insane and they threw their rocks at each other. It was war.

Willie finally died from his diseases. His funeral procession consisted of his stone casket followed by a 26-oxen caravan carting his possessions, including his wives that he had ordered his administrator to bury with him in his tomb.

Willie had been right; his mony would be stolen after his death. His administrator placed old food in his tomb that turned into a fungus mold that would eventually be used to make penicillin, and kept all of Willie's wives and his loot for himself. Willie never wrote a book and history did not remember his name. He was the unknown character that willed the world his wants, banks, monopolies, greed, assessing value, mass production and currency manipulation. He left behind the blueprint for the division of labor and predatory economics. He also left the world with an accidental cure for his disease. And how does a person benefit if he or she gains the whole world and loses their soul in the process? For is anything worth more than his or her soul (Mark 8:36-37)?

CHAPTER THIRTEEN

True Atonement

EXCLUSIVITY

There are times Christian believers take for granted that those who have little or no knowledge of Jesus understand the most elementary components of our faith. When we say things such as "I am blessed," "I am a child of God" or "Jesus loves me" we should not be surprised by the quizzical look on the faces of those who do not know Christ.

We should be aware that some people will become defensive and are not ready to accept our point of view. We should also be aware that we have turned some people away from God by claiming exclusivity. If our attempt was to bring non-Christians into the faith, we have failed by implying that we are more blessed, more spiritually favored than non-Christians or others with little or no knowledge of our religion.

By appearances alone it is understandable that non-Christians think we are placing ourselves above others in a special category of relationship with God. When we say we are children of God, it can easily be interpreted and implied that the person we are speaking to is *not* a child of God. Every day the Christian right and left engage in religious rhetoric that turn people off from joining the faith. When you factor in the behavior they see from Christians and multiply the roadblocks Christians impose on other people's beliefs, it is not hard to understand why some perceive Christianity today as not that much different from the religion of the Pharisee who sincerely prayed: "Thank God I am not a sinner like other men."

WORTH MORE THAN MONEY

No matter what faith we believe in from time to time we are in need of true atonement. When we petition God for His atoning grace we become acutely aware of our "selves." We are far from being entitled to God's righteousness because self often gets in the way. When we seek atonement we experience the righteousness of Jesus and share His entry into the Kingdom of God. Through sincere atonement we can face the ultimate judgment of God and honestly know we tried. Even when we fall short we have been touched by God.

The sincerity of atonement is connected to the tender heart of God. It is worth more than money. It does not matter what paths you have traveled in the past. It has nothing to do with other people's acceptance of you. Sincere atonement is paved with a special path that travels directly to Jesus sitting at the right hand of God. Only one thing is certain: there are no guarantees in this world, but rest assured, all paths lead to God.

In John 18:37-38 we encounter a profound conversation between Pontius Pilate and Jesus. This conversation is essential for clarity. We need to understand in this age of mass media there is still a multitude of people on this earth who cannot conceive Jesus as the Christ, as God's Son and as Savior. He is still seen by many as a myth, a historical figure or too far-fetched to be real.

> *Pilate therefore said to Him, "Are you a king then?" Jesus answered, "You say rightly that I am a King. For this cause I was born, and for this cause I have come into the world, that I should bear witness to the truth. Everyone who is of the truth hears My voice." Pilate said to Jesus, "What is truth?"*

(John 18:37-38)

WHAT IS TRUTH?

Jesus did not answer Pilate and I ask: why not? Pilate is not alone in the question: what is the truth? On a daily basis it seems that truth is on a holiday while lies and deceptions reign as king. The truth is getting harder and harder to come by.

Pilate was in a no-win situation. He was the governor of a province whose citizens were divided. He was responsible for overseeing an occupied territory of the Roman Empire. He was in the same position as our generals are today in occupied Iraq: not fully understanding the customs or religion of the people and not really wanting to be there. When a leader in occupied territory stands between factions and infighting within those factions, the situation eventually takes it toll on the soul of the commanding officer. The true dilemma is when the various factions join forces, which is a tip-off that something terrible is about to happen.

The united factions requested that Jesus be condemned to death. Pilate could not uncover any offense on the part of Jesus that fit such punishment. To further complicate matters, Pilate became frightened after his wife, who was obviously a very spiritual person, had a dream warning him not to touch Jesus. In Pilate's judgment Jesus' only crime was He claimed to be a King who professed the truth. In Pilate's world Jesus was considered a poor, insignificant man according to Roman standards, yet he deeply admired Jesus because He was unmoved by the threat of impending death. I doubt many of us would have acted any differently than Pilate, considering past revolts and the potential for riot if he did not comply with the wishes of the political and church leaders who had incited the crowd.

Back at home in Rome, Pilate's leadership was being questioned and this was probably his last chance to prove he was worthy to lead under Caesar. But Pilate was no fool; he knew something was amiss, so he gave the religious leaders every opportunity to avoid crucifying Jesus. Pilate's fate would rest on a political situation. Where there are politics there is bureaucracy; one is indispensable without the other, a sure potion for blurring the truth.

A GESTURE OF ATONEMENT

When Pilate asked Jesus "What is the truth?" he asked the question with sarcasm, having no use for Jesus' answer. According to William James, psychologist and philosopher, "we disbelieve all facts and theories for which we have no use." So whatever Jesus would have said, Pilate had no use for His answer.

So Pilate symbolically washed his hands of the situation as a gesture of atonement. He washed in protest, claiming no blood rested upon his hands regarding Jesus. But his hands had too much blood on them and did not truly come clean. As Pilate proclaimed his innocence and attempted to reconcile with God, he was partly fearful, not fully understanding why this man must die. So he engaged in strategic politics, employing part reasoning and part theatrics, where a strange twist of fate would seal his doom. Pilate stated his case against the will of a fickle crowd by saying, "He is not guilty of any crime; He is innocent." He then attempted to release Jesus but the mass psychosis of the crowd hungered for the pleasure of seeing Jesus dead; they chanted a roll-call death sentence, a vote of democracy, justified by majority rule.

THE SEARCH FOR TRUTH

My reason for writing this book was to search for the truth. I had to examine my own beliefs as well as the beliefs of others in order to arrive at conclusions of what I believe are true. There are very few things in this world that can hurt you, especially the courage to admit that some of your beliefs were false and need to change. The only things in this world that can harm you and stop you from achieving prosperity are fear and to proceed through life on false premises that contribute to false truths.

It is not a lack of faith to ask, "Is what I believe real or a falsehood?" To ask "what is the truth?" is not a lack of faith but an act of solidifying one's faith. An unexamined religion is a religion that may not withstand the test of storm winds, diseases that ravage the body or abandonment by friends and family. Nor will false beliefs stand strong when facing creditors who threaten you or quiet your worries when your leaky roof collapses. Falsehoods will not help you during your loss of loved ones or when your employer and your insurer betray you and refuse to pay for medical treatment that can save your life. Falsehoods certainly will not withstand the perils of war, this time on your home soil.

Beware of those who label and scold you for examining your religious beliefs. You must constantly examine your religious beliefs in order to discard old ideas that are no longer useful. I still encounter people who dream of prosperity by opening a mom-and-pop store, a BBQ restaurant or a neighborhood bar. These ideas on the subject of prosperity through business ventures are outdated; the profit margin is less than the effort. It is time to aspire to higher thoughts and venture onto untried paths. It is not enough to think outside the box; throw the box away, think outside the universe and experience the vastness of God's truth.

PERCEPTION IS REALITY

In the past I would cringe every time I heard the phrase "reality is what you make it" or "perception is reality." Nowadays I just smile and not say a word. The truth is the area between the perception of an idea and what God has in mind is colored with expectations. Many of us approach ideas with rationalized learning that contains expectations as a form of wishful thinking and therefore bears elements of deception or illusions. Expectations without the proper mixture of practical knowledge and God can serve as a springboard for developing a prosperity consciousness but will later fizzle under pressure, not having a solid foundation that can only be found in Jesus.

We should wish for the best and expect the best for ourselves and our neighbors. What we should understand is the universe is founded on many dimensions, vastly different from our perception based on our expectations. Expectations are but one dimension of the vast dimensions of God's reality. If we truly want to experience the life and real living that are the essence of prosperity we should perceive God as the only realty and let Him guide us from there. This does not mean, however, that we exclude all that is contained in this world, because we must live and become part of the physical world as well as the spiritual. We need the material aspects of the physical world as well as the spiritual.

We must be constantly aware that life on this physical plane is only a part of God's vastness. As we maneuver through this world it is best to develop the temperament of a dove (peaceful) and the instincts of a seasoned general (warrior) while marching through the mine fields of the many thoughts that are contrary to what Jesus instructed.

IT'S A TEST

Our journey here on Earth is but a test of our stewardship of our own life as well as others. We are the best stewards at controlling our thoughts and behavior. It is through our thoughts and feelings that we connect with God.

We have not yet arrived at the point of being trusted by God to handle the full power of spiritual energy. We have the ability to reconfigure matter into products that serve our needs; we have not reached the point of manufacturing matter directly from dark invisible energy contained in the universe that is all around us, nor can we travel backward or forward in time. To be able to do so would place us in direct conflict with God because we are not mature enough to handle such spiritual power. If time travel were possible you can bet there are some who would use this vehicle to erase the birth and existence of Jesus.

The other reality is we can conceive ideas but must combine them with God's spirit and physical work in order to make a life for ourselves and serve the betterment of others, thus assisting

Jesus in the department of creating light burdens. We do not have the ability to control the elements, recreate the function of the soul or conquer the heavens. The truth is we are far from being God. Our progressive growth and future would be in jeopardy if left to our own free will and self-interest.

The truth is we do self-destructive things that skirt suicide and God is constantly working at keeping us alive. Yes, we are limited and even more limited when we proclaim perception as reality and truth. When we believe that perception is reality, we limit ourselves to a one-dimensional consciousness of the physical senses of sight, touch, taste, smell and hearing – all grounded in appearance. No wonder it is so easy to lose sight of God.

WISDOM LEADS TO TRUTH

On the path toward prosperity you must lose sight of your impaired vision and shortsightedness by asking God to allow you to see through His mind's eye and experience His wisdom. You must learn to touch things with your soul, taste love through noble thoughts, smell with your intuition and hear with your discerning mind – all are gifts from God. To do so is to stay in the righteousness of Jesus because you are seeking things from the spiritual realm, things that require constant atonement and constant unadulterated awareness of the times you are living in.

Psalm 51:6, NKJ gives us a clue as to why we seek the truth, *Behold, You desire truth in the inward parts, and in the hidden part You will make me to know wisdom." In The Living Bible it says, "You deserve honesty from the heart; yes, utter sincerity and truthfulness. Oh, give me this wisdom.*

Does wisdom lead to truth? Yes but even wisdom has limits.

OUR INWARD PARTS

The inward parts of our being are far different than those outer things of food, clothing and shelter. What are those inward parts? Do our inward parts consist merely of cells that carry motion and nutrition? Are we more than the skin, called epithelium, that covers the surface of our body, protecting our digestive, respiratory and genital-urinary systems, closed vessels, acini, ducts, glands, ventricles, the brain, central canals, the spinal cord and pituitary and thyroid glands?

Can we transcend our veins that carry our blood through to our heart – the greatest pump and muscle ever conceived, a work of supreme engineering, an automatic function ignited by a power source far better than electricity or fossil fuels? Are we more advanced than our skeletal structure with bones able to grow until the body acquires full completion, able to run, stretch, push, pull, go forward, backward and sideways – one of the most perfect and efficient works of mechanical engineering?

Did Jesus know we are more than a bundle of muscles or flattened bands – a fine network communicating action, tuned to the rhythm of life? How much greater are we than our nervous system connected to our spinal cord and brain, allowing us to feel and touch the beauty and wonderment of this physical world prepared for us by God?

Are we more conscious than our inward parts where we have eyes to see, ears to experience sound – our very own home theater, a nose to experience the rich scents of this world? What greatness beyond what we know is contained in our brain's center, where stimuli from the outside world shapes the power of reasoning, our language, personality, interpretation of sound and education by transmitting information from our senses to our temperament?

Just our inward parts alone are enough to know this truth: we are wonderfully made by a higher intelligence. Who could have conceived such a specimen as a human being with the ability to create and replicate? The truth is we are made of the exact same substance as Jesus in every way possible, yet so many of us cannot conceive of our relationship with divinity. The truth lives in our hidden parts where there is no separation from God. It is true that one of our hidden parts consists of our mind that allows us to formulate ideas and act in the five-dimensional physical world: making, feeling, knowing, pondering and sadly, fearing.

WHERE WE KNOW THE TRUTH

It is in the hidden parts of our minds that we become conscious of life and its ability to advance before our eyes. In the hidden parts of the mind we become aware of time and space, longing for our own space to carve out a destiny, where time is both a necessary friend and a foe. It is in the hidden parts of our minds we can see infinity through filtered light and shadows, visions and sightings. How do we explain the physical response to our thoughts while describing love as a unique feeling?

In the hidden part, on a completely different dimension, there is the sensation of the soul. The soul is a source of magnetic attraction that leaves us in a state of understanding. We are souls connected to a prominent source, released from worries, in a state of bliss, longing for proximity to God. That breath tied to the soul is God's suggestion, a whisper to live an awe-inspiring life. These are the inward and hidden parts where we know the truth. These are the inward and hidden parts where we become one with God, where we meet God, where God is pleased when we act in His image. In our inward parts we find the hidden imprint of ourselves. It is then that we recognize wisdom through reverence to God.

IT IS FINISHED

If the truth were grounded in the physical world, then Jesus' death would have been the finale. His physical death created a derivative value by multiplying His spiritual energy. His spiritual energy is released to all who come to Him: a spiritual energy that is in the Son as the Son is in us.

Jesus died a physical death with three final words, "it is finished," then released the bottled-up pure spiritual energy that was in the Father and in Him. No wonder the earth shook, day turned to night, the elements thundered in protest and the curtain in the temple split down the center! The curtain, separating holy from unholy, was no longer needed. There could be no release of raw spiritual power where this power does not exist.

The Spirit is what stands behind the energy of Jesus' words. His words will remain forever, even unto the end of this time. Each word and each parable will be renewed with new interpretation as time proves and reproves His meaning. His death released His loving spirit that multiplied and became the source of power behind abundant living.

It is no mystery that the explosion of ideas spread more rapidly after Jesus' death than all the years before Him. God's decree of abundant living is the true source of prosperity. The power of Jesus' teaching was intended to bring us back into the fold of God so that we may experience the apex of our existence.

TO MAKE AMENDS

What is true atonement? Atonement is defined as giving satisfaction for a wrong or injury, to make amends, being one of one accord. Finally, atonement is defined as the reconciliation of God with sinners through the death of Jesus. Through prayer, meditation and understanding of the Scriptures we get a clear picture of what atonement is and what it is not.

There is no need to strive for doctorate degrees to know that atonement is not in the clever ways of the world, that says: "as long as I give to the needy there is no need to be kind or hospitable, it is not important."

A child asked his parent: "Is it true we are to love our neighbor just as we should love God?"

The parent responded, "Yes, but you don't necessarily have to like them."

We know atonement is not in the false religion of cruelty, where the dogma says "my way or the highway" to those seeking guidance and understanding of God. Atonement does not fall into the depiction of Hamlet's stepfather who stole his ascension to the throne and said: "my prayers go up but my thoughts remain below." If your prayers go up while your thoughts remain below then you are not engaging in reverence to the Lord and there can be no atonement without acknowledging your shortcomings and making amends for your wrongs.

A BETTER LIFE

The shoeshine boy roamed the streets in search of money to fulfill his dream of making life better for him and his mother. His mother worked evenings caring for people in hospitals and care giving; she had no idea her son was being exposed to things no child should see at the age of 11. He gathered wood and nails and made a shoeshine box, not the best, but useful. He used soda bottle deposits to finance his inventory and set out with a plan to solicit. He loitered in pool halls, speakeasies and red light district street corners, engaging pimps and hustlers: "shoeshine, Mister. I will shine your shoes good"; a scene repeated daily in the summer and after school when weather permitted.

His advertisement was echoed in the early darkness, ever aware that he must return home before his mother arrived so that his after-school activities would remain a secret. He was robbed and beaten twice by older teenaged youths lurking and counting his money before relieving him of his keep at the day's end. His robbers ranged in age from middle to late teens, the age where they have not lived enough to understand that the pleasure derived from fatally hurting little children is wrong. There was no reason to seek atonement because they felt they did no wrong.

One day he advertised all day, but saw not one customer. Like any good businessman he thought: some money is better than none, so he advertised a sale: "Shoeshines, half price. Come and get your shoes shined." An old lady heard the young man's call for hire and offered to pay him to carry her groceries home. He carried her groceries along with his shoeshine box for several blocks. The old lady rewarded him with the unjust wage of a nickel. He took his wage and pressed on: "come and get your shoes shined, half price. I'll shine your shoes good; have them shining like new."

As night drew near the shoeshine boy started to lose his enthusiasm; a full day's effort had netted only a nickel. A Cadillac pulled up beside him and a manicured, well-dressed figure emerged from the vehicle: a man of leisure – some call him a pimp, some say he is a player, some see him as the scum of the earth. He greeted the shoeshine boy with: "Hey Young Blood, it is kind of late for you to be out here."

The shoeshine boy responded "I have to keep working, Man. I did not make any money today." They talked. The boy liked hearing the adventures of the men of leisure. He liked hearing tall tales of street pimps and hustlers. He was considerate and even listened to those who posed as important street players in their own minds. It was better and more colorful to hear their stories than to watch the television set at home that worked on some occasions when the coat-hanger antenna's reception was good.

THE SHOESHINE BOY IS TRUSTWORTHY

The shoeshine boy was accepted as one of the junior "fellas"; he earned their trust when a numbers banker on the run from the police put the money and betting slips in his shoeshine box. Stashing the money was a lesser evil than the beating the police administered upon the numbers bankers for not having their weekly tribute. When retrieving their belongings after making bail, the money was often short or gone altogether. When this particular numbers banker got out of jail all the money was accounted for; the word on the streets was the shoeshine boy was trustworthy.

The street players, especially the egotistical ones, told tall tales of how magnificent their words were. Some thought it was their main asset and entry into the world of pimps and prostitutes. Their world was divided, you were either a player or a trick (a customer) if you were not part of their game.

Some players thought their rap and their game (style) was the lure that turned their women out into the world of prostitution. The women took the dim view of lowered expectations, a cruel way out. So the players played on the woman's need to fix her dire situation. There are times that lies have more situational power than the truth. The pimp promised a better way of life through prostitution, but the promise came crashing down when the pimp insisted on production quotas and asked his women to recruit other women to join his stable. In the stable, favoritism reared its ugly head. But where do you go when all you ever see is prostitution as your profession, never conceiving that you could be anything more?

CRIMES OF THE HEART

Their seeds of entry into the world of prostitution is the where the real crimes of the heart took place. Some streetwalkers had to flee their mother's house because the house was not big enough for two female egos or a high concentration of adverse hormones. Some were forced from their mother's house because mother was overbearing or had a new man and the daughter was in the way. Some were sexually abused and treated with the same heavy burden as a Cinderella stepchild.

Others had to leave because their parent's philosophy called for children to leave home at a specific age and so they were pushed into the slapping hands of the pimp. In some cases deviant behavior made it best that the young girl leave the house but the results of the punishment did not fit the deviance. The thought that perception is reality contributed to the heyday of street prostitution, where young girls were forced from the homes of parents or guardians.

Then there were the young girls who refused to sell their bodies on the streets, so they did the next best thing: they married men with jobs or military allotments that the old folks called a "living," providing them with shelter they could call their own. Some parents and guardians instigated these marriage arrangements to get young girls out of the house.

Today we are witnessing the by-products of these marriages fueled by the impetus to get out of mama's house. A great number of these marriages where not rooted in God's love but in the perception that God will bless the child that got his or her own. But divorce rates around 50% and more if you factor in separations that continue for decades prove that perception wrong. Families produced from these false premises miss the substance of love. Divorcees fight bitter battles in court for material possessions; some even pray to God for a favorable court ruling regarding who gets the house and the car.

THE GAME ON THE LINE

Even little children practiced perception as reality. Judy and Butch, the self-appointed leaders of the neighborhood boys versus girl's baseball game, met on the pitcher's mound and plotted the outcome: the girls would win and the boys would be rewarded with a kiss.

On the right side of the baseball diamond at first base Choochie was whispering in April's ear. He boldly said to her, "After I hit the ball over the fence I will come home for a kiss." Choochie was the last boy at bat with the game on the line in the bottom of the ninth. He prayed to God, "Make my life a homerun so that I may be a winner." He hit the ball over the fence and trotted home to get his kiss from April.

Judy told Butch she would never play with him again because she plays to win. Butch said "That's okay because you were never my friend." Butch and the other boys asked Choochie why he had not gone along with the plan.

Choochie looked them in the eye and said, "Not all fairytales start with 'once upon a time,' some start with 'when we are married' or 'when I am elected, I promise.' I made no such deal of affection. I was at first base trying to hit a home run, so I invited God into my world and asked Him if April could be my girl."

DO GUYS LIKE ME HAVE A CHANCE?

So the shoeshine boy and the pimp sat in his Cadillac and talked about life. The pimp asked what he had learned in school and the shoeshine boy told him. He also told the pimp he had gone to Vacation Bible School last summer and learned that God forgives us our sins if we repent. The pimp asked the shoeshine boy if he thought God would forgive him. The shoeshine boy responded, "Yeah because you are my main man and I'll ask God for you."

The pimp smiled and asked the shoeshine boy, "Do you think a guy like me has a chance?"

The shoeshine boy told the pimp, "Jesus said the least of us will get to Heaven before those who think themselves good."

The pimp asked, "Why is that?"

The shoeshine replied, "I don't know, I guess it is because we know we are flawed."

In the silence on this cold evening the shoeshine boy reflected on the things he had seen on the streets. When his father had died, the boy had set out to make money to buy his own school clothing, keep money in his pocket and one day earn enough so his mother would not have to work so hard for little money. The shoeshine boy thought to himself: there must be a better way for people to make a living in this world instead of by sins of the flesh, drugs, pain and falsehoods.

DON'T BE LIKE ME

The melancholy pimp said to the shoeshine boy, "You don't care what I am, do you?"

The shoeshine boy said, "I look up to you because you have the ride, the money, the fine clothes and the ladies.

So the pimp said to the shoeshine boy, "You cannot be like me; you are too smart. You would make a good lawyer. No matter what you decide to be in life, don't be like me."

The shoeshine boy said, "Yeah I can be your lawyer; I'll keep you out of jail."

The pimp smiled and replied, "Yeah, you grow up and be my lawyer. Whatever you decide, don't be like me."

The pimp highlighted his life and said to the shoeshine boy, "There are no material trappings in this world that could convince a woman to sell her body. Women lie to us and play on the egos of men: having us believe she desires to sell her body because she loves us. But in reality she had entertained thoughts and dreams of a glamorous life before she met dudes like me.

"It is our job to absorb much of the risk. It is our job as pimps to attend to the health and welfare of the women in our stable. It is in our job description to bail them out of jail. We must take them to the doctor and arrange treatment for disease and abortions. We are required to burst into rooms when they scream or give a signal that some crazed customer has gone too far with an unreasonable sex act or a beating. When we burst through the door we have no idea what the sick customer is armed with. I have seen all kinds of weapons. Every day my life is in danger.

"We must be on constant lookout for the fathers, brothers, aunts, uncles, mothers and especially those imaginary boyfriends with no connection to our women but through their imagination claim her as their own. These people are dangerous because in their minds they are certain that we convinced these women to sell their bodies for us. They seek to beat us or even kill us.

"We are forced to pay the police, greedy judges and other public officials, hotel bellhops and hotel security personnel. The lawyers take us for a ride with higher-than-normal legal fees and we are in constant danger of being killed by rival pimps. Worst of all, we are disowned by our families; it hurts most when your mother disowns you. My question to you, my little friend, is this: who is the pimp and who is the whore?"

It did not take the shoeshine boy long to answer, "You are the whore!"

HAVE PITY ON ME

The man of leisure pulled out a wad of money, handed the shoeshine boy a dollar and said, "Here you go. Go home now, Young Blood." The shoeshine boy knew it was better not to be indebted to anyone on the streets so he told the man of leisure that the dollar was prepayment on future shoe shines; they shook hands in agreement. The last words the pimp said to him were, "I have to make things right with God and maybe He will have pity on me."

So the shoeshine boy went home and hopped into bed in the nick of time, just before his mother came home. She was weary from caring for others and he was sad that today's profit was not more. His mother asked if he had done his homework and gave him her usual speech on the importance of education. She told him she loved him and kissed him good night. He lied to his mother and said he had done his homework. In reality he would have to do his homework on the way to school, a habit that would cause his grades to decline. In his mind the business of shining shoes and hustling for money was his homework.

Before spring his friend the pimp was murdered: shot through the heart. The shoeshine boy did not know how he would repay the pimp for his prepaid shoeshine. The shoeshine boy went about his business shining shoes and running errands for street people and old ladies.

LIFE ON THE STREETS

The number men sold long-shot dreams of prosperity in three-digit numbers: straight or boxed hunches that never came. The drug dealers persuaded many that it was better to escape from this world into the abyss where they would benefit from the misery of others. The speakeasy operators sold legal drugs, called alcohol, after hours; the deck and dice were stacked in favor of the house. Factory workers and hustlers visited before going home with their money, hoping to get in on the action – not conscious that they *were* the action. As the dice rolled and the cards shuffled, kids went without shoes. Some fathers did not understand that going home and loving and hugging their children were the actions of real winners.

The shoeshine boy returned home exhausted from all that he had seen and heard. He prayed to God, "The pimps and their prostitutes shame us. So do the drug dealers with their poison, and let's not forget the proprietors of the speakeasies. The police, judges, doctors, lawyers and the customers of the prostitutes shame us.

"Shame on the mothers and fathers who forced their daughters out of the home and into prostitution and bad marriages as means to a shelter! Shame on the fathers who refused to be real fathers and gambled their children's well being away! Shame on the priestly father who molested my childhood friend! And shame on my friend's mother who refused to believe that a man of the cloth would do such a thing. Shame on the Christians that look down and away when they see me coming and tell their children not to play with me because I interact with the street people."

He still had the dollar the pimp had given him for a shoeshine months ago. He did not know what to do with the unearned money. The shoeshine boy counted his money: 50 dollars plus the nickel the old lady had paid him months ago. He subtracted the dollar the pimp had prepaid him; if he located one of the pimp's family members, he would give it back. He thought about how close he was to contributing to his mother's retirement and buying her one of God's mansions he had learned about in Vacation Bible School.

The shoeshine boy was brimming with positive thoughts: he needed a million dollars, which he thought he could make before Christmas. He cried, however, when he thought about his buddy the pimp, and wondered if he had made amends with God. He got onto his knees and prayed, "Please, God, so many people are weary and so many are dying; there must be a better way of life than this. Please, God, come quickly and change things!" He fell asleep without doing his homework, with his money in his hand.

RECONCILIATION

The ultimate act of atonement occurred at Calvary as Jesus voluntarily laid down His life for our sins. True atonement involves reconciling with God for wrongs and injuries we have committed. We commit wrongs and injury to others on a daily basis without a second thought or even acknowledging the injury when we do become aware of our actions. Pride stops us from truly attempting to atone for wrongs done onto others; pride that comes in the form of refusing to admit we committed a wrong or injury.

We go through our daily routine refusing to speak to others or acknowledge them as human beings. We misjudge people by the way they look, and cross to the other side of the street when we see a rough-looking person come toward us. We say we are blessed with an arrogance that says to others they are not. We pronounce ourselves as a child of God as if we have a special spiritual genetic connection with God that others don't have. We advertise how we are saved as if others can only receive God's saving grace by being affiliated with us, our church, our religion and our beliefs; implying that God is one-dimensional according to our perception.

We justify our wrongs by substituting one wrong for another wrong. We use our busyness as a cover for not acknowledging the wrongs we inflict on others. Wrong is wrong no matter what techniques we use to camouflage our wrongs. Our claims of innocence through amnesia fail because God has many ways of letting us know we are wrong.

The truth is there is a lot of sickness in this world and we need daily atonement to receive Christ's healing. We can atone for our own sickness by making amends for the wrongs we commit through our words, actions, thoughts, discriminations, pompous attitudes and hatreds.

On the path to prosperity it is important that we seek healing from God and become conscious of the legions of sicknesses already in the world. Let our daily prayers become praises to God for His atoning grace. We make the world a better place by ridding ourselves of our daily sicknesses through God's atoning grace.

THE TRUE MEANING OF ATONEMENT

When we move out of our habitual comfort zone, we experience things we do not want to experience. The place where we are most uncomfortable is where God blesses us. As we meditate on God's Words we are better able to focus on the true meaning of atonement.

The more we seek atonement the more we see God's grand plan unfold and the uncertainty of life is diminished. It is through speaking in the silence of our heart that God reconciles us to Him and without a doubt blesses us. It is better to be silent and uncover the realness of our soul than to speak too much. It works by saying to God: "Here I am; I release my soul to You. Let my will become Your will." The secret to prosperity is to let God share His will and His goodness with us. When we release the energy in our souls we are asking God for His assistance with a sincere and honest heart.

The soul is sensitive and therefore susceptible to being easily disturbed. The sensitivity of the soul makes it liable to change and to become mildly dizzy and fickle. In times of trouble the soul is hasty to flee and easily tricked into being insincere. This reminds us that even though we are dedicating our life and works to Jesus our prayers are our witness and our hearts are in constant need of cleansing. We are always in danger of following the desires of our heart instead of God's will.

When your mind becomes distracted by the things of this world, concentrate on returning to Jesus through the silence of being one with God. In these necessary moments, we seek true atonement from God. Thanksgiving is a wonderful thing: it opens the heart and allows us to become more receptive to God's loving grace. Atonement is the substance of a repented heart where our souls fuse with God's forgiving grace.

EVERY DAY IS A HOLIDAY

Atonement cleanses the soul and sharpens the mind, keeping us from being cut off from the redemptive power of Jesus. Atonement keeps us mindful of Jesus' gift to all of us. Redemption comes first, then salvation, then atonement. Jesus took care of our redemption and the Holy Spirit is there for our salvation. It is up to us to stay in the spirit of God through daily atonement. Atonement puts us in direct contact with spiritual discipline, and discipline is the only way to reach God on a continuous basis. We must be disciplined if we truly desire prosperity. Set aside every day as a holiday for seeking atonement with God.

There are advocates that would say we need a holiday to celebrate a day of atonement. Holidays are nice but establishing holidays to help us concentrate on atonement is not the answer. Our holidays eventually lose their intent and become more commercial than sincere.

We can engage in daily atonement by paying back the money our grandparents and others gave us to help with down payments for new cars and homes. While we are at it, set aside a day on the calendar to pay all our friends and relatives and significant others money we would not repay in the past. Your success did not or will not happen in a vacuum. Someone helped you along the way. At this very moment God is sending someone your way to help you find prosperity with a word, advice, mentoring or some unexpected money. Every successful person has an unmentioned someone in their life who was instrumental in his or her success.

If the people you owe refuse the money, ask them for information on their favorite charity and make a contribution in their name. Make amends with money or gratitude to those you owe a great deal. This is important; it is through atonement in the Spirit of God that we make amends. Just remember, some of those people who helped you gave to you from the heart. Give back in the same way, from the heart, and watch how many blessings gravitate your way.

MAKE AMENDS

Money is not the only way to atonement. Some long-time friends and family members don't talk or interact with one another anymore because someone crossed sexual lines that should not have been crossed. When Jesus said "Mothers will be against daughters and fathers against sons for My sake," who would have thought it was because one close friend or relative attempted or succeeded at having a sexual relationship with a close friend or relative or someone else's mate who should have been off limits? More people are estranged from one another for reasons of sexual impropriety than for money disputes.

It takes sexual integrity to control our minds and thus combat the temptation of coveting the mates of friends, family and associates. It may look and feel good but there are so many instances where we must practice sexual abstinence. To engage in dangerous sex with another who should be off limits is only adding to unresolved issues that both participants bring with them before consummating the act. Remember, sex is more than engaging the participants in a bodily function because each person comes with a mind and a soul that is inseparable from the act.

We should not succumb to our sexual temptations because to do so thwarts prosperity, dissipates it, splitting up families and friends forever. Here is yet another act that will cause you to answer to God. It is dangerous and could get you killed. This may be the hardest thing you will ever do. You must go back and make amends to those you have harmed by way of sexual impropriety.

Remember the more you reach out to God in sincere heart-felt atonement the more God will change your character so when you do reach out to others to make amends for past sexual improprieties you are not the same person.

Jesus showed us the way to make amends with God at Calvary. We tend to focus more so on the cruelty of the crucifixion missing the four steps of release that Jesus performed.

1. When Jesus released the care of his mother to his disciple John he released his earthly care and concern.

2. When Jesus said "Father forgive them" he released our sins.

3. When Jesus committed his spirit to the Father, he released back to God what belongs to God his soul.

4. When Jesus said, "It is finished," he released God.

These four steps of release work whether you are seeking atonement, prosperity; health concerns; or feel the need to be close to God. The forth step of releasing God is very important. Sometimes we cling on to God too tightly to the point where we must release Him in order to receive answered prayers.

HOPE IS IN THE AIR

The church held its first service since the former pastor died. This was a special service that took years in the making. It was a service of atonement. The former pastor had plunged the church into deep debt by building a mega church at a time when the church's finances were not sufficient to take on such a project. The building project became a monument in the image of the pastor. The new church building greatly exceeded the capacity of current members and new members did not join because hundreds of members who left the church carried with them a negative message.

Several dedicated members had left the church in previous years because the pastor had harmed them by hurling verbal spears at them through sermons of criticism. The deceased pastor had held strong to his staunch position of "my way or the highway." At one point an entire choir left the church along with three assistant pastors. The church was in deep financial depression. Members that had stayed had loathed the deceased pastor but refused to be forced from their church.

There was a sense of hope in the air, especially from the members who had stayed and endured the deceased pastor's antics. He had misread their behavior and thought they approved of his actions but in truth they were simply tolerating him. Then there were those members who had seen no wrong in the deceased pastor. All that tantalized their minds was that the minister nailed his segue on time. And gullible members loved preachers that rhyme.

God heard the members' prayers as things got worse. There were clauses in the church by-laws put there by the founding pastor who had feared being removed from the pulpit: a fear founded from past experience where he was once ousted in the midst of a previous church's political coup. The founding pastor's predecessor had started out fine but his political ambitions, vocal eloquence and hard-heartedness clouded his mind to the point where sickness set in.

The deceased pastor had once told one of his political cronies that he would rather die than change. His lapse of judgment sent vibratory waves out into the universe where God's laws were established before the creation of the world, where vows and strong emotional requests gather spiritual forces that either justify or condemn. Like so many biblical characters, the pastor was convicted by his own words. God's laws had no choice but to smite his mind, so that every decision he made boomeranged, planting seeds that served his self-interest and eventually his demise.

BANDING TOGETHER

Finally the day came when God recalled the pastor's weary soul home. After the pomp and circumstance of a political circus funeral the small membership group banded together to make important decisions. The first thing they had to do was take back their beloved church from the entanglements of the deceased pastor's political allies and those with a vested interest in seeing the church continue as it was: divided and in disarray. A strong core of members formed a bond to repel the political faction of the deceased pastor.

The first item was to change the by-laws: never again should a pastor be appointed for life. They also installed other checks and balances, especially where accountability of money was involved. The next thing this band of strong, faithful members did was search for a new pastor: a pastor who would minister to the people, who would visit the sick and genuinely care about his flock, who would pay less attention to his press and the exploits that struck at the heart of the deceased pastor's integrity.

They found a young pastor who was thoughtful and kind with no other agenda but to see her ministry as fulfilling God's work. She was determined to do God's work with all her mind and soul and to serve the people, thus enabling them to live and walk with God. Her temperament was such that she loved the people and wanted only the best for them. She taught them to go back to the mandate of Jesus: loving one another as the foundation of the church, the essence of what made the church unique.

SHE'S THE ONE

The church was packed; something that had rarely happened in the waning days of the former pastor. A large procession of former members who had left the church years before returned for the first service of the new pastor. Some had vowed they would never return until the deceased pastor left. No one had predicted he would die at the same age and from the same disease as the founding pastor. He had had ample time to change his ways but could not do so, so God had no choice but to rest his soul because he was tired. The sermon hit home and the people knew this was the pastor they had longed for.

The new pastor taught straight out of the Bible and focused on the Word. It was different from the self-aggrandizing speeches they had learned to endure from the deceased pastor, sermons they had quickly forgotten after the service. The new pastor spoke of God in His glory and righteousness, that there is none greater than God, no power exceeds His force. The new pastor emphasized that atonement comes easier with a willing heart. Jesus' blood sacrifice was the one true atonement, redeeming all wrongs and conquering death so that spiritual healing could take place. She spoke of the love Jesus shared with us that granted us passage into the treasury of God and all its contents therein that we are entitled to share. After hearing the new pastor's sermon and examining her demeanor, the congregation knew God had sent them the pastor they had longed for.

The choir sang like never before, hitting magical notes while the talents of the musicians produced tunes with ease and the congregation sang:

God, give us Your atoning grace.
As we overcome the obstacles we face.
Open our hearts to a better place.
Where heavenly streams of light touch our face.
Oh Lord, give us Your atoning grace.
We seek Your majesty to make amends.
We ask forgiveness for our sins
God, give us your atoning grace.
As we overcome the obstacles we face.
Atonement! Atonement!
With the humility of a dove
We give glory to the Lord above.
We commit to Thee our undying love.
Atonement! Atonement!
The wonderful part of Your love
Atonement! Atonement!
What a wonderful blessing from above.
Atonement! Atonement!
Oh Lord, give us Your atoning grace.

The choir segued into a faster beat and hardly a foot stayed still: pat, pat, pat. An old lady pulled out her tambourine and old man Joe, who had left the church years ago, pulled out his harmonica. The congregation swayed from side to side while the band played on and the choir hit notes that had been absent in the past and the congregation embraced another sermon in song.

THIS TIME WAS DIFFERENT

In the past at this juncture of the service, Brother Thomas customarily had to go to the bathroom because of his urinary problems. But on this day his problems went away. He did not have to go and did not want to miss a thing. Mr. James stood up and shook his head and body; for the first time in years his arthritis did not flair up. He did not believe the Holy Ghost was real, just a myth that had never touched him before, but this time was different. Sister Alice felt so good she sang at the top of her voice and her extreme shyness went away that day.

The rhythm of the beat rocked the church. Sweet sounds blew shingles off the roof and the church's thunderous noise reached the heavens. The angels, ever ready to join in with spiritual hymns, hummed tranquil background music while flapping their wings to a chorale ballet. Those souls in transition, waiting at Heaven's gate, danced a gig (although many would be turned away because of Heaven's narrow demands).

The sweet harmonious music from the church penetrated Heaven, ascending to God's throne. The melody was pleasing to God. He snapped his fingers and patted His feet and moved to the rhythmic beat. The saxophone man blew soulful sounds and the piano man, hung over, still dazed from his Saturday night-club jazz gig, twinkle-toed the piano keys to blissful jazz. The drummer felt jazzy and pounded a constant beat, striking cymbal tones pleasing to the ear.

The congregation sang along with the choir: "He is here, God is here. God is in the sanctuary; He came down from heaven and blessed us. He is here in my soul. He is here in the sanctuary of my heart. Praise God, He is here in the sanctuary."

The church clapped when the last note struck its cord and everyone said "Amen."

The angels' mouths flew open: they learned to their surprise on this day God had jammed to gospel jazz. The thunderous voice of God ended the service with an exclamation point; He said, "Yeah!"

The congregation filled the offering baskets to overflowing and departed in great anticipation of next Sunday's Service saying, "Surely God is in the house."

THEY'RE ALL HYPOCRITES

Mrs. Wilkes went home to her husband who had not been to church in years. Mr. Wilkes had parted ways with the church and religion ten years ago. He was a victim of the former pastor's berating; criticism and put downs that had turned him away from church and God. Life had painted him a picture of Christians doing wrongs to others and justifying their actions. Over the years he had observed Christians taking pleasure and rejoicing in the pain and suffering of others, stating: their pain must be because of some sin, why else would they suffer? He saw Christians standing firm in their convictions that they were not like the suffering sinners being punished for their sins. He had developed a perception that all church people engaged in hypocrisy.

It did not help that when Mr. Wilkes was a young child his mother had fed the local preacher in his small southern town at the expense of her children. The preacher ate all that was put before him, Sunday's best. His mother thought God was testing her for future blessings as she fed the greedy preacher. All she got was an empty cupboard and the children went to bed hungry whenever the preacher came visiting, which was often. Mr. Wilkes blamed God for the behavior of Christians on those days he went to bed hungry.

Mrs. Wilkes entered the house with an air of disgust at her unbelieving, heathen husband. She had thought by now he would be in front of the television set with a beer in hand waiting for the football games to start. She thought her husband was too far gone to be touched by God. It is just as well, she thought, that at least one person in this house worships God.

Mr. Wilkes was actually ironing his suit. He greeted his wife with a smile, and then he hugged her and said, "The church was rocking today." She asked him how he knew.

He told her he had fallen asleep and God had awakened him and said, "Check this out."

"Through a vision God showed me what was happening in church. I am ironing my suit to go to church next week to make amends with God for many things."

His wife asked, "A week in advance? Church is a week away."

"I'd better get ready early to get a good seat. The church will be packed next week." Mr. Wilkes went on to say, "A voice spoke to me, saying, 'Your decisions determine your successes and your tragedies. I am the X-factor of all outcomes. The reflection of life is when I see Me in you, that is true atonement and the moments when I am in the house.'"

CHAPTER FOURTEEN

Treasure in Heaven

Don't store up treasures here on Earth where they can erode away or may be stolen. Store them in Heaven where they will never lose their value, and are safe from thieves. If your profits are in Heaven your heart will be there too.

(Matthew 6:19-21, TLB)

ON THAT DAY

On Earth the sky turned brilliant blue as the followers of Jesus removed His body from the cross. The fresh smell of spring permeated the air; it was the smell of seasonal renewal, a season of things to come that dominated the air at Calvary. They wrapped His body in linen cloth saturated with myrrh, aloes and spices, placing His body in a grove near trees where the mixture of smells released a potpourri of tranquility, aromatherapy for the soul.

In Heaven an angel with a golden censer came and stood at the altar, and a great quantity of incense was given to him to mix with the prayers of God's people to offer upon the golden altar before the throne. The perfume of incense mixed with the prayers of the people ascended up to God from the altar where the angel poured them out (Revelation 8:3-4). On that day on Earth as it is in Heaven, smells of sweetness overpowered the stench of death.

On that day at Calvary all things became new through Christ. It was a day that changed the faith of many. It was day marking the beginning of life prevailing over death. An unseen

371

spirit had been released into the world marking the beginning of the Kingdom of Heaven. From that day forth our knowledge of God would increase by leaps and bounds as the angels blew dust from their urn, ushering in the multiplier effect of the Spirit of God.

The Holy Spirit (Comforter) could now reenter human endeavors on a permanent basis. Things had been set right by Jesus, Who is of the same Spirit as the Father, to form a protective covenant between the Father, Son, the Holy Ghost and us. A new covenant was paid for with a blood oath to protect and encourage and gather together the people of God into one Body of Christ.

A future was created based on symbolic new wine, water, blood and bread where the reality of life changed to what is isn't and what isn't is. Up would be down and the last should be first and the least of us would be exalted as children of God. The rich would be revealed as poor and the poor would become aware they are rich. The crooked ways of the world would become straight and straight ways made smooth. The self-righteous would be accused just as they have accused others and the accused would be proven innocent.

The price for all this change cost God His Son in exchange for our souls. The price was high: the life of God's Son in exchange for the redemptive healing of our souls. It was a sacrifice that replaced the doomed ways of old for a new way.

EVERYTHING MADE NEW

On Earth the disciples were uncomfortable with the newness of thoughts Jesus had exposed them to. Their recollection of Him contained magical moments as they had walked the earth with God's Son. Now that Jesus was dead the magic seemed to have vanished and they would have to go at it alone. But they had a choice: they could do the unthinkable and abandon their newfound beliefs altogether.

They met in seclusion out of fear of persecution by political and church leaders and their allies who were determined to eliminate the cult followers of Jesus. They had not fully understood the prophecy that Jesus would return from the dead, yet there was no indication that many of them wanted to quit the movement. Thomas and the women disciples were the brave few who dared to walk the streets while the enemies were hunting them. Neither Thomas nor the women disciples wavered in their beliefs, yet they yearned to know if Jesus was the Son of God.

The political and religious leaders saw Jesus' disciples as a band of cult followers. Cults had existed since man had first conceived the idea of God. The unspoken goal of any dominant established religious order is to control the concept of worshipping God. Even cults believe in worshipping a higher power but they are a threat to the established order of things.

The followers of Jesus resembled a cult in every way: they were resilient, they were focused, they were forceful. They zealously insisted on certain rituals, traits of extremists. Jesus was the focal point of their beliefs. He was the object of their devotion. His followers were obsessed with His person; that can at times color an objective view.

So what is it that separated the disciples of Jesus from the cult thinking of man? The difference is Jesus' intimate contact with the Father and His special knowledge of the internal workings of the heavens. It was Jesus' richness of character and His voluminous treasure of love that placed Him above earthly cult leaders. No other form of worship speaks volumes on the loving Spirit of God who decreed life biased on the side of good.

SEARCHING FOR GOD

What would inspire a small band of people to welcome death for the sake of a man they were not absolutely sure had descended from God? What on Earth would influence this group of men and women called "disciples" who lacked a blessed earthly birth that would allow them to speak out against the established order of things and get away with it? They lacked financing to start a movement. They lacked direction. Yet they wanted to continue working onward to share with the world a new way of thinking.

When Jesus was with them physically, He used His sharp mind, frank matter-of-fact speaking skills and confrontational style along with miracles to render opponents defenseless. It was Jesus' frank style that got Him killed and seemed to remove God's protection from the disciples.

Like many of us, the disciples were searching for God. The more we learn about God the more we develop a Christ-like character that helps us build treasure in Heaven. The character we develop in Christ will help build courage, and it takes courage to look for God.

The disciples saw their unfiltered selves after spending time with Jesus. It was difficult to go back to being fishermen, radical fanatics, tax collectors and laborers. One may return to those professions, but once the heart co-habitats with Jesus, could the heart return to distancing itself from God?

In retrospect their entire lives and relationship with Jesus had changed. They had once thought of Him as their teacher but now that He was dead they were His friends; He had poured His heart out to them but they still did not understand. At one point in their relationship the disciples asked Jesus for free bread and more miracles. This was clearly their attraction and motive for following Jesus, evidence of their lukewarm belief.

PLEASE GOD

When they arrived and found Him, they said, "Sir, how did You get here?"
Jesus replied, "The truth of the matter is that you want to be with Me because I fed you, not because you believe in Me. But you shouldn't be so concerned about perishable things like food. No, spend your energy seeking the eternal life that I, the Mes-

siah, can give you. For God the Father has sent Me for this very purpose."
The disciples replied, "What should we do to satisfy God"?
Jesus told them, "This is the will of God, that you believe in the One He has sent."

(John 6:25-29, TLB)

The disciples again missed the point.

They replied, "You must show us more miracles... Give us free bead every day, like our fathers had while they journeyed through the wilderness! As the Scriptures say, 'Moses gave them bread from Heaven.'"

(John 6:30-31, TLB)

Jesus again attempted to get them to understand.

...I am the Bread of Life. No one coming to Me will ever be hungry again. Those believing in Me will never thirst.

(John 6:35, TLB)

Two things stand out during this interaction between Jesus and the disciples. One: the disciples asked how they could satisfy God. Satisfying God is far different than being obedient and pleasing God. Any attempt to satisfy God is limited. Satisfying God means to do just enough to fulfill some ritualistic requirement wrapped in ceremony. Satisfying God sets limits, confining our beliefs within boundaries as we attempt to interpret what is satisfying to God.

Pleasing God requires a totally different state of mind in that to please God is to be in agreement with Him in order to carry out His will. Another attribute of pleasing God is to delight in His laws. Jesus corrected the disciples later when he said, *"For I have come here from Heaven to do the will of God who sent me, not to have My own way"* (John 6:38, TLB).

SHOW ME A MIRACLE

The second thing that indicates how far the disciples were from fully understanding Jesus was when they asked Him to show them a miracle and supply them with free daily bread. Jesus used miracles to serve as proof of God's power and love. The disciples were looking for miracles to solve the requirement of daily bread.

If you expect a miracle in your prosperity walk you are setting yourself up for failure. Miracles violate the process of natural law. Natural law occurs with a degree of certainty for regulating, sustaining and advancing the universe and beyond. The occurrence of natural law regulates the things of gravity: attraction and repulsion, the regeneration of stars and the creation of new planets and all forms of living things. Any violation of natural law is under the direction of the Father, Son and Holy Spirit, the guardians of natural law who must agree to bypass and regulate the opening of doors and windows in the Kingdom of God. The Kingdom of God is an indescribable place where hope and recognition of blessings are never an issue.

We have the ability to attract things to us from the unseen world by way of our thoughts. When prosperity does become a reality it is not a miracle but faith mixed with thoughts and action that ascended to a higher plane. The occurrence is not beyond the power decreed upon us at the foundation of creation.

If you really want to experience prosperity as God intended for you, stop looking for miracles. It is easy to see God as part wizard, part magician when He is healing you and feeding you from invisible substance. If God were to continue using miracles as the primary source, they would become common place and lose their value. Too much of anything causes confusion. Too many miracles on the part of God would cause us to lose sight of His significance.

When miracles do take place many unseen events are set in motion, including the spirits prompting occurrences that culminate in a physical birth. Therefore the most significant miracle that will take place in most of our lives is you. The fact that you were born means you are the miracle. Prosperity is not a miracle but a promise and God is faithful at keeping His promises.

THE GREATEST KNOWLEDGE

The most revealing clue why the disciples stayed the course after Jesus' death has more to do with their character than their fears. It was no accident that the disciples were chosen because Jesus knew the heart of each one of them. The common bond that attracted each disciple to Jesus was their yearning for life's meaning. They yearned, like many of us, to see life beyond the physical or traditional, beyond the status quo or conventional wisdom. The greatest knowledge is the knowledge of self. And the knowledge of self is a necessity for accurately assessing the times we live in and where we stand in relationship to the times.

The disciples were exposed to loss of life on a daily basis. When Jesus entered their lives, the risk of death increased. When the disciples acknowledged Jesus or boldly preached the Gospel they exposed themselves to the peril of martyrdom. As they steadfastly pushed onward following the death of Jesus in search of life's greater meaning, their souls were being pruned for greater receptiveness to the Holy Spirit. It was then that all the perils of death they faced took a backseat to the inner peace of knowing God through Jesus. On the road to prosperity God must prune our souls for greater receptiveness to the Holy Spirit.

THE DEEPER MEANING

As the disciples searched for deeper life meaning they recalled every subtle thing Jesus had done or said until a picture emerged. They remembered Jesus had spoken of the first being last and the last being first and they realized the Spirit of God has no beginning or end. They reasoned, "If the Father is the alpha and the omega and Jesus is in the Father and Jesus is in us, it makes sense that we are of the same substance at the soul level." With each discussion the disciples began to understand with soaring confidence that the eternity Jesus spoke of was a continuous circle where death or any other interruption is impossible at the center point of the circle.

God becomes rich when we dedicate our souls to Him. In return, He shares with us material riches in response to our human experience where the material is necessary. God enlists all of us to lend a hand and play a role in His grand plan. There are no civilians; we are all soldiers. We are enlisted to fight the battle against death and tears, fears and years magnified by cold-heartedness. If we fight the good fight we store up treasure in Heaven. Our good works offered to God in a spirit of loving Him and pleasing Him is a deposit in our heavenly bank account in the treasury of God.

If the wages of sin is death then the righteousness of God is your prosperity salary. Every time you commit yourself to God in sincere service without the motive of receiving free bread through a miracle, you become part of the mix of God's people where prayers are blended with the perfume of the Spirit and poured out into the heavens, returning infinite blessing.

WORKING IN GOD'S TREASURY

A new angel arrived in Heaven. He was to report to God's treasury and receive further instructions. He could not contain his joy because on Earth he had dreamed of working for the government of his country in the treasury department. But each time he had applied he was rejected. He had spent his entire career performing financial audits, uncovering the theft and cover-up of men which eventually took its toll on his health, his faith and his longing for honesty. God monitored the sincerity of his heart, and when the time came for him to leave this world his sleep was peaceful.

The treasury of God was located in a huge mansion in the east wing of the heavens. Upon entering the treasury the angel was blinded by the sparkling gleam emanating from transparent gold, bright pearls, diamonds, emerald, sapphires, amethysts and many other precious gems the size of baseballs. The angels working in God's treasury were playing a game of stick ball with the precious gems, to the horror of the new auditor general angel.

The angels stopped playing to welcome their new auditor general and he asked them to explain why they played games with precious gems. So the angels explained to the new auditor that they were working and the best way to sort the gems into piles was to have fun while they worked and sort by playing stick ball. The auditor's blood pressure increased and his next question was: when do you count the gems and assess a value? The angels were silent. So the auditor angel asked again: why aren't the gems counted? The angels remained silent until one angel stepped forward and said, "The gems continuously multiply when the children of God act in accordance with the teachings of Jesus. The gems are manufactured from the invisible ether in the Kingdom, they never stop multiplying. The more treasure the children of God store up in Heaven, the more gems are produced."

MULTIPLICATION WITHOUT END

The auditor angel still could not understand why the gems were not counted. He thought to himself: the ways of Heaven are inefficient. It is a good thing he was appointed auditor general to clean up the mess. What if he was called upon by God to give account of the value of the treasury?

The new auditor general asked again: why are the gems not counted? The angels remained silent until one angel stepped forward and said, "The only way to explain it is to use the bad word."

The auditor angel asked, "What bad word?" The angels replied that it was the same word the hecklers used at Calvary as Jesus hung on the cross; the word that causes a thunderous storm in Heaven as it does on Earth. The auditor thought for a while, then he said, "Do you mean the word can't?" The angels were distressed that he had said the bad word.

One angel said, "That is a bad word in the Kingdom. Besides, there is no number yet conceived on Earth as it is in the Kingdom to place a value on the treasure stored up in Heaven."

The auditor angel then asked "Does the treasury multiply to no end?"

A worker angel replied, "Some of it is released to those who give themselves to the understanding of God, the rest keep multiplying and stand in waiting for those who are in training to be able to handle God's abundant blessings."

The auditor angel then asked: "What will become of it all?"

Another worker angel replied, "We'll have to build more rooms in the mansions to store it." The worker angels gave their new auditor general a stick and he too sorted the gems by playing stick ball.

THE HOLY SPIRIT DESCENDS

The disciples received a spiritual boost, a spark of mental confidence when Jesus appeared to them as they hid behind locked doors before the ascension. This may have solidified their courage to die for Jesus' sake. Following Jesus is not a life of ease or without problems. All people have problems, whether they believe in Jesus or not, whether they are rich or poor. We cannot ignore the call to mercy, compassion, obedience and honesty that is God's peace. We are to develop an attitude of service to our fellow human beings and serve as caretakers for Earth and spiritual things that are of God.

When the time was right at Pentecost a portal opened windows of Heaven and the Holy Spirit descended among the disciples. God arose in the affairs of men by sending the Holy Spirit to speak for us in more profound words than any linguistic dialect developed by man. The Holy Spirit intervened and spoke for us in tongues. This intervention by the Holy Spirit is as necessary today as it was in days gone by. Now we could petition God directly in Jesus' name through doors opened in Heaven as they are on Earth. It was a radical change in thinking: God could now enter our lives by way of request on demand.

The disciples spent hours discussing the meaning of Jesus' thoughts, words and parables. A light went off in their minds as they began to understand the meaning of what Jesus meant when He said, "When doors are opened on Earth they are opened in Heaven and when they are closed on Earth they are closed in Heaven." They began to understand the key to opening and closing doors and windows in both Heaven and Earth rested on our thoughts, our prayers and meditations and our deeds that are assets we store up in the treasury of Heaven. From that point on the disciples knew that their time on Earth would be diminished because the knowledge they now possessed from the teaching of the Holy Spirit was removing them from dependence on this world.

A BETTER LIFE

The point is this: God is willing and able to grant you a better life. He is willing to meet you wherever you are. If you feel down in the dumps, God can go there to get you. If you are in pain, God can go there to get you. If you have been dealt an injustice, God can go there to get you. If you are rich, God can go there to get you. If life has beaten you down and you are poor, God can go there to get you.

It does not matter where you are at this moment, God can go there to get you. The only obstacle to God's entry into your life is you. There was a cigarette commercial in the days the tobacco industry could advertise on television. The commercial gave us a visual of a person with a black eye and the name of the cigarette. The person said, "I would rather fight than switch." There are some God invites to a better life who would rather fight than switch. Fighting God is a huge factor in why many spiritual blessings are blocked and prosperity is denied. So instead it is, "we will always have the poor among us until the end of this time or at least when all of us stop fighting God."

There are some people that thought or have said, "If God decreed prosperity for us why can't He just give it to us without strings attached?" The answer is prosperity is a naturally occurring by-product of giving God your undivided attention, thus first place in your life. It is contrary to divine law for you to receive God's prosperity when your mind and heart reside somewhere else.

Our free will blessing is a choice. We can choose to be happy, we can choose to let the bad things of this world dominate us or we can choose the goodness of God. Sound reasoning would ask the question: why sell our souls in conformity to a harsh world that ultimately will dispose of us when our usefulness is up? The other option is God asks us to give Him our souls for usefulness here and eternally.

THE CHOICE IS OURS

Both selling and giving are a three-fold process. In the parable of the rich man who could not enter Heaven, Jesus asked him to sell all he had, give the proceeds to the poor and follow Him. The rich man could not see himself selling his estate, generally sold at a discount for a quick sale at no profit (a loss in his mind), then giving the proceeds to the poor (a greater loss in his mind). So it is easier, symbolically, for a camel to go through the eye of a needle than to connect with Heaven when the thought of foregoing anything earthly dominates the mind. By free will the choice is ours.

The disciples developed a rudimentary system of storing up treasure by requiring believers to bring all their material wealth into the storehouse to be distributed in the concept of a new church. This communal act was called "The Way" before the term "Christianity" was used. The system of dividing the collective goods of the people was not new, it had been tried before. The idea was retrieved by the disciples and retried in modern times under the name of community socialism.

The disciples experienced many missteps in the development of the Christianity we see today. This is expected as remnants from their former life left them with no previous experience at handling prosperity. The disciples had a difficult time getting a handle on being responsible for large numbers of people and money, never having had previous occasions of dealing with largeness. The disciples had it right in one respect: communal worship gives practical support to collective minds that better enable us to unravel meanings and better understand clues to God's will. Jesus' simplistic meanings have stumped us for centuries, sentencing us to debates that are sometimes disharmonious and divisive. All signs point to the true purpose of Jesus' mission: to reconcile us to God and divide us from loving ourselves and this world so much.

STEADFAST LOVE OF THE LAW

Christianity would have come about differently had it not been for Jesus spotting Paul, the messenger whose pain was used to carry his words further. Paul was an unlikely disciple; in fact, he was a hit man for the Pharisees. Paul possessed personality traits that the other disciples did not have. He had an unashamed desire for protecting man-made laws. In fact, he loved the law and its principles more than people. To be a killer you must have contempt for people to justify with ease the necessity for killing. It was Paul's steadfast love of the law and its principles that led his soul to possess the personality of "Saul": a personality that Jesus would transform into Paul.

Jesus had to give Saul a new name to replace the man-made laws and principles in him with Jesus' love, so He wrote His passion in Paul's heart and used Saul's pain as a lightening rod. Paul believed the fulfillment of the law and its protection came about through intelligent effort and duty. He had an ironclad will and a keen, concentrated focus to stay the course and press on in search of Jesus after coming in contact with Him on the road to Damascus.

If you really want prosperity, you must allow Jesus to write His laws, principles and passion in your heart and use your pain as a lightening rod. You must feel comfortable with Jesus using you and boldly acquire a taste for prosperity while loving God above all things. You must affix firmly in your mind that prosperity comes from God through intelligent effort, work and practicing the principles Jesus will give you.

Christianity would have indeed come about differently had Paul not been the choice and voice that carried Jesus' message. God does not stop at one person to fulfill His prophecy, with the exception of the Son. There is no doubt there was another waiting in the wings had Paul refused to cooperate with Jesus.

I tell my friends the best stories in life are the ones where we start out as smug fools, fickle with false beliefs and a lost cause, then on the road to Damascus a bolt of lightening strikes us in the butt and we change into trusting children of God. If we start out as unconscious fools without developing a noble cause we die just as we lived. What kind of life story is that? No punch line, no dramatic turn of events, no heartfelt examples of interaction with God, no beauty, no truth; we just lived as a fool and died as a fool – now that is sad life story.

SEEING THE LIGHT

A flash of light blinded Paul and in his blindness he saw the light. The light is not physical sight but inner vision, the sight of the soul which draws us near and dear to Jesus. There we derive pleasure from the source of our souls. There Jesus says, "Look! I have been standing at the door and I am constantly knocking. If any one hears Me calling him and opens the door, I will come in and fellowship with him and he with Me. I will let everyone who conquers sit beside Me on My throne, just as I took My place with My Father on His throne when I had conquered" (Revelation 3:20-21).

To become a decent disciple requires enormous discipline. To truly concentrate on God you have to make Him the central figure in your life. Paul was more disciplined than the other disciples. No other disciple had enough discipline to take the words and ways of Jesus to the rest of the world. Peter wavered a lot; James and John were hung up on who would sit at the right hand of Jesus when He came into His throne. Thomas still needed proof, but once he got started, his faith was unshakable – however, he lacked the charisma to excite the masses. The remaining disciples could not get past the strong personalities of the beforehand mentioned disciples.

Paul was both a free thinker and a staunch follower of the cause. Paul was different from most free thinkers, who are usually rebellious and certainly uncooperative and unfocused. Paul had a rare combination of cooperation working within the framework of the group and he humbled himself. More importantly, Paul had a concentration so focused on Jesus that he would hardly notice if the building was burning. The other disciples had a tendency to become timid and drift during periods of confusion. Paul was neither timid nor confused once he truly grabbed hold of the Spirit of Jesus and boldly preached the Gospel. You must develop a boldness in Christ to achieve prosperity.

It was hard for the other disciples to readily accept Paul. One of Paul's biggest obstacles was the other disciples' distrust of him. They distrusted him for a number of reasons: primarily because he had been the hit man for the other side. It's hard to trust someone who had vowed to kill you in the past. Paul was undisturbed by what the other disciples thought of him.

BREAKING RANK

Note on the road to prosperity you cannot get caught up in what other people think of you. You must develop a clear estimate of yourself noting the good, the bad and the ugly and refining yourself in the name of Jesus. Your goal is to ask God to change the bad to a greater good, eliminate the ugly and to change you into what He wants you to be. This is exactly what Paul did: on the road and in the silence of his dark room he pushed on, keeping his eyes on the prize: Jesus. With all Paul's refinement of soul, violence and mistrust still followed him all the remaining days of his life. He had a pain in his body: a reminder of past sins, a pain recorded in the deep tissues of darkness.

The growth of Christianity rested on the disciple James' decision. James was known for his stubbornness, a stubbornness that would turn the tide of things and release the multiplier effect of Jesus' Spirit. James broke rank with the other disciples and sided with Paul on the decision to offer the Gospel of Jesus to the Gentiles (people not of the Jewish Faith).

There will be times in your prosperity walk where you must break rank with conventional wisdom and political pressure in order to do God's will. Christianity flourished with the decision and was absorbed into the greater civilization of the Roman Empire, where the Gospel of Jesus could gain greater exposure by planting seeds that multiplied. It did not matter that the greater masses did not fully understand what Jesus meant; what did matter was they understood basic concepts. God knew others would come along later in the same Spirit of Jesus to add new challenges to the basic concepts and overcome conventional wisdom and political pressures.

WE ARE CHILDREN OF GOD

When dissension arose in the church of Galatia, Paul wrote his finest thoughts on the direction of Christianity. Paul dealt with many carnal customs of the church:

> *Let me put it another way. The Jewish laws were our teacher and guide until Christ came to give us right standing with God through faith. But now that Christ has come, we don't need those laws any longer to guard us and lead us to Him. For now we are all children of God through faith in Jesus*

Christ, and we who have been baptized into union with Christ are enveloped by Him. We are no longer Jews or Greeks or slaves or free men or even merely men or women, but we are all the same - we are Christians; we are one in Christ Jesus.

(Galatians 3:24-29, TLB)

Paul carried the message "our business with God is better business" a step further when he said,

...Because of that cross my interest in all the attractive things of the world was killed long ago, and the world's interest in me is also long dead.

(Galatians 6:14, TLB)

Our connection to the sacrifice at Calvary was driven home with the statement,

So overflowing is His kindness towards us that He took away all our sins through the blood of His Son, by whom we are saved; and He has showered down upon us the richness of His grace.

(Ephesians 1:7, TLB)

He goes on to say,

...I want you [us] to realize that God has been made rich because we who are Christ's have been given to Him! I pray that you begin to understand how incredibly great His power is to help those who believe Him...

(Ephesians 1:18-19, TLB)

THE MULTIPLYING EFFECT

The Spirit of Jesus multiplied into the greatest story ever told of a religious movement that began from an unlikely seed planted in the unfertilized minds of devoted common men, and more importantly, women. Christianity is now a worldwide religion with over a billion followers. There is no greater story of the multiplying effect in action than the legacy of Jesus.

Jesus spoke extensively on the subject of prosperity as a direct blessing from God. In the past as it is today many people did not believe we are entitled to share in God's treasure. Even now there is debate on the importance of prosperity in the scheme of things.

The importance of prosperity has to do with how you view the world. From the stand point of the individual, I know of many individuals who want to be assured of their daily bread. I know many individual who want good health. I know some individual who suffer from severe mental depression who wants to maintain a consistent positive attitude. In the scheme of things prosperity is important to our health, welfare and over-all positive attitudes. When the Father, the Son and the Holy Spirit (Comforter) smiles upon (show favor) you, you receive prosperity by inclusion into a sacred covenant with God. There is nothing more important than being included in God inner circle. Somewhere on the path to prosperity you must become grounded in the belief that God comes first, then healing, then development and then prosperity.

STORING YOUR TREASURE

We do not have to look far to begin storing up treasure in Heaven. We can store up treasure in Heaven right where we are in life and find a multitude of outlets. The businessman can dedicate his company to the service of God and treat employees with respect, dignity, compassion and empathy, and still prosper on the bottom line.

There is a difference between profit-centered companies and companies that treat their employees with Christ-centered values. The Christ-centered companies perform better over the long run in areas of productivity, employee motivation and profits than profit-centered companies that attempt to profit by any means necessary. Christ-centered companies weather the storms of economic downturns better than profit-only motivated companies. Employees are happier at Christ-centered companies and thus achieve a higher level of customer service, retention and satisfaction as a measurement of productivity. You rarely if at all hear of Christ-centered companies involved in financial shenanigans and corruption that can destroy prosperity.

Public officials who steal and misappropriate funds should stop because this action does not store up treasure in Heaven. On occasion I have engaged appointed and elected officials on the subject of corruption. We hear stories of money disappearing, unaccounted for. I have heard some public officials justify corruption as the cost of doing business. They say America was built on corruption; other people stole before we did. My response was and is: if people jumped out of windows during the stock market crash of 1929, does that mean you should do the same?

I would respond to these appointed and elected officials that in other communities the theft is usually from their surplus. I went on to say if you break into the home of a little old woman of limited means and steal the incremental rent money she saved which is all she had, as opposed to breaking into the home of a wealthy individual and steal a fortune in jewelry, who is most affected? The answer is the old woman because she had to save the monthly rent in increments therefore she is more susceptible to small losses without much hope of recovery; whereas the wealthy individual that lost their excess more than likely is insured. If the wealthy individual had replacement cost insurance it is even possible for them to reap more than the historical value of the stolen jewelry due to appreciation. The poor also require more effort and resources. So when resources are stolen from those who can least afford a theft, we propel that person or community further into the grip of poverty.

Christ-centered politicians can store up treasure in Heaven by no longer stealing and misappropriating public funds. Politicians can spend their energy and devote their careers to producing change through issues that set the courses of people's life on positive paths for the better. They can change things by fighting legislation that places hardships on the people and those unable to fight the battle of influence through money.

Christ-centered politicians can be steadfast at protecting our God-given rights to life, liberty and the pursuit of happiness and can stand as a deterrent to tyranny. In spite of opposition, Christ-centered politicians must press on, ignoring labels such as being called a "liberal." Life is liberal. If the progression of life were to stop, life as we know it would die from stagnation and lack of ever-expanding ideas. The proof is in the ever-expanding universe. Only a fool or one with the motives of preserving their idealized way of life would refuse to see that God is all-encompassing, all-knowing and all-focused on human growth so that we can fit into the vastness of His thoughts and stop reducing Him to our limited conservative ideas, contradictions and rational analysis.

OUTSIDE THE BOX

To conserve old ideas is to think inside the box. The richness of life is liberal and certainly lived outside the many barriers of entry to life. The beauty of God's plan is that liberalism, conservatism, fundamentalism and any other man-made doctrine will fall short. No doctrine is the answer because this creation is not complete, and oh what glory God is moving into position. This whole business of business and government would fail if not for the grace of God. If you release yourself to God and trust that He has a plan in store for you, a whole new world will open up to you and you will store up treasure in Heaven.

Schoolteachers can store up treasure in Heaven by returning to the true meaning of why they are there in the first place: to teach the children. Some teachers have lost their salt; Jesus said salt with no flavor is useless. Today a number of teachers in the profession never intended to be teachers; to them it is just a job. We are seeing teachers whose performance was rated unsatisfactory for years become principals and administrators and given greater responsibility to continue spreading their ineptitude.

When your heart is not in it the necessary commitment of intensity and passion is not there and the children, being of keen perception, sense insincerity and lack respect. The important thing about teaching is you should never keep the children away from the core teachings of Jesus.

It is important to examine your actions and motives to assess if they are contrary to the teachings of Jesus. If they are contrary to Christ's teaching you are doing more harm than good. It is most important that you approach the duties of your position with greater responsibility and faith.

FINDING GOD

Teaching is a circle where minds and spirits meet on a continuum in search of finding God. It does not matter if God is never mentioned in the classroom; we are all in search of God. The better educated we are, the sooner we will marvel at the knowledge of God while He is waiting on us to catch up. The road to God is through knowledge, you acknowledge Him by being responsible at teaching the children. Teachers have a unique opportunity to convey thoughts on the subject of formulating, retaining and managing ideas. By teaching a child to think you are helping that child find God.

When teachers in the profession are there for the money or with an attitude that it is just a job, true prosperity will pass them by. They will end their career as financially broke as they were when they started and spiritually in debt. When a child is inferiorly educated, he or she may be ill-equipped to deal with God's Word and the ways of the world.

Yes, teaching is a frustrating job. However, the biggest obstacle is not the students with their multi-faceted set of problems. The biggest obstacles are the parents who expect the educational system and teachers to raise their children, they lost control of at age two when the temper tantrums starting. Parents request the system instill values and behavior clues that should be learned at home. The other set of problems are pompous administrators who shoot themselves in the foot with additional burdens they place on teachers.

Cuts in public school funding and layoffs due to declining enrollment start at the top. Enrollment declines when the quality of educational experience and the building facilities decline. The other factor is school violence and crime and an unnecessarily high degree of bureaucracy. The best students in academics, citizenship and finance end up leaving the system. Administrative incompetence and bureaucracy, along with the threat of layoffs, motivates the best teachers to flee the system and those who are left are not the best. The downward spiral continues until eventually the school system ends up in state-controlled receivership. Both the parents and administration have ulterior motives; both are willing to pass the buck onto the teachers for their own shortfalls.

LIFE DEPENDS ON IT

The greatness of God is His accuracy of judgment. He judges us by our motives; educators are judged by a different set of rules. This prompted Jesus to say that when our day of judgment comes, He would judge rightly.

Teachers must overcome parents and administrators to teach children as if their lives depended on it. In essence it does; the irony of life is that the child you give up on may be the same child who ends up causing acts of destruction, thus highlighting your shortcomings through neglect. Teach the children well and do no harm to their minds, body and souls. To do so is to store up treasure in Heaven. Teach the children with all your heart and watch God bless you beyond your wildest dreams.

The church and the ministers can store up treasure in Heaven by no longer camouflaging political meetings and fundraisers, nor flowering heavy praise on other pastors and those who can grant favors. We need to stop pursuing personal gain and worldly endeavors; above all we need stop worshipping each other and instead worship God.

The sins of the church are piled up high. The majority of the people of this world are relying on some form of religion to bring meaning to their lives and to help them place peace in their hearts, enabling them to go to God. Financial decisions and questions of life and death hinge on religious development, and they shape the formulation of ideas on how we see God and ourselves.

Religion is the central mechanism people use to aid them in coping with unexplained circumstances of this world that put them in crutches and cause them pain. Those times when God does not make sense, when dreams are shattered and when death comes knocking at the door can be faced with courage, hope and strength in the presence of an inner knowledge that there is something bigger and better than the perils of this world.

You Can't Bring It with You

A friend once commented that in the heyday of the city there were a large number of prostitutes and pimps and every shyster imaginable on the scene; where had they all gone? My comment was they had gone into the church, certainly a place where they belong, but sadly, so many of them had brought their games with them. The former street folks discovered pimping parishioners was easier than street life; they also bought with them havoc in the form of constant strife, the residual effects of a former life.

That slick deacon or trustee was once a master shyster. Some repented; others simply changed the venue of their game: the church. Churches today have gone the way of the corporation; reasoning that we need the material things of this world to the extent that the church should be run as a business. On the other hand, God's business is not the business of man. God's business is better business. The inner sanctuary of God is not a business nor should it be run like one. There is a reason Jesus chased the businessmen from the church, His Father's house.

SUCCESS DEPENDS ON THE HEART

The church should employ some of the practices of the business community but maintain its love of God, which is immeasurable and certainly cannot be managed in the same manner as running a business. The middle ground is to place Jesus at the forefront of church operations and the same should be applied to the corporation. The middle ground is acts of compassion, empathy, treating people right and going a step farther by loving one another instead of embracing a cutthroat environment that has invaded both the church and the corporation.

Your success depends on your heart. The bottom lines of the church and the corporation will take care of themselves, if those in charge do the right things in the eyes of God. The pastor, corporate executives and all the rest will get what is coming to them if God is given first place in their operations. The church and corporation will prosper beyond their wildest dreams if they do the right thing in the name and Spirit of Jesus.

All churches and all religious adaptations of what God has truly decreed have failed miserably at enabling the multitude to heal themselves. The sins of the church are piled high, but there is still hope by going back to the true meaning of Christ and christening the church and its spirit as the sanctuary of the Father, the Son and the Holy Spirit. Jesus called the church His Father's house. When factions fight over who has the right to control the church, an ironic twist is taking place; how can any side claim exclusivity and ownership to what belongs to God and is freely given to all of God's children?

THE GOD OF JUSTICE

Protectors of the law can store up treasure in Heaven by being intolerant of corruption. God is a God of justice. In the legal systems of man, justice is not blind: it sometimes peeps with one eye open. On other occasions justice merely pretends to be blind. If you wave some money or influence near the nose of justice, the aroma opens its eyes.

In too many cases the compromised equation of justice and money gives justice a black eye. I have seen enough cases to make me sick at the people that were guilty as Hell but granted clemency because they had money or their family was well-connected socially and politically.

There is no other profession where those blessed to judge others in the courts of men must engage God every single day, all day. To sentence another human being to life in jail or to death carries with it the ultimate load of piling up sins and potential sins. It only takes one bribe, one mistake or one act of indifference to lose your soul. Sentencing the sons or daughters of a well-connected family to probation or a suspended sentence while sentencing a minority or someone poor to the harshest sentence for the same crime is not only a crime against God, but a crime against humanity.

To say a corrupt prosecutor is exempt from being punished for his crime of creating and withholding evidence or engaging in a conspiracy to convict a human being is a crime against God and humanity.

If you are a prison guard or warden, stand firm that you will not tolerate corruption. You must not fall prey to money for extorted favors that are inherent in the prison system. There is prisoner-on-prisoner abuse that must be stopped and guard-on-prisoner abuse that should not be.

Remember, the devil despises corruption; he has but one plan: to sell you out in the end. When prison officers engage in unjust cruelty it is a crime against God and humanity; even the devil thinks less of you when you add to the burdens of over-burdened fellow human beings. In time he will destroy your soul because he sees you as morally unworthy, untrustworthy, despicable and not entitled to live in God's power where human beings are endowed with the ability to fuse with God through Christ and thus enter into the Kingdom of God.

Those in law enforcement can store up treasures in Heaven by simply obeying the law themselves, by showing compassion and empathy and by practicing the real justice as outlined by

Jesus. There are some people who really should be in jail but there are also many who do *not* belong there. What is sad is some law enforcement officers know who the innocent are because they helped put them in jail. God is truly a God of justice and truth pressed to ground (a lie covered up) will rise again (be revealed).

WISHING YOU THE BEST

No matter how poor you are, you can store up treasure in Heaven by helping someone else as poor as you or poorer than you. Help a single mom while she works by babysitting, and let her know you do not want to be taken advantage of because we have a propensity to use one another up. You can build up treasure in Heaven by being truly happy when someone in your socio-economic category receives a blessing that will help them better themselves.

Don't engage in envy or jealousy or say mean things, but instead be genuinely happy for other people's success. Be kind and wish only the best for others. See the best in all people. Think only good for people. Do whatever you can to help others and yourself develop your talents.

Give when you can; it is not the amount you give but the spirit in which you give that will bring you more blessings than you can imagine. Don't fall into the trap of believing that you can only give when your ship comes in. Give for the sheer joy of giving. Be open-minded and willing to learn at every opportunity. People are more willing to inform you if you are not stubborn or hiding behind an attitude that knows it all. Stop putting on a million-dollar front when you are living at or below poverty.

Have you ever wondered why immigrants from other countries come to America and within one generation lift themselves out of poverty? It is because they are willing and eager to learn and to use what they have learned to make life better for themselves and their families. I have seen some immigrants who cannot speak fluent English but stress to their children to learn the language. And every day they ask their children to explain what they learned that day. What these immigrants are doing is learning from their children. They then use what they have learned from those conversations to start a business or engage in some activity to improve themselves.

EAGER TO LEARN AT EVERY TURN

Education is the key. I am not speaking of attending university; the university is not for everyone. Be eager to learn at *every* turn. Ask good questions. Formulate your questions with greater thought to gain the maximum amount of knowledge. Learn to ask the right questions instead of asking questions for the sake of saying something.

Alter your behavior so that people will have respect for you even though you are poor. Behavior and manners have played a significant role in lifting so many people up from poverty. Spend a lot of time developing and honing your manners and the manners of your children.

Good manners are acceptable to both God and man. The rich and the poor alike admire good manners. You will be surprised how far good manners will take you, especially in today's world where ill manners seem to rule the social scene. What good manners do is place you in a unique position and separate you from the increasing population of the ill-mannered.

If you are a gang member there are surely one or more youths in the gang, or who want to be in the gang, who are not cut out for this life. Do all you can to discourage them from joining your gang or any other gang. Talk to them; show them there is another way of life. If it becomes necessary you might have to protect them from harm or find a way to get them out of the gang. By doing this you will store up treasure in Heaven. A loving God will not forget that you helped someone headed for a bad life change his or her path.

If you are in jail for a crime you know you committed, God has not forgotten you; you can store up treasure in Heaven by protecting those who are there because they are innocent. You know who the innocent are as opposed to the guilty. Protect those who made a mistake but are good at heart; they may have gotten caught up at the wrong place at the wrong time or with the wrong friends or relatives. Stop them from being beaten, extorted or sodomized.

When this happens, men and women who were victims of circumstance are again victims, this time of prison abuse; some will never be the same after being victimized again. Families and loved ones also become victims when they witness the spiritual decline of jailed loved ones victimized in prison. You can right some wrongs in your own life by stopping some of the evils that go on right where you are in jail.

A HELP IN TIME OF NEED

We can store up treasure in Heaven by not contributing to the further demise of sweet people: the individuals willing to help anyone in need. I have notice a decline in the number of sweet people in the world today. Nowadays they are a dying breed as they exchange their sweetness for a hard-core attitude, cooling their love in order to survive in a world that constantly uses them up. Practical knowledge should lead us to understand that with the decline of sweet people who else would minister to the increasing number of strange and lonely individuals this new world age is producing. Where the internet and electronic messaging is eliminating close social contact. By not contributing to the demise of this endangered species you are storing up treasure in Heaven.

A great many of us can store up treasure in Heaven by no longer being mean, hyper-critical, hateful and ornery, nor causing strife. We can store up treasure in Heaven by no longer using one another without care or concern. We can store up treasure in Heaven by no longer lying, being deceptive or killing one another.

We can also store up treasure in Heaven by learning more about God, by working toward perfecting our talents and our stewardship, and by improving our overall behavior. We store up treasure in Heaven by loving God, ourselves and our neighbors. Best of all we store up treasure in Heaven by releasing ourselves totally to God. It is in the releasing where we totally trust God to do with us as He wills. In releasing ourselves we have no concern about our health and welfare.

The more we practice releasing ourselves the more able we are to achieve total release into the hands of God because during those moments all is well and we are in Heaven. The secret to prosperity and living an abundant life is learning to "let go and let God." We should learn to download the things of God into our hearts and upload what we have learned. In that way we store up treasure in Heaven. Where your heart is so is your treasure; let your heart reside in God's heart and notice how you gradually prosper.

THE SPIRITUAL FUNERAL

Jesus came to divide the dead from the living. The only way the dead can bury the dead is by laying them to rest through a spiritual funeral. The spiritually dead buries its own by throwing spiritual soil on dead, negative thoughts. Be respectful by sending flowers to dead religions and laying a wreath at the foot of dead ideas; say a eulogy to fears.

After burying all this deadness, the soul becomes alive again and you can breathe the breath of God and be born again in Christ. The only way to reconnect with God is through spiritual transformation. It is contrary to natural law for human beings to be born again in the physical. When we engage in real living through Christ, the transition from this world to the next is a spiritual journey, not a physical one.

God will not give you prosperity for you to have your own way. It is important that you spend your life seeking to please Him, not engaging in lukewarm acts of merely satisfying Him.

Your prosperity is to be used as blessings for others. Use it to heal the sick and uplift the poor, to replenish the earth and fight injustice. Spend your prosperity fighting for those that are held captive and speaking out against the oppressed. Most of all, use your words, actions and deeds to announce that God is willing to give blessings to all who come to Him. Your prosperity is to be used to further the Kingdom of God.

We should use our prosperity to right the wrongs of this world and to aid in solving problems of humanity, the environment and other living things. These are the things that fund our prosperity accounts in the Kingdom of God and have value as stored-up treasure in Heaven.

EPILOGUE

A Celebration of Many Mansions

THE CHURCH NURSERY

Ms. Doolittle hurried to Sunday early morning service to greet the parents and register their children for nursery service while the parents attended church. She was a young graduate school student unmarried with no children, fresh out of undergraduate school with a degree in sociology. She was ambitious and cunning. At her undergraduate university the students nicknamed her "Gold-digger" because she had a male friend who drove her wherever she wanted to go. She had another male friend who researched and wrote her papers and a professor that took care of her financial and other needs. She was physically attractive and traded on her looks.

This summer she had returned home to work at her church. She thought she would serve the Lord through the nursery ministry, plus the graduate school she would attend in the fall required her to have so many hours of community service before being officially accepted into the program. She told everyone who would listen she wanted to have an impact on the children's development through the biblical Word. Ms. Doolittle was looking for a subject on which to write her graduate school thesis.

The children piled into the small room the church set aside for the children. Some parents felt uneasy leaving their child with Ms. Doolittle, she was so young, with no child of her own. Some parents thought Ms. Doolittle would do just fine; it is no big deal to watch the children for approximately an hour or more.

The children, like most children, needed help with cleanliness and help getting something to eat. They needed someone to play with them and teach them with patience. On this Sunday five children entered the church nursery: Kyle was four, Alfonso was four, Audrey was four, Susan was three and a half and Terrance was six months. Ms. Doolittle welcomed the children, introducing herself as their new Sunday school teacher.

Kyle asked Ms. Doolittle what had happened to their other teacher, Mrs. Flowers. Ms. Doolittle told the children she wasn't aware of what had happened to Mrs. Flowers. The truth was Ms. Doolittle had approached the pastor in the privacy of his office in a loosely-clad dress. Focused on her good looks and figure, the pastor lost all sense and sensibility as she flattered him and his mind took flight with thoughts of future rendezvous. So the pastor made a decision he thought was of sound mind but which was actually influenced by Ms. Doolittle. He dismissed Mrs. Flowers in favor of Ms. Doolittle.

Alfonso volunteered that Mrs. Flowers had quit because she did not like the children.

Ms. Doolittle: We don't know if that is true, Alfonso. As Christians we must be careful not to make false accusations, speaking only on information we know as fact.

Kyle: He is speaking a fact; Mrs. Flowers said to our faces last week that she could not stand us. She was so mad she tried to pull that door open so hard on her way out but the door got stuck. It was funny and we laughed as she struggled to open a door that would not open.

Ms. Doolittle was at a loss for words and said nothing else on the subject of Mrs. Flowers. She asked the children "What are some of things you liked doing with your other teacher?"

Susan: We played and talked about Jesus

Kyle: And we did other fun things

Audrey: We studied the Bible.

Ms. Doolittle: What book were you studying with Mrs. Flowers?

Alfonso: The Book of Revelation.

Ms. Doolittle: You mean the end of the world?

Kyle: The book where John saw Jesus in a vision, the beginning.

Ms. Doolittle: Well let's talk about Jesus. You tell me what you know about Jesus. Then we will proceed from there.

Susan: Jesus is cool!

Ms. Doolittle: Okay we have "Jesus is cool." Does anyone else have anything to add?

Kyle: My brother Terrence said Jesus is the resurrection and the truth. He was born to fulfill God's plan of salvation.

Ms. Doolittle: I don't think Terrence can talk yet. What is he, about six months old?

Kyle: He can talk, but most of the time he must remain silent so I speak for him.

Ms. Doolittle: In time he will speak for himself and not need you to interpret for him, Kyle.

The door to the nursery opened; an elderly church member calling himself "the General" entered the room.

The General: Soldiers, fall in line, this is your general speaking! Troops fall in line. Hut two, three, four.

The children fell into formation and marched to the general's command.

The General: Hut two, three, and four. Left, left, left right left.

Ms. Doolittle: Who are you?

The General: I am the General; I am responsible for whipping these recruits into shape. They are in boot camp, soon to be soldiers in God's army. We are at war, Young Lady.

Ms. Doolittle: But this is a church and you are dressed up in a military uniform.

The General: Protocol, Young Lady, protocol. No self-respecting general would be caught dead without his uniform. Let us begin, Kiddies. We must be prepared to fight the good fight. The fate of the world hangs in the balance. To win this war for God we must be prepared. We must be physically fit and mentally prepared; above all we must be spiritually grounded in God's Word. You recruits give me ten push-ups.

The children got down on the floor and did ten push-ups.

Ms. Doolittle: I was not aware that we are to engage the children in physical exercise.

The General: Any soldier under my command had better be physically fit. The battle is not always won by the swift at deeds or those strategically cleaver but by those with the stamina to endure until the end. We know not when this battle will end and good soldiers are prepared to go the distance. Okay you kiddos, give me ten abdominal crunches; nothing sorrier than a fat-bellied soldier.

Ms. Doolittle: General, the children and I were about to have a discussion about Jesus. This is a church; it is rude to disrupt and interrupt my class.

The General: Nonsense, Young Lady, Jesus is with us as we prepare to get strong. Our goal is clear: we pray that God would open our eyes to the wonderful things in His Word. For we were chosen to do the right thing.

Ms. Doolittle: But General, I don't understand what you are doing here.

The General: Young Lady, we are preparing for war. We must fight the battle for life. War is about the business of mortality and immortality. If we must die, let it be for a place of honor in God's Kingdom. We owe this life to God. If we are victorious we live in an honored seat of the blessed. The disciple John said, *"I heard a voice in the heavens above me saying... At last the time has come for His martyrs to enter into their full reward. Yes, says the Spirit, they are blest indeed, for now they shall rest from all their toils and trials; for their good deeds follow them to heaven"* (Revelation 14:13, TLB)!

Ms. Doolittle: I am sure you mean well, General, but your methods seem too crude for these children.

The General: Nonsense, Young Lady, this is a tough bunch. They may be kids but they are fierce warriors. Okay, Troops, time for hand-to-hand combat training. Wars are won in the trenches. Bombs have their impact and bio chemicals float along, eclipsing humane sanity for cruelty. It is in the trenches, up close and personal, where soldiers see the enemy's eyes and victory is decided. A soldier must react and respond, using their wit, their hands, the toughness of their hearts and instincts as weapons of saving grace.

We are soldiers in God's army, soldier of noteworthy acclaim. We fight, we live, we fight, and we grow stronger. When we fight for God we raise the ceiling of our limitations. We fight for God in hope of gaining His favor in our weakest moments on the battlefield surrounded by death. When we see God He is with us, and we fight for a much higher calling: the Kingdom of God.

Ms. Doolittle: General Sir, by whose authority do you march these children into the art of war?

The General: In the spirit world I act on orders from the supreme commander-in-chief, Jesus. Here on Earth where we engage in the physical, I act on the authority of the pastor. I am commissioned to get these kids in shape; it is they who fight our wars. Old men like me can only provide strategies and suffer when we send the young off to die.

Alfonso: General Sir, why do we speak so often of death when Jesus is about life?

The General: Because to honor God with all our hearts we must die to self and give in to the will of God; this is the path that leads to victory, prosperity and good fortune. All right, Troops, no more chit-chat, we must train to engage demons in hand-to-hand combat.

The General: Fall in line, Troops, get in first position. Now kick, kick, kick high, Audrey and Susan, you young ladies kick low, strike where it matters, strike and never quit. Sharpen your knuckles and thrust a deadly blow. Have no mercy on demons; if they plead mercy, fight until they are completely subdued. Remember the words of Jesus: when a demon is vanquished he returns with seven more deadly demons. So fight hard and when these fighting techniques from the Far East fail, resort to street fighting. Hit those demons with a left hook and shoot a right jab.

The best fight is a one-punch fight: it frees you up for greater warfare. Jab and jab, then come with the right or left hook. Fight until the end, never give up and never relent, fight, fight, fight! Hit those demons dead in the eye; give the demon a black eye. It just may be a demon of profound vanity, ashamed that others see them with a black eye. It will retreat and refrain from battle for a week, or fight with sunglasses and give us an advantage.

The General: Now, Troops, give me ten jumping jacks. You too, Terrance; age is not a factor in the war of the spirit world. When we are in formation you should be with us. I am not fooled by your infant ways I can see past your appearance; I know you are an old soul from God.

The General: All right you troopers: attention! Ms. Doolittle, I am turning these troops over to you for additional training. Train their minds with the knowledge of God. I trust you will carry on with the same intense discipline I expect from my recruits. Should one or more of them disobey an order, I want a report on my desk immediately. Troops, stand tall and never slouch. You too, Terrance, and take the pacifier out of your mouth. If the demons from Hell discover you are hooked on the pacifier they will exploit your every weakness. At ease, Troops. This is our strategy session. Are there any questions?

Alfonso: I have a question.

The General: What is your question, Trooper?

Alfonso: Shall we engage the enemy with conversational prose or just cuss them out?

The General: That is a good question. Some demons require a good tongue-lashing and others you should politely dismiss.

Alfonso: That brings me to my second question. Under the art of war, should we warn the demons first or proceed to kick their butt?

The General: Another good question. Some demons will back off when you warn them because they understand you are under God's authority and you mean business. Other demons require that you walk up and commence kicking their butts without a word. It depends on the situation. There is a time for every response to every situation. Are there anymore questions? Troopers, you are dismissed. Carry on, Ms. Doolittle. I am leaving this battalion with you fit for duty.

The General saluted the troops and exited the room.

Ms. Doolittle: Well, Children, the General is certainly entertaining. He is quite a character. Does anyone know if he really was a general in the military?

Susan: He was an honored soldier in the war.

Ms. Doolittle wrote notes on her writing pad.

Alfonso: What are you writing?

Ms. Doolittle: Just a note to myself. Does anyone remember where we stopped?

Aubrey: We were talking about Jesus.

Kyle: Terrance said we should study Revelation.

Ms. Doolittle: Kyle I know you are trying to pull my leg; Terrance is not old enough to talk yet.

Kyle: No, Ms. Doolittle. I may be a kid but I don't kid around; life is too serious to play silly games.

Audrey: Ms. Doolittle, don't pay them any attention, they are just acting up, trying to be grown.

Ms. Doolittle: Let's continue talking about Jesus.

Susan: He said unless you are like us – children, you can't get to Heaven.

Ms. Doolittle: I believe Jesus said we must be as trusting as little children in order to get to Heaven.

Audrey: I am not worried about going to Heaven. I know I am going.

Alfonso: You don't know where Heaven is.

Audrey: Yes I do. Heaven is where the beautiful people go like California, Hawaii, and Miami.

Kyle: My brother Terrance said the greatness of Jesus is He died at Calvary for unworthy people like us. His death allowed us to experience the Kingdom of Heaven here on Earth and opened the doors for the Holy Spirit to touch our souls.

Ms. Doolittle: I told you Terrance is not able to talk at this time. He has no knowledge of God and he certainly cannot read.

Kyle: And I told you he could. He talks to God all the time. He has only been in this world a short time; he still has heavenly insights. He can see God and angels ascending and descending the heavens. I was at that point once; now I seek grown up things and seem to have lost my way. I have graduated to wanting to be a man so I can take care of myself. I kind of regret it because I lost some of my heavenly privileges by being cast down here on Earth.

Ms. Doolittle: I don't believe you, Kyle.

Kyle: Then believe in Terrance's innocence. Look at him, he was born helpless, needing everything and surely God has made a way for him. We must teach him the things of this world.

Susan: Jesus likes babies.

Alfonso: Jesus hears babies when they cry and when they hurt. If you listen closely they sound like a lamb. It seems strange that the Lamb of God is a man.

Ms. Doolittle decided at that moment on the subject of her thesis. She would write her paper on the subject of early childhood development.

Ms. Doolittle: Would it be all right to change the topic for a moment and talk about what you all want to be when you grow up?

Susan: I want to be the President and bring peace to the world and make everyone happy.

Alfonso: No girl can be President; that is a man's job. How are you going to deal with dropping bombs on people and countries? Do you have what it takes to lie again and again with a straight face?

Audrey: Women are better liars than men. We can do anything better than men.

Ms. Doolittle: I want to continue but let's respect each other's choices and not criticize someone else's views. Who else would like to share with the group what they want to be when they grow up?

Audrey and Alfonso: I do.

Ms. Doolittle: Alfonso we will let Audrey go first. Ladies first.

Kyle: Jesus said the first shall be last.

Ms. Doolittle: Yes, Kyle, but we have to put Jesus on hold for now. It is appropriate and polite to let ladies go first.

Alfonso: You just said we are putting Jesus on hold. God don't like it when we put Jesus on hold.

Susan: Remember Ms. Doolittle is our substitute teacher so she may not know any better.

Audrey: That's okay. Understudies can become stars.

Ms. Doolittle: Children! Children, we are getting off track and out of hand. We may need a period of time out.

Kyle: Yeah, my brother Terrance needs a time out. Do you smell that?

Ms. Doolittle: You mean his diaper needs to be changed?

Alfonso: You got that right. What are you going to do?

Ms. Doolittle: I am not sure if I am allowed to change his diaper under the church by-laws. I'll have to check with the pastor. Let me make a note.

Susan: Yeah, she is just a sub.

Kyle: Mrs. Flowers changed all of our diapers.

Ms. Doolittle: Well I am new at this, so I had better check first.

Audrey: I need your help to stay clean, I am just a child. That is something Jesus would say.

Alfonso: Jesus would also say "little children cry when their needs are not met." I need your help.

Ms. Doolittle: Church will be over soon. Terrance's mother may want to change her child. Shall we continue? Audrey what do you want to be when you grow up?

Audrey: I want to be a glamorous star and give love to all my fans.

Alfonso: What kind of career is that? She really wants to be a drama queen.

Kyle: They are one and the same.

Ms. Doolittle: Alfonso, Kyle, remember we don't comment on other people's choices. It's their choice and they are entitled to it. What do you want to be, Kyle?

Kyle: I want to a businessman. I figured this success equation out; prosperity equals entrepreneurship, plus economy, plus giving, plus God.

Ms. Doolittle: Are you sure the ministry is not one of your choices? I see "pastor" in your personality.

Kyle: No I cannot be a preacher; I would have to take the hypocritical oath.

Ms. Doolittle: That is not the oath they take.

Alfonso: He said it right.

Kyle: Terrance said he is a prophet.

Ms. Doolittle: I am not sure Terrance knows what a prophet is.

Kyle: Yes he does, I told you he is a new arrival from the Kingdom of God and still maintains his mansion and connections there.

Ms. Doolittle: Alfonso what do you want to be when you grow up?

Alfonso: I want to be myself. I want to experience the true meaning of life. I want to know Jesus and spend all my days with Him. Early in the morning I want to pray how much I trust the Lord. I will ask the Lord to make me understand what He wants. I want to know my hidden self. I will not be the fool by falling sleep at the wheel of my self-directed ego, thinking I am a king, preferring money to obedience to God. I will not be a stupid king, busy ruling over the subjects of my talents, accomplishments, education and certificates of merit. I seek to avoid worshiping all things that block my entry into the Kingdom of God. I seek to stand in the here and now with my eyes wide open focused on my final resting place in the Kingdom of God.

And if that is not enough I seek to expel some of my ministry, to purge my conditional love, to see God as my wealth and the granter of my temporary possessions. And when I fall short I will applaud the correction God gives me as the best thing that could have happened to me for it taught me to pay attention to His laws. His laws are my joyous treasure. Surround me with Your tender mercies that I may live. God's laws are my delight. I will have communion with God. I will love Him. Jesus is my brother. When asked what my career choice is I will say I am the brother man of Jesus, and therein lives my identity.

Ms Doolittle was stunned by Alfonso's remarks; it was far from what she had expected. He spoke boldly and quoted parts of Psalms 119 at age four.

Ms. Doolittle: You children don't act or speak like normal children at your age. According to my studies in psychology the things you speak of are impossible for children your age to know. Can anyone explain?

Audrey: It's because we have been here before.

Ms. Doolittle: You mean you've been to the nursery on other occasions?

Audrey: No, Ms. Doolittle. We have been in this world before. We are the arisen of the first resurrection.

Ms. Doolittle: I do not understand.

The children's parents arrived as church service ended. Ms. Doolittle smiled and told each parent how wonderful his or her child had behaved. Ms. Doolittle said good-bye to the children and parents and told the children they would continue their discussion next week.

On the way out of the church nursery Kyle said to Ms. Doolittle, "My brother Terrance said he is not sure about you."

Ms. Doolittle said, "Good-bye, Kyle."

Ms. Doolittle pulled out her pen and paper and began taking notes. She thought about her encounter with the children. An idea crossed her mind to write her graduate school thesis in the style of a matter-of-fact novel. She thought about the possibilities: the latitude she could cover by writing her paper in this style. As thoughts raced through her mind she said "Maybe I should write a book about the children." She said to herself: I am rich. She then wrote more notes:

Susan: She has a social-worker mentality with a Mother Teresa slant. She has a need to nurture and be nurtured. This is a result of low self-esteem. A good subject for my paper; she has many variables to exploit.

Aubrey: She has movie star illusions dominated by an ego of self. She is very selfish and cannot function without an audience. She needs constant praise. Her range as a subject is limited, not much substance.

Kyle: He is delusional with a propensity for exaggeration, an early sign of mental illness, obsessed with infant brother. He may be a potential child predator. A good subject: many dysfunctional psychological avenues to explore.

Alfonso: A natural-born leader; he has a rough edge with a hoodlum bent, if not a civil rights leader destined for jail. He is socially un-integrate-able. He could do a lot of good or cause great destruction and misery. A very good subject: he is both villainous and a saint.

Terrance: A strange baby with stinky feces.

CHURCH NURSERY: WEEK TWO

The parents dropped off their children in the small room retrofitted for a church nursery. The room had been thrown together because the church pastor did not want the little children and infants interrupting his sermons. Ms. Doolittle greeted the parents this week with greater enthusiasm; she was sure this Sunday would be special.

Susan spotted a baby doll, picked it up and played with it. Kyle tossed a ball he had found on the floor into the air. Audrey admired herself in a mirror she spotted hanging on the wall. Alfonso saluted a picture of Dr. Martin Luther King in which he was pointing at the Washington Monument while giving his "I Have a Dream Speech." And Terrance cried because he did not want to be apart from his mother; he needed to be loved.

Ms. Doolittle welcomed the children by reigniting last week's conversation.

Ms. Doolittle: Children, why don't we start today's discussion where we stopped last week? I believe we ended with Audrey speaking about being children of the first resurrection. What did you mean by that statement, Audrey?

Alfonso: Ms. Doolittle, can't you see that Audrey is busy? She is looking in the mirror again and worshipping herself. She is part vanity and part of God within.

Aubrey: Ms. Doolittle, tell Alfonso to leave me alone.

Ms. Doolittle: Alfonso, would you be so kind as to keep your opinion to yourself and let Audrey and anyone else speak without you teasing them.

Kyle: When we look in the mirror, it is like looking at God's good work.

Ms. Doolittle: Kyle, I would appreciate it if you would wait your turn before commenting. Could you do something to comfort your brother's crying?

Kyle: Children cry when they need help. He needs someone to hold him; to be human is to be touched. To comfort one another is to acknowledge God. To have faith in one another is the cornerstone of continuing our race. He is among us and yet alone; won't you look at him, see his Christ-like qualities? Will you hold him?

Ms. Doolittle: I think it may be best if Terrance's mother holds him. I have to check with church policy to see if holding your brother is appropriate.

Susan: I am not sure about you, Ms. Doolittle.

Alfonso: You noticed that, Susan.

Ms. Doolittle: I have nothing against any of you children. I choose to serve by serving in this capacity. In the performance of any ministry one should seek to do the right thing. Since I am not sure of church policy it is better to err on the side of caution than to throw caution to the wind.

Kyle: Did you hear that? Sounds like fancy talk to me coming from bureaucratic lips.

Audrey: It sounds like a contradiction of political rhetoric.

Ms. Doolittle: I think we are getting off the subject, Children.

Alfonso: Why do we have to talk about anything? I understand it is best to be still and know that God is God.

Ms. Doolittle: I am curious what Audrey meant when she said that you are the children of the first resurrection.

Audrey: The first resurrection changed time from BC to AD to set in motion the final outcome of God's plan. We are the children of happiness and health and good desires, we are the children of God.

Ms. Doolittle: Okay, I understand, but you said *we* are the children implying that yourself, Terrance, Alfonso, Susan and Kyle share a special bond.

Kyle: We do.

Ms. Doolittle: How so?

Susan: We were born of God's blood He spilled on Earth through the sacrifice of His Son. We have within us certain spiritual genes with the purifying DNA of God running through our souls.

Ms Doolittle took out her pen and wrote more notes: These children are possessed. It is worth exploring to discover if they are on drugs.

Alfonso: Why are you talking notes? And where is the General? He should be here by now.

Ms. Doolittle: Just writing myself some reminders. The General is not coming today.

Kyle: What kind of reminders? And why is the General not coming?

Ms. Doolittle: Just notes. The pastor and I decided the General's role was inappropriate for this church setting.

Aubrey: We love the General. Where is he?

Ms. Doolittle could not tell the children she had spoken privately to the pastor with the goal of eliminating the General. This is standard warfare within churches: a place where ordinary people can administer departments or projects and gain importance and attention that may be absent in their family structure or at work. The church is the place where unqualified people can volunteer and proclaim they did this or that apart from God. It is a place where individual goals become paramount and the goals of spiritual obligations to God are secondary to their committee, their speech, their fundraising and their praise, where some connive and commit crimes of the heart.

In the privacy of the pastor's office she had approached him in a saucy, provocative, suggestive way and the General was immediately relieved of his duties. She whispered in the pastor's ear, saying, "In today's world children are searching for meaning and gratification through gadgetry and exposure to mass media; old dinosaurs like the General are no longer effective at aiding children in self-discovery." With a look of passion in her eyes and with hips protruding, hips that touched the pastor's body providing innuendoes of future sex, she had suggested that the General be relieved of his duties. She had learned at an early age that some men, such as the pastor, were prone to suggestive overtures. The General did not have a chance.

The pastor, like those sleazy old men, had charted Ms. Doolittle's growth since she was a pre-teen, waiting on babies to come of age. He was married but recited certain biblical passages that helped him justify his exemptions from contemplated sins, under the protective covenant of Jesus' righteousness. He planned to covet future booty with the young Ms. Doolittle. He would pray afterwards then repent, and if the situation permitted do it again and start the repenting all over again.

So he called the General on the telephone and informed him that the church was moving in a different direction and his services were no longer needed. He thanked the General and said he would send him a certificate of appreciation in the mail. The General was heartbroken; he lived for the time he spent with the children. He looked forward to church on Sundays; the children gave him a reason to live although his body and soul were weary.

Kyle: The General has never missed a Sunday of being with us. Where is he?

Ms. Doolittle: The pastor and I discussed the General's role in the ministry of the church nursery and we felt his methods were inappropriate and outdated for what we are attempting to do.

Alfonso: So you got rid of the General?

Ms. Doolittle: I would not say we got rid of him. He is still a member of the church. What I am saying is we believe the General would better serve in another church capacity.

Susan: That means you got rid of the General.

Audrey: Have you all noticed Ms. Doolittle never gives us a direct answer to a direct question?

Ms. Doolittle: Why am I explaining myself to children?

Alfonso: Why are you asking so many questions and providing no answers?

Ms. Doolittle: It is part of my ministry to others, you know, just interacting with people, sharing our commonality.

Audrey: When we interact with one another we are folksier. We talk straight, letting our yes be yes and our no be no, saying we like this or we don't like that, calling a spade a spade. What kind of nonsense is this? These are the things we learned from the General. We ask questions for the sake of what we don't know and for clarity but you, Ms. Doolittle, you probe.

Ms. Doolittle: I did not to mean to intrude. Why don't we just sit in silence without saying a word?

Susan: It would be nice if you would just attend to Terrance's needs; he's still crying.

Kyle: My brother is hungry and needs to be fed; he is messy and cannot clean himself. While so young he is more dependent on God and other human beings. He shares one of the two phrases of life where you are prone to be messed over. This world messes over you when you are very young and very old. He is at the mercy of other human beings. It is especially true that in those two phases of life we must cling to Jesus. Why won't you attend to Terrance's needs?

Ms. Doolittle: Maybe I should go get one of the church elders who would be more acquainted with church procedures.

Alfonso: Ms. Doolittle, why are you here? You don't seem to know anything and you refuse to do anything.

Ms. Doolittle: Remember, Children, we agreed to sit in silence.

Susan: I have some questions for you, Ms. Doolittle. Why did you see the General as a threat? When were you born, where were you born and why were you born?

Ms. Doolittle: I was born in Arkansas and why I was born is a question none of us can answer. I think the answer to such a question is ongoing; we were born for this moment and all our moments add up to the sum total of a life. To answer your other question I discovered the General was not a General at all but a master sergeant with 21 years in the Marines. I have a problem with people that misrepresent their titles. It is the equivalent of telling a lie.

Audrey: That is the first question Ms. Doolittle really answered.

Alfonso: There may still be hope for her. But we still love the General. What harm did it do to let an old man think he is a General? He was a sergeant in Vietnam. It was the sergeants that brought our troops home while the generals lost the war. The sergeants were fierce warriors. They were stuck in the middle between the enemy and the bad strategies of generals and politicians.

Kyle: My brother Terrance said your religion is superficial and since you are part of the problem you cannot solve the problem.

Ms. Doolittle: We are not going to start that again, Kyle. Terrance is too young to speak.

Kyle: And I say he can talk.

Audrey: I am bored with this talk of motives. All motives are the same: mine and yours, yours and mine. God cannot reside in our motives, only His.

Ms. Doolittle: Let me ask you, Audrey. Why were you born?

Audrey: I was born to live my mother's dreams of stardom, dreams lost with lovers that went awry and a pregnancy that altered her direction. So I dance, practice the piano and take singing lessons in hope of exposing some hidden talent. My life is her life. Her dreams are my path. Her regrets are my mandate. She is I and I am she and to be a star is where we are. Yet God knows if this scene were to be relived I would be an aborted dream.

Susan: I was born because my mother could not have any more abortions. I am just afterbirth of the legions of this era. There is hope God is watching from His throne; He sees the vast hearts of the unwanted. We are blessed with certain insights. We know our circumstances yet cling to a yearning for love. Our love is of self, though we try to break free from the spirit of our conception. I see me, we see more of me and God sees my soul.

I have feelings that run deep. Jesus tells us "I love you, I love you and I will carry your pain. Just believe in Me."

Kyle: I was born to be a guardian to lead the way for my brother. It is road of little reward: others will claim all the credit. I am destined to sow where I will not reap, to blaze trails that I will never travel. This is a birth of many complications and uneasy delivery. I was equipped like the prophet Jeremiah; God blessed me in the womb. As the sun sets on God's will, it will bring me labor without the authority to deliver the final blow. My time is the time of John the Baptist. I am my brother's keeper, chosen to be His trailblazer and my end will be without fanfare.

Alfonso: I am a mistake, a mistake in the name of freedom. I was too late to be disposed of. I am an embarrassment of those ashamed to admit their error. In God's corrective nature, freedom is the path assigned to me, to tread among a hostile race bearing a message that Jesus loves you and there is prosperity in harmony. It is a battle to correct too many injustices. Note the irony of a mistake assigned to correct other's grave mistakes.

I do not understand why the General's thoughts are becoming my thoughts and the General's ways are becoming my ways. Jesus is his commander-in-chief and mine. There is only one mission: to fight injustice against God's people. My mission is to restore our God-given right to live and to spark men to valor, men of conviction and honor willing to sacrifice it all. There will be no victory, only a seat at the "Table of the After Life." I cannot describe those moments at my lowest points when Heaven opens up and pours out blessings, reviving my courage in the name of God. I hate every false teaching. I am determined to obey God until I die.

Let all others join me, who trust and fear God, as we discuss His laws. I pray to God to help me love His every wish; then I will never have to be ashamed of myself. God will never forget me and will bless me with overflowing abundance, just as He promised. I know that God loves me.

Ms. Doolittle wrote more notes: these kids are the products of abuse. Alfonso has an obsession for reciting Psalms. The children's minds are saturated with illusions of grand achievement, a by-product of kids seeking love through imagination. These kids are in need of counseling. It may be in their best interest that they be removed from their parent's homes and placed in foster care as wards of the state.

Audrey: Look, Ms. Doolittle is doing a pencil job on us. She is penciling us in as misfits.

Kyle: I knew she was using us.

Susan: She is an opportunist.

Alfonso: Come on, Y'all, we are out of here. She is using us as guinea pigs.

Susan picked up stinky Terrance and the children headed for the door. Before they reached the door, it opened. Mrs. Flowers entered the room.

Mrs. Flowers: I came to tell you all that the General died last night. He died from a massive heart attack, but I know he died from a broken heart.

Mrs. Flowers, speaking to Ms. Doolittle: It was bad enough when you convinced the pastor to replace me. The time I spent with the children had its moments. Sometimes it was fun; other times we experienced great joy. There were other times the children got on my nerves and I let them know they were getting on my nerves.

What troubles me is how you will live with yourself after manipulating the pastor, a man with dreams of lustful fun, dreams that turned into a nightmare and in the process you took away the one thing an old man loved. You broke the cardinal rule of the Lord when you attempted to use the children. *"Let the children come to me, and don't prevent them. For of such is the Kingdom of Heaven."* In the process you hammered the nail as the final blow for a good man to die. These children were the reason the General wanted to live.

Ms. Doolittle: Children, where are you going? You cannot leave the nursery without your parents signing you out. Children come back. Where are you going?

Audrey speaking to the other children: She is a witch.

Alfonso: I've got another name but we are in church.

Mrs. Flowers: The members of the church are divided: some say your sexual teasing is evil, other members say you are just a child acting out what you were taught at an early age. Others have their opinion that your implication of sex mixed with charm is the men's fault for being so gullible.

No wonder the church is silent on the subject of sex. Personally, I have no illusions or confusion. In my job as a school system consultant I witness parents express amazement at their children's behavior. They complain and murmur about how bad the system is; never acknowledging their child made in their image is a major part of the problem. They refuse to acknowledge that their children are the products of what they laid down with and conceived. It is no mystery when you put trash in an empty receptacle that it maturates into garbage. So it is when you came into the church speaking of ministering to the children.

You are too young to understand that our every action produces a vibratory reaction in the universe. Take war for instance: when we are at war killing innocent men, women and children abroad, that violence resonates back home as the mass psychosis of citizens take hold of war. Gradually homicides increase so do rapes and all kinds of sexual perversions, robbery and other violent acts. The increase in crimes is blamed on everything else except where it should be: on the vibratory affects of war. Our fate lives in the spiritual genetics of every innocent man, woman and child killed in war. Those deaths on foreign soil begot innocent men, women and babies killed at home.

I am not sure you realize what you have done. First you helped me confirm that it is time for me and members like me to leave this church. You managed to place the pastor's career at this church in jeopardy. You have managed to plant seeds that will destroy and alter the lives of many people.

I don't think you understand that true success is improving yourself by investing yourself in God and perfecting your talent in accordance with the behavior of Christ; that is the way to the one true path to happiness and prosperity. When we connive to get others to include us in their worlds or base our success on the opinions or judgment of others we are bound to fail and live a life of unhappiness.

You set a wicked trap along forbidden paths, Young Lady. You have earned your medals in the devil's evil army. You do not understand, Young Lady, that what you do here on Earth has a multiplying effect in the heavens. Look at how the children reject you! My advice to you is to learn as soon as possible that the evil plans we pursue in life always go awry because life is biased on the side of good.

Ms. Doolittle: I am sure our Lord said we are not to judge others; we should be concerned with our own faults.

Mrs. Flowers: In reality it is impossible not to judge. God gave us a mind to distinguish between right and wrong, to do so is to judge. When we ask God for a discerning mind we are asking for sound judgment. To think is to judge, so is the focus of our faith, to choose is to judge. I do not take lightly what Jesus said, that I should not judge the sinfulness of others, but in this case I stand accused yet justified for judging your sinfulness.

Ms. Doolittle: Children, where are you going? This is highly unusual.

Ms. Doolittle wrote a note in her journal before she forgot the thought: The children are exhibiting riotous behavior. This situation is stressful and could turn critical. I will observe the children and monitor their behavior. At this point it seems their behavior is escalating into a riot. I will flee for my life if the children start looting and burning vehicles. She followed the children as they walked out of the nursery, asking Susan, who was carrying Terrence, where they were going.

Susan stopped and shifted Terrance from one hip to another. "I will let Terrance answer you."

Ms. Doolittle: Terrance.

Terrance: You say, "I am rich, with everything I want; I don't need a thing!" And you don't realize that spiritually you are wretched and miserable and poor and blind and naked.

My advice to you is to buy pure gold from Jesus, gold purified by fire – only then will you truly be rich (Revelation 3:17-18).

Susan turned and walked away. Ms. Doolittle was not conscious of what had just happened. So she asked again, "Children where are you going?"

Terrance: We are going into the Holy Sanctuary of God where you cannot go to place our hearts in God's depository, storing up treasure in Heaven where blessings multiply into the everlasting!

When Ms. Doolittle finally realized that Terrance had spoken, she fainted.

THE RIDE HOME

Terrance rode home in his car seat in the family vehicle. He was visibly upset over what had happened in the church nursery. His pacifier had fallen from his mouth when he had spoken to Ms. Doolittle; without it his peace was interrupted. So Terrance did what children do after a long day of activity and stress, he fell asleep.

In his sleep he made contact with the Spirit of God, a calming voice that said "Terrance; Come up here." So Terrance took a spiritual flight to the Kingdom of God where he stood before the throne of the Spirit. He was blinded by the glitter of gold, diamonds and other gems emanating from the throne, a light so bright he had to look away.

A voice said to Terrance, "Come, My Son, and sit on My lap." Terrance, being a trusting child, sat on the lap of the One who had summoned him. "May I get you anything?" the voice said.

Terrance responded "Kool-Aid would be fine." The Spirit on the throne summoned an angel to bring two royal golden, jeweled-encrusted goblets of Kool-Aid. The Spirit proposed a toast to Terrance, a toast of things to come.

Then the Spirit asked Terrance, "What is it that you seek from Me?"

Terrance thought about the question and answered, "I seek a Way."

The Spirit on the throne said, "I will make a way; there is always a way. I am the way and I promise a way has been granted." Then the Spirit said to Terrance, "You must learn to hold your tongue. People who do not know Me or you will exploit your ability to speak, especially at such an age. Beware of flattery and too much praise. Only the Father, Son and the Holy Spirit is worthy of all-encompassing praise. All things are possible in the name of My Son, including the ability to see invisible things on Earth and invisible things in the heavens."

So Terrance thought about what the Spirit had said to him and decided he wanted to meet the Son. The Spirit knew Terrance's thoughts and said: "My Son is unavailable at this time. He suffers so much and endures His pain. When one of my children is harmed on Earth the Son experiences the crucifixion again and again until the end of this time. He is doing what He loves to do: saving lives."

Terrance was curious. The Spirit knew his thoughts and said "You want to know how the Father, the Son and Holy Spirit became one.

Terrance said "Yes."

THE VIDEO

The Spirit on the throne said, "Would you like to see the video?" Terrance did. "We installed video after the Garden of Eden when My children became separated from Me; I needed to keep an eye on their visible sins. I still have not figured out why so many of My children hide from Me. They are forever closing windows and doors on Earth: doors that lead to Me. After the Tower of Babel we included audio to record separations from Me that involve the tongue. We've had audio and video for a while now. It keeps me busy; I have never been unemployed: too many of My children have broken My heart. I lift them up and they try to take My place and be god."

A tear rolled down the cheek of the Spirit. Terrance used his oversized bib, stained with milk and Kool-Aid, and wiped the tears off the face of God.

The Spirit nodded, giving the command to another angel to start the movie. The wide-screen video projected itself onto luminous bright space. It could not be described as a sky, because a sky is not needed in God's Kingdom. It was space without perimeters, picture perfect, the envy of earth's media device manufacturers as they strive to be first to perfect real vision.

The movie started with no credits or title. The storyline on Earth was the clouds at Calvary moving rapidly in the sky, ushering in grayness followed by darker overcast clouds. The sun was absent, consumed by impending darkness and the earth shook. As Earth's surface rocked and rolled, a brilliant light was released from Jesus' body with swirling off-shoots ascending in many directions upward. The light then descended downward onto the living and the dead.

In the Kingdom of God dimness was in its final hour as God gathered His composure after being weakened by the heart-drenching love expelled from His soul as He embraced His Son, shielding Him from each blow. Each blow thrust upon the Son was a blow that landed on the Father. This blow released medicine of healing and forgave individual categories of our sins. That blow released healing for sins piled up against humanity. That blow landed in the protective center of the circle where death cannot crossover.

With each blow the beat of heavenly drums pounded: cleansers of forgiveness, guilt would no longer be needed. The curtain in the temple split; it was no longer needed to stand between God and His children. As each blow lashed upon the Son, the Father held His Son tighter in admiration for His heroism for volunteering to die to make things right again. Man did not know his blows intended for the Son actually landed on the Father, so he beat God with the wrath of human error. And neither the Father nor the Son cried out in pain.

The Kingdom of God held strong under its temporary dimness while loaning its light, Jesus, to human salvation. As the light from Jesus' body reached the heavens, the glitter of the Kingdom returned. The light gravitated and touched the Holy Spirit; the Holy Spirit became more powerful in preparation for departure to live among God's people on Earth as it lives in the heavens, and thus multiplying.

The inhabitants of the Kingdom of God lit their lamps with stored oil set aside for the Festival. Lighting their lamps signaled the beginning of the Festival leading to the Feast and then the Wedding of all things new. The angels put on their ceremonial robes and joined in while the choir of infinite numbers sang:

> The Lord is King;
> Praise Him up.
> Sing Him up.
> Pray Him up.
> Release Him up.
> Give Him up.
> Live Him up.
> Laugh Him up.
> Love Him up
> Store Him up.
> The Lord is King

NON-STOP CELEBRATION

The angels celebrated non-stop; fatigue was never a factor while they praised God forever. The more they praised the Father and the Son the more spiritual energy was released. The angels sang and danced to music that flowed seamlessly from one venue to the next. Gospel songs and songs of praise were mixed with varieties of praise music.

Some angels who had boogie in their souls boogied non-stop. The slow dancers did their thing and hoe-downers danced a country jig without any signs of being out of breath. The hip hoppers were there and they stepped all night.

The best wine in the universe flowed from golden fountains without ever being refilled and the inhabitants of God's Kingdom drank as much as their hearts desired without the sidebar sins of celebrations down here on Earth.

Terrance could not believe what he was seeing. He saw a special fountain called the Fountain of Salvation dispensing living water, and other fountains ever-flowing with sprinkling streams of milk, honey and Kool-Aid. The Spirit knew that Terrence's eyes were affixed on the Kool-Aid fountains and the fountains of milk and honey. Terrance's mind was so focused on what he saw he forgot he had lost his pacifier. The Spirit felt Terrance's excitement. He whispered in Terrance's ear: "We do things big up here. This is the real deal. We call this the big time!"

MYSTIC SMOKE

Terrance saw an angel fly by carrying a canister and a white garment rapped in a purple cloth and he asked the Spirit on the Throne who the angel was. The Spirit said, "He is the one dispatched to carry my Son's cross on Earth. He asked that his life be one of significant contribution and My promise to him was fulfilled.

Terrance then asked; "Where is he going now?"

The Spirit on the throne said, "He is going to Earth to attend to My Son."

On Earth the angel opened the canister of mystic smoke and waved it in the faces of the guards guarding Jesus' tomb; they fell into a deep sleep. The angel then prayed and the boulder sealing the tomb rolled aside, allowing the angel to enter and perform the sacred spiritual embalming of Jesus' earthly body. The canister of mystic smoke was released mixing with sacred words and prayer.

In the Kingdom of God the angel sang louder and the Holy Spirit grew stronger and God meditated on things to come and the rebirth of His creation. On Earth the angel clothed Jesus in the white garment brought from Heaven and placed the purple accessories on Jesus' body. At the appointed moment he was joined by another angel who read from the Holy Scroll over the body of Jesus.

The angel left the tomb with the canister of mystic smoke, went to the home of Caiaphas the High Priest and blew smoke from the canister on him while he slept. He then went to the home of Pilate and blew smoke from the canister on him while he slept. He then went to home of the chief priest and blew smoke from the canister on him. The angel went to the soldiers and false witnesses who had convicted, beaten, humiliated and crucified Jesus and blew smoke from the canister upon them, sealing the doom of all those spirits not of Heaven that received the mystical smoke.

TIME FOR A FEAST

In the Kingdom of God the harps played, signaling the Feast. The citizens sat at the banquet table stretching from one end of Heaven to the other. They ate in merriment while still singing praises to the Father, the Son and the Holy Spirit. They ate until full and gathered up the excess so there would be no waste. The festivities continued as the angels praised the fusion of the Trinity and danced while ushering in the new.

On Earth the angels in Jesus' tomb completed the reading of the words brought down from God's Kingdom. The angel with the canister and robe retuned to the Kingdom, joining the cele-bration now in full swing.

Out of the corner of his eye Terrance saw another angel fly across the Kingdom. He carried a military uniform on a royal purple pillow with an officer's hat in tow. The angel met with three other angels dressed in full military uniform with the rank of general. Through a crack in the circle of uniformed men Terrance saw a man lying on Heaven's floor of clouds. The man was lying prostrate, face down and seemed to be dead. The gen-erals stood erect, swords holstered in preparation to strike a knighted touch on one worthy of joining their rank. They were proud men, members of an elite cause stuck on doing what is right. The generals were men of grave decisions surrounded by doubt with faith in the chaos of war.

The circle of generals opened and Terrance saw the man that appeared to be dead rise, dressed in the general's uniform brought by the messenger angel. The man lifted himself up to his knees, head bowed downward in humility as the general angels in God's Army conferred upon him the rank of general.

Terrance smiled with an overjoyed spirit, knowing his nurs-ery boot camp instructor really was a general. In Terrance's silent words he said, "I knew it! Death was defeated on that faithful day at Calvary. Life is truly biased on the side of good."

Terrance watched as each general tapped his nursery instructor on each shoulder with the blades of their weapons. The General then rose to his feet and an angel placed three golden stars on the General's uniform. The angel then read this message: By royal decree from God on the throne it is announced that the honor of general in God's army has been bestowed upon the General.

The General turned and winked at Terrance.

Terrance was proud. He said, "I am proud of you, My Friend," as a tear rolled down his cheek. "I will miss you where I am down on Earth. Farewell, My Friend, I am happy for you. Who would ask a dear friend to give up his heavenly arrival? If our lot is to be blessed again, we pray that there will be another one just like you. It was willed by God and does not matter that you were denied a generalship on Earth. God has decreed, 'I will accept you and so honor you to be a general in My army.'"

Another angel arrived with four horses and a special horse that was red. The General mounted a grey stallion and joined the other three generals, and the four of them galloped in flight to unknown mansions in the Kingdom of God.

Terrance was again distracted from watching the video. Out of the corner of his eyes he saw a lady with dreadlocked braided hair; she looked like Mrs. Flowers. He heard an angel address her as the administrative assistant of the Godhead. She was telling the angels to clean up their mansions after the celebrations. Her reputation was she did not take any stuff from anyone. Even the Angel of Time avoided her in debates. Her name was Sister Girl, the most respected angel in God's kingdom.

Terrance's attention returned to the video. He saw a messenger angel fly across the Kingdom in a hurry and knock on the door of the Angel of Time's mansion, who did not take kindly to being disturbed.

The Angel of Time called out "Who dares come knocking at my door as a time robber? Only a fool would provoke me, I will set my mark on you, hunt you down and take away your time. I am not the sort of fellow you want to mess with. Mine is the King David complex; I will slay a thousand enemies and retreat to writing God a flowery poem." The messenger angel knocked again at the door and announced that the time had come. The Angel of Time went into action, opening the Chamber of Doom containing the chest that housed the Book of Sins and tossing it in the Holy fire.

He then announced that the consciousness of the Kingdom of the heavens and entry into the Kingdom of God had been reopened. With the help of the messenger angel they pulled the lever that reset the universal clock, synchronizing a change of time on Earth as it is in the heavens, opening the portal that we can travel through to contact God directly.

The messenger angel asked the Angel of Time, "Now what?"

The Angel of Time replied, "The sacrifice of Jesus is a conscious gift to man in recognition of the variation of the physical world extending human insight into the heavens where the Father, Son and Holy Spirit will meet them there. Now those who come to their senses may find their way back home to the Father."

The Angel of Time was still on probation for being anti-social, so he said, "The time has come, I am now unemployed. I have worked myself out of a job. It was my job to keep time from the beginning of the old ways to the beginning of the new ways at the completion of Jesus' mission. I pushed this button and we pulled this lever and burned the book of sins. Only the Father knows the appointed hour of the passing of this world and the ushering in of the world to come of no more tears."

So the messenger angel asked, "What is to become of us?"

"I will wait on God to see me through. In the meantime I will discard my smug attitude of importance now that I am just an unemployed timekeeper. I will learn to be all right with myself. And then I can be all right with others. You and I, we will start right now, and learn what is to become of us. Let us for once put aside our sense of duty and party non-stop like we just don't care, joining in with the other angels."

So the messenger angel and the Angel of Time drank wine, danced and shook their wings, made friends with other angels, got a kiss from two female angels and staggered throughout the Kingdom of God singing the happy songs of drunks, "New wine is the best."

On Earth, Jesus' disciples met, hiding from those who would kill them, to speak of what Jesus meant to them individually. The room was full of sadness, confusion and fear with the looming question: what shall we do? The question drifted to: what if? What if Jesus had lived longer? What if Jesus had advocated violence? Would things have been different if we had fought the enemy with force instead of loving him? What if Jesus had taught us in plain, simple language that we could better understand? Should we stay or should we flee? Should we feel enriched by the time we had with Him or should we feel destitute by His departure?

On Earth in the tomb, the angel recited another set of secret sacred words mixed with prayers and songs of the angels fused with the hopes of God's people. The momentum overflowed from the heavens and the light of Jesus returned to the tomb. When Jesus' earthly body absorbed His returning light, more powerful by being sanitized in the Kingdom, Jesus heard the sacred words, the songs and prayers and He awoke!

Mary Magdalene heard sounds coming from the spirit world in the heavens and she dropped what she was doing and ran to the tomb.

The video ended with Jesus ascending to His throne in God's Kingdom. God noticed Terrance had fallen asleep on Earth and in his dreams as it is in Heaven. God then smiled and said; "In the true spirit of God's disciples and prophets you fall asleep at crucial moments. That is why I sent My Son!"

The Spirit then kissed Terrance and showered him with love.

REFERENCES

Journal Science website, www.sciencemag.org

United States. NASA, "The Chandra Chronicles," Revised January 10, 2005, Harvard-Smithsonian Center for Astrophysics, website, www.chandra.harvard.edu.

United States. *Government Human Genome Project Report*, 1999 release, website, www.genome.gov

Complete Gray's Anatomy, Sixteenth Edition, Dr. R. A. Bolam, Longmans, Green & Company Publishing, 1905.

Robert B. Ekslund and Robert F. He`bert, *A History of Economic Theory and Methods*, Fourth Edition, Waveland Press Inc., 1997, 2004.

Huston Smith, *The Religions of Man*, Harper Row, 1958.

Charles Fillmore, *Prosperity*, Unity Books, 1936.

United States, Major Congressional Action, Congressional Almanac, Environment / Energy Legislation, 1980-1987.

Six Theories of Human Development, The Teaching Company.

Erdman Harris, *God's Image, Man's Imagination*, Charles Scribner's Son, 1959.

"The Bible through the Ages," *The Readers Digest*, subtitled printed word Modern Biblical Scholarship.

J. R. Porter, *The Lost Bible, Forgotten Scriptures Revealed*, University of Chicago Press, 1921.

Leo F. Buscaglia, *Love*, C.B Slack Publisher, 1972.

Aristotle, *Nicomachean Ethics*, Oxford University.

"Inner Seed," *Living Waters Ministry*, Volume 5.
William Foxwell Albright, *From Stone Age to Christianity*, John Hopkins Press, 1940.

Lee J. Colan, *Sticking to It, the Art of Adherence, How to Consistently Execute Your Plans*, Corner Stone Leadership Institute, September, October 2004, issue.

Larry Schweikart, *The Entrepreneurial Adventure, a History of Business in the United States*, Harcourt College Publishing, 2000.

Douglas Greenwald, *Encyclopedia of Economics*, Economist, "Irving Fisher's Money Illusion Theory."

E. M. Bounds, *The Essentials of Prayer*, Whitaker House Press, 1994.

W. G. Clark and Aldis Wright, Editors, *The Complete Works of William Shakespeare*, Nelson Doubleday, Volume Two.

"Utilities Facing a Pinch," *Detroit Free Press*, June 10, 1982, page 12D.

"A Measure before the Legislature Would Abolish Automatic Rate Hikes Full Review of All Proposed Increases," *Detroit Free Press*, June 21, 1982, page 1E.

"Utilities Proposition the Hottest Pros and Cons of Michigan's Ballot Proposal," *Detroit Free Press*, October 4, 1982, page 3A.

"3 Utilities Fined $3 Million for '82 Ballot Fight," *Detroit Free Press*, April 10, 1985, page 1A.

"Utilities Employees Paid to Lobby Polls," *Detroit Free Press*, November 2, 1983, page 3A.

"Utilities Use Subtle Offense to Win at the Polls \ Slick campaigns Cost $4.4 Million," *Detroit Free Press*, November 7, 1982, page 3A.

"Reagan Aides Say Natural Gas Plan Would Boost Price 5% at Most," *Detroit Free Press*, January 11, 1983, page 11A.

"Major Reorganization MichCon Trim Middle Ranks," *Detroit Free Press*, January 11, 1983, page 3B.

"Firing of Execs Just the Start Layoff Drama," *Detroit Free Press*, January 22, 1983, page 1A.

"MichCon Tells 300 They'll Lose Their Jobs," *Detroit Free Press*, January 26, 1983, page 10A.

"Primark Earnings Rise," *Detroit Free Press*, February 4, 1983, page 4B.

"Decontrol Gas Prices – Reagan," *Detroit Free Press*, February 27, 1983, page 1A.

"New Ventures to Flow into Primark Pipeline," *Detroit Free Press*, April 17, 1983, page 1B.

"Utilities Should Refund Cost of Voter Drive, Auditor Says," *Detroit Free Press*, June 2, 1983, page 1A.

"Michigan Firm Sue in U.S. Court Utilities Challenge Campaign Ceilings," *Detroit Free Press*, June 14, 1983, page 8A.

"MichCon to Shuffle Top Management," *Detroit Free Press*, December 10, 1983, page 10A.

"ANR, MichCon Are at Odds," *Detroit Free Press*, September 1, 1985, page 1A.

"Two Detroit Ministers Charged," *Detroit Free Press*, June 15, 1985, page 1A

"Fired Employee File Age Bias Suit against MichCon," *Detroit Free Press*, January 24, 1986, page 7A.

"Primark Holders Vote to Spin-Off MichCon, *Detroit Free Press*, May, 17, 1988, page 5C.

"Utilities Ballot Spending Legalized," *Detroit Free Press*, July 12, 1986, page 1A.

"MichCon Chairman Disputes Allegations," *Detroit Free Press*, October 4, 1985, page 8A.

About the Author

CALVIN L. SWINDELL was born in Detroit, Michigan. In addition to writing this book, he has written three other unpublished books on various topics which he plans to release in the future. Calvin helped found a children's charity and established a marketing firm and an insurance agency. He received his Bachelor's Degree in Economics from Marygrove College in Detroit, Michigan. He later received a Masters Degree in Finance from Walsh College in Troy, Michigan, followed by a Masters Degree in Economics from Walsh College, with postgraduate studies at Harvard University, John F. Kennedy School of Government.

He lives in the Detroit area with his wife, Paulette, and their two sons. He served on the trustee board of a multi-million dollar church for 15 years.